The Emperor
and the Peasant

The Emperor and the Peasant

*Two Men at the Start
of the Great War and the End
of the Habsburg Empire*

KENNETH JANDA

McFarland & Company, Inc., Publishers
Jefferson, North Carolina

ISBN (print) 978-1-4766-6957-1 ∞
ISBN (ebook) 978-1-4766-3118-9

LIBRARY OF CONGRESS CATALOGUING DATA ARE AVAILABLE

BRITISH LIBRARY CATALOGUING DATA ARE AVAILABLE

Front cover: Emperor Franz Joseph I (*left*, photograph by Carl Pietzner)
and Samuel Mozolák, 1905 (Wendel Photographic Art Studio);
background: Austro-Hungarian prisoners
from the Battle of Vittorio Veneto (Italian Army)

Printed in the United States of America

*McFarland & Company, Inc., Publishers
Box 611, Jefferson, North Carolina 28640
www.mcfarlandpub.com*

To John Mozolak, Jr.
and
Ann Mozolak Janda,
the peasant's second-generation
Slovak-American grandchildren

Table of Contents

Acknowledgments

Inspiration for writing this book came from British television and from my brother-in-law, John Mozolak. London Weekend Television's 1970s series *Upstairs, Downstairs,* and the popular 2010s series *Downton Abbey,* impressed me with their penetrating views of life early in the 20th century from the top and bottom of society. My Slovak-American brother-in-law's research into his genealogy and into the military history of his grandfather, Samuel Mozolák, inspired me to tell his grandfather's story in an "upstairs, downstairs" style—juxtaposing the Slovak peasant's life and death alongside the life and death of Austro-Hungarian Emperor Franz Josef and his empire.

John Mozolak provided virtually all of my information on the Mozolák family, on Samuel Mozolák's military experiences, and on his home village of Krajné. A great deal about that small village was in John's collection of Slovak books, sections of which my wife Ann (Mozolak) Janda translated for me. Other scholars and students of Slovakia furnished valuable additional information on the land and the people. A family friend from Krajné, Milan Pagač, helped John in his research in Slovakia and assisted me in securing information and permissions.

University of Washington professor John Palka, whose grandfather was Czechoslovakia's prime minister from 1935 to 1938, patiently read my manuscript and advised how to improve it. Professor M. Mark Stolarik, an expert in Slovak emigration at the University of Ottawa, closely read sections of the manuscript, correcting errors and expanding on parts. Daniel Nečas in the Immigration History Research Center at the University of Minnesota patiently answered many questions. Ryan Mattke and Dana Peterson in the University's Map Library turned up several maps for the book. Professors Winston Chrislock (University of St. Thomas) advised me early in my writing, as did Stanislav Kirschbauum (York University). Kevin Hurbanis and Suzette Steppe, respectively vice-president and president of the Czechoslovak Genealogical Society International, also made useful comments, as did Professor Jana Reshová (Charles University in Prague). Ed Chandla of the American Sokol library in New York helped identify Czech and Slovak organizations early in the 20th century. Kevin McNamara (Drexel University) answered questions about the Czech and Slovak Legionnaires fighting in Russia.

My observations on Hungary were influenced by spending 1993–94 as a Fulbright Fellow in the political science department of the Budapest University of Economic Sciences at the invitation of Professor Attila Ágh. My current writing was encouraged and advised by former departmental colleagues Gabriella Ilonszki and Láslo Váss, by Antal Örkény at Eötvös Loránd University, and by my former Ph.D. student at the Central European University, Gabriela Borz. In Minnesota, Zsolt Nagy (St. Thomas University) kindly took time to talk with me about the project. Bernard Tomas (Valdosta State) provided helpful comments and shared some of his family experiences with Magyarization in Hungary. Carl Kotlarchik, who maintains a website on Austro-Hungarian Army Records, confirmed some information on Samuel Mozolák's military life. Michael Dreyer (Friedrich Schiller University in Jena, Germany) interpreted some German texts.

Living in retirement in the Twin Cities proved little handicap to research. The excellent interlibrary loan system at the Roseville Branch of the Ramsey County Library in Minnesota allowed me to order and obtain scores of books on the Habsburg empire, World War I, and international immigration—many of which came from the fine collection at the University of Minnesota Library. The Roseville Library also sponsored a helpful series of talks by World War I historian Janet Woolman, who also read and commented on my manuscript. Thanks to its digital archive of League of Nations documents, my former library at Northwestern University provided a rich source of statistical data on the belligerent nations before and after World War I that I could access online. Northwestern also provided online access to print materials in electronic form, such as scholarly journals and back issues of the *New York Times* before and during the war.

Concerning World War I and its aftermath, Professor James Sheehan (Stanford University) helped define targets and sources very early in my research. Professor Gregory Ference (Salisbury State University) answered several queries about Slovak-American support of the war in the United States. Zora Bútorová and Radka Skalická at the Center for Public Opinion Research in the Czech Republic provided data on polls prior to the 1993 division of Czechoslovakia into the Czech and Slovak republics. My Northwestern colleague, Andrew Roberts, also helped with poll data. Special thanks goes to Professor Geoffrey Wawro (University of North Texas) for sharing his anonymous review of my draft manuscript and encouraging me to proceed. Wawro's 2014 book *A Mad Catastrophe* greatly informed my writing. Another reviewer, who chose to remain anonymous, suggested several lines of revision that led to a better book.

Concerning the processes of writing my manuscript, I benefited greatly from the suggestion by Professor Thomas Ort (New York's Queens College) to incorporate into my narrative insights from novels, such as Jaroslav Hasek's *Good Soldier Svejk* and Joseph Roth's *The Radetzky March*. Anthropologist Janet Pollak (William Paterson University) gave similar advice. As an academic who previously wrote only scholarly books and articles on political science, I never would have thought to use fiction to elaborate facts. Jerry Goldman, my departmental colleague at Northwestern University, my co-author of *The Challenge of Democracy* (an American government textbook), and my dear friend, plowed through 300 pages of an early draft of a manuscript on topics far from his own interests and identified several aspects of my text that needed improvement. My best friend, my wife Ann, unwearyingly read my text and made it better in so many ways, as she has done for decades.

As for publishing my manuscript, John Palka shared his own experiences in publishing his own book, *My Slovakia, My Family*, which sustained me when I received rejection emails. Other good friends—Irving Rockwood (former editor and publisher of *Choice*) and Nader Dareshori (former chairman and CEO of Houghton Mifflin)—advised me on contractual issues. Thanks to their assistance, this book is being published in time to commemorate the 100th anniversary of the end of World War I and the deaths of Samuel Mozolák and the Habsburg empire.

Preface

This book is unlike any I have written before. Those were either specialized books for political science professionals or textbooks for students taking courses in political science. This is a historical narrative—a nonfiction work informed by research—written for broader audiences. It aims at two categories of readers.

The first is the general reader who wants to know more about the "Great War" from the standpoint of the Eastern Theater of operations—as opposed to the many, many books about the Western Front. World War I actually began in the east, when Austria-Hungary declared war on Serbia and shelled Belgrade. The war also lasted somewhat longer in the east, and it killed more soldiers—and probably more people. Unlike other histories, my account of the war and Austria-Hungary delves into the foppish nature of the upper society in the Habsburg empire. It focuses on Emperor Franz Josef, who ruled the country for almost 68 years and—against his better judgment at almost age 84, but in keeping with his antiquated conception of honor—started World War I on July 28, 1914.

Throughout his long reign over an opulent court, Franz Josef was in many ways quite ignorant of the lives and aspirations of his subjects. My treatment expands to include the other ill-informed autocrats of the principal belligerent nations—German Kaiser Wilhelm II and Russian Tsar Nicholas II—who were equally unprepared to guide their nations in the 20th century. Although experientially ignorant of their subjects' lives and of public affairs within their nations, they were constitutionally empowered to declare war. And they did.

My second intended audience consists of those who wish to learn how the emperor's actions affected his peasants who fought his war. The book recounts the life and times of my wife's grandfather, Samuel Mozolák, a Slovak peasant in Austria-Hungary. In 1902, at age 20, Samuel emigrated to New York, intending to make his fortune and to return a wealthy man to his village of Krajné. In 1905, he met and married an immigrant woman from a nearby Slovak village. In 1906, she gave birth to twins—a boy and girl. They took their twin U.S. citizens to Slovakia in the spring of 1906 to be raised by Grandma, and then sailed back to New York to work for seven more years. Eight years later, the twins' parents returned to Austria-Hungary in May 1914, just weeks before the emperor's heir, Archduke Franz Ferdinand, was assassinated in Sarajevo. Samuel was conscripted into the army, won a medal for bravery under fire, but was killed in Italy in June 1918.

Samuel's story provides the thread that ties together the larger story of peasant life in Austria-Hungary before and during the war. Among the millions of the emperor's subjects who emigrated to seek a better life elsewhere were hundreds of thousands of

Slovaks who sailed to America. Why they left, how they left, where they went, and how they fared in the New World may interest this second audience. In addition to statistical graphs documenting the large-scale movement of people across and within nations, the peasants' lives and journeys are illustrated with scores of quotations from novels of the era, allowing fiction to illuminate fact.

This book is presented as both a scholarly account of the Eastern Theater of the Great War and as a personal story of the lives of those forced to fight it for their emperor.

Prologue: The Habsburg Empire and the Great War

The Emperor and the Peasant tells parallel stories about two men at opposite ends of the social scale living in separate societies in the same country at the same time. The country was the Austro-Hungarian Empire. The time was over one hundred years ago, at the end of the 19th and the beginning of the 20th centuries.

The emperor was Franz Josef I, by the grace of God Emperor of Austria; Apostolic King of Hungary; King of Bohemia, Dalmatia, Croatia, Slavonia, Galicia, Lodomeria, Illyria; King of Jerusalem, etc.; Archduke of Austria; Grand Duke of Tuscany, Crakow; Duke of Lorraine, Salzburg, Styria, Carinthia, Carniola, the Bukovina; Grand Prince of Transylvania; Margrave of Moravia; Duke of the Upper and Lower Silesia, Modena, Parma, Piacenza, Guastalla, Oswiecin, Zator, Cieszyn, Friuli, Ragusa, Zara; Princely Count of Habsburg, Tyrol, Kyburg, Gorizia, Gradisca; Prince of Trent, Brixen; Margrave of the Upper and Lower Lusatia, in Istria; Count of Hohenems, Feldkirch, Bregenz, Sonnenberg, etc.; Lord of Triest, Kotor, the Wendish March; Grand Voivode of the Voivodship of Serbia, etc., etc.[1]

The peasant was my wife's grandfather, Samuel Mozolák, who lived in Krajné, a Slovak village in Hungary, one-half of the Austro-Hungarian Empire. Although they never met, Franz Josef's life profoundly affected Samuel Mozolák's. It is inconceivable that the peasant ever did anything to harm the emperor. The emperor, however, did much to harm him. By declaring war against Serbia, Franz Josef personally made the decision that led to his subject's death. So began World War I, innocently known then as the Great War—the war to end all wars.

Franz Josef resided in his Austrian palaces and visited Hungary as little as possible. Living in different places and with no common acquaintances, the two men traveled together on nonintersecting paths toward World War I. The story about Franz Josef is based entirely on historical records. Samuel Mozolák's story is based on family documents, histories of Slovaks in Hungary, reports of Slovaks emigrating to the United States, immigrants' personal accounts, and novels of the era. It threads together the description of Slovaks' lives as subjects in Hungary and as immigrants in America.

Chapter 1 begins the emperor's story, which continues over the odd-numbered chapters. Chapter 2 and subsequent even-numbered chapters tell about the Slovak peasant who crossed the ocean at 20 years of age to work in New York City and who returned to Slovakia in time to fight in Franz Josef's war. Those chapters also tell why hundreds of thousands of Slovaks fled the empire, how they traveled to the United States, where they settled, and what they did as immigrants. The Epilogue evaluates more broadly the pattern and extent of immigration in the United States from the 19th to the 21st century.

The Habsburg Empire

Our story about Emperor Franz Josef is also about the Habsburg empire of Austria-Hungary, little-known to most readers today, but early in the 20th century it was the second largest country in Europe. Map P.1 shows its sprawling expanse of territory, which one writer described as a "great blotch of a single color on the European map."[2]

According to League of Nation statistics, Austria-Hungary covered 625,000 square kilometers and had 50.6 million inhabitants. Only Russia, at 21,745,000 square kilometers and 173 million people, was larger. Germany was larger in population at 67 million but not in area.[3] Separately, Austria and Hungary were about equal in size—Hungary being slightly larger (325,000 vs. 300,000 square kilometers), but Austria having more people (29 vs. 21.5 million).[4] Physically, the empire's two components were well matched.

Map P.1: THE BOUNDARIES OF THE HABSBURG EMPIRE IN 1914. At the beginning of the 20th century, Austria-Hungary was the largest country in Europe outside of Russia. This map shows the boundaries and major cities of the Habsburg empire at the time it entered the First World War in August 1914. Credit: Map produced by Geographx with research assistance from Damien Fenton and Caroline Lord. Available at www.nzhistory.net.nz. Used with permission.

Austria and Hungary also were similar in another respect: they were mainly agricultural economies. Figure P.1 compares Austria and Hungary separately with France, Germany, and Britain. Majorities of the workforce in Austria-Hungary were engaged in agriculture: 57 percent in Austria and 64 percent in Hungary. Both workforces clearly differed from those in Germany and Britain, where more people worked in industry or mining than agriculture. Although a plurality of France's workforce was also agricultural, its proportions in industry and mining were not far behind those of Germany and Britain.

Austria and Hungary were dissimilar, however, in language and ethnicity. German was the predominant language in Austria, the mother tongue of about 37 percent of the population, with about 70 percent knowing some German.[5] The Magyar language—functionally unrelated to any other of the world's languages—predominated in Hungary. It was the mother tongue of about half the population, with ten other mother tongues spoken by the rest of its people. So the empire's problem was twofold: (1) Most people in one country could not communicate in the same language with people in the other one; and (2) substantial percentages of people within both countries could not communicate in the same language with one another. Language barriers caused huge political problems between Austria and Hungary, and within Austria and Hungary.

Austria-Hungary's Dual Monarchy

Heading the long list of Franz Josef's titles were "Emperor of Austria" and "King of Hungary." How did it happen that two countries with predominantly different languages were joined under one person with the title of emperor in one country and king in the other? The Austro-Hungarian "Dual Monarchy" has been described and analyzed in

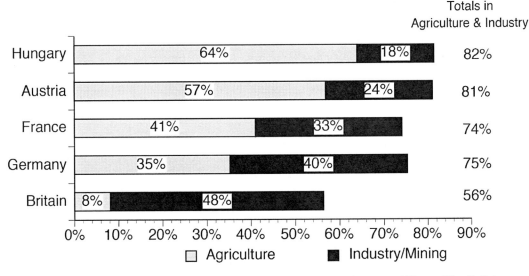

Figure P.1: Percent Employment in Agriculture and Industry Prior to World War I. Prior to World War I, more than half the workers in the three leading countries in Western Europe were engaged in agriculture, while both Austria and Hungary were predominantly agricultural. Data: League of Nations, Economic and Financial Section, *International Statistical Year-Book, 1927* (Geneva: Publications of the League of Nations, 1928), pp. 44–45.

many books, most of them dusty and unread.[6] Alan Sked, who authored one, admitted as much: "[F]ew people today know or care to know very much about the Habsburgs. History students rush towards doors or even windows when the subject is mentioned. The names involved are too difficult; the geography no less so; the evolution of events apparently complicated. The story, in any case, is one of retreat and dissolution, and therefore lacks appeal."[7] But, Sked said, to study the Habsburg empire is "to study the problems involved in ruling a large number of peoples of disparate and often mutually hostile cultures, in finding some bond of loyalty between them, and in retaining that loyalty in a world full of internal and external challenges. The Habsburgs did, moreover, rule more of Europe, and for a longer period, than anyone else in modern times. Hence if Europe is to unite it may still prove possible to learn from their mistakes."[8]

For centuries, Austria had been ruled by one of the most famous European dynasties, the House of Habsburg (occasionally spelled Hapsburg).[9] A.J.P. Taylor's history *The Habsburg Monarchy* said, "No other family has endured so long or left so deep a mark upon Europe: the Habsburgs were the greatest dynasty of modern history, and the history of central Europe revolves round them, not they round it."[10] The name came from Habsburg Castle, the 11th-century Swiss home of an early ancestor. Generations later, in 1273, Rudolph of Habsburg became King of Germany and moved from Habsburg Castle to the Duchy of Austria.[11] When Rudolph became Duke of Austria in 1276, he started the continuous string of Habsburg rulers of Austria that lasted until 1918.

This paragraph and the next four summarize the last three centuries of that "continuous string" of Habsburg rule. The string actually divided into two strands in 1556, when Charles V—head of the House of Habsburg, Holy Roman Emperor, and King of Spain to boot—abdicated in favor of two heirs: his son, Philip II, *and* his brother, Ferdinand I. Philip got Spain, its New World colonies, the Netherlands, and its Italian possessions—making Spain a global power.[12] Ferdinand as Archduke of Austria received the extensive Austrian and German lands in continental Europe—making Austria a European land power.[13] Thus, historians refer to the Spanish and Austrian branches of the House of Habsburg.

Ferdinand I in Austria was also named Holy Roman Emperor, an elected office chosen by a handful of princes. The Holy Roman Empire was a loose collection of territories in central Europe ritualistically blessed by the Pope and said to have descended from the Roman Empire. Often described as neither Holy nor Roman, it wielded little power but conferred great prestige to its emperors, who henceforth were usually Habsburgs.

Genealogical purists contend that the dynasty was extinguished in the 18th century with its lack of male heirs. Spain's Habsburg ruler, Charles II, died in 1700, childless and heirless, leading to the War of the Spanish Succession. Alerted to Spain's succession problem, Austrian Archduke and Holy Roman Emperor Charles VI in 1713 issued an edict known as the "Pragmatic Sanction" that allowed his daughter to inherit his Habsburg possessions in the absence of male heirs. Before dying in 1740, he persuaded foreign governments to recognize his edict, but after his 23-year-old daughter, Maria Theresa, claimed the throne, some reneged. The resulting War of the Austrian Succession cost Austria some territory, but Maria Theresa retained her crown, thanks in part to support from Hungary, which earned itself special treatment during her reign. She is known today as "Maria Theresa, Empress of Austria," but her biographer Robert Pick has noted, "The title [Empress] was unknown in her own day, as indeed was an 'Austrian Empire.'"[14]

Maria Theresa continued the line of Habsburg rulers through marriage to Francis

I, Duke of Lorraine, which created a Habsburg-Lorraine heritage for their male offspring. Her father's death allowed a non–Habsburg to be chosen Holy Roman Emperor, but the interloper lived for only two years. Then the "Empress of Austria" connived to elect her husband to the post, restoring that title to the House of Habsburg-Lorraine. On her death in 1780, Maria Theresa was succeeded by their sons: first Joseph II, who ruled until dying in 1790, and then Leopold II, who died in 1792. Both succeeded their father in election as Holy Roman Emperors. Thus, non-purists grant continuation of the Habsburg line, modified as Habsburg-Lorraine.

Leopold II's son, Francis II, reigned after his father. Thus, Habsburgs of one type or another occupied the throne of the Holy Roman Empire from 1438 to 1806—with the brief exception following Charles VI's death. In 1806, however, Napoleon crushed the Austrian armies, which forced Francis II to abdicate as Holy Roman Emperor and dissolve the Empire. Napoleon graciously allowed Francis II, the last Holy Roman Emperor, to proclaim himself Francis I, the first Emperor of Austria. Counting this as a continuance of office, the House of Habsburg supplied Europe with functioning emperors for over 600 years.

In a nutshell, that encapsulates the origin and history of the Hapsburg-Lorraine dynasty up to the 19th century. Few people today employ the modified name, Habsburg-Lorraine, referring refer simply to the Habsburg dynasty. In 2015, for example, museums in Minneapolis, Houston, and Atlanta billed the traveling and "astonishing" art exhibition from Vienna's Kunsthistorisches Museum as "Habsburg Splendor: Masterpieces from Vienna's Imperial Collection."[15]

Over centuries of marriages and conquests (mostly marriages), the Habsburgs vastly expanded their domain. A common epigram of the time was, "Let others make wars, thou happy Austria, marry!"[16] One historian plotted some fifty territory increments and decrements from 1282 to 1918.[17] Although the result from centuries of marriages and wars is easier to visualize on a map than explain in words,[18] Map P.2, which shows the periodic gains and occasional losses of Habsburg territories in Central Europe, is complex enough.[19]

Austria acquired the territory of Hungary in 1699. That date marks the treaty that ended war with Turkey, and which ceded European territories to those already held under Habsburg rule, however limited that rule. Hungarian nobility, for example, had extracted considerable autonomy to govern the kingdom under their own laws. Hungarians defended and preserved their autonomy throughout the time they were formally ruled by the Habsburgs.

Despite having a numerical advantage in troops and a favorable tactical environment, Austria and its Emperor Franz Josef suffered a humiliating defeat by Prussia in the 1866 Battle of Königgrätz.[20] This was terrible news for Austria but not necessarily for Hungary. The Hungarian historian Oscar Jászi wrote, "According to a tradition, when Francis Deak, the great liberal Hungarian leader, heard the first news of the Austrian defeat, he exclaimed, 'We lost the war! … we are now victorious.'"[21]

Deák saw opportunity in Austria's defeat. Not only did Prussia absorb Austria's small German allies, but it also excluded Austria from the nascent German Confederation.[22] Defeated and snubbed, Austria sought support from, and a stable relationship with, its Hungarian half. In 1867 Franz Josef agreed to a proposal floated in the Hungarian Diet— a parliament dominated by the Magyar plurality—for a "Dual Monarchy." He would reign and rule as Emperor of Austria and would reign, but not really rule, as King of Hungary.

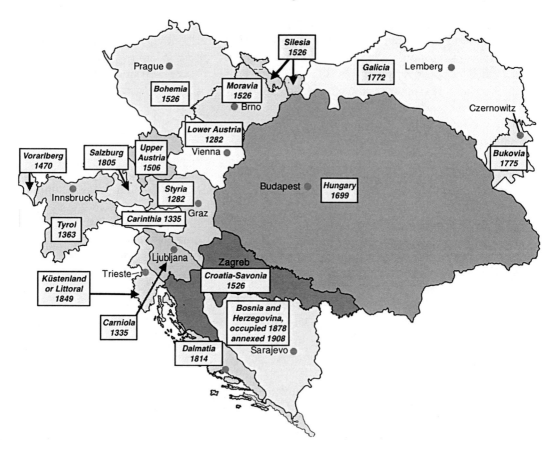

Map P.2: The Growth of the Habsburg Empire, 1282 to 1918. In 1282, the Habsburg possessions consisted only of Lower Austria and adjacent Styria. By 1526, they had extended northward to include Bohemia, Moravia, and Silesia, and southward to embrace Croatia. Hungary was acquired in 1699, doubling Habsburg territory. By 1918, Austria-Hungary had expanded to include Tyrol and other lands to the west and Bosnia-Herzegovina and Dalmatia to the south. Credit: Based on the map at https://commons.wikimedia.org/wiki/File:Austria-Hungary_map. svg in the public domain tagged with information in Gordon Brook-Shepherd, *The Austrians: A Thousand-Year Odyssey* (New York: Carroll & Graf Publishers, 1998), pp. xiv–xv.

Hungarians—i.e., Magyars—could rule themselves through their Diet in Budapest. As Emperor and King, however, Franz Josef would oversee the foreign affairs and defense of both countries under a joint budget acceptable to both Budapest and Vienna. The arrangement became known as the 1867 Compromise (*Ausgleich* in German, and *Kiegyezés* in Magyar).

With the Compromise of 1867, Vienna effectively relinquished the government of Hungary to its strong Magyar plurality. Henceforth, Franz Josef would act as their monarch only when Hungary faced external threats. Unlike republican France, where successful rebels lopped off the heads of aristocrats, Hungary's Magyars, who had rebelled against the monarchy in 1848, were themselves aristocrats with monarchist sympathies. As King of Hungary under the Dual Monarchy, Franz Josef seemed to be their type of king. Living in Vienna, he could be revered in absentia while not present to interfere with how the Magyar aristocratic leaders governed the country. One writer likened the unique polity to an egg with two yolks.[23] Contained within its own membrane, the Hungarian yolk was protected from being scrambled with the Austrian one.

Perhaps the new creation is better described as conjoined twins: two adjacent states that could function fully, given the other's cooperation. Consider the so-called "Siamese twins," Thai-Americans Chang and Eng Bunker, who were joined at the sternum.[24] Born in 1811, they cooperated well enough to father twenty-one children (eleven and ten respectively) through marriages to two sisters. The Bunker twins led full and respected lives until Chang suffered a stroke in 1870, declined in health, and began drinking heavily. Due to separate cardiovascular systems, Chang's drinking did not affect Eng. Nevertheless, Eng died about three hours after Chang's death in 1874. Still, they survived as conjoined twins for 62 years—longer than the 51 years of union between Austria and Hungary, which started in 1867 and ended in 1918.

Unfortunately for their marriage, the Austria-Hungary twins did not cooperate as well as the Bunkers. Austria—home of enchanting Vienna and centuries-long seat of the Holy Roman Empire—was the more illustrious of the two states. It was also the more willing to cooperate with its jealous partner, often giving in to Hungary's demands. Hungary already enjoyed special treatment since backing Maria Theresa during the War of the Austrian Succession in 1741. Pieter Judson said, "Her personal relationship to Hungary was tinged most obviously by the gratitude she felt throughout her reign for the critical support the Hungarian Diet had offered her in her moment of abject weakness."[25] Moreover, the Hungarian nobility, mostly but not all Magyars, claimed that they led a "Hungarian nation" that had certain rights, including the right to crown their own king. Indeed, Maria Theresa herself was crowned King of Hungary in 1741 (women were thought unfit to rule so her title was adjusted accordingly).[26] More than a century later, the Compromise of 1867 formalized the Hungarian nobilities' aspirations in a unique monarchical union.

To continue the marriage analogy: the Compromise was a loveless one that proved to be bad for both spouses. Austria and Hungary had little to unite them except survival in European politics, and much to divide them. The Dual Monarchy joined two countries dominated by two proud ethnic groups—Germans in Austria and Magyars in Hungary. While Austria did not lead Europe in political modernity, it was far ahead of Hungary in extending citizenship rights to its inhabitants. Moreover, both partners were unwilling to share power with the nine other ethnic minorities in their lands, and even unwilling to cooperate constructively with each other. In his two-volume work, *The Passing of the Hapsburg Monarchy, 1914–1918*, Arthur May wrote: "[T]he crowning astonishment is not that the multinationality realm of the Hapsburgs burst asunder, but that in an age of perfervid nationalism this heritage from an earlier historical era survived so long as it did."[27] When the empire did collapse at the end of the Great War, May marveled at the event: "Here was a strange realm of over fifty-two millions, almost bewildering in its linguistic complexity, lying in the heart of Europe, possessed of great armies and rich material resources.... Sober writers have been known to compare the resounding break-up of the Danube Monarchy in 1918 to the disappearance of ancient Babylon or Assyria or even of imperial Rome."[28] Unfortunately for Franz Josef (and for his empire), he denied to the end that it was a bad marriage. As is often the case in a bad one, the children suffered the most. In this case, that means the empire's non–German and non–Magyar subjects—the Czechs, Poles, Ruthenes,[29] Slovaks, Serbs, Croats, Slovenes, Romanians and Italians.

The Great War

The Great War began on July 28, 1914, when Austria-Hungary declared war on Serbia for the assassination in June of Archduke Franz Ferdinand on the streets of Sarajevo, Bosnia. During the ensuing century, thousands of books detailed the worldwide inferno. Most people in Western Europe and the United States learned about the war from the "Western Front" perspective. Barbara Tuchman adopted that perspective in her enthralling 1962 book *The Guns of August*, winner of a Pulitzer Prize for nonfiction and a favorite of President John F. Kennedy. Tuchman's book made for fascinating reading but presented a myopic view of the war. Tuchman wrote only about Germany fighting against France, Britain, Belgium, and Russia—and mainly on the Western Front. She said virtually nothing about the causes of the war and barely mentioned Germany's ally, Austria-Hungary, which actually ignited the conflagration. Tuchman devoted only eight sentences to the Austro-Hungarian Empire and Emperor Franz Josef; they occurred on just 7 pages out of 524.[30] Aware of this neglect, she explained:

> To the reader I must explain that the omission of Austria-Hungary, Serbia, and the Russo-Austrian and Serbo-Austrian fronts was not entirely arbitrary. The inexhaustible problem of the Balkans divides itself naturally from the rest of the war. Moreover, operations on the Austrian front during the first thirty-one days were purely preliminary and did not reach a climax, with effect on the war as a whole, until the Battle of Lemberg against the Russians and the Battle of the Drina against the Serbs. These took place between September 8 and 17, outside my chronological limits, and it seemed to me there was unity without it and the prospect of tiresome length if it were included.[31]

If Tuchman dismissed "the omission of Austria-Hungary" from her account of the Great War, her omission fit into historiography up to the 1970s. Historian James Sheehan wrote that until then, "scholarly consensus had assigned Germany a predominant share of the blame for starting the war."[32] Writing in the early 2000s, British historian Alan Sked—reflecting the revised historiography—laid responsibility for the war squarely on the Habsburg regime, saying, "The Monarch deliberately started a world war rather than compromise internally or externally on the South Slav question" in the Balkans.[33] In fact, Austria-Hungary had declared war on Serbia and fired on Belgrade before fighting began between Germany and the Allied powers.

A series of recent books—James Sheehan reviewed four—reinforced Austria-Hungary's role in starting the war.[34] In *The End of Tsarist Russia*, Dominic Lieven in 2015 reflected historiography's recognition that the war originated outside of Germany, stating: "[The war's] immediate origins lay in the murder of the Austrian heir at Sarajevo in southeastern Europe. The assassination of Franz Ferdinand on June 28, 1914, led to a confrontation between Austria and Russia, eastern Europe's two great empires. France and Britain were drawn into what started as a conflict in eastern Europe above all because of fears for their own security: the victory of the Austro-German alliance over Russia would tilt the European balance of power decisively toward Berlin and Vienna."[35] Lieven went further: "Contrary to the near-universal assumption in the English-speaking world, the war was first and foremost an eastern European conflict."[36] Not only did Austria-Hungary start the war in central Europe, but most of the fighting occurred outside of Western Europe over a greater area of land. Writing about both military arenas, Winston Churchill said, "In the West the armies were too big for the country; in the East the country was too big for the armies. The enormous masses of men which were repeatedly flung at each other were dwarfed and isolated by the scale of the landscape."[37]

Historians read history books. Ordinary people read novels and watch movies, allowing the popular media to shape their understanding of the war. Soon after the war, people in North America and Western Europe read novels and saw films portraying how Britain, France, and the United States fought against Germany. A prime example is *All Quiet on the Western Front*, the English title of a 1929 novel by a German soldier and survivor made into a 1930 movie, which won two awards from the United States Academy of Motion Picture Arts and Science.[38] Remade for television in 1979, its images were revived in Steven Spielberg's 2011 acclaimed World War I movie *War Horse*. It told the story of a cavalry officer's mount performing heroic deeds as a workhorse on the Western Front, when cavalry proved outdated for trench warfare.

Movies about the Great War were made even as it was fought. Social historian Maureen Healy said that Vienna had 160 cinemas (kinos) in 1918.[39] A weekly compilation of war footage, the *Kriegswochenschau* (weekly war show or war newsreel), was very popular.[40] However, many comedies and dramas—even those from enemy countries—entertained war-weary citizens. Healy said, "If their content was deemed acceptable, all signs of their 'enemy origin'—titles, subtitles, credits—had to be removed."[41] That proved relatively easy to do, given that they were silent films.

Since then, scores of movies have shaped the public's view about the Great War. Over one hundred and thirty films from 1918 to 2015 were produced in more than twenty countries.[42] Many films created in one language were released in another via subtitles or voice dubbing. Some important films were remade for different audiences. For example, the 1918 Hungarian silent film *Hotel Imperial*, which recounted international intrigue along the Russian-Austrian border at the end of the war, was remade in 1927 in the United States as a silent film under the same title. In 1939, it was remade in Hollywood as a sound film, again as *Hotel Imperial*.

World War I attracted filmmakers worldwide. The United States produced only one-third of those movies, the United Kingdom only another tenth. Other countries made more than half. Not surprisingly, most movies—almost 30 percent—were filmed in the 1930s when the motion picture industry had matured. Surprisingly, the second most prolific decade was the 2000s (12 percent). By 2015, fifteen World War I films (10 percent) were listed for the 2010s, putting the present decade on track to produce the most movies about the Great War since the 1930s.

A hundred years after its conclusion, the Great War continues to fascinate filmmakers and viewers. The war's causes were nuanced and debatable and its belligerents motivationally and sociologically complex. World War I offered filmmakers more options than World War II. World War I had scheming imperialists on both sides, but World War II was constrained by an ideological dualism: autocracy versus democracy. The monochromatic films of World War I rendered events in many shades of gray, but even color films of World War II portrayed conflicts in black and white.[43] Whereas motion pictures about the Second World War glamorized action and adventure in defeating the Axis powers, less than twenty percent of films about the First World War were action or adventure. Two-thirds were dramas.

In his chapter "Films of the War," American historian J.M. Winter classified war movies in six categories—(1) Mythologies of War, (2) Landscapes of Battles, (3) Camaraderie of Arms, (4) Romantic Themes, (5) Noble Warriors, comic and otherwise, and (6) Pacifism and the Pity of War.[44] In the "Camaraderie of Arms" category, Winter placed Frenchman Jean Renoir's 1937 film *The Grand Illusion*, which dramatized the attempt of

French soldiers to escape from a German prison, and called it "perhaps the greatest" of all. By portraying World War I solely in terms of the Western Front, with French and British soldiers pitted against Germans, *The Grand Illusion* once again fueled a view of the war that neglected the conflict in Eastern Europe, where almost a million more soldiers died than in Western Europe.[45] Thoroughly familiar with portrayals of trench warfare in Belgium and France, western audiences are less familiar with other theaters of operation in World War I.

They may be only dimly aware that Germany and Austria-Hungary, the two main Central Powers, also fought on an "Eastern Front" against Russia until 1917, when the Bolsheviks withdrew from the war. The fifth and final volume of Winston Churchill's history of the war was titled *The Unknown War: The Eastern Front*, which he called "incomparably the greatest war in history. In its scale, in its slaughter, in the exertions of the combatants, in its military kaleidoscope, it far surpasses by magnitude and intensity all similar human episodes."[46] As fighting on the west and east flanked the countries of northern Europe, battles occurred on at least five other fronts to the south and east (see Map P.3).

Although the conflict on the Eastern Front was treated in various versions of *Hotel Imperial*, that film was made many decades ago. The more recent British television mini-series *The Fall of Eagles* dramatized events in the Eastern Front, but few people today know of that outstanding 1974 production. Only Romanian speakers or those truly dedicated to the cinema are likely to have seen *The Death Triangle* (*Triunghiul Mortii*), a 1999 film set in Romania on the Eastern Front in the Great War. More readily available to English readers is the powerful 2009 novel *The Linden and the Oak*, which described the destruction wrought on innocent Rusyn villagers (sometimes called Ruthenes). Although some films and novels address military operations in the Eastern Front, they are little known. Other well-known films set in Russia during World War I, like *Doctor Zhivago*, focused more on domestic Russian politics.

The pickings are slim for World War I movies and books on other fronts than the Western Front—in the Balkans, Italy, the Caucasus, the Middle East, and Palestine.[47] One 1981 Academy Award–winning film was set in the far edges of the Balkan Front. *Gallipoli* dramatized how the Turks, occupying the high ground, fired relentlessly on thousands of Brits, Australians, and New Zealanders landing on the beaches below—leading to a military disaster. Readers today may have even less information about fighting toward the Mediterranean, where the Central Powers fought against Italy on the Italian Front. However, they may have read Ernest Hemingway's 1929 romantic novel *A Farewell to Arms*, or seen the 1932 or 1957 film adaptations by the same name.

Knowing about the Italian Front answers a question raised by *The Sound of Music*, the 1965 "Best Picture" about the von Trapp family of singers in Austria. In the movie, Nazi officials in the 1930s wanted Baron von Trapp, the family head and former Austrian naval officer, to join the German navy. *Question:* When did Austria, a land-locked country, have a navy? *Answer:* When it was part of the Austro-Hungarian Empire and bordered on the Adriatic Sea. *The Sound of Music* did not explain that von Trapp had been a distinguished U-boat commander in World War I. Indeed, the English-language media generally said little about troops dying on the Italian and Balkan Fronts.

For the record, battles also raged thousands of miles east on three fronts spread across a thousand miles from north to south. On the Palestine Front, the British confronted combatants from the Ottoman Empire, while on the Middle East Front, the British

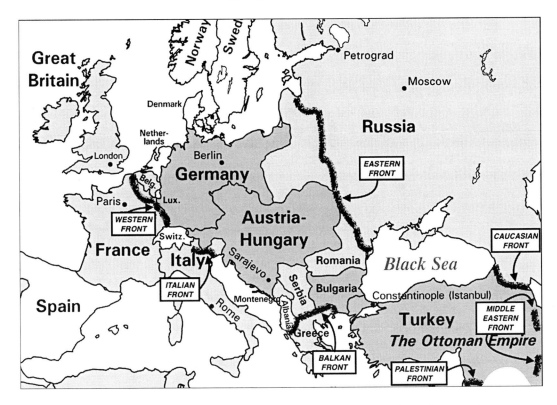

Map P.3: Seven Fronts in the Great War. This map approximates where the seven fronts—main battle areas—stood at the end of World War I. Most English-language readers know about the Western Front and may have heard a little about the Eastern Front, but few know anything about the Italian and Balkan Fronts, not to mention the Caucasian, Middle East, and Palestine Fronts. Note that the Central Powers (in dark gray) generally occupied lands within the territories of the Allied Powers (lighter gray), who formally won the war. Credit: Original for this book, drawn according to the fronts as portrayed in Alan Palmer, *The Gardeners of Salonika* (New York: Simon & Schuster, 1965), inside cover.

and the Russians faced Turkish forces supported by Germany. The public experienced fighting on these fronts in the 1962 Oscar-winning film, *Lawrence of Arabia*. On the "Caucasian" Front to the north, Russia and Britain fought Turkey, the leading power in the declining Ottoman Empire. Few Americans got insights into the Caucasian Front, except for the handful who saw the 2008 Turkish film *120*, about 120 Turkish children who died carrying ammunition to soldiers fighting Russians in the 1915 Battle of Sarikamis.

To complete the record, World War I also spread across the North Sea, the Mediterranean Sea, the Atlantic Ocean, and even the Pacific Ocean. The British navy ruled over the seas, but German submarines ruled under them, particularly in the Atlantic Ocean. The war also extended to Africa. The 1951 Academy Award–winning film *The African Queen*, starring Humphrey Bogart and Katharine Hepburn, was set in German East Africa at the outbreak of the war. Fitting their decrepit river launch *African Queen* with torpedoes, they managed to sink a German gunboat commanding a strategic lake and waterway. The war's reach into Asia could be seen in the 2006 Japanese movie *Ode to Joy*, in which German soldiers, captured from German territories in the Far East, were transported to a Japanese prison camp.

Mentioning these far-flung battle theaters underscores the scope and complexity of the Great War, the First World War. Like these war movies in exotic settings, the intertwined stories about the emperor and the peasant may reveal aspects of the Great War and the lives of its combatants that have escaped the average citizen's attention a century after Franz Josef died and the war ended.

Relating Samuel Mozolák's story alongside Franz Josef's tells how one subject among the emperor's Slovak minority escaped the empire's grip. In 1902 Samuel Mozolák emigrated from the empire to New York, where he married a Slovak immigrant from a nearby village in Hungary. Giving birth to twins, they took their infant U.S. citizens back to Hungary to be raised by grandma while they returned to earn money in New York. Samuel and his wife returned to Hungary in the spring of 1914, shortly before Archduke Franz Ferdinand was assassinated in Sarajevo.

Within weeks, Samuel was conscripted to fight in the Great War. Although he paid the ultimate price for returning to his children, he may have been satisfied knowing how things eventually turned out for his homeland and his descendants. His American twins, and another son conceived in the U.S. but born in Hungary, eventually followed him to New York, where they gave birth to their own children, all natural-born United States citizens. Samuel Mozolák's story serves as a vehicle for telling the story of Slovak immigration to America, a story that should resonate with the many millions of European immigrants who came to the United States seeking better lives for their families than they experienced in the old country.

1

The Emperor in Vienna

Franz Josef I was Emperor of Austria only in the English language. In German, Austria's official language, he was *Kaiser* Franz Josef I. Readers may think that only Germany had kaisers. Kaiser of course derives from Caesar, which the Romans called their rulers starting with Julius Caesar, their first de facto emperor. Tsar (or Czar) in Russian derives from Caesar too, so tsar also means emperor. While Austrian emperors are kaisers in German texts, they are emperors in English texts. That linguistic code helps in writing about the Austrian, German, and Russian imperial houses—about the emperor, the kaiser, and the tsar.[1]

The title of emperor goes back to Roman times. In 44 BC, Gaius Julius Caesar, to use his full name, was proclaimed "dictator in perpetuity" of the Roman Republic before it became the Roman Empire. Historians credit his adopted son Octavius, who ruled as "Augustus" from 63 BC to AD 14, as being the first Roman emperor.[2] "Empire" itself is an imprecise term. It refers to a political system that unites different lands under a single person (personage is important) who rules through central political institutions.[3]

If any monarch deserved an imperial title in the last half of the 19th century, it was Queen Victoria, whose 400 million subjects were spread across nearly one-quarter of the world's land mass. Piqued that lesser monarchs (including her erratic German grandson, Wilhelm II) had grander titles than she had, yet knowing that Parliament would not make her a British Empress, Victoria contrived to become Empress of India in 1877, the same year she celebrated her 40th year as "merely" Queen of the United Kingdom of Great Britain and Ireland.[4]

Franz Josef's rule as Emperor of Austria (Photo 1.1) began almost twenty years before he was crowned King of Hungary. Born August 18, 1830, Franz Josef was emperor for 11 days short of 68 years—from December 2, 1848, to his death on November 21, 1916. At the outbreak of World War I, he had reigned longer than all living European monarchs. (Queen Victoria died in 1901 after 63 years and 217 days on the British throne.) On September 9, 2015, when Queen Elizabeth II at 89 surpassed Queen Victoria's reign as Britain's longest-serving monarch, she was still four years short of Franz Josef's reign. And unlike either British queen, Franz Josef could claim among his ancestors a long line of Holy Roman Emperors. By longevity and pedigree, Franz Josef I of Austria was an emperor's emperor.

To historians, however, Franz Josef was only a run-of-the-mill emperor. Biographer Joseph Redlich referred to him as "a good specimen of the average prince."[5] Describing Franz Josef as an average emperor is not citing him for having special abilities, like a typical winner of a Nobel Prize or a representative inductee to a sports Hall of Fame. Perhaps

15

in earlier eras, individuals with titles like emperor, king, tsar, sultan, or other appellations actually merited their status. But decades if not centuries of inbreeding through hereditary succession impaired the royal gene pool. As a biographer of George V, Nicholas II, and Wilhelm II pointed out: "Kaiser Wilhelm was Queen Victoria's eldest grandson. George's father was Wilhelm's uncle; his mother was Nicholas's aunt; Wilhelm and Nicholas, meanwhile, were both second and third cousins, through the marriage of a great-aunt, and a shared great-great-grandfather, the mad Tsar Paul of Russia."[6] Indeed, the network of Queen Victoria's relatives extended further. Her golden jubilee in 1887, which commemorated her 50 years of rule, was attended by 50 members of royalty—thirty-two of whom were related to her.[7] Contemporary zookeepers worry more about bloodlines for breeding giraffes than royal families did about producing heirs to monarchies.

Franz Josef found himself embroiled in an extended family conflict among three cousins in World War I. He fought alongside Germany's Kaiser Wilhelm II but against two of Wilhelm's cousins, Russian Tsar Nicholas II and Britain's King George V—all three related, by birth or marriage, to Queen Victoria. Such was the inbreeding among European monarchies, which abounded at the beginning of the 20th century. Of the fourteen key European countries involved in World War I, thirteen were monarchies. In alphabetical order, they were Austro-Hungary, Belgium, Britain, Bulgaria, Denmark, Germany, Greece, Holland, Italy, Romania, Russia, Serbia, and Turkey—more properly, the Ottoman Empire. France stood alone as a republic, the only government without a hereditary head of state.

Some of these countries, most notably Britain, had a constitutional monarchy, the king functioning as a nonpolitical head of state within written or unwritten constitutional boundaries. Walter Bagehot's *The English Constitution*, published in 1867, same year the Dual Monarchy was formed, claimed that the English sovereign had just "three rights"—"the right to be consulted, the right to encourage, the right to warn."[8] In contrast, the three key monarchs in World War I recognized no limits to their authority. Franz Josef, like Kaiser Wilhelm II of Germany and Tsar Nicholas II of Russia, believed in rule by divine right. Accordingly, all three ruled as autocrats, dismissing attempts by fledgling governmental institutions to constrain their powers.

Unlike King George V, who understood that he was merely Britain's symbolic head of state and not its ruler, Kaiser Wilhelm II in particular made

Photo 1.1: EMPEROR FRANZ JOSEF I IN 1851. Portrait of Emperor Franz Josef I by Eduard Klieber, painted in 1851, when the emperor was about twenty years of age and in his third year on the throne. Credit: In the public domain; available at https://commons.wikimedia.org/w/index.php?title=File:Eduard_Klieber_Franz_Joseph_I.jpg&oldid=182056121.

decisions that conflicted with advice from his generals and ministers. Tsar Nicholas II often autocratically changed his mind after making a decision, or simply failed to decide. Emperor Franz Josef imperiously ignored key problems, such as Hungarian obstructionism, that threatened his empire and that no one but the emperor could have confronted. As we will see, none of these three emperors made history for his intellectual abilities or governmental skills.

Franz Josef reached legal maturity at age 18 on August 18, 1848, just months after the start of the 1848–1849 revolutionary period. The Austrian emperor then was childlike Ferdinand I.[9] His father, Francis II, and mother were cousins, and Ferdinand suffered from various medical aliments, including epileptic seizures. Ferdinand I governed through a regency council while occupying the throne from 1835 to 1848. Historians often characterize him by citing his response when told he could not have apricot dumplings because apricots were out of season: "I'm the Emperor, and I want dumplings!" When liberal forces rebelled within his empire in 1848, he reportedly asked, "But are they allowed to do that?"[10] Naturally, key council members anxiously awaited Franz Josef's 18th birthday. Once Franz became of age, they could maneuver him onto the throne to replace Ferdinand, thus restoring strength to the monarchy and order to the state.

To understand Franz Josef's place in the politics of the Austro-Hungarian Empire, one needs to know something about the circumstances surrounding his coronation. Here is an abbreviated recap of key developments at that time.

- Across Europe in 1848, threats to established rulers were real, including in Austria. In March, the emperor's troops suppressed students in Vienna demonstrating for political reforms. Armed conflict broke out after workers joined the demonstrators. Rebellion against Austrian rule occurred as well in Italy, and Hungary declared itself an independent kingdom in April.[11] Acceding to demands and directed by his regency council, Ferdinand dismissed conservative Chancellor Clemens Metternich, the famous statesman and council member. Despite the crown's concessions, street protests became more violent, forcing Ferdinand to flee to Innsbruck. Returning after order was restored, Ferdinand sent troops to crush the Hungarian revolt, only to lose a battle to the revolutionaries. On October 6, Viennese citizens again took to the streets, protesting the conflict with Hungary. A mob seized the war minister Count Latour-Baillet, killed him, and hanged his body on a lamppost. The Emperor and his government again fled the city, this time to Olmütz (Olomouc) in Moravia.
- Prince Felix of Schwarzenberg, Chancellor Metternich's latest replacement, agreed to serve on the regency council only if it agreed to replace the incompetent Emperor Ferdinand with his young nephew, Archduke Franz Josef. Although informed of the plan several weeks before it occurred, the young emperor-in-waiting did not instigate his uncle's replacement.[12] To implement his extraordinary coup, Prince Schwarzenberg required key royal players to agree on three steps:
  - First, the young Franz Josef must agree to accept the crown. He was willing to do that, but not more willing than his mother, Archduchess Sophia, who groomed him for the throne.
  - Second, Archduke Francis Charles, Franz Josef's father and next in line for the throne, must renounce his claim to the throne. Described as a "kindly

> nonentity,"[13] the Archduke was willing to do that, but not more willing than his wife, Archduchess Sophia, who longed for her son to be emperor.
> - Third, Ferdinand himself must agree to abdicate. He was willing to do that, and so was his plain and dutiful wife, Empress Anna Maria, who suffered at court in a loveless and childless marriage.
> - On December 2, 1848, in a chamber of the Archbishop's palace in Olmütz before a small gathering of the Imperial family, Emperor Ferdinand haltingly read the Abdication Act handed to him by Prince Schwarzenberg. Archduke Francis Charles obediently stood aside, and Franz Josef politely accepted the crown. Accounts differ on exactly what Ferdinand said, but they agree that uncle and nephew embraced when the emperor surrendered his throne.[14]

Thus concluded the amicable coup that placed the teenage Franz Josef on the throne to begin his long reign. Unhappily for the new emperor, the court remained stuck in Olmütz, the situation in Vienna being judged unstable and dangerous. Franz Josef remained there until May 1849, when he returned to Vienna as emperor and supreme commander of the army.[15]

Neither side in the revolution was inspired by the persona of weak Ferdinand I, whose "sickly frame sometimes cut a sharply unvirile figure,"[16] or by the untested youth, Franz Josef. Nevertheless—and ironically—forces on both sides *favored* Habsburg rule. Slovak historian Victor Mamatey wrote that "the Magyars fought paradoxically *in the name* of the King *against* the King."[17] In fact, some troops fought each other under the emperor's banner, and Franz Josef awarded medals for bravery on opposing sides. Loyalty in the 1848–49 revolution lay little to the emperor as a person, more to the prestige of the Habsburgs, and most to monarchy as the accepted mode of government. To his good fortune, the new emperor got assistance from two different individuals: General Radetzky, who prevailed over the Italians in the First Italian War for Independence, and Russian Tsar Nicholas I, who provided troops to help defeat the Magyar forces challenging rule from Vienna.

Following the end of the Magyar revolt, the young Emperor ignored advice from European leaders and, heeding his advisers, cracked down on its ringleaders, participants, and likely suspects, imprisoning thousands and executing hundreds.[18] Claiming that Hungary had forfeited its rights and special governmental status, the crown created a bureaucratic police state under centralized rule from Vienna, which relied on informers and spies to underscore its absolute rule.[19]

Ironically, during this period of absolute rule, Vienna proposed and imposed major liberal reforms in the empire's neo-feudal sociopolitical system. A new (and short-lived) constitution in 1849 contained liberal clauses that

> 1. freed the serfs ["every kind of feudal subjection is now and for ever abolished"];
> 2. gave citizens equal rights ["All Austrian citizens are equal in the eye of the law"]; and
> 3. accorded equal rights to races ["Equal justice will be given to all races, and each race has the inviolable right of preserving and maintaining its own nationality and language"].[20]

Although some Magyar liberals had proposed similar reforms in their 1848 revolution, many other Magyars resented their imposition from Vienna, especially the business about equal rights for all races—read: non–Magyars. R.W. Seton-Watson's celebrated and controversial 1908 book *Racial Problems in Hungary* described how Magyars mistreated Slovaks, Serbs, Romanians, Italians, and other nationalities.[21] People then in Europe—and in the United States—often spoke of nationalities as representing different "races."[22] Categorizing people by race suggested that they differed biologically, not just culturally. So not being in the dominant white nationality in the 19th century cut more deeply than it does today.

These events during 1848–1849 preceded the 1867 Compromise that created the Dual Monarchs—separate ones for Austria and Hungary. Historian John Deak also said that it "created two states, each with their own parliament, government, and judicial system."[23] The rebellious kingdom would govern itself through its own parliament in Budapest, but Franz Josef would oversee the foreign affairs and defense of both countries. However unwieldy this odd coupling proved to be, Franz Josef remained unalterably committed to the Dual Monarchy into the Great War, and to his death.

Meanwhile, Emperor Franz Josef had an imperial life to lead, one that required producing an heir. At 23 years of age, he rebelled against the carefully formulated marriage plans of his formidable mother, Archduchess Sophia, who had schemed to place him on the throne in the first place. (Some called her "the only man at court" during Ferdinand's ill-starred reign.) The Archduchess had decided that her son should marry Bavarian Princess Helene, who came from her own distinguished House of Wittelsbach. Not coincidentally, Princess Helene was her sister's eldest daughter, thus her niece and Franz Josef's cousin. In 1853, Helene at 19 was only four years younger than Franz Josef. Surely, that was a heaven-made match for her divine son.

In keeping with his mother's interpretation of God's plan, Franz Josef dutifully agreed to meet his cousin Helene at a family gathering. At the event, he was captivated by Helene's 15-year-old sister, Elisabeth, known as "Sisi" by the family. Defying his mother, he decided to marry Sisi and did so after she turned 16. In a simple royal ceremony (portrayed in Figure 1.1), Franz Josef followed dynastic custom and married within the family, as responsible monarchs did, on April 23, 1854.

The wedding was attended by the empire's finest people in their fanciest civilian attire and most ornamental military dress. Just as tailored tuxedos adorned Fred Astaire movies in the 1930s, resplendent uniforms formed backdrops for Viennese social affairs in the 19th century. The decor was reflected in contemporary operettas, usually featuring comic themes, which were very popular in central Europe. Writing about Budapest in 1900, John Jukacs called it the "golden age" of operetta.[24] *The Merry Widow*, by Hungarian composer Franz Lehár, debuted in Vienna in 1905 to great success. Lehár's operetta involved counts, barons, dukes, and diplomats in the fictional Grand Duchy of Pontevedro, presumably within the Austro-Hungarian Empire or perhaps in Montenegro. In 1908, Viennese composer Oscar Straus's successful *The Chocolate Soldier* was set in the neighboring Balkans and satirized war between Bulgaria and Serbia, which became no laughing matter during the Balkan Wars of 1912 and 1913.

According to cultural historian Fredrik Lindström, comic operettas were serious reflections of contemporary Austro-Hungarian politics. His book *Empire and Identity* devoted seven pages to *Der Rosenkavalier*, which premiered in Dresden in 1911. The operetta had music by Richard Strauss and a libretto by Hugo von Hofmannsthal, a prominent Viennese essayist. Although it was set earlier in the 18th century, Lindström said that Hofmannsthal intended his message for its contemporary audience, just before the war. The message reflected the "Austrian idea"—that only a "great empire" could produce

Figure 1.1: WEDDING OF FRANZ JOSEF AND ELISABETH (SISI). Emperor Franz Josef, age 24, married his cousin, Elisabeth Amalie Eugenie, Duchess of Bavaria, age 16, in Vienna on April 24, 1854. Credit: In the public domain; available at http://erzsebet-kiralyne.blog.cz/0808/zivotopis-1-cast.

"the cooperation and partial integration of the spirits of all [its] different peoples."[25] Hofmannsthal truly believed that the aristocracy promoted the social integration of disparate nationalities.

Operettas were performed even after the Great War started and continued long after it ended. Messages in comic art form often stressed society's frivolity rather than its social integration. In 1916, a Hungarian silent comedy film *Mágnás Miska* (*Magnate Mike*) spoofed the magnates who ruled prewar Hungary. In 1949, *Mágnás Miska* was remade into a musical comedy/operetta. The film's humor played well during the Communist era in the 1950s, when the term "magnate" became a nickname for degenerate aristocrats and greedy nobility. Clips from the film, which remains popular today, can be viewed on YouTube.[26]

The popular 2014 film *The Grand Budapest Hotel*, set between the two world wars in the fictional Republic of Zubrowka, also portrayed images of an elegant and class-conscious Austria-Hungary. In fact, the rolling credits at the film's end acknowledged that the screenplay was "Inspired by the writings of Stefan Zweig," a famous Viennese author at the time of the Great War. Zweig's 1941 autobiography *The World of Yesterday* furnished insights into life in central Europe at that time.[27]

Operettas with central European settings also drew enthusiastic audiences to stage and movie theaters across America in the early decades of the 20th century. Appreciative fans admired the florid costumes worn by court ladies and especially by dashing soldiers decked out with polished buttons, epaulettes, chin straps, and parade caps festooned with plumes and decorated visors. Sigmund Romberg's *The Student Prince*, set in the fictional kingdom of Karlsberg (probably German; maybe Austrian), exemplified the genre on stage and became the longest-running Broadway show in the 1920s. In the 1930s, the popular Marx Brothers' film *Duck Soup* parodied these operettas through foppish court scenes in the fictional European nations of Freedonia and Sylvania. The movie ended with a comic clash of their armies marked by a melee of flying fruit. (The film's impact on the American psyche is reflected in *Duck Soup*'s 1990 selection for preservation in the National Film Registry of the United States.)

Reflecting on dress in 1900, Zweig wrote in 1941: "We need merely look at the fashions, the modes of a century, with their trends in visual taste, unintentionally also reveal its morals. It is no mere chance that today, in the year 1941, when men and women of society of the year 1900 are shown on the cinema screen in the costumes of their time, audiences in every city and in every village of Europe or America break out into uncontrolled laughter. Even the most naive persons of today laugh at them as caricatures. These strange figures of yesteryear appear as unnaturally, uncomfortably, unhygienically, and unpractically dressed fools."[28]

Americans could find another reason for poking fun at the Austro-Hungarian Empire. Not only did its court—and especially its soldiers—look like they modeled for a 19th century operetta, but so did its political map. What to call all the new lands united under the Dual Monarchy?[29] Austria and Hungary wouldn't do, because those terms included only two entities (Archduchy of Austria and Kingdom of Hungary) among many within the new empire. Architects of the new government seized upon the little Leitha River (really a stream) that flowed close enough to the border between Austria and Hungary to represent a division of some sort. They duly proclaimed that all the lands west of the Leitha River (Austrian side) were to be known as "Cisleithania" and everything to its east (Hungarian side) as "Transleithania."[30] (In Latin, "cis" means "this side of" and "trans" means "across.")[31] At least in *Duck Soup*, the mythical country of Freedonia invoked the idea of freedom and Sylvania the image of woods. The names Cisleithania and Transleithania never caught favor in the United States. A computer search of the *New York Times* from 1867 to 1922 turned up only five stories that mentioned either term.

Less amusing but certainly more curious was the Dual Monarchy's concatenation of governmental forms, joining an autocracy with an oligarchy. By tradition and intent, Austria was an autocracy. Franz Josef clung to the Habsburg dynasty's belief in the divine right of kingship and, by extension, in monarchs' divine right to unfettered rule.[32] In today's world, we may not realize that many citizens then regarded their monarchs as deities, or close to it. Robert Musil's 1930 novel *The Man without Qualities* relates how even that amoral and indifferent man was awed when ushered into an audience with Emperor Franz Josef. "Till then he had taken the term 'Majesty' for a meaningless word that was kept in use from sheer habit, just as one can be an atheist and yet say 'Thank God.'"[33]

A novel about the era, Joseph Roth's *The Radetzky March*, described an Austrian officer's shock when someone referred to the Emperor as "Franz Josef " instead of "His Majesty."[34] In *The Emperor's Bust*, Roth recounted the plight of a high-ranking Austrian officer who survived the Great War only to find that his landed estate in the province of Galicia was no longer in Austria, but in a country called Poland. Ordered to remove from his property a bust of his beloved and deceased Emperor, he instead buried the bust with military honors, and requested to be buried alongside it.[35] Three decades later, Japanese soldiers died for Emperor Hirohito in World War II even though they had never heard him speak. After the war, Japanese citizens still dared not look at the Emperor's person.

Franz Josef, like most hereditary rulers, never experienced ordinary human existence. In *To the Last Man: A Novel of the First World War*, Jeff Shaara attributed to German Field Marshal Paul von Hindenburg this explanation of the German Kaiser's behavior: "You must understand that royalty are like children. They awake each morning to birds singing and servants fluttering around them. Their milk is always cold, their bread is always warm, and their beefsteak is always tender. They do not live in a world of inconvenience."[36] Monarchs typically held audiences before well-fed and well-dressed citizens of high status. They had an excuse for thinking that all their citizens resembled those who came before them. They literally did not *see* the great masses of their subjects who were ill-fed and ill-clothed.

Drawing on his subjects' reverence for royalty, the teen-aged Franz Josef naturally governed autocratically when he ascended to the throne in 1848. Although he promulgated a new constitution with a parliament, the document gave him complete control of government. He could veto legislation, appoint and dismiss ministers, dissolve parliament, and even rule by decree in emergencies.[37] While the crown occasionally made concessions and adjustments to deal with rebellions in 1848–1849 in both Austria and Hungary, Franz Josef opposed real constitutional reforms during 1860 and 1861 to counter unrest in Hungary. Governmental decisions remained firmly in the hands of Emperor Franz Josef and his ministers.

In essence, the Dual Monarchy resembled a shotgun marriage between fundamentally incompatible spouses. German guns forced the marriage by defeating Austria at the Battle of Königgrätz in 1866. Acting jointly to preserve their existence after the defeat, Austria and Hungary negotiated the Compromise of 1867, in which Austria permitted Hungary to govern itself internally while allowing Austria to direct both nations' foreign policy and defense. The stratagem for accomplishing this was the Dual Monarchy—the same person being the ruling emperor of Austria but only the symbolic king of Hungary, empowered to command the countries' joint forces in war, however. This marriage of convenience between two spouses was never intended to be consummated except in case of war.

The spouses were physically compatible in size but incompatible in other key aspects of a political marriage. They had not only different forms of government but different governmental orientations. Despite being an absolute monarchy, Austria recognized the liberalizing trends in Europe and made some effort to reflect them. It tried to achieve some equity in parliamentary representation of its territories, expanding voting rights for males in 1897 and granting universal male suffrage in 1907.[38] Austria was an autocracy with a little democratic gilding.

Despite Franz Josef's attempts to introduce universal suffrage at the same time in Hungary, the Magyars were not ready for that European political innovation.[39] Hungary simply did not look to Europe, to the west, for inspiration. While incorrect to imply that it looked to the east—to the Russian or Ottoman Empires—the Hungarian component of the Dual Monarchy was more inclined (like the Russians and the Turks) to keep their own inferior subjects (i.e., the non–Magyars) under their Magyar thumbs.

Which brings up another element of marital incompatibility. The two partners did not speak the same language. Literally. Austria's official language was German and Hungary's was Magyar. Within Austria, other nationalities—especially the Czechs—pressed to have their languages recognized and used in governmental affairs. So too in Hungary. In 1868, right after the Compromise, the Hungarian Parliament passed a "Law of the Equal Rights of Nationalities," allowing non–Magyar nationalities to develop their own language and culture. They could supposedly conduct local proceedings in the local mother tongue as well as Magyar and educate their children in their mother tongue at local schools.[40] But this law was largely ignored. By 1875, the only three Slovak high schools were closed.

Not only were Austria and Hungary incompatible partners linguistically, they were emotionally estranged. Historians portray many of Austria's top leaders as anti–Hungarian, including Archduke Franz Ferdinand, the Emperor's heir, and Count Franz Conrad von Hötzendorf, chief of staff preceding and during World War I.[41] Franz Josef himself traveled to Hungary as little as possible, despite the fact that he spoke good Magyar—as well as some Czech and Serbo-Croat.[42] He usually stayed close to enchanting Vienna.

In 1900, Vienna was one of the largest cities in the world. Estimated to have a population of 1.7 million, it ranked just behind London, New York, Paris, Berlin, and Chicago—in that order.[43] Vienna had majestic public buildings in its palaces, parliament, town hall, natural history museums, fine arts museums, concert hall, theater, and opera house—all bedecked with gold, marble, frescoes, and sculptures fit for the capital of an empire.[44] Zweig rhapsodized: "There is hardly a city in Europe where the drive towards cultural ideals was as passionate as it was in Vienna."[45] Vienna was an enchanting destination for visitors, and Franz Josef seldom left its surroundings.

Franz Josef had three major palaces of his own in or near Vienna and another about 160 miles west of Vienna at the Kaiservilla (Imperial Villa) in Ischl (later Bad Ischl), where he spent summers, especially later in life. The Habsburgs' established principal winter residence was sprawling Hofburg Palace (with 2,600 rooms) in the center of Vienna (Photo 1.2).[46] The 1,400-room Schönbrunn Palace on the outskirts of Vienna was another favorite summer residence (Photo 1.3). The Emperor also relaxed for periods at Laxenburg Castle just outside of Vienna. Perhaps Franz Josef avoided living inside Vienna because he cared little for its artistic offerings. The writer and intellectual Zweig sniffed that Franz Josef "had never read a book other than the Army Register, or even taken one in his hand, [and] evidenced moreover a definite antipathy to music."[47]

Franz Josef's wife, Empress Elisabeth, was more sympathetic to the arts, but her real passion was horseback riding, and she became a truly fine equestrian. Elisabeth was also enamored with Hungary, much to Franz Josef's dislike. She chose to learn Magyar well and delighted in wearing Hungarian national dress on her numerous visits. The appreciative Hungarians in 1867 officially crowned her Queen of Hungary when Franz Josef became King of Hungary, and they gave the royal couple Gödöllő Palace outside of Budapest.[48] To Franz Josef's annoyance, Elisabeth used it often—too often—leaving him in Vienna for weeks while she spent time in Budapest with her children.

With a population of about 800,000, Budapest was half the size of Vienna.[49] Although smaller in population, Budapest's history was comparably illustrious and its name more exotic. Budapest arose from two towns, Buda and Pest, situated respectively on the west and east sides of the Danube River. Buda Castle stood far above the west bank of the storied Danube River, roughly on the site of a destroyed castle from the 13th century. Austrian

Photo 1.2: HOFBURG PALACE ABOUT 1900. Historical panorama of the Michaelertrakt wing of the Imperial Hofburg Palace in Vienna (between 1890 and 1900). Credit: LC-DIG-ppmse-09210 from Library of Congress, Prints and Photographs Division, in public domain.

Photo 1.3: SCHÖNBRUNN PALACE ABOUT 1900. **Panorama of Schönbrunn Palace, summer home of Emperor Franz Joseph. Credit: LC-DIG-ppmsc-09213 (digital file from original) in the Library of Congress, Prints and Photographs Division; in public domain.**

Queen Maria Theresa built a new castle in the 18th century in return for the Hungarians' support of her effort to keep the throne as a woman monarch in the House of Habsburg. However, she had no intention of reigning from Budapest instead of Vienna.

After Buda Castle was built, it was used as a nunnery, a university, a palace for various archdukes, and an army headquarters—damaged when Austrians suppressed the Hungarian revolt in 1849. Rebuilt and enlarged, the grand building was the site of Franz Josef's coronation as King of Hungary in 1867 after the creation of the Dual Monarchy. Grand as it was, Buda Castle was regarded as too small for great royal celebrations, and further enlargements followed. Although the first floor had a wing of royal apartments, Franz Josef never used them for any extended period. After World War II, the building housed the Hungarian National Gallery, the national art museum.

Vienna and Budapest—the Dual Monarchy's two royal cities—were both technologically modern for the start of the 20th century. Most people today have only a hazy view of when new technologies became commonplace. In the early 1800s, Britain led in developing railroad technology, moving cargo and people with horses prior to using steam locomotives. By the 1830s, commercial railroads operated on the continent. By the 1840s, Austria and Hungary had railroad lines, as did Russia by the 1850s. Construction began on the Trans-Siberian railway in 1891.[50] As early as 1833, railroads transported troops into battle.[51] By World War I, every European country had railroad networks for moving troops and supplies, but some—as we will see—had far more extensive and effective networks than others.

Inventors also experimented with telegraphy in the early 1800s. Samuel Morse's method of expressing pulses of electrical current as dots and dashes was demonstrated in 1838. In 1847, Vienna had telegraph connections with Prague in Bohemia and Brno in Moravia, with Buda in Hungary connected the next year.[52] Austria was linked with the German states in 1850, and companies soon laid cables under the seas to connect to other continents, including Australia by 1872.[53] By 1883, people in Europe could read about the volcanic eruption (and destruction) of Krakatoa, an island between Sumatra and Java, the day after it happened.[54]

As the telegraph sent text messages over long distances, the telephone allowed people to talk to one another over shorter distances. Vienna and Budapest had telephone exchanges in 1881. By the end of the century, telephone lines connected virtually all cities and towns in Austria and Hungary.[55] Experiments with electricity as a source of light also began in the early 1800s but took time to be commercially productive. Although electric arc lighting appeared at the 1878 Paris Exposition, it was impractical for residential use. About that time, various inventors, including Thomas Edison, had designed incandescent bulbs that lit when transmitting electric current. In 1904, two residents of Austria-Hungary patented a tungsten filament lamp that lasted longer and glowed brighter than Edison's carbon filament. The bulb was marketed in Europe the same year (and in the U.S. two years later).[56]

So in the years prior to World War I, people in large European cities—certainly well-off citizens in Vienna and Budapest—could keep abreast of news across the globe via the telegraph; communicate with family, friends, and business partners via telegram and telephone; travel comfortably via the railroad to most cities in continental Europe (and by steamship to Britain and even to the United States); and spend time in the evenings talking with friends, reading, or working in relatively well-lit homes. They could also travel easily across their cities via the new subway systems that opened in Budapest in 1896 and in Vienna in 1898.

These technological achievements of the 19th century were showcased at the 1900 Paris Universal Exposition, during which Paris opened its own subway. As befits a Dual Monarchy, Austria-Hungary had not one but two pavilions at the Exposition. The Austrian pavilion was ornately decorated in the flowing lines and floral motifs of Art Nouveau style and embellished with fountains, statues, gold leaf, and marble accouterments. It naturally honored the Habsburg family but also showed exhibits by Czechs, Poles, and South Slavs among the Empire's many ethnic groups. In contrast, the Hungarian pavilion was strongly nationalistic, celebrating Magyar victories and paying little attention to the millions of non–Magyars living within Hungary's borders.[57] Even in deciding what to celebrate from their past and present, Austria and Hungary were at odds with each other.

Living in Vienna in 1900 at age 70, Franz Josef had a comfortable life, albeit one already marked by three personal tragedies. In 1867, his younger brother Maximilian was executed in Mexico after an aborted attempt to become its emperor. In 1889, his son and heir, the intelligent but psychologically troubled Crown Prince Rudolph, shot his mistress and committed suicide the same evening. In 1898, his wife, Empress Elisabeth—his beloved Sisi—was assassinated in a random act of anarchism. Franz Josef was already venerated by many of his subjects as a kindly ruler, as rulers go, and his family tragedies made him seem more human for being so unlucky. Given that his subjects typically regarded themselves as unlucky, many bonded to Franz Josef through his family misfortunes.

Unlucky, yes, but Franz Josef in 1900 had his duty to continue as Emperor, which he had been discharging for 52 years since his coronation in 1848. Only Britain's Queen Victoria, crowned in 1837, had served longer at that time. Victoria died in 1901, after more than 63 years on the throne. On June 12, 1908, the city of Vienna celebrated Franz Josef's Diamond Jubilee, marking his 60th year on the throne. In a book published the following year, Geoffrey Drage described that the procession "lasted more than three hours as 12,000 of his subjects, of all races and tongues, in costumes of all the historic periods of his house, shouting their loyal greetings," passed before the emperor: "Nobles and warriors have assembled before the monarch before, but never has there been so complete a muster of the peoples of the Empire. The Austrians, who are a nation without knowing it, found themselves that morning, and the people of Vienna cheered each race and clan, in the consciousness that not only common loyalty to a common dynasty personified in a venerable Sovereign, but also a common history, common interests, common enemies, and a common destiny, unite them all."[58] Franz Josef would reign for eleven days short of 68 years. He had been Emperor for so long that his people wondered what they would do without him. Franz Josef's likeness was prominently displayed in public places and in private homes of residents above the peasant class.

In the 21st century, we can observe the affection that British citizens, especially the English, feel for Queen Elizabeth II, who on September 9, 2015, became the longest-serving British monarch, breaking the record of her great-great-grandmother, Queen Victoria, of 63 years and seven months.[59] Since she is the longtime head of state, Queen Elizabeth's inevitable death will be felt in her subjects' hearts. But it will not necessarily be felt in their pocketbooks, for she, as a constitutional monarch, does not head her own government. British citizens can be assured that government, in the hands of parliament and the prime minister, will continue on course with the next monarch.

Not so with an absolute ruler like Franz Josef. Who knew what would follow after his death? When the emperor passed his 80th year in 1910, Stefan Zweig observed, "A mystical feeling began to spread universally that after his passing the dissolution of the thousand-year-old monarchy could no longer be stayed."[60] Given that most citizens in the Dual Monarchy had adjusted to life under kindly, stable old Franz Josef, few looked forward to his passing. They harbored little hope of getting a better deal under the new regime.

Franz Josef, who experienced the unnatural deaths of his brother, son, and wife during his long reign, even as an octogenarian unflinchingly accepted his duty to continue as emperor. He did so knowing that his succession was settled, although not to his liking. He had little choice. Franz Josef's younger brother and son, both certified heirs, had died violently—by execution and suicide, respectively. His youngest brother, Archduke Franz Karl, was next in line, but Franz Karl had renounced his claim in order to advance his own son, Franz Ferdinand. Unfortunately, Franz Josef never liked his nephew and new heir. He disliked Franz Ferdinand even more after he married a "common" countess, Sophie Chotek of Bohemia. Franz Josef conceded that Countess Sophie was of "noble birth," but he claimed that she was not of "equal birth." The emperor consented only to a morganatic marriage, meaning that Franz Ferdinand could not pass the throne to their offspring. Other Habsburg kin stood in line to inherit it on Franz Ferdinand's death.

So Franz Josef continued his reign as Emperor of Austria and King of Hungary, living in his beloved Vienna and seldom traveling to Budapest. Even if not living an emperor's life in an emperor's palace, today's readers might find life in Vienna or Budapest in 1900 familiar and even pleasantly livable. Going outside those great cities into the Austrian or Hungarian countryside, however, they would encounter unfamiliar and unlivable conditions, more medieval than modern. Moreover, the vast bulk of the population in both Austria and Hungary lived a traditional existence in villages and towns outside Vienna and Budapest. Samuel Mozolák lived in such a village.

2

The Peasant in Krajné

Samuel is not a common name among Slovaks. Still, a branch of the Mozolák family living in Krajné in the 19th century sometimes named boys Samuel. We will call their son Samko, using the familiar form. Samko Mozolák lived in the small village of Krajné, in a region of Slovakia in the Hungarian half of Austria-Hungary depicted in Map 2.1. After the war, Slovakia combined with the regions of Bohemia and Moravia (and a portion of Silesia) in 1918 to form Czechoslovakia.

Krajné exists today, as it has for more than six centuries, in Nitra County in the western part of Slovakia just south of the border with Moravia. It lies in the foothills of the White Carpathian Mountains about eight miles east of Myjava, the closest large town shown on most maps. The rolling landscape surrounding the village was well suited to farming, as it is today. An American visitor from southern Minnesota might think it looks just like home. In fact, Minneapolis is almost at the same latitude as the center of Slovakia, and Minneapolis's average annual temperature of 46° almost matches Slovakia's 48°. However, Minnesota is roughly 4.5 times bigger in square miles.

Krajné is a typical yet remarkable Slovak village. Remarkable in that we know a great deal about it thanks to *Krajné: 1392–1992*, a well-researched book celebrating the village's 600-year history.[1] To substantiate Krajné's existence in 1392, the book cites a March 7 decree from Hungarian King Sigismund on the disposition of villages surrounding Čachtice Castle, just five miles away. Those fascinated by morbid tales may be intrigued by Krajné's proximity to Čachtice Castle and its connection to the infamous Countess Elizabeth Báthory of the noble Hungarian Báthory family.

Legend says that the Countess kept herself young by bathing in the blood of virgins plucked from surrounding villages. Whether she actually did is unknown, but the Countess and accomplices were formally accused of torturing and killing hundreds of girls. After a trial in 1611, she was imprisoned in Čachtice Castle, where she lived and died in her own rooms, sealed behind a brick wall. The castle fell into ruins long ago, but visitors can still see its remnants. The more sedentarily curious can choose from over thirty movies referring to or detailing the "Blood Countess," who also has been featured in a dozen stage plays and celebrated in numerous songs and video games.[2]

Mentioning the Báthory tale from the 1600s underscores Krajné's medieval history. Just citing Krajné's origin as 1392 is not as impressive as fixing it one hundred years before Columbus discovered America. Over Krajné's centuries of existence, it did not grow much. A 1753 Hungarian census counted 1,600 persons from 259 serf families.[3] An 1828 census reported 2,260 at 368 houses.[4] In 1869, a more comprehensive count that included the surrounding hills and valleys identified 2,732 people in 506 households. Samko's

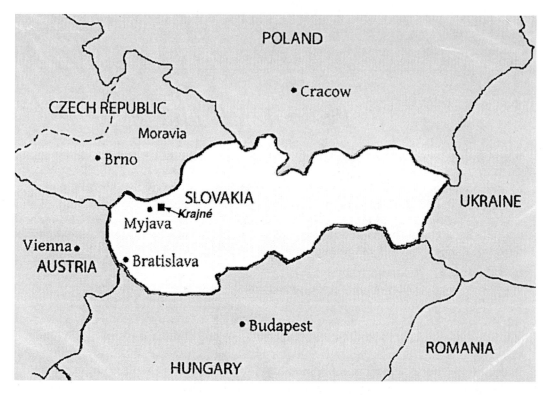

Map 2.1: KRAJNÉ'S LOCATION IN SLOVAKIA TODAY. The village of Krajné lies in the northwestern part of Slovakia, about eight miles east of Myjava, the closest town shown on most maps. Slovakia became an independent nation in 1993, when Czechoslovakia peacefully separated into two nations, the other becoming the Czech Republic. Credit: Adapted from the map in John Palka, *My Slovakia, My Family* (Minneapolis: Kirk House, 2012), p. 324. Used with permission.

ancestral family name, Mozolák, appeared in all these censuses. They reported that most of Krajné's inhabitants were Slovaks, but there were Hungarians, Germans, and some Jews—a census category then. Figure 2.1 suggests how Krajné appeared a century ago.

Krajné never grew much afterward. A census in 1895 put its population at 2,736. Twenty-five years later in 1919, it remained virtually the same: 2,727 people in 550 houses.[5] Krajné's inhabitants then were almost entirely Slovaks with fewer than 25 Magyars.[6] With 1,700 inhabitants in 2014, Krajné today is actually smaller in population than it was a century ago. It has about the same number of dwellings, but they house fewer children.

While Krajné's population stagnated, its larger neighbor, Myjava, grew more rapidly and increased its population over time. Founded in 1586, almost two hundred years after Krajné, Myjava had nearly 10,000 inhabitants in 1910[7] and 12,500 in 2014.[8] Myjava was large enough in the mid–19th century to play a significant role during the confusing 1848–1849 revolutionary period. Despite the fact that Austrian troops disrupted the Slavic Congress in Prague in the summer of 1848, Slovaks extracted support from Austria for grievances against their Magyar rulers in Hungary.[9] Gregory Ference wrote that the Viennese government granted Slovaks permission to use Vienna as a base of operation.[10] Slovak leaders formed a Slovak National Council and organized a volunteer corps to wrest rights from the Magyar leadership. About 1,000 Slovak volunteers marched to Myjava in September for the first national assembly of Slovaks.[11] The assembly renounced

Figure 2.1: DRAWING OF THE VILLAGE OF KRAJNÉ. **Drawing of the village of Krajné as it appeared early in the 20th century. It has about as many homes in the 21st century but fewer people. Credit: Drawn by Štefan Pavelka and used with permission.**

obedience to the Magyar regime and urged Slovaks not to pay taxes to the government nor provide troops to its army.

Despite the monarchy's early support, Habsburg forces soon engaged the Slovak volunteers. After some initial victories in skirmishes, their armed revolt ended within weeks. Although a second Slovak Volunteer Corps fought with the Austrian army against the Magyars in the chaotic 1848–1849 revolution, that action occurred far away from Myjava and Krajné. Local Slovaks' involvement in the uprising was documented in *Krajné: 1392–1992,* which reproduced a handwritten list of 29 names of participants from thirteen villages who fought under a Captain Štefanovič in the 1848 conflict. Thirteen names were from nearby Krajné.[12]

Certainly those who lived in Krajné around 1900 had fewer modern conveniences than residents in Budapest, the Hungarian capital, which had electric lighting in 1873.[13] The city's population in 1900 was over 700,000, growing to almost 900,000 in 1910.[14] Fed by grain grown by Hungarian peasants, Budapest was the world leader in milling until 1900, when it was surpassed by Minneapolis,[15] which milled grain grown by Minnesota's immigrant farmers on land like Slovakia's. In 1896, Budapest's subway system was second only to London's, and Budapest's was the first to use electricity.[16] Historian John Lukacs wrote: "Foreign visitors arriving in that unknown portion of Europe, east of Vienna, were astounded to find a modern city with first-class hotels, plate-glass windows, electric tram-cars, elegant men and women, the largest Parliament building in the world about to be completed."[17] The palatial Hungarian parliament was opened in 1901 on the Pest side of the Danube, across from the Royal Castle, last rebuilt in 1905 on ancient grounds of earlier castles.[18] In the mid–2010s, television commercials for Viking River Cruises often showed a cruise ship sailing past Budapest's ornately gorgeous parliament on the bank of the Danube River.

Living in Vienna, a jeweled city with its own subway, Franz Josef seldom visited his Royal Castle in Budapest. Nominally King of Hungary, he was excluded from Hungarian government under terms of the Dual Monarchy. Nevertheless, he was content if Hungarians did not trouble him. Otherwise, he took little active interest in their affairs and their well-being.

Everywhere and always, hereditary monarchs lived in a different world from their subjects. So it was with Emperor Franz Josef, whose Hofburg Palace in Vienna could almost accommodate Krajné's turn-of-century population of 2,700 individually in its 2,600 rooms. Today, democratically elected presidents and prime ministers also live in a world of comfort and luxury, but they usually grow up in the ordinary world and gain some sense of how most citizens live. Monarchs in the 19th century had virtually no understanding of the lives led by most of their subjects.

Most 19th-century Slovak peasants in Krajné and the rest of Hungary lived in small but surprisingly solid houses, as in Photo 2.1.[19] Foundations were typically of stone with walls of clay brick, often with straw binder.[20] Floors were usually earthen. Building dimensions varied in a range around 15' by 50' and were usually divided into two or three rooms, often including space for farm animals.

One researcher offered this account of houses in the Slovak Carpathian hills: "The homes were compact containing living quarters as well as stable, grain storage and food storage integrated under one roof. Thus, the living space was protected from cold winter winds by the stable to the west, and the grain and hay storage to the north. The living area was located at the southeast corner of the house. In some cases a cellar was located

Photo 2.1: Early Example of a Peasant Building. **Example of a 19th century building constructed with stone foundation and brick walls. This one was in the Konkušova Valley outside of Krajné. Other homes then and certainly later were much more substantial, with stuccoed walls, interior and exterior. Credit: Zuzana Bielikova and Ján Kubíček,** Krajné v spomienkach **[Krajné Memories] (Krajné, Slovakia: City of Krajné, 2010), p. 12. Used with permission.**

under the house to maintain a constant temperature for preserving vegetables."[21] A wood stove with oven was in the living space. Smoke was vented into an adjoining room, which served as a smokehouse, before escaping through a hole in the roof.

Strictly speaking, the Mozolák family didn't live in the village of Krajné, but on a hill bordering it on the east. Villagers knew that *Mozoláci* (Mozoláks) had lived there for decades. The family name Mozolák was derived from *mozol*, the Slovak word for callus, as on the hand. From their hill, the Mozoláks looked down on the village, but villagers did not necessarily look up to them. In the Slovak language, people who lived in the hills were known locally as *kopaničiari*. Though not "hillbillies" in the derogatory American sense of the term, *kopaničiari* did not have equal social standing with people who lived in the village.

In Krajné, as across the globe, villagers often felt superior to people who lived in and off the countryside. Some villagers worked on farms, but others engaged in trade and crafts. They were merchants, butchers, blacksmiths, millers, laborers, and so on. Although they also worked with their hands, they were often skilled hands, unlike the callused hands of those in the countryside. Other villagers derived status from living in town, in proximity to their skilled neighbors. They didn't live in the woods and labor on the lands. Most farmers owned the small plots of land they worked, but some worked on other people's land. Even the small landowners found farm labor hard and the rewards negligible. And the Mozoláks were, by name and occupation, agricultural laborers.

Krajné villagers and people in the surrounding countryside had a hard living. They married young and had many children, some of whom even managed to survive. Early marriage at least favored survival of both bride and groom, as husbands and wives could share the burden of living. Spouses frequently remarried after the other died. Having a spouse and begetting many children was dictated by economic realities, by biology, and by God. Samko Mozolák's family history was not uncommon in Krajné. Describing it in some detail may illustrate the patterns of life and death in that time and place.

Samko's father, Ján Mozolák, was born in 1831, married in 1854 at age 23, and died in 1896, just short of his 65th birthday. Along the way, he sired 18 children with four wives.[22] His first wife died at age 21, and his second in childbirth at 38. The fate of his third wife is unclear (they may not have been formally married), and only his fourth survived him for certain. Ten of the 18 children (one named Samuel) died before the age of 7, and another at 17. Only seven Mozolák children (including Samko) survived their father, Ján.

Samko was born on February 23, 1882. At his father's death in 1896, he was 14 years old and the youngest of three sons. Samko's half-brother Ján was 25, and his brother Martin, 22. Two half-sisters were also older. Of his two full sisters, one was older, the other younger. In any event, Ján's four daughters could not share in inheriting his property, and by the standards of the time, father Ján Mozolák was well off. According to the 1869 Hungarian census, his property consisted of one mare, one gelding, one cow, three calves, three sheep, two breeding pigs, and a beehive. The census did not report the number of rooms in his domicile, number K129a, but it said that it had two storerooms and two stables, and that Ján owned one half of a barn.[23] Ján's first son would inherit property of some value. Unfortunately for Samko, he stood at the bottom of the inheritance totem pole.

Samko's family owned a little land, but not much. Most of the rich agricultural land in 1895 was owned by a few families, many as absent landlords. Even fortunate farmers with small plots of land, like the Mozolák family, consumed most of their own produce. Left with little to sell in the market, they lived in a semi-subsistence economy.[24] Rising costs of production and falling prices for produce squeezed everyone dependent on the agricultural economy, and there was little economic opportunity in the area besides agriculture. Some did leave for seasonal work in neighboring counties and even in Austria.[25] Austria-Hungary was building railroads, but at a pace far behind Germany, and no lines came close to Krajné.

Scholars who debate the definition of "peasant" might argue over whether Samko Mozolák was really a peasant.[26] The term applies most properly to farmers or farm laborers in pre-industrial societies. It conjures up images of farmhands toiling for large landowners, a view better fitted to medieval Europe under serfdom than to Hungary at the turn of the century. Unlike a serf (serfdom was formally ended in the mid–19th century[27])—who was bound to work his lord's land—a peasant owned his own land, however small the plot.

Certainly by the 20th century, being a "peasant" was more likely to indicate one's low place in society than one's position in the agricultural economy. Keely Stauter-Halsted's study of peasants in Galicia in Austria-Hungary included those "actively involved in working the soil as a primary occupation, or whose family and hence cultural identity are attached to work on the land and to interactions within the village community."[28] Werner Roesener's *The Peasantry of Europe* cited five criteria defining a peasant.[29] Then he continued, "In addition to these purely economic criteria there are traits that project an image of the peasant rooted in everyday speech: they have to do above all with the way rustics live and behave."[30] In that sense—and certainly in the eyes of Franz Josef—Samko was definitely a peasant.

Historian Bernard Wasserstein wrote that even by 1914 the peasant was "the representative European social type" and "the village the basic social milieu."[31] Village life was brutish compared with even poor city-dwellers. "Hardly any villages had paved ways, electricity, or piped water."

> Clothing was simple, often sordid and filthy. The colourful "traditional" costumes that we associate with peasant life in east-central Europe were worn only on special occasions; in some cases they were nationalist revivals, in others inventions. In the more prosperous country areas of Britain, France, and Germany ready-made clothing was becoming available by 1914, undergarments were increasingly popular, and nightgowns were replacing unchanged dayclothes in bed. Elsewhere clothing was generally home-made spun and sewn by women or woven by men. Most male peasants wore undyed, colourless smocks or floppy shirts over loose trousers. Worn clothes were patched rather than replaced. Children would wear hand-downs. Washing of clothes, as of persons, was rare.[32]

Wasserman also noted that better-off men might have one Sunday suit, which often lasted the rest of their lives, while poorer peasants dressed in rags and sometimes lacked shoes. If they had shoes, they were often worn mainly to church. As for housing: "Rural housing remained rudimentary. Poor peasants, sharecroppers, and landless labourers might live in mud huts or log cabins with dirt floors. Outside western Europe glass windows were found only in more recently built homes."[33]

Few Hungarian peasants owned any land, and most who did, like the Mozolák family, owned very little. According to one source, just 0.2 percent of all proprietors had property of 1,000 acres or more, and they consumed over 30 percent of all the land.[34] Over half of all proprietors had plots under five acres, accounting for less than 6 percent of total acreage. Ference cited 1896 data showing that 36 percent of Hungarian land was held by

800 families in holdings of 1,000 or more acres in 1896.[35] About half of farmers (52 percent) worked farms of five acres or less. Analyzing the 1896 data in another way (and with more precision than either necessary or defensible), Spiesz found "9.44 percent of the population as landless, 11.53 percent with less than 1.5 acres, 31.1 percent with 1.5 to 5 acres, 21.26 percent with 5 to 10 acres, 16.9 percent with 10 to 20 acres, and 7.6 percent with 20 to 50 acres. There were 1,529 estate owners with 100 to 200 acres, 768 with 200 to 500 acres, and 806 with more than 1,000 acres."[36] In 1910, according to Spiesz, the large landholders in Slovakia specifically were mainly Magyars. They also owned the commercially productive larger farms, while Slovaks owned the small plots suited to subsistence farming. Figure 2.2 portrays the distribution of landholdings by size and nationalities. Magyars owned over 80 percent of the largest holdings; Slovaks owned over 70 percent of the smallest holdings. Spiesz described Slovakia as "essentially a country of small farms and large landed estates."

Hungarian peasants farming small plots lived under the thumb of wealthy and influential personages called "magnates," a Latin-based term referring to people with great landed wealth and high social position. Back in 1900, the American press called John D. Rockefeller a magnate, and the term is sometimes applied to industry leaders today. However, we seldom think of magnates as a political group pursuing common interests. Not so in Hungary. Writings on Hungarian politics from medieval times to the early twentieth century referred to the magnates' organized influence. Magnates arose from the few dozen great landowners in the 15th century who provided private armies to support the king.[37] A parliamentary act in 1608 created a bicameral legislature, the Diet, consisting of a Magnates' Table and a Lower Table. The Magnates' Table included the aristocracy, ecclesiastical leaders, and descendants of powerful landowners—often overlapping categories.[38]

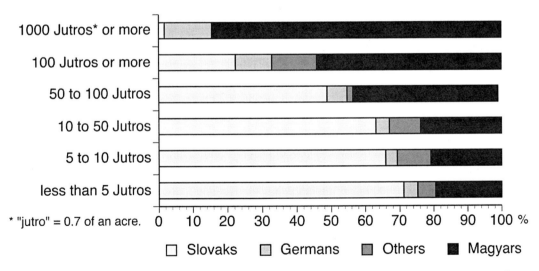

Figure 2.2: Percent Distribution of Landholdings in Hungary by Size and Nationality. Land ownership in Hungary was distributed very unequally by ethnicity. Magyars owned over 89 percent of the largest holdings, while Slovaks owned over 70 percent of the smallest. Data: Anton Spiesz, "The Era of a Dual Monarchy (1867–1918)," in Ladislaus J. Bolchazy (ed.), *Illustrated Slovak History: A Struggle for Sovereignty in Central Europe* (Wauconda, IL: Bolchazy-Carducci Publishers, 2006), p. 173.

The magnates' influence was reasserted in an 1848 public law that created a new Diet with a House of Representatives and a House of Lords, known informally but widely as the House of Magnates. Their influence continued over time. One source said that in 1896 its members consisted of "17 archdukes, 29 Catholic and 8 Orthodox or Byzantine bishops, 10 high Protestant clergy, 7 dukes, 143 counts and 41 barons, all from among the Hungarian nobility, and lastly, 75 life-time appointees of the king."[39] The House of Representatives was scarcely more representative of the population. As shown in Figure 2.3, only about 30 percent of the representatives who served from 1887 to 1910 were "commoners," and a majority were nobles with historical titles.

How many magnates were there in Hungary? Estimates vary, but most writers fixed the number at less than 5 percent of the population.[40] Despite their small numbers, magnates held approximately 20 percent of the land; again, estimates vary.[41] Magyar landowners treated their peasants poorly, regardless of the peasants' nationality. The celebrated Magyar writer Móricz Zsigmund wrote about the harsh life of Magyar peasants. His 1917 novel *A Fáklya* (*The Torch*), focused on the life of a new Calvinist minister in a Magyar village. A local teacher explained why Magyar peasants were so obstinate: "They have been educated to this for many centuries. Their taskmasters stood with the lash behind their backs, and the peasants learned to bite as well as to bark. They have been exploited and now they are paying back the debt. They are more enlightened and more civilized than other peasants and it is the inexcusable crime of our governing classes that instead of elevating them to their own level they want to push them back into the mire where the peasantry of other countries is floundering. Primarily it is the crime of our aristocrats."[42]

Later, the minister from a nearby town elaborated: "The gentry rule, friend, merely carries out the will of the landed barons, and the barons are not even grateful for the help.... The burghers are the real supporters of the gentry, because they are ignorant of the real situation. And the gentry disdain the burghers, which is sufficient cause for the burghers to idolize the gentry.... They are part of the political gang that monopolizes public offices in this country."[43]

Few Slovaks held public office, and their Magyar rulers certainly understood that Slovak peasants lived even worse lives than Magyar peasants, but their rulers also did not care. Scholar Suzanna Mikula estimated that around that time, among 46,449 people who "had positions of civil authority in Slovakia, only 132 acknowledged themselves as Slovaks."[44] This fits with Gregory Ference's statement: "In 1910, Slovaks accounted for only 184 out of 3,683 judicial officials throughout Hungary and 164 among the remaining 6,185 Hungarian governmental employees."[45] In villages like Krajné, the office of notary

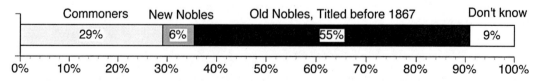

Figure 2.3: SOCIAL COMPOSITION OF HUNGARY'S HOUSE OF REPRESENTATIVES, 1887–1910. **Over more than two decades up to 1910, the nobility dominated Hungary's House of Representatives, with commoners holding less than one-third of its seats. Data: Table 16 in Andrew C. Janos,** *The Politics of Backwardness in Hungary, 1825–1945* **(Princeton, NJ: Princeton University Press, 1982), p. 137. Calculated for 1,121 deputies serving 1887–92, 1897–1901, and 1910–18.**

"collected taxes, conducted elections (which were by open balloting), and in general over-saw the public affairs of the people. Of 5,313 notaries in Slovakia, only 38 were Slovaks."[46]

The notary in Krajné was Alojz Nozdrovický, who was appointed in 1899 and held office until 1919. His name was apt to be ethnically Slovak rather than Magyar. Some Slovaks became Magyarones—assimilated Magyars—for status and profit. In his 1906 book *The Slovaks of Hungary*, Thomas Čapek wrote, "notaries are uncompromising apostles of Magyarization." He continued, "In many instances he is the local postmaster, and keeps a record of births, marriages, and deaths. The notary, by reason of his official position, possesses information within reach of no other inhabitant in the place. Nothing escapes him. He knows accurately what newspapers and books you read, whether you order your goods from 'patriotic' or Slavonian firms. The local priests and teachers, if they be Slovaks, must be on guard before the notary, knowing that he watches and reports their every action. Even the butcher, the innkeeper, and the tailor find it profitable to court the notary's favor. Elections without his assistance or interference are unthinkable."[47] Lukačka's history of Krajné also reported that notary Nozdrovický and his all-powerful wife "decided everything."[48] Krajné folks understood who buttered the notary's bread.

Assuming that Slovakia had teenagers back then, Samko was an intelligent but uneducated 14-year-old teenager when his father died. He had been sent to primary school to learn how to read and write, but that was in Magyar—the language spoken by Hungarians. In Hungarian legal theory, Slovak children should have been taught in Slovak. Nevertheless, Hungarian government data submitted to the 1919 Paris Peace Conference showed otherwise.[49] Of its 17,378 elementary schools, 81 percent were taught in Magyar and 15 percent in Romanian. The Romanian percentage matched the 16 percent of Romanian-speaking population, nearly all of whom were in the eastern province of Transylvania. The 11 percent of Hungarians whose mother tongue was Slovak, however, had only 322 primary schools (2 percent of the total) in the entire country. Hungary also had a Slovak kindergarten, just one. The three Slovak high schools had been closed in 1875.

Although 10 percent of Hungary's population was German, Magyar magnates did not encourage people to learn German, the official language of their Dual Monarchy partner (and rival). As in the Slovak case, only 2 percent of the elementary schools were taught in German, but there were 18 German kindergartens and a smattering of schools above the primary level. No schools offering higher education were taught in Slovak in all of Hungary. In fact, 98 percent of all high schools were taught in Magyar. So nearly all children who showed intellectual ability in primary school could only advance by learning Magyar, which funneled them into the state bureaucracy. Nevertheless, Hungary did a good job in teaching people to read and write. By 1910, 80 percent of its male population was literate in some language, primarily Magyar.[50] Recall, however, that about half the population was Magyar. Viewed another way, only about 20 percent of the other 8.3 million knew Magyar.[51]

Samko learned to read and write, but he could not be called educated. Like most of his classmates, he disliked learning Magyar. It was not the language his family spoke, nor one spoken by most Krajné residents. Learning Magyar was like learning a foreign language in a foreign language. Moreover, there was little attraction to learning the language. How could knowing Magyar help Sam? People in his world spoke Slovak. When would a Slovak peasant like him ever be in a world where he spoke only Magyar? It was like requiring a high school student in rural Nebraska to learn Latin, except insofar as

Nebraskans had nothing against the ancient Romans. In contrast, Slovaks then did not like Magyars, and vice versa.

So Samko as a child attended the one-room local school in Krajné, but only as much as required. His Magyar teacher in the school of Slovak children was probably as good an instructor as one might expect from a man of superior education who longed for a better governmental position and who regarded his students as ethnically inferior. That Samko was not the bookish type did not help his learning Magyar or learning much else. Moreover, teachers then enjoyed substantial latitude in methods of instruction. Motivation to learn, or at least to listen, was often instilled through the threat of pain. A favored technique was to ask an unruly or inattentive student to make a pear with his fist (in Slovak: *Tvorí hruška s rukou*; in Magyar: *hogy a körte a kezével*) so that the fingers pointed upward. When the student (usually a boy) did so, he was struck with a stick (usually a ruler) on his fingertips. According to the prevailing pedagogical theory, learning commenced promptly afterward.

Samko's lively intelligence was not captured by such discipline, nor by spelling and grammar rules, nor by mathematical equations, and certainly not by historical accounts of the 11th century reign of Stephen I, the first King of Hungary, canonized as Saint Stephen by the Pope. Perhaps that was because the Mozoláks were Lutheran. They attended Krajné's Lutheran church, where the Mozoláks had their own pew, not its Catholic church, which had relatively few congregants in the mostly Lutheran village. More likely, Samko was simply uninterested in Magyar history, not even in the great Magyar military victories in the 15th centuries.

Geography was one subject likely to interest Samko, but not the geography of Europe. The "new world," particularly the United States, drew young people's attention then— like space travel today. Samko knew that new steamships could sail across the Atlantic Ocean to reach the United States in only two weeks. In fact, he heard that young men from his village had already embarked on the journey. They headed for a port in northern Germany, aiming to sail to America, but no one had heard from them since they left. Samko had heard of others leaving from nearby villages. Historical statistics claim that 1,124 people from Nitra, Krajné's home county, had immigrated to the United States in 1893 alone.[52]

Further east in the much smaller county of Spiš, just south of Galicia, Slovak emigration started earlier and proceeded faster. Almost 20,000 left in the decade of 1880–90.[53] Joseph Grisak, who immigrated to America in 1901, wrote decades later in his autobiography: "The type of existence that prevailed among the peasants in the villages and throughout the entire area, with its feudal system of dominance by the 'haves' over the 'have-nots,' and with no possibility of upgrading their living standards, gave cause for the migration of the masses to America to seek a better life."[54] Samko was too young to plan his departure, but he was not too young to imagine the adventure.

So his instructor pretended to teach him in Magyar while Samko pretended to learn. Samko's schooling, such as it was, ended at the primary level years before he turned 14. Eventually, Samko did learn to read and write, but his proficiency was not high. He learned Magyar about as well as Hungarian students learned Russian after World War II when forced to study it under communist rule. Most Hungarians then learned enough Russian to pass their examinations, then left the language in the classroom. At least they studied other subjects in their own language. If Samko had thirsted to continue his education, he would have had to continue in Magyar, for the nationalists had closed the only Slovak higher schools in Slovakia.[55]

Earlier we assumed that prewar Hungary had teenagers. When Samko's father died in 1896, Samko at 14 was in his teens, but there were no teenagers then, as we think of them today. Chronological teenagers assumed their place in the labor force. For years, Samko performed his own chores on the family's little farm. As a young boy he surely performed the usual chores: gathering eggs in the chicken coop, hauling water from the pump, pulling weeds from the garden, and filling the wood box. As he grew older, he must have milked cows, fed livestock, and harnessed horses. By age 14, he certainly toiled in the fields, doing whatever he was told to do by his older brothers, Ján and Martin. Samko probably derived satisfaction from bossing hired field workers, but he was smart and imaginative enough to want more.

At their father's death, Samko's half-brother Ján was 25 and had already completed his three-year compulsory military service. As his father's namesake and eldest son, Ján was destined to inherit his father's property. Even if Ján fell ill and died (a real possibility), Martin at 22 (probably engaged in fulfilling his military obligation) would be next in line for inheritance. Samko got along all right with his brother Martin and even with his half-brother Ján, but Samko could see that he was likely to work for them on the farm as long as they lived. By the time they died, he would not have much time left to be a landowner himself.

Samko lived in a small house with his mother, two brothers, and youngest sister—the older sisters already having married and moved out. But in 1898, two years after his father's death, Samko's home life became encumbered with new relatives. His oldest brother Ján took a wife, and children followed. Martin had also married in 1899, but moved into a small house newly built on the small family property. Samko wondered whether there would there be enough space on the property for him, should he marry. In 1900 at age 18, Samko began to contemplate the obligation imposed on all the Emperor's male subjects: to receive three years of military training and then to remain in the military reserves for another ten years.

Three years compulsory service by all males was required in 1867 when the Dual Monarchy was formed. If he had reported for service when he was 20, Samko probably would have been placed in the *Magyar király Honvédseg* (Royal Hungarian Armed Forces), commonly called *Honvéd* (the army), and have been trained at Army Corps District V, based in Pozsony. That was the city's Magyar name, but Slovaks knew it as Prešporok and Germans as Pressburg. (After the war, Prešporok became known as Bratislava.) Pozsony/Prešporok/Pressburg was the largest city in the region of Slovakia.

Going to Pozsony held some attraction. In 1900, the county's population of about 370,000 was 45 percent Slovak, 38 percent Magyar, and the rest mainly German.[56] The county seat was in the city of Pozsony. With a population about 75,000, Pozsony was an urban metropolis compared with Krajné's 2,000 people and about 10,000 in Myjava, the closest large town. Pozsony's bright lights probably appealed to a young man from a dark village. Even its range of foreign tongues may have had some allure. Pozsony had far fewer Slovaks, with the bulk of its population divided almost equally between Magyars and Germans. Samko might have a chance to use the Magyar language forced on him in elementary school.

Indeed, some Slovak youths looked forward to their military service, which they viewed as a welcome change from rural drudgery. John Keegan, a World War I historian, said that "for three years of a young conscript's life" military service "provided an enjoyable diversion from the routine of workshop or plough." Keegan adds, "Annual manoeuvres were a pleasurable summer holiday. Regimental anniversaries, when the band played, wine flowed, and the honorary colonel, an archduke, a prince, perhaps the Emperor him-self, came to visit, were joyous feasts. The return home, time expired, brought more cel-ebration and adult respect. The reality of war was a distant eventuality."[57] Nevertheless, Samko was not stirred by the prospects of awakening to a camp bugler. As he contem-plated serving for three years in the Hungarian part of the Emperor's army, Samko won-dered whether he might escape his obligation entirely by sailing to the United States.

3

The Emperor's Subjects

Were people in Austria-Hungary the emperor's *subjects* or the empire's *citizens*? The answer given depended on who you asked, when you asked, and where you asked. In the second half of the 18th century, Pieter Judson wrote that Maria Theresa and her emperor sons, Joseph II and Leopold II, sought to redefine their "subjects (*Untertanen*) as citizens (*Staatsbürger*)—that is, as individual men and women with common legal rights and obligations anchored in their unmediated relationship to a central state."[1]

Maria Theresa and sons acted more out of self-interest than enlightenment. In his penetrating analysis of the empire's government, Judson contended that Maria Theresa understood that its wealth "ultimately rested on the productivity and wealth of the peasantry, and because the peasantry bore most of the tax burden, the state took an increasing interest in improving the situation of the peasantry."[2] Improving the peasants' situation put the crown into conflict with its nobility and landowners, who would need to "give up personal control over the peasantry, along with their rights to unpaid peasant labor, to the administration of local justice, and to their own tax-free status."[3]

Contemporary readers may visualize politics in feudal empires as a two-sided conflict: monarchs v. peasants. Monarchs, however, had more trouble dealing with powerful nobles than with powerless peasants. The Habsburgs' attempts to centralize their power were resisted by local and regional nobles who controlled taxation, administration of justice, and military conscription through regional assemblies, or diets, with which the crown had to negotiate.[4] In Austria and Hungary during the late 18th century, according to Judson, "many peasants thought of the central state or imperial power as a handy counterweight to the authority of the local nobility."[5]

As landowners fended off Vienna's attempts to centralize power, the nobles sought to extract as much benefit as possible from their peasantry's labor. Aware of conflict between the crown and the nobility, peasants appealed for help from distant Vienna to improve their local situation. Judson said that peasants began to imbue the Habsburg ruler with "an almost mythical power" who exercised "a fatherly concern for their well-being. If the emperor had known what exactly was going on in Galicia, according to peasant lore, he would not have allowed things to continue."[6]

Indeed, Maria Theresa and her emperor sons had already enacted reforms, if unevenly enforced, to improve the peasants' lot. Legally, landlords could no longer personally whip their peasants or prevent them from marrying; they could not require peasants to work free for more than three days a week; and they had to allow peasants to pay obligations in cash, rather than crops—which (not incidentally) allowed the state to share in the payments.[7] Given these interventions by early Habsburg emperors, there was some basis for the dynasty's popularity within the peasantry in the second half of the 18th century.

When Franz Josef assumed Austria's throne in 1848, the Habsburgs and the empire continued to enjoy popularity and respect among the peasants, while still clashing with the nobility over the distribution of power. But by that time, the conflict had become multifaceted. In addition to conflicting interests of the crown, the nobility, and the peasantry, according to Judson, there were "competing demands made by ethnic nationalists, crownland patriots, civil rights liberals, and bureaucratic centralizers."[8] The conflict had fewer facets within Hungary, where nobles, nationalists, and urban liberals had united against the crown's centralizing policies.[9] Governing the various parts of their empire continually posed challenges to its Habsburg rulers, but governing Hungary proved particularly vexing.

Hungarians believed they deserved a special place in the empire. Not only was Hungary far larger than any other territorial component, but since 1687 it had also crowned its own king, who had to swear in Latin to protect the collected rights of *natio Hungarica*. This "Hungarian Nation," Judson said, "was constituted from those members of the nobility who sat in the two chambers of the diet, those who had the right to elect its deputies, and those who also, by definition, remained exempt from taxation."[10] So Hungarian nobles regarded themselves, not their peasants, as the citizens of Hungary.

Applying terms "citizens" to a nation's adult inhabitants eligible to participate in government and "subjects" to those who cannot participate finds more subjects than citizens across the empire throughout the 19th century. Through political reforms, the proportion of citizens tended to grow over time outside of Hungary, but the proportion of subjects remained high in Hungary, where relatively few inhabitants became citizens. Margaret MacMillan reported that by 1870 Austria had elected one half of its parliament by universal male suffrage, whereas in Hungary "the franchise was restricted to about 6 percent of the population,"[11] where it remained to the start of the war.[12]

Franz Josef's Austro-Hungarian Empire was an odd polity. At the top, it fit the definition of an empire: a political system uniting different lands under a single person ruling through central political institutions.[13] Following the 1867 Compromise between Austria and Hungary that created the empire, Emperor Franz Josef decreed in 1868 that the new political entity should be known in short as *Die Österreichisch-Ungarische Monarchie* (the Austro-Hungarian Monarchy). Its full name, *Die im Reichsrat vertretenen Königreiche und Länder und die Länder der Heiligen Ungarischen Stephanskrone*, translated into English as "The Kingdoms and Lands Represented in the Imperial Council and the Lands of the Hungarian Holy Crown of St. Stephen."[14] Over time, it became known in English as the Austro-Hungarian Empire, or simply Austria-Hungary.[15]

Just below its top, the empire consisted of two lands with the comic operetta names of Cisleithania and Transleithania, centering respectively around Austria and Hungary. Cisleithania included Austria and its neighboring provinces of Bohemia, Moravia, Carniola, Carinthia, Tyrol, and Croatia, in addition to its more distant provinces of Silesia, Istria, Dalmatia, Galicia, and Bukovina. Transleithania encompassed Hungary and its bordering provinces of Slovakia, Transylvania, and Banat. Bosnia-Herzegovina, which also adjoined Hungary, belonged to the Ottoman Empire in 1867. Austria-Hungary gained administrative control of the territory in 1878 and abruptly annexed it in 1908, nearly triggering a war with neighboring Serbia. Cisleithania and Transleithania did not include Bosnia-Herzegovina, which was separately administered..

Austria and Hungary themselves qualified as countries according to both of the term's historical meanings: "an expanse of land" and "the territory or land of a nation."[16] Today, "country" and "nation" are interchangeable in informal usage. In political usage, however, nation has a more specific meaning: that the people being governed have a common language, ethnic origin, culture, and historical tradition. Austria and Hungary housed such a diversity of peoples that neither country could be called a nation.[17] Nor could the Austro-Hungarian Empire, a conglomerate of at least eleven different language groups. Figure 3.1 reports how they were distributed in the 1910 census by percentages within the empire overall and within each half. Map 3.1 shows where the nationality groups clustered in the Empire.

Habsburg historian Arthur May invited readers to imagine the United States ethnically divided like Austria-Hungary:

> If an American, taking into account the disparity in size between the United States and the Danube Monarchy, could imagine German-speaking folk predominating in the Pacific seaboard states and eastward from California, Czechs in Montana, the Dakotas, and Minnesota, Slovaks in Wisconsin and Michigan, Poles and Ukrainians in New York and New England, Slovenes in Texas, Croats and Serbs in much of the Deep South (Florida corresponding to Bosnia-Herzegovina), Italians in Louisiana, Magyars in the Middle West with Chicago as their capital, Rumanians in Pennsylvania and the border states, he would then have a crude approximation of the variety and distribution of the national groupings embraced in the Hapsburg Monarchy of 1914.[18]

Austria's ethnic problem was intricate but manageable. Almost 40 percent of its population spoke German as their mother tongue. Czech was the mother tongue of another 25 percent.[19] Polish, Ukrainian/Ruthenian, and Slovene accounted for nearly everyone else, but more than 70 percent spoke some German. The nationality problem was worse in Hungary. While about 55 percent of Hungarians spoke Magyar,[20] the language was difficult for non–Magyars to learn. Only another 10 percent spoke Magyar in addition to their native Romanian, Slovak, German, Serbian, Croatian, Ruthenian, or other language.[21]

Here is how the empire's name, "Austria-Hungary," translated into the empire's eleven officially recognized languages, ordered according to their percentage distribution:

German: *Österreich-Ungarn*
Magyar: *Osztrák-Magyar Monarchia*
Czech: *Rakousko-Uhersko*
Polish: *Austro-Węgry*
Ruthenian: Австро-Угорщина (transliterated: *Avstro-Uhorshchyna*)[22]
Romanian: *Austro-Ungaria*
Croatian: *Austro-Ugarska*
Serbian: Аустро-Угарска (transliterated: *Austro-Ugarska*)
Slovak: *Rakúsko-Uhorsko*
Slovene: *Avstro-Ogrska*
Italian: *Austria-Ungheria*[23]

Some of these languages were similar to others, but Magyar was different from all of them. One measure of language similarity is "lexical distance," the percentage of noncognate words between two languages. The greater the distance the less similar their vocabularies; the smaller the distance, the more similar the languages. Figure 3.2 charts the lexical distances among European languages. It shows Hungarian (Magyar) alone at

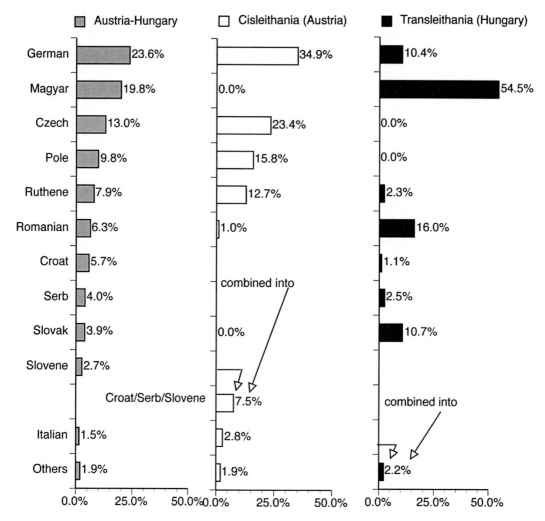

Figure 3.1: PERCENT DISTRIBUTION OF LANGUAGE GROUPS IN 1910 AUSTRIA-HUNGARY. More than eleven different languages were spoken in the Austro-Hungarian Empire. Here is how they were distributed across the empire and across its two halves, Austria and Hungary. Measureable numbers of some ethnic groups—Magyars, Czechs, Poles, and Slovaks—resided in only one of the two countries. Data: Gordon Brook-Shepherd, *Royal Sunset: The European Dynasties and the Great War* (Garden City, NY: Doubleday, 1987), p. 131; Felix Klezl, "Austria," in Walter F. Willcox (ed.), *International Migrations, Volume II: Interpretations* (Washington: National Bureau of Economic Research, 1931), p. 391; and https://en.wikipedia.org/wiki/Austria-Hungary#Linguistic_distribution. Zero percentages indicate negligible numbers that round to zero.

the upper-right, far from all the others. Slovak, Ruthenian (Ukrainian), Serbian, and Croatian—the four main Slavic languages in Hungary—are relatively close to one another, as is Czech, widely spoken in Austria but not Hungary. German and Romanian also stand far from the Slavic grouping.

Austria was also more religiously homogeneous than Hungary. Over 90 percent of its population was Roman Catholic. The rest split among Jewish (5 percent), Orthodox, or Lutheran faiths. Hungary was about 60 percent Roman or Orthodox Catholic, but almost 15 percent were Calvinist and more than 10 percent each Orthodox Catholic and

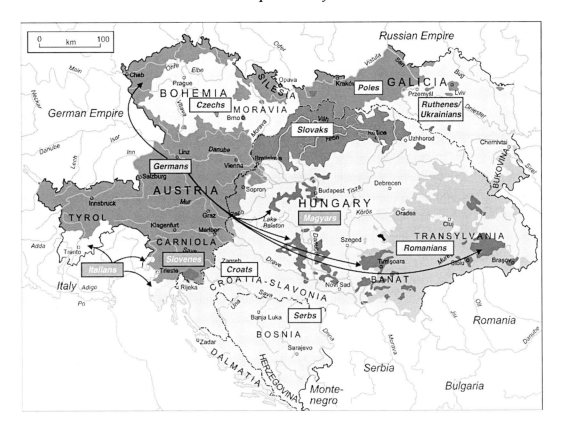

Map 3.1: Ethnic Divisions of Austria-Hungary Prior to World War I. The Austrian lands (Cisleithania) held most of the Germans, Czechs, Poles, Ruthenes, and Italians, but pockets of Germans were found everywhere, as arrows indicate. The Hungarian lands (Transleithania) had nearly all the Hungarians, Romanians, Slovaks, Croats, and Serbs. Credit: Adapted from William R. Shepherd, "The Distribution of Races in Austria-Hungary," in *Historical Atlas* (New York: Henry Holt and Company, 1911), p. 168. In public domain.

Lutheran. Again, about 5 percent were Jewish. Austria was also more ethnically homogeneous on other cultural indicators. Its German majority and substantial Czech minority had similar tastes in food and drink (e.g., dumplings, beer) and listened to similar music (e.g., polkas, brass instruments). Although ethnic groups in Hungary shared some tastes in food and drink (e.g., goulash, slivovitz) and music (e.g., czardas, violins), the groups' cultural similarities varied according to their proximity. Poles and Slovaks in the north, for example, were culturally closer to each other than to Romanians (who spoke a Romance language) in the southeast and even to fellow-Slav Croats to the south.

Finally, nationality groups in Austria were more politically compatible than in Hungary. Austria's Czechs even figured in Habsburg and Holy Roman Empire history. Among other connections, Habsburg Rudolph II in the early 17th century was Archduke of Austria and King of Bohemia—in addition being King of Hungary and Holy Roman Emperor. In contrast, the various Hungarian minorities savored few historical moments with their Magyar conquerors. Usually, their remembrances clashed. For example, Magyars celebrated the defeat of a Slavic king early in the 10th century, which Slovaks mourned as the end of a Slavic Great Moravia and the beginning of their rule by Magyars.[24]

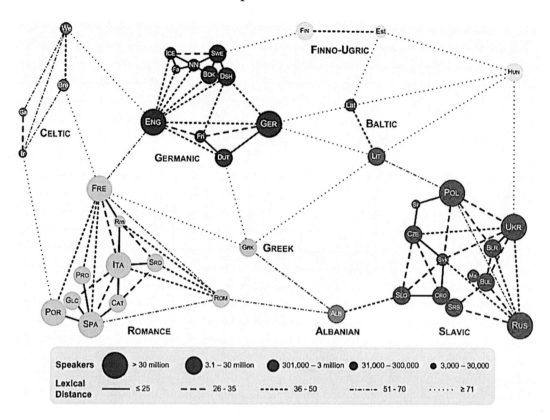

Figure 3.2: LEXICAL DISTANCES AMONG EUROPEAN LANGUAGES. According to a measure of lexical distance used in linguistics, Magyar stood far from other languages in Austria-Hungary. Credit: Created by Teresa Elms, *Etymologikon* (March 4, 2008), from data published in Kostiantyn Tyshchenko, *Metateoriia movoznavstva [Metatheory of Linguistics]* (Kiev, 1999) at https://elms. wordpress.com/2008/03/04/lexical-distance-among-languages-of-europe/. Used with permission.

In summary, neither Austria nor Hungary, as individual countries, qualified as nations. They fell far short of governing people with a common language, ethnic origin, culture, and historical tradition. No wonder Prussian President Otto von Bismarck in 1867 excluded Franz Josef's Empire from the North German Confederation prior to creating a united Germany. Bismarck would have diluted his homogenous German Protestant population with millions of Catholic Germans, Slavs, Romanians, and other ethnic groups. How could he fashion a German nation from such an assortment of peoples?

At the beginning of his rule in 1848, Franz Josef and his Viennese advisors struggled to control the Empire's non–German nationalities, a struggle that continued throughout his reign. The large Czech minority caused the most trouble for Austria. Czechs demanded that their language be used as a governmental language, and they even rioted in Prague against Vienna's rule. Over time, Franz Josef made concessions to bring them along. In 1880, he allowed Czech in official dealings within the bureaucracy.[25] In 1890, his government proposed that more than half of the Supreme Court had to be bilingual in Czech and German.[26] Although the non–Czech majority in parliament defeated that proposal, Franz Josef made some effort to accommodate Austria's most vexing minority.

In Hungary, the monarchy confronted threats from both Magyars and non–Magyars. The majority Magyars took up arms against Austrian rule in 1848. With Russian help, the young monarch crushed the rebellion in 1849. Instead of adjusting to the Magyars' desire for autonomy, Franz Josef imposed a form of absolutist rule from Vienna. Decades later, faced with (a) the Magyars' continuing resistance, (b) Austria's humiliating military defeat by Germany in 1866, and (c) Bismarck's subsequent exclusion of Austria from the German Confederation, a chastened Franz Josef agreed to the Magyar plan for the 1867 Compromise: a Dual Monarchy, making him Austria's ruling emperor but only Hungary's symbolic king, leaving rule to the Magyar magnates.

After the Compromise, Franz Josef hoped that the Magyars would improve the status of non–Magyar Hungarian nationalities, thus removing from the Empire further sources of ethnic disturbance. Indeed, Hungary's 1868 Nationalities Act acknowledged that "all nationalities—Magyars, Slovaks, Rumanians, Serbians and Ruthenes—[had] equal rights."[27] Moreover, paragraph 17 of the 1868 Law of Nationalities, stated: "[S]ince from the standpoint of general culture and well-being, the success of public instruction is one of the highest aims of the State also, the State is, therefore, bound to ensure that citizens living together in considerable numbers, of whatever nationality, shall be able to obtain instruction in the neighbourhood in their mother-tongue, up to the point where the higher academic education begins."[28] In proclaiming the right to instruction in the local language, Franz Josef was following Maria Theresa's decree in 1774 that children of both sexes of age six through twelve attend school conducted in the vernacular.[29] Even Maria Theresa waited until 1777 to apply the requirement to Hungary, which insisted on instruction in Magyar. Later, Hungary also ignored the 1868 law and within a decade placed new emphasis on the old practice of "Magyarization"—assimilation of non–Magyars into the Magyar culture and language.[30]

Magyarization had its roots in 18th-century attitudes and actions.[31] In 1784, Maria Theresa's son, Emperor Joseph II, decreed that German would replace Latin as the official language of the empire, an act that was fiercely opposed in Hungary, where German was already spoken by increasing numbers of immigrants, especially in Budapest. Nobles resisted German cultural hegemony by favoring the Magyar language.

Inevitably, favoring the Magyar language meant favoring Magyars. During the 1848 revolution against Austrian rule, Lajos Kossuth, Hungary's regent-president, won fame for demanding parliamentary and electoral reforms, but only to benefit Magyars. Concerning Hungary's other nationality groups, he was quoted as saying: "In Hungary everything—land, laws, story—is exclusively Magyar. Slovaks, Romanians, Serbs, Rusyns are only 'peoples,' they are not nations. In Hungary only Magyars have the right and the duty to be a nation."[32]

Magyarization, however, truly blossomed as government policy in the fourth quarter of the 19th century, focusing first on increasing usage of the Magyar language by all citizens. Magyarization went far beyond encouraging or rewarding them to learn Magyar. Contrary to paragraph 17 of the Law of Nationalities, the government restructured the educational system so that most children could get an elementary education only in Magyar. Legislation in 1875 aimed "to increase the number of subjects taught to non–Magyars in the Magyar language."[33] After 1896, the policy spread to changing place and family names in other languages to Magyar—e.g., Závada to Zenynye, Handlová to Hunyad, and even Krajné (the name of Samko's village) to Széles.[34] (Krajné means extreme or edge in Slovak; Széles in Magyar means broad or wide.)

Although these policies impacted all non–Magyars in Hungary, they had less impact on the quarter of the population that was German and Romanian. Hungarian Germans took comfort that King Franz Josef was German, which is how he regarded himself. Identification with the ruler gave the Germans some status and protection, and the Magyar magnates themselves looked to Germany for protection against their Austrian partners. Ethnic Romanians benefitted somewhat from their majority status in Transylvania, which had for centuries enjoyed some degree of autonomy under the Habsburgs. While Transylvania lost its autonomy under the Compromise, Romanians somehow managed to buck Magyarization in their schools, perhaps because Transylvania bordered on Romania, a separate country, albeit a weak one.

Before examining Magyarization's harsh consequences for non–Magyars, we should, for perspective, recall what was occurring in the United States during the same period. After the Civil War, the U.S. Congress in 1870–71 passed three "Enforcement Acts" that protected African Americans' right to vote, to hold office, to serve on juries, and to receive equal protection of laws. Like the 1868 Hungarian Law of Nationalities, those noble U.S. laws were nullified by subsequent events, beginning with its own "Compromise of 1877"— an informal political deal that decided the 1876 presidential election—coming just ten years after the Compromise of 1867 between Austria and Hungary.

In 1876, Democrat Samuel Tilden won more popular votes than Republican Rutherford Hayes, but Tilden lacked a majority in the electoral college, where 20 votes were hopelessly disputed. Under a deal in 1877, Hayes became president; the Enforcement Acts went unenforced; Republicans withdrew federal troops from the South; Democrats took back their control of the South; and Southern blacks suffered for decades under white supremacy. So in the fourth quarter of the 19th century, treatment of the racial minority in America's southern states resembled the treatment of Hungary's ethnic minorities. In both countries, laws mandating equal treatment were not enforced.

Magyarization in education had its greatest effect on the quarter of Hungarians who were Slavic—the Slovaks, Ruthenes, Croats, and Serbs. Both the Germans in Austria and the Magyars in Hungary tended to exhibit a "master-race" mentality toward Slavs. The German (and communist) Friedrich Engels had dismissed European Slavs as "a people without a history"—always ruled by others. The Czechs could confidently dismiss Engels's charge. Prague, their magnificent city in Bohemia, had been home to early monarchs of the Holy Roman Empire. Moreover, Czechs had a written literature and had so for centuries. Slovaks had no such defense. Although they had a distinct culture, it had been perpetuated through an oral tradition of stories, songs, and poems. Little was written down.[35] Until the middle of the 19th century, Slovaks usually wrote in modified Czech. Not until 1852 did Catholic and Lutheran leaders agree on publishing a concise Slovak grammar.[36]

Magyarization's effect on the language of instruction in elementary schools, based on official Hungarian statistics, is displayed in Figure 3.3.[37] In 1869, instruction in Magyar and Slovak occurred respectively at 42 and 13 percent of elementary schools, which roughly matched the percentages of the two nationalities. By 1905, instruction in Magyar had soared to 71 percent of the schools, and in Slovak had plunged to less than 2 percent. The number of Romanian schools remained about the same, while the percentage of German schools fell from 9 to 2 percent.

Defenders of Magyarization in elementary education might have argued that they were helping non–Magyar children improve their adult lives. Magyar was the official

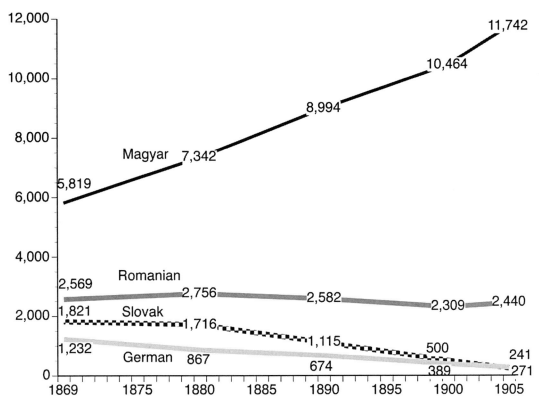

Figure 3.3: LANGUAGE OF INSTRUCTION IN HUNGARIAN PRIMARY SCHOOLS, 1869–1905. In 1869, instruction in Magyar and Slovak occurred respectively at 42 and 13 percent of elementary schools, which roughly matched the percentages of the two nationalities. By 1905, instruction in Magyar had soared to 71 percent of the schools, and in Slovak had plunged to less than 2 percent. The number of Romanian schools remained about the same, while the percentage of German schools fell from 9 to 2 percent. Data: R.W. Seton-Watson, *Racial Problems in Hungary* (New York: Howard Fertig, 1972 edition, originally published 1908). p. 437.

language of government and politics. It was the language in which the magnates conversed, ran their farms and businesses, and governed the country. One could not advance in Hungarian government, politics, or society without being fluent in Magyar. Learning Magyar while young, when language learning was easy, would prepare them for life later. Left unsaid was that not offering instruction in local tongues would depress their usage at home and lead to their extinction. What was said—and understood—was that developing Magyar as a common language in Hungary would aid developing Hungary as a Magyar nation. By 1905 over 90 percent of all academically oriented grammar schools, gymnasia, and commercial/industrial schools were Magyar.[38]

Hungary made no attempt to decorate its oligarchy with democratic trappings. Compared with other European countries to its west—England, France, Austria, and even Germany—Hungary was backward in its economic, social, and political development. Andrew Janos elaborated the argument in *The Politics of Backwardness in Hungary, 1825–1945*.[39] Hungary—but not necessarily Austria—lagged behind the western countries in industrial capacity, ethnic integration, and political inclusiveness. Returning to the metaphor of Austria-Hungary as conjoined twins may be helpful here. Austria and

Hungary were really separate states joined together as Austria-Hungary. On the "back-wardness" charge, John Deak said, "For a long time, the history of imperial Austria in the modern era has been a story of backwardness, a failure to innovate, and thus a story of decline and fall."[40] Deak's more optimistic book, *Forging a Multinational State*, was about the Austrian twin, not the Hungarian one. Whereas Austria elected parliamentary delegates by universal male suffrage in 1907, Hungary limited the franchise to about 6 percent of its population.[41] In 1912, an electoral reform bill raised the proportion of Hungarians who could vote from 6 to 10 percent of the population, but in other countries 25 to 30 percent could vote.[42] Compared with countries to its east and south—Russia, Romania, Bulgaria, Serbia, and Albania—Hungary may have been moderately progressive, but the Habsburgs' referent nations in Europe were to the west and north.

Not only was Hungary backward compared with Western European countries at the turn of the century, it was backward with itself across time. According to Judson, Hungary in the eighteenth century had "remarkable reform rulers" in Maria Theresa and her emperor sons, Joseph II and Leopold.[43] Maria Theresa in the 1770s required all children from six to twelve to attend school in their vernacular language, and in 1869, primary school language instruction did correspond well with the population distribution. By the time of the Great War, however, elementary school instruction was almost exclusively in Magyar. According to statistics submitted to the 1919 Paris Peace Conference, prewar Hungary had 2,264 kindergarten schools, of which 98 percent were taught in Magyar, the mother tongue of only half the population.[44]

Magyar, of course, was Hungary's official language; the language of government and politics; the language in which the magnates conversed, ran their farms and businesses, and governed the country. Austria also had an official language, German, but an 1880 law admitted Czech in the "outer service" of Austria's administration, e.g., the bureaucracy and courts.[45] German was still required in the "inner service" of its top level of government. By contrast, Hungary moved in the other direction, passing laws requiring Hungarian even in local government and more schools subject to be taught in Hungarian instead of local languages.[46]

If this picture of Magyar rule before the Great War seems overdrawn, readers should know that most writers today see it that way, even Magyar writers. Consider the judgment of Peter Zombory-Moldován, who a hundred years later lovingly translated and published the memoir of his Magyar grandfather, Béla Zombory-Moldován, an officer in the Austro-Hungarian army. His grandson wrote in his introduction: "The greatest political tension in pre–1914 Austria-Hungary, however, stemmed from the refusal of the Magyar (the ethnically Hungarian) political establishment to meet the aspirations of the kingdom's minority nationalities—especially the Slovaks in the north, the Serbs in the south, and the Romanians in the southeast—to a measure of cultural and political autonomy. Hungarians were fearful of becoming outnumbered in their own country, of losing their privileged position within the empire, and, worst of all, of the prospect of the historic Magyar lands being parceled out among the various nationalities that had settled in them."[47]

Few non–Magyars residents saw much political, educational, or economic future in Hungary. In his 1909 book *Austria-Hungary*, the British writer and Conservative Party politician Geoffrey Drage concluded: "The Magyars, in fact, have treated the non–Magyars as political helots, regarding their own interests as the common, and indeed the only, interests of the State. All public institutions are made instruments of Magyarization, whether posts, telegraphs, railways, or law courts; finally, the hoped-for Hungarian army is to complete the process."[48] Slovaks, nearly all of whom lived within the boundaries of Hungary, felt especially oppressed.[49] Forced to learn Magyar as the cost of elementary education and left to till small plots of land to support themselves, substantial numbers of Slovaks opted to emigrate. Some chose to move to a western European country; others chose to travel to North or South America. Writing at the time, Drage said, "The villager now looks for a larger life, and places his hopes beyond the seas."[50]

Overseas emigration was a drastic solution to life's problems. First and foremost, emigration typically meant leaving family and friends, perhaps forever. Second, emigration was risky to life and limb. Third, emigration risked worsening one's life chances if the grass abroad were not greener than at home. Fourth, emigration cost money to pay the agent arranging the trip and the cost of the travel itself. Emigration abroad was for the courageous or the desperate, and even the desperate needed courage to undertake an ocean voyage.

Scholars estimate that over two million people left Hungary prior to World War I. Emigration statistics for the period are not ideal, and the "shortcomings of the statistical data" are well known.[51] After the war, the League of Nations collected and published reputable statistics on prewar demographics and economics, but its migration data for Austria and Hungary began only postwar, at 1920.[52] Writing in the early part of the 20th century, several scholars reported migration data culled from various documents, but mainly from official Hungarian sources of questionable accuracy.

R.W. Seton-Watson relied on official statistics in his controversial 1908 book, *Racial Problems in Hungary*.[53] He claimed the government's own data provided "an overwhelming case against the present racial policy of the Magyars"—especially against the Slovaks. His compilations, despite various small errors, are still cited by scholars today.[54] Seton-Watson proved to be more than a British scholar who changed from being an "admirer" of the Hungarian government to one of its harshest critics.[55] Years later during the Great War, he worked in Britain's Ministry of Information on propaganda campaigns against Austria-Hungary.[56]

The scope of emigration out of Hungary at the turn of the century is not a matter of much dispute. Figure 3.4 reports Hungarian emigration data for 1896–1906. The decade saw increasing numbers of courageous or desperate inhabitants leaving Hungary. According to available data from official sources, the total number of emigrants increased by sevenfold, from under 25,000 in 1896 to over 178,000 in 1906.

Historian Z.A.B. Zeman reported that Hungary passed an Agricultural Labourers Act in 1907 "intended to check the flow of emigration from Hungary to the United States, and tie down the agricultural labourer more securely to his landlord and to the land he cultivated."[57] Writing from Vienna about that act, the *London Times* correspondent explained that, among other provisions, the legislation forbade workers to leave the farm without permission and prohibited passports for emigration "to a farm servant until 'all relations of service between him and his master have been ended.'" The effect was to empower a master "to prevent servants from saving the little capital requisite for emigration."[58]

Most emigrants were men, but over one-quarter in 1905 and 1906 were women, equally courageous and comparably desperate. Seton-Watson's breakdown by gender for two years prior to the Great War is given in Figure 3.5. In the decade prior to World War I, Slovaks emigrated at a higher rate per 1,000 people than any other of Hungary's major ethnic groups, as shown in Figure 3.6. These rates support Seton-Watson's depiction of Slovak life under Magyar rule.

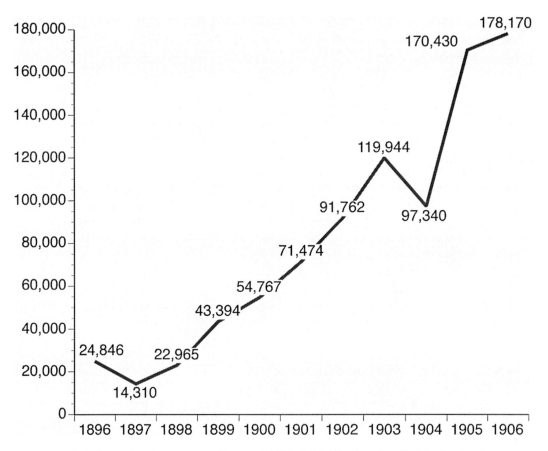

Figure 3.4: TOTAL EMIGRATION FROM HUNGARY, 1896–1906. The decade of 1896–1906 saw increasing numbers of courageous or desperate inhabitants leaving Hungary. The total number of emigrants increased by seven-fold from under 25,000 in 1896 to over 178,000 in 1906. Data: R.W. Seton-Watson, *Racial Problems in Hungary* (New York: Howard Fertig, 1972 edition, originally published 1908). Appendix XIII, p. 47.

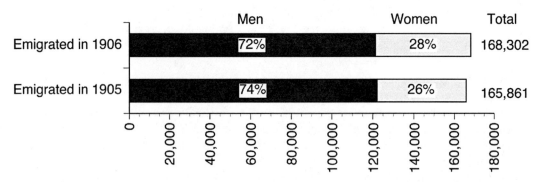

Figure 3.5: DISTRIBUTION OF HUNGARIAN EMIGRANTS BY GENDER, 1905 AND 1906. Most Hungarian emigrants were men, especially at first, but in the first decade of the 20th century, about one-quarter were women. (The totals differ slightly from those in Figure 3.4.) Data: R.W. Seton-Watson, *Racial Problems in Hungary*, Appendix XIII, p. 470. Seton-Watson's data by gender produce lower numbers than his total emigration data. He did not explain the discrepancy.

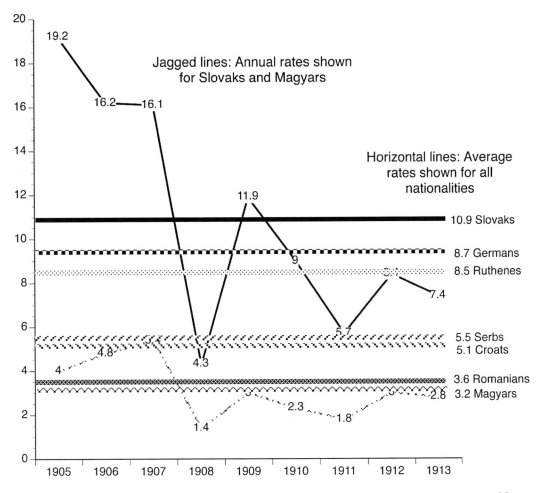

Figure 3.6: Hungarian Emigration Rates per 1,000 by Nationality, 1905–1913. Prior to World War I, Slovaks left Hungary at a higher rate than residents of any other nationality. Data: Gustave Thirring, "Hungarian Migration of Modern Times," in Walter F. Willcox, ed., *International Migrations, Volume II: Interpretations* (Washington: National Bureau of Economic Research, 1931), p. 411.

Additional data on emigration came from another scholar, Konštantín Čulen, who also attacked the Hungarian government. Although an anti–Semite who blamed much of Slovak misfortune on Jews, Čulen provided detailed data on Slovak migration not available in Seton-Watson's book. Čulen's book, *Dejiny Slovákov v Amerike* [*History of Slovaks in America*], is cited less often than Seton-Watson's, probably because Čulen's 1942 Slovak edition was not widely available until an English translation was published in 2007.[59] Figures in Seton-Watson and Čulen mainly agree when they addressed the same topic.[60]

Čulen provided more detail on Slovak emigration, especially as it varied by region and time. Initially, emigration started in the poorer eastern counties and spread to the west and south, soon coming to the western county of Nitra, where Sam Mozolák lived in Krajné. In 1900, Nitra had a population of 428,246.[61] According to annual figures for 1900 to 1909, 22,544 of Nitra's people emigrated over the decade. That amounted to almost 6 percent of the county's population.

According to sources already cited, one-quarter or more of the emigrants were women. Data show that of 36,934 Slovaks emigrating in 1901–1902, 89 percent were of working age, from 14 to 45. Very few (3 percent) were over 45 and only about 8 percent were children under 14.[62] One infers that few Slovak families emigrated together before the Great War. Almost 90 percent were employable men and women who planned to work and prosper away from Hungary—and perhaps to return to live in Slovakia with the wealth they earned. Statistics show that many did indeed return. Čulen estimated that about 25 percent of all Slovaks who left eventually returned.[63] Seton-Watson's data reported that Slovaks who returned in 1905 were 10 percent of those who left, and that returnees were 20 percent of emigrants in 1906.[64] A contemporary scholar estimates that 35 to 40 percent of all Hungarian emigrants returned "after spending some years in the United States."[65] All experts contend that most emigrants planned only to make enough money to live better in their home country. And many fulfilled their plans.

Some Slovak emigrants, especially those living in Nitra County, did not travel far. The city of Nitra was only about 60 miles from the Austrian border and about 100 miles from Vienna, which offered nonagricultural employment that promised better pay and easier living than on the farm in Slovakia. Čulen said that Vienna was the "main destination" for Nitra emigrants. They were among thousands of *Záhoráks* or *Záhoráci*, referring to emigrants from *Záhorie*, the western region in Slovakia that included Myjava and other nearby areas.[66] He wrote, "They found jobs especially as industrial workers, craftsmen and small storekeepers, particularly greengrocers." Although the 100 miles between Nitra and Vienna does not seem far today, Slovak peasants unable to afford train fare did not easily nor often travel that distance. If not desperate about their lives, they had to fear lack of opportunity and be courageous to leave village life for the big city. Those who envisioned immigrating to America needed much more courage to make the move. Many demonstrated that courage: 28 percent of all immigrants to the United States in 1902 came from Austria-Hungary.[67]

Two factors—poverty and discrimination—motivated most Austro-Hungarians to leave their homes. This was especially true of the Slavic peoples—Czechs, Poles, Ruthenians, Croats, Slovaks, Serbs, and Slovenians, who constituted almost half (47 percent) of the inhabitants in the Austro-Hungarian empire. In Austria, most minorities accepted German rule and did not emigrate. In Hungary, more suffered from Magyar rule and chose to leave.

Although obscured since by the passage of time, Seton-Watson's book on the nature and extent of Magyar oppression of Slavs caused a political stir when it appeared. Historian Geoffrey Wawro wrote: "Franz Josef recoiled at the publication (and international sensation) of Oxford scholar R.W. Seton-Watson's *Racial Problems in Hungary*, detailing myriad abuses of non–Hungarians in Transleithania.[68] On July 30, 1914, on the eve of World War I, the *New York Times* printed remarks by the Serbian honorary consul-general in New York, who charged that the Austrian Empire treated its Serb subjects with "repressive measures" that "according to Seton-Watson, cannot be found in the annals of any other European country."[69] Seton-Watson's political message even surfaced in a nonpolitical 1930 travel book, *The Road Through Czechoslovakia*,[70] and his indictment of Hungary's nationality policy is duly noted by contemporary scholars.[71]

Some Magyar scholars at the time also severely criticized government policy toward non–Magyar nationalities. In his book on the Habsburg monarchy, Arthur May wrote, "No one had surpassed the Hungarian sociologist and publicist, Oscar Jászi, in condemnation of the iniquities of Magyarization and in advocacy of humane policies toward the nationalities."[72] May quoted the prominent Magyar leader, Mihály Károlyi, as charging, "It is a sad fact that among … our foreign slanderers the Magyar Oszkar Jászi has taken the place of the English Scotus Viator [the pen name used by R.W. Seton-Watson]."[73]

In *The Dissolution of the Habsburg Monarchy*, which Jászi published in 1929 while at Oberlin College in the United States, he said he was not alone in his criticism: "Many of the best statesmen, poets, scholars, and publicists were unanimous in the understanding that the empire of the Habsburgs had become an anachronistic impossibility, that it was doomed to death or at least could have been saved only by a major operation."[74] For the next six pages, Jászi then reported the critical views of other scholars and politicians in the empire who shared his views.

Seton-Watson had once been Hungary's strong supporter, as was Henry Wickham Steed, who had lived for a decade in Vienna as the *London Times* correspondent before becoming its foreign editor in 1914. Steed's 1913 book *The Hapsburg Monarchy* also denounced Hungary's "policy of ruthless Magyarization."[75] Before the war, British policy had supported the Habsburg monarchy as a bulwark against Germany. Back in London at the *Times*, Steed used his position to influence Britain's policy against the Habsburgs.[76] Later, Steed joined his fellow Magyar critic, Seton-Watson, in Britain's Ministry of Information in a propaganda campaign to dismantle the Austro-Hungarian Empire.

Steed, Seton-Watson, and others documented the plight of Hungary's non–Magyar peasants. Because Slovaks and other Slavs were living poorly and treated badly, Gregory Ference said, "It is easy to make the deductions that they would search for a way to escape this oppression and that is why they emigrated." He continued, however, "nothing can be further from the truth."[77] Instead, he attributed their emigration to overpopulation, a lack of farmland, unemployment, and poverty. They were not refugees who fled from ethnic strife. In today's parlance, most Slovak immigrants were economic migrants, not political refugees.[78]

In contrast to the Slovaks, who lived almost wholly in Hungary, the Czechs lived almost wholly in Austria. Historians writing about Czech emigration from Austria paint a somewhat different picture. First, large numbers of Czechs immigrated to the United States earlier, starting in the mid–1800s, than large numbers of Slovaks. Second, early Czech emigration from Austria was politically motivated. Stephanie Saxon-Ford said, "Bohemian intellectuals who had participated in the nationalist revival of the 1840s and 1850s … left their homeland by the score to escape the repression of Hapsburg rule."[79] By 1850 about 500 members of the Czech intelligentsia—doctors, professors, composers, and journalists—immigrated to the United States.

Afterward, from 1850 to 1890, Czechs did emigrate because of economic deprivation and not political repression. U.S. Census data for 1890–1899 show some 268,000 immigrants from Austria versus 203,000 from Hungary. By 1900–1909, these totals were doubled and reversed: some 685,000 from Hungary versus 532,000 for Austria.[80] Czechs and Slovaks were not the only peoples who emigrated from Austria and Hungary, but no counts are available for specific ethnic groups. Immigrants were not tallied by "mother tongue" until 1910. Certainly Austrian immigrants included many German speakers, and Hungarian immigrants included many Magyars.

Had Franz Josef paid more attention to the welfare of his peasants, he might have commanded more support from them when he ordered them to defend his empire. Certainly Slovaks did not leave their homeland prior to 1914 because of warfare. Indeed, historian Margaret MacMillan described the century since the end of the Napoleonic Wars in 1815 as "the most peaceful one Europe had known since the Roman Empire."[81] European countries had engaged in wars, but usually elsewhere: against the Zulus and Boers in southern Africa, with Japan or China in the Far East, and on Europe's periphery in Crimea. The 1866 Austro-Prussian War and the 1870 Franco-Prussian War were contained, decisive, and short—the first lasting seven weeks and the second less than a year. Accordingly, MacMillan titled her masterful book about World War I *The War That Ended Peace*. Samko Mozolák did not fear for his life when he decided to sail to America.

4

The Peasant's Voyage

In 1901, Samko decided to risk traveling to America. His situation in the Mozolák family home in Krajné did not hold much promise. Four years had passed since his father died. His mother was still alive, but his oldest brother, Ján, headed the family. While everyone worked the farm, agricultural prices had dropped, making for hard times everywhere. Samko's older brother, Martin, stood ahead in prospects for inheritance. The Mozoláks were not poor, and Samko could work on the family farm, of course, but he was young, single, and blessed with a sense of adventure.

Earlier, he had heard that some young men from Krajné had left for America. He since learned that they eventually reached New York City, that they wrote their families periodically, and that they sent home American money. If they could travel to America and make money, why couldn't he? He would need financing for the voyage, but he could borrow that from his brothers and pay them back handsomely from his earnings. After he made enough money in America, he could return to Krajné, or maybe move to Myjava and live in style.

Western civilization thrives on such youthful heroic fantasies. Most never materialize, but those that do sometimes pay off. Millions of Europeans during Samko Mozolák's time had similar visions of life in America. And millions in Ireland, Norway, Sweden, Germany, Italy, Greece, and elsewhere in Europe acted out their visions. In countless Slovak villages across Hungary, other young men and young women—whose personal situations may have differed from Samko's—were thinking along the same lines. Thoughts about emigrating were so pervasive that Slovaks called those who had committed to the voyage "our Americans." Some villages used *Američan* (with č pronounced as "ch") for residents of America but *Amerikán* for Slovaks going there or even those who returned.[1]

Novelists of that era described how Slovaks responded to emigration fever sweeping over their villages. Here is how Božena Slančiková, whose pen name was Timrava, wrote about it in her 1907 short story, "That Alluring Land," after a rumor spread through the village of Polievec that someone was going to America.

"Who's in there?"

"The Americans," the old woman said maliciously. She loved to dominate every conversation, but now the noise of the tavern was so great that she could not be heard, so she had left it. "We just call them the Americans now, the ones going off across the ocean. They say even Srnec is going. The whole village would go if it could. They think they'll be gentlemen there, and have nothing to do but load their pockets with gold. It's Privoda that baits them like that. Till now he just lured them to carouse around, but now it's to America! That fellow could sweet-talk the devil. He says there's a harvest right now in America."[2]

When a mother worried about her son's intention to be gone for two years, he replied: "That's not so long, not so long as when I was in the emperor's army. I stayed three years, and you got along without me. They pay good wages in America. In Ružovka, when I went for the young ox we put out to feed with Bolec, I heard that a man from there made two thousand [Kronen] in just two years. He came back and built a fine house—I saw it myself. Almost as good as ours here."[3]

Later the Americans met at the tavern, their expectations enhanced by the bottle on the table. "[W]hile they drank, they talked about that wondrous land across the ocean which provided mankind with such blessings. It had four harvests a year with no taxes, and money fell everywhere like dust. That land glittered magically before their eyes. It was covered by luxuriant ears of grain strewn with the dollars that rained down abundantly upon the working man and jingled together like music. The jingling heard at the table in the tavern went to everyone's head, and in each man's heart the desire to go off with Paľo Privoda flared up."[4]

One can imagine a similar scene in Krajné when Samko walked down Mozolák hill to the local *hostinec* or tavern. If he hadn't already made up his mind to emigrate, tavern talk certainly fortified his intentions. His mother, Anna, may have wanted him to stay, as mothers always do. But she had two other sons at home and, at age 55, could expect to see him return after a few years. Also, it would be good to have a prosperous *Amerikán* in the family. Unlike other mothers who mourned their children leaving the village, she gave Samko her blessing, and her other sons advanced Samko the needed funds.

By the second half of the 19th century, travel to America was a big business. As early as 1849, German and Czech newspapers advertised the offerings by steamship companies and travel agents. In 1849, a Czech paper, *Pražský Večerní List*, carried these advertisements:

> May 22. Travelers to America are conveyed by vessels on the 15th of every month by S.H.P. Schröder in Bremen. Agent C. Poppe, Prague, Koňksý Trh, No, 833
> June 30. Announcements to Travelers to America. The firm of Lüdering & Co., in Bremen, ships emigrants on the 1st and 15th of every month by fast going vessels. Agent, F.F. Dattelzeir, Klatovy (Klattau).[5]

As time passed, the travel-abroad business grew in Europe, drawn by the boom in America. Manufacturers in the east wanted factory workers and miners. Western states needed population, especially farmers. Cities, states, and railroad companies advertised for immigrants. Enough money was involved that Minnesota's Secretary of State, Hans Mattson, resigned his position to become a promoter for the Northern Pacific Railroad, urging Swedes and Norwegians to come to America.[6]

Emigrants needed money for several purposes even before landing in America. First, most needed (or wanted) some city clothing for the journey and the New World. Then, they had to pay for travel to the point of embarkation, the closest to Slovakia being the German port cities of Hamburg and Bremen. Finally, and most costly, they needed money for the voyage. That cost the equivalent of about $30 in 1900, typically paid in advance to the travel agent, who also arranged for passports. M. Mark Stolarik, an expert on Slovak immigration, estimated that the entire trip cost $80.[7] Additional money was necessary for living in America after landing, but that varied widely according to who—if anyone—awaited the immigrant in America.

Samko had no one special waiting for him in America. That meant he could not count on support when arriving, but he was free to choose where he wanted to go. Most people he knew talked about New York City, so why not go there? Applying for permission to emigrate, Sam—who was small for his 19 years of age—claimed he was 17, probably to evade the issue of future military service at home.[8] Samko booked passage on a ship leaving from Bremen, about 600 miles from Krajné.[9] (Bremen was the most popular port of departure for Slovak emigrants, accounting for about 60 percent at the time.[10]) He probably traveled by wagon to Pozsony (Bratislava), then by train to Vienna, changing for the long haul to the city of Bremen for processing before taking another train for 40 miles to the actual harbor at Bremerhaven.

On the 60-mile wagon ride from Krajné to Pozsony, Samko was joined by others headed for embarkation. Few had proper luggage. Most had battered suitcases or bags containing only what they thought they would need in the New World. The train ride from Pozsony to Bremen itself took over a day of living and sleeping in very close quarters. On arrival in Bremen, the prospective passengers had to pass a health screening. This was not perfunctory. They would be screened again on arrival in New York, and those who did not pass were denied entry and returned to the port of embarkation at the expense of the steamship company. So the company took the screening seriously.

Just six months earlier, Joseph Grisak, a Slovak from the eastern county of Spiš, was in Bremen awaiting his crossing in June 1901. As he recalled in his autobiography:

> In Bremen there were agents looking for our identifications when we arrived since we made a deposit for passage on an ocean liner back in Ratibor. These agents took us to the Mislera Company head-quarters where we were served a meal and given lodging. It was a place where immigrants were passing thru—some arriving and others departing. The next morning breakfast was served to this huge crowd at tables. After breakfast we went into a large adjoining hall where people relaxed to music and dancing awaiting to be examined by doctors and to receive vaccinations.
>
> We were also served our noon and evening meals, and there was plenty to eat. The following day we made arrangements to purchase our passage and to pay for our meals and lodging. My total bill amounted to 110 Zlaty. This included my deposit and transportation all the way to my final destination which was Horatio, Pa. I had 40 Zlaty left which I changed into American money for a total of $18.00.[11]

Carrying passengers across the Atlantic became big business. Ships had improved dramatically from 1900 to the start of the Great War, as one source recounts:

> Three or four funnels, three or four screws, turbine propulsion, speeds of twenty-five knots, three-deck superstructures, all appeared. In 1907, Cunard's record-breaking *Mauretania* entered service. Her tonnage was 31,938, with a length of 762 feet and beam of 88, and she carried 563 first, 464 second, and 1,138 third, in conditions considerably better than the traditional steerage. White Star's *Olympic* of 1911, 45,324 tons, with a length of 852 feet and beam of 92, was the only vessel ever to carry as many first-class passengers as third-class—a little over 1,000 each—together with 500 second. Hamburg-America's *Imperator*, the biggest ship to go into service before war broke out, measured 883 feet by 98, had a gross tonnage of 51,969, and was designed to carry 700 first, 600 second, 1,000 third, as well as 1,800 steerage.[12]

The *Imperator* was actually 24 feet longer than the *Titanic*.

On January 18, 1902, Samko boarded the SS *Rhein* sailing to the port of New York under the North German Lloyd line. Built in 1899, the *Rhein* was a fairly new ship of 10,200 registered gross tonnage, 501' long and 58' wide.[13] While not huge like the *Imperator*, the *Rhein* (Photo 4.1) was a big ship. It accommodated 140 passengers in 1st class, 150 in 2nd class, and 2,500 in steerage—space below the waterline even less commodious than third class. Samko sailed below the waterline.[14]

Although smaller than the *Imperator*, the 501' *Rhein* was nearly half as long as today's

Photo 4.1: S.S. *RHEIN*. Samuel Mozolák sailed from Bremerhaven, Germany, to New York City on the SS *Rhein* in 1902. Credit: National Archives at http://www.navsource.org/archives/12/ 1217301607.jpg. In the public domain.

largest aircraft carrier, the 1,100' USS *Gerald R. Ford*. How much space did the *Rhein* provide for passengers below the waterline? Some rough calculations are sobering. Not allowing for narrowing at the bow and stern and simply multiplying the ship's length by its width yields an area of 30,000 square feet. Not allowing for machinery, bulkheads, crew, and so on, that computes to 12 square feet for each of 2,500 passengers in steerage when full. The typical crossing from northwestern European ports was 12 days.[15] So for an ocean voyager lasting almost two weeks, passengers in steerage averaged living spaces of 12 square feet. This worked by sleeping in bunk beds.

Samko left no description of his voyage, but a writer described the general pattern of emigration from Europe to America in steerage:

> Iron bunks with straw mattresses but no pillows were their berths. Wooden floors sprinkled with sand, two washrooms open to both sexes, a small basin and a dishpan and other cans used for laundry were typical equipment for steerage. In cases of seasickness, quite common during such voyages, conditions became especially filthy and malodorous, relieved occasionally by the salt breezes of the ocean. By journey's end, everything was dirty and disagreeable. Rough voyages were even worse as no facilities were available for personal cleanliness. All passengers lacked space and privacy. No open deck space was available in steerage, no dining room, and little drinking water.[16]

By transporting 2,500 passengers at $30 each in steerage on a fully booked run, the *Rhein* would return $75,000 in fares to the North German Lloyd line. That would be in addition to fares from its 140 1st-class and 150 2nd-class passengers. For that time period, the North German Line was making good money on emigration to America. From 1900 to 1909, more immigrants (24.4 percent) entered the United States from Austria-Hungary than from any other country, exceeding even Italy (23.5 percent).[17]

Those who sailed in third class or steerage often complained about travel conditions. A published complaint about the Cunard line, which had an emigration contract with the Hungarian government, was cited in a 1904 letter written by Hungarian-Americans to Count Apponyi, a Hungarian government minister. According to Konštantín Čulen, the letter charged that Hungarian emigrants traveling on the Cunard Line "are treated much worse than cattle." It continued, in part: "Honorable Count, there are dozens and dozens of honest countrymen who testified under oath. A few months ago, the majority of these testimonials were published in a pamphlet entitled: *A cunard vonal és a kivándorlás Magyarországból* (The Cunard Line and Emigration from Hungary). These testimonials provide undeniable evidence of the terrible fact that the Hungarian government failed to respect the interests of the emigrants, or any Hungarian general interests, when it made the agreement with the Cunard Line. We, the Hungarian immigrants, are deeply ashamed of these facts."[18]

Prior to the Great War, immigrants could enter the United States without passports. Craig Robertson's history of the American passport stated, "The first attempt to legally control the entry of aliens to the United states came in a joint order of July 26, 1917, issued by the State and Labor Departments."[19] That order only required all aliens to have a visa issued by a U.S. consul. Passports were not required until after Congress enacted the Passport Control Act in 1918. During the preceding decades, when millions of immigrants poured into the country, the U.S. government depended on information in steamship passenger lists, called manifests, to learn who was coming from where. As Robertson put it, the government relied on steamship companies to "compensate for the limitations of U.S. administration and bureaucracy abroad."[20]

In the Passenger Act of 1882, Congress required steamship companies to compile and furnish, on arrival, manifests with information on passengers' "names, sex, calling, country of citizenship, and number of pieces of baggage belonging to each."[21] As concern over immigration grew, Congress in 1893 passed another law "requiring much additional information and setting forth in detail the procedure to be followed"—specifying that the manifests were not to exceed thirty lines of names. Later laws required additional information.

Robertson described the standard steamship company manifest in 1918, saying it "was a large sheet of paper, ruled with horizontal lines and vertical columns. There were thirty lines intended to record thirty names, with twenty-nine numbered vertical columns for steamship officials to record the information immigration officials required to ascertain admission."[22] From 1919 to 1925, the government demanded more information as it sought to control immigration, and it instructed companies to expand manifests to 33 columns.[23] After 1925, as the government clamped down harder on immigration from Asia and from southern and eastern Europe, manifests expanded to 36 columns.[24]

Exhibiting handwriting skills unpracticed today, steamship officials neatly crammed immigrants' data into tiny rectangles. Despite the expert penmanship, entries often became unreadable. Steamship companies, however, strived to provide accurate information so that their passengers were admitted to the country. It was not good business to return them home. Some companies did cut corners to save money, such as listing more than 30 immigrants on a single manifest page—not to save paper but to reduce per-page notary costs.[25]

When Samko sailed in 1902, the U.S. government requested little information about immigrants, and its manifest (reproduced in Figure 4.1) had only 22 columns.[26] The SS *Rhein* docked in New York on February 3, after 16 days of travel from Bremen, longer than the usual 12 days. Passengers who traveled first or second class often landed in New Jersey for transport directly to New York, for ship doctors had examined them on board. Those in steerage were taken to the main immigration facility on Ellis Island in Upper

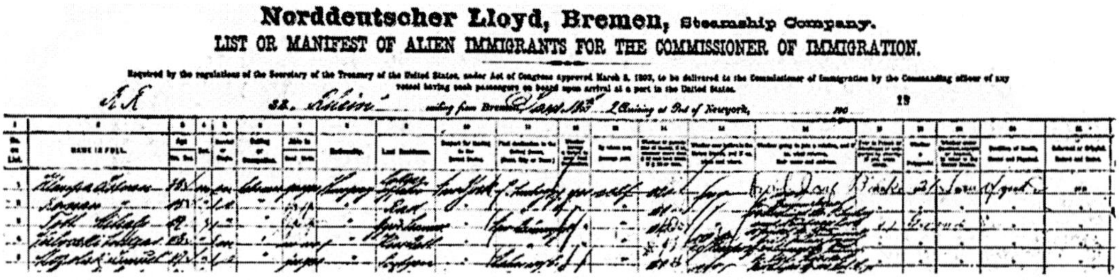

Interpretation of Information in the 22 columns

1	No. on List	*5*
2	NAME IN FULL	*Mozolak Samuel*
3	Age: Yrs. Mos.	*17*
4	Sex	*m*
5	Married or Single	*s*
6	Calling or Occupation	*Labourer*
7	Able to: Read, Write	*Yes, Yes*
8	Nationality	*Hungary*
9	Last Residence	*Pöstyn*
10	Seaport for Landing In the United States	*New York*
11	Final destination in the United States (State, City or Town)	*illegible*
12	Whether having a ticket to destination	*" (yes)*

13	By whom was passage paid	*" (self)*
14	Whether in possession of money, if so, whether more than $30 and how much if $30 or less	*4*
15	Whether ever before in the United States, and if so, when and where	*no*
16	Whether going to join a relative, and if so, what relative, their name and address	*illegible*
17	Ever in Prison or Almshouse or supported by charity. If yes, state which	*" (no)*
18	Whether a Polygamist	*" (no)*
19	Whether an anarchist?	*" (no)*
20	Whether under Contract, express or implied, to labor in the United States	*" (no)*
21	Condition of Health, Mental and Physical	*" (good)*
22	Deformed or Crippled, Nature and Causes	*" (no)*

Figure 4.1: S.S. *RHEIN* PASSENGER MANIFEST, FEBRUARY 3, 1902. The U.S. government required steamships to collect immigration data, specifying information to be recorded on passenger manifests. The entries were often hard to read. The entries on line 4 for *Mozolák, Samuel,* are interpreted here. Credit: Ancestry.com. In public domain.

New York Bay to disembark for three to five hours of questioning and medical inspection for contagious diseases. An immigration inspector asked questions working from the ship's manifest, for example:

> *"What is your name?"*
> *"What is your age?"*
> *"Are you married?"*
> *"What is your occupation?"*
> *"Where are you from?"*
> *"Why have you come to the United States?"*
> *"How much money do you have?"*

The manifest listed Samko's age as 17; later that month he would turn 20. Instead of Krajné as his origin, Samko gave Pöstyn (Hungarian for Piešťany, a large town 25 miles away). It indicated that he would join someone named Mozolák in the city; who that was is unknown. Writing down $4 for Samko's fortune on arrival, the officer allowed him to enter New York City.

By 1902, there were enough Slovaks in New York to assist "greenhorns" just off the boat. The 1910 U.S. Census counted 10,324 people of Slovak stock in the city.[27] Samko took lodging in an apartment building at 26 E. 165th Street in the Bronx managed by a Slovak family. Some New York Slovaks came from villages in Nitra County, where Krajné was located. Many earlier Slovak immigrants came from eastern counties (e.g., Joseph Grisak from Spiš). Although they too were peasants, most soon left the city to work on the railroads and in mines and mills in Pennsylvania. Emigrating from Hungary for economic, not political reasons, few Slovak immigrants to the United States could be regarded as "educated."[28] Gregory Ference reported that only 52 percent of Slovaks in Hungary were literate in 1910.[29] Nevertheless, some educated Slovaks did emigrate from the old country to play important roles in their new one. Two categories are of special note: journalists (or budding journalists) and clergy.

Back in Hungary, newspapers were not important to Slovaks. Almost half were illiterate and the government censored the press anyway. In the United States, Slovak-language newspapers increased in importance. Ference's study of the Slovak-American press found that most immigrant organizations "published newspapers for their members, which expressed opinions and ideas that reflected the ideology of the parent society." They "became powerful tools to express grievances against the Magyars and conditions in the Habsburg Monarchy, as well as covering controversial issues that arose in America."[30] Ference said, "At the beginning of the twentieth century, Slovak language journals and newspapers published about 80,000 copies a week."[31] By 1910, twelve Slovak-American newspapers "published 112,500 copies a week, whereas the twenty Slovak weeklies in Hungary issued a total of 48,300."[32] "In Pennsylvania alone twenty-five new Slovak language journals were launched between 1914 and 1918."[33]

Slovak immigrant clergy soon began to serve the spiritual needs of their different flocks. Unlike other Slavs, Slovak Christians split across four religious groups: Roman Catholic, Lutheran, Calvinists, and Byzantine-Rite Catholics. In 1910, 70 percent were estimated to be Roman Catholic and 14 percent Lutheran, the other denominations dividing the remaining 16 percent.[34] A Roman Catholic church conducting services in Slovak was founded in Manhattan's Yorkville area in 1891 and two more in other parts of the city in 1895. In 1902, the year Samko arrived, the protestant Holy Trinity Slovak Lutheran Church was founded at 288 East 10th Street in lower Manhattan.[35] Immigrants from Nitra County attended there, and its Slovak services would fulfill Samko's minimal religious needs.

Samko's social needs may have been more pressing. Alone in a strange city, he certainly sought the company of fellow Slovaks, or at least the company of Czechs, whose language he could understand. Because large numbers of Czechs had immigrated early to the United States, they had already established social institutions in the new world to address needs of Slavic immigrants from Austria-Hungary. As early as 1854 in St. Louis, Czechs formed the *Česko-Slovanská Podporující Společnost,* or C.S.P.S. (the Czech-Slavic Protective Society).[36] C.S.P.S. and other fraternal-beneficial societies offered inexpensive life and disability insurance. Czechs and Slovaks, usually separately, built halls that soon became centers of social activity, organizing picnics, dances, theatrical productions, and athletic events. Historian Gregory Ference said that forty different Slovak fraternal organizations existed by 1890, and the majority of these later associated or merged with one of the larger, stronger national societies.[37]

Separate from the benevolent societies were the "Sokol" athletic organizations (sokol means falcon) that sprang up across the country. One was formed in New York in 1867, and a Czech Sokol Hall was built in 1896 at 420 East 71st Street, where it operates today.[38] Three other Sokols thrived in Manhattan when Samko arrived in 1902. They were the STJ (*Slovenská Tělocvičná Jednota*—Slovak Athletic Union), the DA (*Delnicko-Americký*—American Worker) Sokol, and the Sokol Catholic Orel [Eagle] Sokol.[39] Usually welcoming Czechs and Slovaks alike, Sokols were places where Samko could have enjoyed a social life.

Of special importance to New York Czechs and Slovaks was the *Národní Budova*

(National Hall), which opened in 1896 on East 73rd Street. Making the successful case for its designation as a New York City Landmark in 1994, the president of the Landmark Preservation Commission said that for one hundred years, "Bohemian National Hall has been an important center for Czech and Slovak culture in New York City."[40] The ground floor of the four-story building "held a restaurant and bar, the upper floors individual club rooms, and the top floor a ballroom/theater."[41] (In 2001, the building was sold for $1 to the Czech government. Completely renovated on the inside, it now houses the Czech Consulate.)

If Samko had little desire for religious guidance, he had even less for information about European politics. He never followed politics closely in Austria-Hungary and—even if he had—he would not have paid much attention to a bizarre event on June 11, 1903, in the small country on Austria-Hungary's southeastern border that made the front page of the *New York Times* as "KING AND QUEEN OF SERVIA SLAIN." At the time, Serbia was commonly spelled "Servia."

As detailed later by historian Christopher Clark, Serbia's King Alexandar and Queen Draga were attacked, murdered, and butchered in their royal apartments by their own soldiers.[42] Plenty of reasons—scandals, sexual depravity, deceit, public extravagance, political repression, constitutional manipulations—motivated the regicide. Moreover, it proved popular with the citizenry, who later welcomed Petar Karadjordević, the head of a rival dynasty, as Serbia's king. The bloody coup d'état was generally applauded in Serbia.

It drew little applause in Austria-Hungary, which regarded the murdered king as the empire's friend. That was one reason that the Serbian military wished him dead; another reason to murder him was that he failed to strengthen the Serbian army. Although Austria-Hungary courteously recognized the new king, Karadjordević's government shifted toward greater independence. The two countries fought over trade policies, leading Serbia to turn away from Austria-Hungary and turn to France for financial and diplomatic support.

No longer tied to Austria-Hungary, an independent Serbia became a political threat, standing as a possible homeland for two million Serbs in the Dual Monarchy. Later, Serbia would emerge as a military threat in disputes over Bosnia-Herzegovina. Ultimately, the 1903 regicide planted the seeds for the 1914 assassination in Sarajevo of Archduke Franz Ferdinand, Franz Josef's heir. Clark wrote: "Above all, the conspiratorial network that had come together to murder the royal family did not simply melt away, but remained an important force in Serbian politics and public life. The provisional revolutionary government formed

---

KING·AND·QUEEN·OF· SERVIA·SLAIN·¶

——— ¶

Killed·by·Revolutionists·in· Belgrade·Palace¶

——— ¶

MINISTERS·ASSASSINATED.¶

——— ¶

Queen·Draga's·Relatives·also· Put·to·Death.¶

——— ¶

Prince·Peter·Karageorgevitch,· the·Pretender·to·the·Throne,· Proclaimed·King—Servians· Approve·the·Coup·d'Etat.¶

——— ¶

New·York·Times¶ June·12,·1903,·p.·1¶

on the day after the assassinations included four conspirators (among them the ministers of war, public works and economics) and six party politicians."[43] One of the key conspirators, Dragutin Dimitrijević, known as "Apis" (after the Egyptian bull-god), was appointed head of the General Staff's intelligence division in 1913 and became principal architect of the assassination plot that sparked World War I.[44]

So the 1903 murder of the Serbian king and queen not only transformed the relationship between Serbia and Austria-Hungary from friendly to adversarial, but also laid the groundwork for war a decade later. Even if Samko had not read the *New York Times* story about the assassination, he surely heard about the regicide from the Slovak community. However, he could not have imagined how it would eventually affect him.

There is no record of what work Samko did in New York and for what pay. Classified as a laborer on the *Rhein*'s manifest, he probably took any job he could find in the city, which—next to London—was the biggest in the world in 1900.[45] At a population of 4.2 million, New York had a million more people than Paris, and 1.5 million more than Berlin. New York was more than twice the size of Vienna, and more than five times the size of Budapest—the largest city that Krajné's villagers might ever imagine visiting. Whereas Krajné offered no gainful employment, New York was a huge and growing metropolis that needed lots of workers. Most Slovaks, however, did not stay in the city but moved to mines and steel mills in Pennsylvania.[46] The 1910 census counted 22,515 people of foreign stock whose mother tongue was Slovak in the entire state of New York. In contrast, Pennsylvania had 140,894—amounting to half of all the 281,707 Slovaks counted in America![47]

Although nearly all Slovaks worked in agriculture in Hungary, most avoided farming when coming to America. In his *History of Slovaks in America,* Čulen wrote: "Most of the early Slovak immigrants settled in the industrial and mining areas of Pennsylvania. Here, two main centers developed. One was in the hard coal (anthracite) mining region (or in the Slovak slang 'v tvardouhoľtnej okolici'—'the hardie coal circle'), the other in the soft coal mining region. The first settlements formed around the mines. Later, they formed around large industrial complexes, particularly around iron and steel mills."[48]

Mill cities of Pittsburgh, Pennsylvania, and nearby Cleveland, Ohio, soon attracted thousands of Slovaks and other Eastern Europeans to backbreaking but remunerative work in their factories. Working conditions in the mines and mills were dirty and dangerous. According to Čulen, "More than one Slovak immigrant had to struggle harder in America than he did in Slovakia. A peasant who had never been deep underground, became a miner overnight. Another peasant, who had never before seen liquid iron, was earning his bread the morning after his arrival by doing the difficult job of a steelworker. Only a few Slovaks settled as farmers. Farming was not the quickest way to make money."[49]

M. Mark Stolarik's more recent research found that Slovaks accounted for 13.1 percent of all steel workers and 12.8 percent of bituminous coal miners. They sought out such dirty and dangerous jobs to make more money, as much as $18.00 in a six-day week, but usually about $13.26 a week, which amounted to about $690 a year.[50] For comparison, consider the $760 earnings of a New York shipping clerk in 1900, as reported by economist Robert Gordon.[51] While the comparison is problematic, it suggests that a recent European immigrant with little or no knowledge of English might make almost as much in one year as an American citizen. Of course, there was no comparison in the conditions of employment and the risk to life and limb.

Thomas Bell's 1941 novel *Out of This Furnace* described the mean existence eked out in the steel mills by generations of George Kracha's family. Kracha "came to America in the fall of 1881, by way of Budapest and Bremen … bound for the hard-coal country of northeastern Pennsylvania, where his brother-in-law had a job on a railroad section gang."[52] Settling in Pennsylvania like half of all Slovak immigrants, Kracha "fought brush fires in dry weather and floodwaters in wet. Storms made silt of ballast, threatened trestles, uprooted trees and telegraph poles; in winter the ballast froze, the switches froze, spikes snapped like glass, snow choked the flangeways and drifted into white hills across the tracks. His wages were ten cents an hour, and when bad times came and the company cut wages, nine. It was an excellent month when he made as much as twenty-five dollars."[53]

Lured by the prospect of earning higher wages for more dangerous work in the steel industry, Kracha moved to Braddock, east of Pittsburgh, to work in Andrew Carnegie's Edgar Thomson Steel Works.

> [I]n Braddock he helped produce the metal from the raw ore. He was a very minor factor in the extensive, highly involved process of supplying a nation with steel, though it cannot be said that he ever thought of himself in just that way. Mills existed to provide men with jobs and men worked in mills because they had to work somewhere. Kracha did what he was told and was paid for it every two weeks; his interest ended there. There was little about his work to make him feel it was important or necessary; on the contrary, the company lost no opportunity to press upon him that his services could be dispensed with at any time, that it was really doing him an enormous favor by letting him work at all.[54]

Bell's novel portrayed the struggles of Slovak "peasants and shepherds" thrust "into the blast furnaces and rolling mills," many of them paying "with their lives for their unfamiliarity with machinery and the English language."[55]

> Even more bewildering were the hostility and contempt of their neighbors, the men they worked with.
>   That hostility, that contempt, epitomized in the epithet "Hunky," was the most profound and lasting influence on their personal lives the Slovaks of the steel towns encountered in America.[56]

By choosing to settle in New York, Samko worked in less dangerous jobs, but also made less money than his countrymen working in steel mills and in mining. Family history suggests that Samko washed dishes, and he most likely dug ditches and toiled on building sites, carrying materials on and trash off. It is reasonable to assume that he earned about the same as other immigrants at the time. Roberts's 1912 study of data from the previous decade quoted a report from the United States Immigration Commission on immigrant wages: "It is a striking fact that of the total number of foreign-born wage earners, 77.9 percent received under $600 per year, and 43.5 percent under $400.' But these figures do not bring out the more striking fact that 27 percent of the men of the newer immigration receive less than $200 per year, and 70.1 percent receive less than $400, and 92.5 percent less than $600, while none of them reached the $1000 mark."[57] The report also states that Slovaks made about the immigrant averages: 43.7 percent made less than $400 and 83.0 percent less than $600 annually.[58]

Let's return to the estimated $760 in annual earnings of a New York shipping clerk in 1900. Suppose that after Samko's first full year of work in 1906, he earned $400, which was less than Slovaks working in mines and mills, about the average for Slovak immigrants generally, yet nearly half that of the American shipping clerk. What would $400 be worth in 2015? Calculating inflation over time is an inexact practice, but Internet inflation calculators extrapolate $400 in 1906 to $10,600 in 2015.[59] (The shipping clerk's $760 projects to about $20,000 in 2015, less than the $28,000 median for a single worker.[60]) Given that

$11,770 marked the poverty guideline for a single person in 2015, Samko would be regarded as poor today. He would have been relatively poor as well in 1906, when $400 would be only about 80 percent of an estimated U.S. median income of about $500.[61] In his 1912 book, Roberts said: "The Immigration Commission found that the average income per annum of foreign-born husbands living in cities was $452. The man and his family must live on $1.50 a day, and 45 percent of the men studied had to keep house on $400 a year. From this wage they must pay each month an average of $2.86 per room for rent, which consumes fully one-fourth of the family income. Under these conditions it is impossible for the foreigner to keep the wolf from the door unless the income is supplemented by the rent paid by boarders or the earnings of the wife and children."[62]

Having no wife or children, Samko was better off than many immigrants. Income comparisons over a century cannot be carried very far, for people lived quite differently then. They did not demand indoor toilets, hot and cold running water, refrigerators, ranges, and so on. The inflation calculation, however, helps to remind us that $400 was a lot of money in 1906. At the official exchange rate in 1913, $1 was worth about 5 Austro-Hungarian Kronen, so $400 would amount to 2,000 Kronen.[63] Villagers back in Krajné simply could not make that kind of money by farming. According to Oscar Jászi, the Hungarian sociologist living after the war in the United States, "the average yearly income of a Hungarian agricultural laborer before the war varied between 60 and 100 dollars."[64]

Of course, Samko wrote back to his mother Anna, and his brothers Ján and Martin, about his new life in New York. Emigrants from Hungary to America tended to write two types of letters. Some were sad accounts of misfortune, even despair. A short story published in 1907 by a Slovak novelist dramatized such a letter: "Here it's not like people at home said it would be. Just don't believe it's so good. It's very difficult here, very hard. True, we get three dollars a day, but we work by the open furnace where the iron ore is melted. Just the two of us—old Duro Tankel' didn't last there even two days and had to quit. Now he's working by the train, hauling coal in a wheelbarrow for the engine. He said he's going home as soon as he gets enough money for the ticket. Srnec went down into the mine because he didn't last by the furnace, either. We work in leather gloves so the flames won't burn our hands, and we have glasses over our eyes."[65]

But most emigrants sent home positive messages, stressing the writers' good fortune in the new land. Scholars today credit such letters with stimulating emigration to the United States. About these letters, Ference said that they "often contained large sums of money to build homes with tiled, instead of thatched, roofs. This newfound prosperity in a poverty-stricken area further enticed others to emigrate."[66] Samko probably wrote positive accounts of his experiences and very good news about his earnings. He almost certainly sent his family money, perhaps hidden in packages of clothing to foil theft of money sent in envelopes—a common immigrant practice. Ján and Martin learned that their little brother was not only surviving in the foreign city but might return as a *boháč*—a rich man. Perhaps they harbored thoughts about leaving the farm and working in New York for a while, like Sam.

Like many immigrants expecting to return, Samko saved his meager earnings; unlike some countrymen, he did not regularly frequent the local taverns. But like most young men, he did seek feminine companionship. After arriving, he met Anna Dlhy from the tiny village of Hrachovište, only three miles northeast of Krajné. We have no record of how they met, but it was likely to have been at one of the Sokol halls. They were places where Slovaks gathered to celebrate special occasions, especially weddings, which allowed unattached young men and women to meet one another. Although Anna, born July 8, 1878, was four years older than Samko, he probably knew her through Krajné's Lutheran church, which also served Hrachovište. In her late twenties, Anna was exiting the age range when most women were married. However, she was a pretty, diminutive woman stuffed with gumption and determination, which probably explained why she had not yet married. Like Samko, she also had courage. After all, she sailed across the ocean as a single woman.

On April 30, 1905, Anna and Samko, then 23, were married at the Holy Trinity Slovak Lutheran Church at 117 First Avenue. (His age was incorrectly stated in their marriage certificate in Figure 4.2.) Why they married in that church, less than a half mile from the first Slovak Lutheran church at 288 East 10th Street, is unknown.

Regardless of their choice of churches, their marriage conformed to Slovak immigrant practice. Stolarik's study of Slovak congregational records found "that men who had come to America single very often married sweethearts from the same or neighboring village, just as would likely have been the case had they remained in the Old Country."[67] Photo 4.2 shows them on their wedding day.

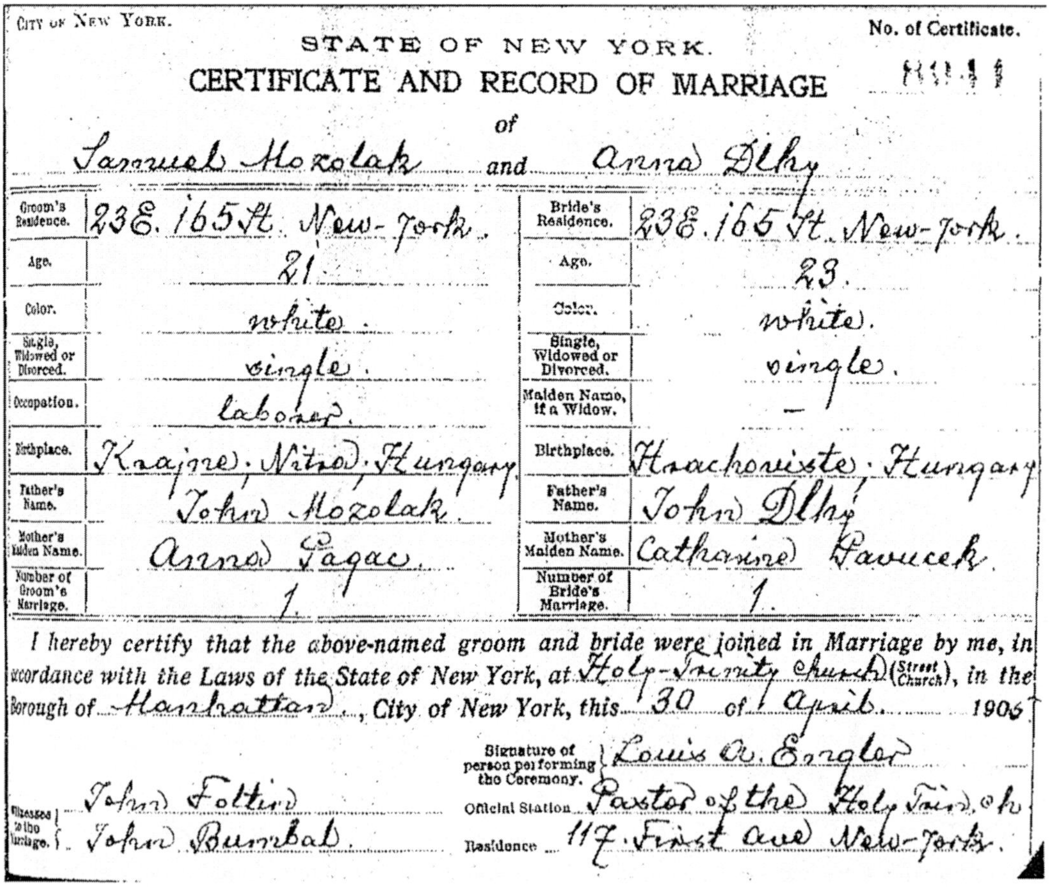

City of New York. No. of Certificate. 8011

STATE OF NEW YORK.

CERTIFICATE AND RECORD OF MARRIAGE

of

Samuel Mozolak and Anna Dlhy

Groom's Residence.	23 E. 165 St. New-York.	Bride's Residence.	23 E. 165 St. New-York.
Age.	21	Age.	23.
Color.	white.	Color.	white.
Single, Widowed or Divorced.	single.	Single, Widowed or Divorced.	single.
Occupation.	laborer.	Maiden Name, if a Widow.	—
Birthplace.	Krajne, Nitra, Hungary	Birthplace.	Hrachoviste. Hungary
Father's Name.	John Mozolak.	Father's Name.	John Dlhy
Mother's Maiden Name.	Anna Pagac.	Mother's Maiden Name.	Catharine Pavucek.
Number of Groom's Marriage.	1.	Number of Bride's Marriage.	1.

I hereby certify that the above-named groom and bride were joined in Marriage by me, in accordance with the Laws of the State of New York, at Holy-Trinity church *(Street / Church), in the Borough of* Manhattan*, City of New York, this* 30 *of* April 1905

Signature of person performing the Ceremony. Louis A. Engler

Official Station Pastor of the Holy Trinity ch.

Residence 117 First ave New-York.

Witnesses to the Marriage. John Foltin, John Bumbal.

Figure 4.2: Samuel Mozolák and Anna Dlhy Marriage Certificate. **The marriage certificate of Samuel Mozolák to Anna Dlhy lists his age as 21 and hers as 23, but he was really 23 and she 27. Clerks wrote down what they were told. Credit: Family document.**

It is highly unlikely that Samko and Anna read the *New York Times* on their wedding day. Even if they had, they probably ignored the headline on a one-column story with a St. Petersburg dateline: "RUSSIAN RULER GRANTS FREEDOM OF RELIGION." The autocratic Tsar Nicholas II allowed minor social and economic reforms in the spring of 1905, following an unsuccessful revolt against his rule in the winter. The uprising was fed by long-term social unrest and by recent military humiliations.

The most recent defeat occurred on January 2, 1905, when Russia's far eastern seaport, Port Arthur, fell to Japan just months after the Japanese destroyed the Russian fleet in the Battle of the Yellow Sea. When, on January 22, hungry and unarmed demonstrators sought to present a petition to "father Tsar," they were shot and slashed by his Imperial Guard. The *Times'* April 30 story reported on the Czar's feeble attempt to make amends for the slaughter.

No one at the time, much less Samko and Anna, expected those events in Russia to profoundly affect the course of European history. Samko and Anna certainly would not have imagined that the threat of revolution against the Russian Tsar would have any impact on their lives.

Photo 4.2: WEDDING PHOTO OF ANNA DLHY AND SAMUEL MOZOLÁK. **On April 30, 1905, Anna and Samko were married at the Holy Trinity Slovak Lutheran Church at 117 First Avenue. This photo was taken at the Wendel Photographic Art Studio, No. 13 Avenue A, New York.**

5

Imperial Ignorance

From 1803 to 1814, the French empire fought against various European powers in a series of conflicts called the Napoleonic Wars. The 1815 Conference of Vienna, chaired by Austria's foreign minister, Klemens von Metternich, sought to settle national boundaries to achieve long-term peace. The ensuing treaties and subsequent diplomatic maneuvers kept Europe out of major wars for decades afterwards, during which Europe changed through technological developments, improved communications, transportation, manufacturing, and trade. Citizens' views of their rights and government responsibilities had changed too. European leaders, especially the monarchs heading dynasties that had ruled their nations for centuries, did not fully understand these changes; they certainly did not accept their implications.

Historians Richard Hamilton and Holger Herwig wrote, "The training of monarchs, what might be called the social psychology of monarchy, has been generally neglected by the social sciences."[1] They said, "Elites are regularly depicted as well informed, rational, and calculating. But opposite hypotheses are always useful, in this case the possibility that the decision-making coteries were uninformed or ignorant."[2] The ruling monarchs in the decades before World War I—pictured in Photos 5.1–5.4 in their resplendent military uniforms—were often ignorant about important matters regarding their countries. Most did not adequately learn important facts and lessons that could have improved their governance and their handling of foreign affairs. They were not unintelligent, but they were often monumentally slow learners.

These severe judgments of their reigns were distilled from biographies of the principal monarchs and from histories of World War I and its era. Those writings form a literature too vast to be read, much less mastered, by any individual. Fortunately, most biographies[3] and histories[4] are remarkably consistent in their assessments. Accordingly, the descriptions and quotations below from different scholars should be fairly representative of the literature.

Opposite: Photos 5.1–5.4: MONARCHS OF MAJOR BELLIGERENT NATIONS IN WORLD WAR I. *Top left:* Photo 5.1: EMPEROR FRANZ JOSEF I. 12/2/1848 to 11/21/1916. Austria-Hungary. b. 8/18/1830 d.11/21/1916. *Top, right:* Photo 5.2: KAISER WILHELM II. 6/15/1888 to 11/9/1918. Germany. b.1/27/1859 d. 6/4/1941. *Bottom, left:* Photo 5.3: TSAR NICHOLAS II. 11/1/1894 to 5/15/1917. Russia. b. 5/6/1868 d. 7/17/1918. *Bottom, right:* Photo 5.4: KING GEORGE V. 5/6/1910 to 1/20/1936. United Kingdom. b. 6/3/1865 d.1/20/1936.

All four monarchs were often portrayed in military dress. Emperor Franz Josef normally wore uniforms. Note the resemblance of Tsar Nicholas II to his cousin, King George V. Credits: The first three photos came from Wikipedia Commons. That of George V was supplied by Roger Cullingham, Editor@Thamesweb.co.uk. All are in the public domain.

Nineteenth-century monarchs never doubted their ability to rule. To do that would be to question God. Fervently believing that God chose them to rule, they concluded that they were divinely qualified to do so. That belief was instilled in all three emperors of the major belligerent nations, Austria-Hungary, Germany, and Russia, but not in the British king, who—as explained in Chapter 1—was only Emperor of India, a British possession.

Austria-Hungary's Franz Josef not only accepted his heavenly mission to rule his subjects in Austria-Hungary, but he also assumed a sacred responsibility to preserve the 600 years of Habsburg rule. Moreover, he sought to defend monarchism against creeping republicanism, which had already engulfed France. He ascended the throne during the attempted revolution in 1848, when a parliamentary subcommittee charged to write a new constitution dared to state in the first article that "the power of the state proceeds from the people."[5] Knowing their emperor, his ministers struck that heretical idea from the document that emerged in 1849. As Hilde Spiel stated, "The first obsession was the emperor's belief, held by his ancestors and never abandoned by the House of Habsburg, in the divine right of kings."[6]

Since he had been endowed to rule by God, Franz Josef's thinking experienced no serious "reality testing" by others that might question the validity of his judgments.[7] Joseph Redlich, an Austrian parliamentarian who knew Franz Josef personally, said, "Fundamental, here, as in the rest of his outlook, was his conviction that, at bottom, his subjects had nothing to do with government policy, which belonged solely to him, his ministers, and officials, while their business was to attend to their own affairs."[8] As Alan Palmer described the emperor's upbringing: "[W]hile every lesson in history, philosophy and Christian apologetics emphasized to Francis Josef the divine omnipotence of kingship, he was also taught that imperial sovereignty carried obligations and that it was his duty to protect his subjects from injustice as well as to uphold monarchical rule."[9]

One might expect Franz Josef's views on his divine appointment to have changed after a half-century on the throne. Apparently they did not, even when he knew that his views were out of fashion. Meeting with former President Teddy Roosevelt in 1910, he avoided mentioning that the "old system" he represented "rested on divine sanction." Biographer Palmer noted, "For Francis Josef, dynasty and supranational Empire remained twin pillars of a just society based upon a predominantly Christian moral order."[10] Roosevelt would neither understand nor appreciate that rationale.

Germany's Wilhelm II, who ruled from June 15, 1888, to his forced abdication on November 9, 1918, spoke openly about his celestial appointment. Soon after his accession, he was quoted to say, "We Hohenzollerns receive our crown only from Heaven and in the duties connected to it we are responsible only to Heaven."[11] Apparently, he also thought that God personally bestowed crowns on other monarchs, for he too believed deeply in the divine right to rule. According to a biographer, "Wilhelm liked to talk of a 'magic tie uniting him with all other anointed heads. It was a supernatural, a mythic sacrament … the mystic fellowship of monarchs was heaven-ordained.'"[12]

Russia's Nicholas II, who ruled from November 1, 1894, to his forced abdication on March 15, 1917, was probably the most religiously spiritual of the three autocratic monarchs. Miranda Carter wrote:

> Nicholas compensated for his anxious feelings of inadequacy and lack of preparedness by holding tenaciously to his belief in divine right. The moment the crown had touched his head, he had become a vehicle for God's purpose and had magically absorbed a kind of spiritual superiority which made

him, whatever his inadequacies, better equipped than any minister to know what Russia needed. It was a mystical idea far more literal even than the pronouncements about his relationship with God which had brought Wilhelm such derision in Europe, and in Nicholas it encouraged a kind of fatalism which would make him oddly passive in a crisis. It also made him extremely possessive of his authority, and sensitive to anything that could be interpreted as interference.[13]

As fervently as the emperor, the kaiser, and the tsar believed in the divine right of kings, others sensed, in the words of Hamilton and Herwig, "that 'time was running out.'"[14] In fact, time had already run out in Britain more than three centuries earlier.

Britain's Edward VII, who succeeded Queen Victoria in 1901, and **George V,** who became king in 1910, did not claim to rule by the doctrine of divine right—despite its formal exposition in 1598 by Scotland's James VI (later, England's King James I) in *The True Law of Free Monarchies*. James's son, Charles I, carried the doctrine even further, claiming that he was answerable only to God. English citizens proved him wrong. After his defeat in the English Civil War, Charles was beheaded for treason in 1649, and the doctrine of divine right died with him. No British monarch afterward publicly claimed a God-given right to rule. Instead of ruling, later monarchs merely reigned; that is, they occupied the throne. Victoria, Edward, and George all recognized that they were constitutional monarchs who did not govern the country but only presided over it on the sufferance of parliament. In the years leading up to World War I, this constrained the roles that British monarchs played in their country's foreign affairs.

The three emperors who claimed that God ordained them to rule, however, would not countenance constraints on their political authority from any worldly source. They sought to rule as autocrats concerning domestic and foreign policy. Forms of megalomania touched all three. Again, biographers and historians concur on this assessment.

Franz Josef was only 18 years old in 1848 when court elders installed him to replace his feeble-minded uncle as emperor. Within weeks he took personal control of the army. As an untested youth, he accepted advice to govern autocratically, especially in Hungary, where he suspended the constitution and launched what was called "absolutist" rule in 1851.[15] Simply by means of sending a message to his chief minister, Palmer said:

> The Constitution of March 1849 was abolished, without ever having been put into practice; "fundamental rights," conceded by the Emperor under threat of revolution, were annulled (though freedom of worship was guaranteed and no attempt was made to re-impose feudal obligations on the peasantry); and centralization of the administrative system was completed by the abolition of all locally elected councils and the application of Austrian codes of law to every part of the Monarchy, including Hungary. Now at last Francis Josef had achieved his first ambition. He ruled as a benevolent soldier autocrat, Austria's Tsar in his own right, not the nominee of a military camarilla.[16]

Franz Josef's insistence on complete obedience was an ingrained personality trait. He dictated behavior within his own extended family, requiring his own brothers to get his permission to travel, to marry, and even to appear in public.[17] Twenty-first-century readers can gain insight to Franz Josef's proprietary view of his realm by considering how he gave approval in 1857 to opening the city of Vienna to compete with the new boulevards of Paris: "It is My Pleasure that, as soon as possible, preparatory work should begin on the extension of the inner city of Vienna so as to establish an appropriate link with the suburbs, and that, at the same time, consideration should be given to the regulation and embellishment of My Residence and My Capital…. I give My Permission to abolish the walls and fortification of the inner city, as well as their surrounding ditches."[18]

Wilhelm II was comparably autocratic, more outspoken, and more unpredictable.

He once proclaimed: "I am the Supreme War Lord. I do not decide. I command."[19] He also told Norwegian composer Edvard Grieg that he was conducting his famous *Peer Gynt* suite all wrong, and he advised the British admiralty on how to design their ships. Noting that Wilhelm reflected traits of someone never corrected or contradicted, Hamilton and Holger found "no 'controlling' logic to govern his thinking," resulting in "irresolution, vacillation, continuous and unpredictable changes of positions."[20]

Wilhelm's famous outbursts supported Carter's contention that he manifested symptoms of "narcissistic personality" disorder: "arrogance, grandiose self-importance, a mammoth sense of entitlement, fantasies about unlimited success and power; a belief in his own uniqueness and brilliance; a need for endless admiration and reinforcement and a hatred of criticism; proneness to envy; a tendency to regard other people as purely instrumental—in terms of what they could do for him, along with a dispiriting lack of empathy."[21] However, Carter continued: "On the other hand, plenty of royals shared these attributes. It was hard not to have an inflated sense of uniqueness and self-importance, an expectation of constant deference, certain blind selfishness and assumption that others were there only to serve if you had been brought up amidst constant deference."

Nicholas II of Russia exemplified autocracy for the period. Historian MacMillan wrote that in the first decade of his rule (1894–1904), Nicholas "was an absolute monarch who could appoint and dismiss ministers at will, determine policy, and, in wartime, command the armed forces. Before 1905, unlike his cousin Wilhelm in Germany, he did not have to worry about a constitution, an elected parliament, or the rights of his subjects. Even after the concessions of that year, he had greater power than either the Kaiser or the Austrian Emperor, both of whom had to deal with greater control over their governments and over spending from their legislatures and who, in addition, had states inside their empires with strongly entrenched rights of their own."[22]

Even **George V**, whose governmental power as a constitutional monarch was severely limited, demanded obedience from subjects in his non-political world. Carter said, "Where George did have control—over the court and his household—he was an autocrat. What he wanted he got."[23] So even monarchs who did not announce that they were channeling God tended to behave like tyrants, certain of their own judgment, dismissive of alternative views, and intolerant of alternative values.

One might expect royal houses to bring up their royal heirs so that they would govern from knowledge, rather than ignorance, about the world and the lives of the their subjects. Certainly monarchs tried to give their heirs an outstanding education, bringing to their palaces famous tutors and professors to give lectures and to hear recitations. Young emperors-in-waiting—whether archdukes, crown princes, or tsesarevichs[24]—rarely studied with other students, seldom had their ideas subjected to rigorous questioning, and never sat for school examinations. Nevertheless, structured tutoring in isolation seemed to work for learning foreign languages, and speaking them was important for European monarchs.

Franz Josef, as befits the ruler of an empire whose subjects spoke at least eleven languages, could converse in four of their major ones—German, Magyar, Czech, and Italian—plus French, then regarded as the international language of diplomacy.[25] Wilhelm II spoke English fluently, knew some French, and even studied Greek and Latin. Nicholas II also was fluent in English and French and spoke some German.[26] Cousins Wilhelm, Nicholas, and George V communicated among themselves in English, which suited George, who was unable to learn any foreign language due to his severe case of Anglo-Americanism.

Although most imperial heirs managed to learn foreign languages from tutors while sequestered in their palace classrooms, that educational setting tended to turn out flawed products. One of Nicholas's biographers quoted a revealing critique from the royal tutor of Tsesarevich Alexie, Nicholas's son: "The education of a prince tends to make him an incomplete being who finds himself outside life if only because he has not been subject to the common lot in his youth. Such teaching as he receives can only be artificial, tendencious [*sic*], and dogmatic. It often has the absolute and uncompromising character of a catechism."[27] He continued: "A child brought up in such conditions is deprived of something which plays a vital part in the formation of judgment. He is deprived of the knowledge which is acquired out of the schoolroom, knowledge such as comes from life itself, unhampered contact with other children, the diverse and sometimes conflicting influences of environment, direct observation and simple experience of men and affairs— in a word, everything which in the course of years develops the critical faculty and a sense of reality." Finally, "Under such circumstances an individual must be endowed with exceptional gifts to be able to see things as they are, think clearly, and desire the right things."

Some monarchs in history were endowed with exceptional intelligence, vision, and creativity. Russia's Peter the Great (who planned St. Petersburg and created a navy) and Catherine the Great (who corresponded with Voltaire and founded the Hermitage Museum) come to mind. Unfortunately, Franz Josef and the three cousin emperors were not intellectually gifted.[28] Historian T.G. Otte colorfully described "the three eastern monarchies" as headed by "giants with double heads of clay."[29]

Biographers, and historians of the time, agree that the emperors did not have great minds. They did not tolerate opposing thoughts very well, nor were they open to social change or cultural innovations. They varied in their enthusiasm for foreign travel and their ability to benefit from it. None of the four monarchs—with great navies at their disposal—visited the United States, and Franz Josef did not even cross the English Channel.

Franz Josef did travel widely to cities within his far-flung empire, and he also visited Wilhelm in Berlin and Nicholas in St. Petersburg. However, he went to Paris only once, for its 1867 exposition. In 1869, he was uncharacteristically persuaded to attend the opening ceremonies of the Suez Canal, a trip that was expanded to include a stop in Athens, a call on the Sultan in Constantinople, and a pilgrimage to Jerusalem.[30] His travels in the east, which he apparently enjoyed, awakened his interest in economic opportunities there. However, his extensive travel within his own country did not generate much understanding of its problems.

Biographer Redlich said that Franz Josef, while "not without serviceable gifts" for his position, "yet lacked any striking special gift." Moreover, "a complete lack of imagination" was his outstanding intellectual defect.[31] Palmer wrote: "Twelve years of Francis Josef's early life were spent in absorbing the facts presented to him by his tutors but, apart from a desire to widen his vocabulary in the four foreign languages he studied, there was no stirring of intellectual curiosity. By the age of eighteen a fine memory was excellently trained. The mind, however, was not disposed to analyse ideas or to question acknowledged truths."[32]

Franz Josef undoubtedly saw a lot while traveling through his empire but failed to comprehend what he observed. Palmer writes that during his early military service in the Alps and Venetia, the young archduke "recognized that there was a natural antipathy between German-Austrians and Italians. Yet he failed to understand how deeply the people of Lombardy and Venetia resented the presence of the Austrian 'whitecoats' among them."[33] Indeed, he was surprised when Italian battalions rebelled against their Austrian officers in 1848. Franz Josef's contemporary biographer, Redlich, commented: "Nothing is so hard to understand here as his lack of interest in the special characteristics of the various peoples composing his realm, most of whose languages he knew.... None taught him in these formative years to take a deeper view of the historic character of these races, above all the non–German ones, or their special outlook."[34] Palmer quoted Austrian Archduke Rudolph speaking about his own father: "Our Emperor has no friend, his whole character and natural tendency do not permit it. He stands lonely on his peak; he talks to those who serve him of their duties, but he carefully avoids any real conversation. Accordingly he knows little of what people think and feel, their views and opinions."[35] Oscar Jászi, a contemporary Magyar sociologist, wrote that "outside of his magnates and generals, the monarch [never] had a serious conversation with members of the other classes. I do not know of a single case where he was anxious to know the opinion of a scholar, an artist, or a leading man of industry."[36]

Wilhelm II traveled so much he was nicknamed "Reisekaiser," the touring kaiser.[37] Grandson of Queen Victoria, he loved England, went there often, and stayed long (too often and too long for many in the British court). He frequently visited Russia, Austria, North Africa, and Turkey, among other places. But like Franz Josef, he went to Paris only once, for the 1878 exhibition, a decade before becoming kaiser. He said that he did not enjoy his visit, and never wanted to return.[38] Given that the Paris exhibition celebrated France's recovery after its defeat by Germany in the 1870 Franco-Prussian War, it is surprising that he went at all. Nonetheless, Barbara Tuchman said that he longed to visit Paris as kaiser but was never invited.[39]

Compared with the other emperors, Wilhelm was a scholar. He enrolled at Bonn University and studied history, law, government, economics, German literature, art history, physics, and chemistry. But he was never a real university student who attended classes. The professors came to him to deliver their lectures.[40] His early tutor wrote that Wilhelm, while not clever, had "an excellent memory." "On the other hand he believes he understands everything, talks on any subject and makes assertions with such sureness and in such a self-opinionated manner that he effectively prohibits all contradiction." The charge that Wilhelm "believes he understands everything" emerges as a theme in his biographies. A general who knew the young prince reportedly said, "Good heavens, whatever will happen if Prince Wilhelm becomes Kaiser as early as this? He thinks he understands everything, even shipbuilding."[41] Not only was Wilhelm boastfully opinionated, he was erratic and easily distracted.[42]

So the scouting report on Wilhelm before ascending the throne might read: has traveled widely, knows several languages, has broad university-level studies in multiple fields, and is socially gregarious, but also is opinionated, boastful, impulsive, and unpredictable. When Wilhelm became Kaiser, who in Germany would dare advise him?

Nicholas had the richest and the poorest upbringing of any of the four emperors. The richest in that the imperial trappings of the Romanovs, which exceeded the royal treasures of any European monarch, surrounded him. (The Romanovs were said to have 15,000 royal servants at their numerous palaces.[43]) The poorest in that his father, the reactionary Alexander III, kept him isolated from the country and its people. Nicholas and his siblings "assumed that the palace servants, who often served the family for generations and had as little connection to the peasant communes as they did, represented the average Russian peasant."[44] As tsesarevich, he did take a ten-month tour from the Near East to the eastern edge of Siberia, but became bored reading government papers after he returned. The year before he became tsar, his own father, Alexander III, rejected the proposal that Nicholas have more responsibility in state affairs, saying, "He's nothing more than a child. His judgment is infantile. How could he be president of a committee?"[45]

After Nicholas became tsar, he moved fifteen miles outside of St. Petersburg to *Tsarskoe Selo*, "the Tsar's village," where he and his family lived fairly simply—if one can live simply while attended by thousands of servants and protected by thousands of guards.[46] There Nicholas preserved his splendid isolation from his people. As the country's ruler, he had little grasp of economics or even the value of things. Carter relates the tsar's exchange with his chancellor, when he asked whether a gold watch cost more than 25 roubles. Nicholas admitted, "It is one of the big gaps in my education…. I don't know the price of things; I have never had reason to pay for anything myself."[47]

In contrast to Wilhelm, whom biographers described as impulsive—too quick to decide, only to reverse decisions later—Nicholas was said to be indecisive, "not being able to make up his mind, changing his opinion every time he heard someone else expressing theirs, usually taking the advice of the person to speak to him last."[48] Radzinsky, a Russian biographer, said that Nicholas lacked the "powerful will" of a tsar, demonstrating instead a "paralysis of will."[49] Although stubborn, he was unable to say no directly, leaving people to think that he approved their proposals only to learn later that he had not.

George V traveled across the world for three years as midshipman on the HMS *Bacchante*. Biographer Carter describes the excellent adventures of young George, who "saw the Mediterranean, South America, South Africa, Australia, Japan, China, Singapore, Egypt and the Holy Land; shot albatrosses, exchanged photographs with a Zulu chief and his four wives, almost got caught up in the first Boer War, encountered ostriches, saw the twelve Stations of the Cross in Jerusalem, had a dragon tattooed on his arm in Tokyo, met the Mikado, was nearly shipwrecked off southern Australia, experienced the street smells of Peking, travelled in gold barges down the Nile, and adopted a baby kangaroo."[50] However, she continues, "But all this failed to imbue him with a sense of curiosity or excitement about the world." In fact, the Prince of Wales was glad to finish his service, never longed to sail again, and hated going abroad—except to India, where he had enjoyed the maharajah lifestyle in 1905 and returned in 1911 to receive the Imperial Crown as Emperor.[51] Otherwise, George V hobnobbed with "the shooting aristocracy" and "kept himself insulated from the twentieth century, public attention and the messy world of politics."[52]

Recall from Chapter 1 German Field Marshal Hindenburg's explanation of the German Kaiser's behavior: "You must understand that royalty are like children." When Franz Josef, Wilhelm, and Nicholas matured to emperorship, they acted much as they did when children. They played soldiers—but with one difference. As boys, they played with toy soldiers. As adults, they deployed real soldiers.

Even as a boy, one famous emperor used real soldiers. Biographer Massie described the play of Tsesarevich Peter the Great of Russia:

> His favorite game, as it had been from earliest childhood, was war. During Fedor's reign, a small parade ground had been laid out for Peter in the Kremlin where he could drill the boys who were his playmates…. And, unlike most boys who play at war, Peter could draw on a government arsenal to supply his equipment…. In January 1683, he ordered uniforms, banners and two wooden cannon,

their barrels lined with iron, mounted on wheels to allow them to be pulled by horses—all to be furnished immediately. On his eleventh birthday, in June 1683, Peter abandoned wooden cannon for real
cannon with which, under the supervision of artillerymen, he was allowed to fire salutes.

By the time Peter was fourteen and he and his mother had settled permanently at Preobrazhen-
skoe, his martial games had transformed the summer estate into an adolescent military encampment.
Peter's first "soldiers" were the small group of playmates who had been appointed to his service when
he reached the age of five.[53]

Later, he drew on royal attendants and retainers and even built barracks to house the
regiment.

Monarchs have always prized their military. In ancient times, monarchs owed their
rule to battlefield victories and military conquests. In the Roman Empire, Praetorian
Guards both protected and installed their emperors. Even after heredity became the
accepted basis for their rule, monarchs relied on their armed forces to defend their realms
against foreign and domestic enemies. Alexander III, Nicholas's father, was famously
quoted as saying, "We have just two allies in this world … our armies and our navies.
Everybody else will turn on us on a second's notice."[54] Military culture was valued, or at
least respected, across society.[55] Aristocratic families often groomed their sons for military
office; families on the rise viewed an officer's insignia as a social boost; and peasants both
admired and feared soldiers. (Even in today's United States, three-quarters of the public
report having a "quite a lot" or a "great deal" of confidence in their military versus just
7 percent in their Congress.[56])

World War I historian MacMillan wrote, "Like his fellow sovereigns Nicholas II and
Wilhelm II, Franz Josef loved the military life and almost always appeared in uniform.
Like Nicholas and Wilhelm, he was sent into a rage when the details of army uniforms
were wrong."[57] Figure 5.1 showed the four monarchs in military uniforms. (George V
began to wear one regularly only after the outbreak of the war.) Indeed, the emperor,
kaiser, and tsar were obsessed with military uniforms, personally proposing changes in
style and trimmings. Kaiser Wilhelm in particular fancied himself a military clothing
designer and fashion plate. A biographer said that he made thirty-seven changes to army
uniforms between 1888 and 1904 and maintained a wardrobe with 300 German regimental
uniforms.[58] As war clouds formed in the Balkans in 1909, Wilhelm finalized details concerning his soldiers' chinstraps and trouser seams.[59]

Recall that the emperors were living out an era of regal operettas in which uniformed
captains of the guards, lancers, hussars, and dragoons outdid one another in their fancy
buttons, lariats, lanyards, piping, and plumes as they pranced across the royal court. Fas-
cination with military uniforms was not peculiar then to central and eastern European
culture. England had long been (and still is) a world leader in elaborate military dress.
Even republican France revered its military uniforms. French parliamentarians, who dis-
dained Germany's martial culture, refused to replace their troops' 18th-century colorful
blue tunics and red pantaloons with less conspicuous gray or green uniforms. In *The
Guns of August*, Barbara Tuchman describes French outrage at "clothing the French soldier in some muddy, inglorious color." The *Echo de Paris* wrote, "To banish 'all that is
colorful, all that gives the soldier his vivid aspect, is to go contrary both to French taste
and military function.'"[60]

The "military function" of the vivid blue tops and red bottoms, apparently, was to
foster the French spirit of *élan vital*, which Tuchman defined as "the all-conquering will."
Against German power, she described the belief in French *élan*: "The spirit of France

would be the equalizing factor. Her will to win, her *élan* would enable France to defeat her enemy. Her genius was in her spirit, the spirit of *la gloire*, of 1792, of the incomparable 'Marseillaise,' the spirit of General Margueritte's heroic cavalry charge before Sedan when even [Kaiser] Wilhelm I, watching the battle, could not forbear to cry, '*Oh, les braves gens!*'"[61] Their *élan* notwithstanding, the French were badly beaten by Wilhelm I's army at Sedan in 1870, losing the Franco-Prussian War, which led to the formation of a united German nation in 1871.

This lengthy discussion of uniforms and military culture has a point. It illustrates the romantic view of war—dashing uniforms, flashing sabers, and glorious victories— that was widespread among monarchs, aristocrats, statesmen, and other members of the governing classes as the 19th century rolled into the 20th. National pride was celebrated in fancy dress at military parades. A mystical sense of national honor preceded the rational calculation of national interest. Emperors were especially prone to idealizing national honor in dealing with foreign states, a royal prerogative of the times.

During the 19th century, monarchs regularly practiced personal diplomacy among themselves. They cemented ruling ties through marriages, struck alliances, recognized suzerainty over territorial possessions, and settled international disputes—sometimes disputes involving countries other than their own. Regarding military matters and foreign affairs as falling within their royal domain, monarchs often struck deals first and told their generals and ministers later. This practice of diplomacy through monarchs became dysfunctional for modern societies in the 20th century, but Franz Josef, Wilhelm, and Nicholas failed to get the message.

Of the four monarchs among the main belligerents in World War I, only George V was crowned in the 20th century, and he was the only one who had no constitutional authority to engage in monarchical diplomacy. The others were still stuck in the past. Emperor Franz Josef had ruled for 52 years before the 20th century rolled around. Those decades fixed his vision and his resolve. Biographer Redlich said: "He was strong *because* he knew nothing of the ideas of his age, nothing of their historic application, nothing of the power inevitably lent them by the social and economic development of the whole period."[62] Kaiser Wilhelm, who reigned for twelve years in the 19th century before war clouds gathered in 20th, also occupied himself with formalities and niceties of an earlier era.[63] Although Nicholas served only slightly more than five years before the 20th century, he never really made the transition. Even at the time of his abdication in 1917, he behaved like a 19th-century monarch, at the latest.

Although Austria-Hungary, Germany, and Russia had written constitutions, the emperors ruled by skillfully skirting them, with Tsar Nicholas generally ignoring his. Moreover, all three constitutions entrusted the emperor with the power to declare war. Hamilton and Herwig quoted from Austria-Hungary's 1867 "Fundamental Law Concerning the Exercise of Administrative and Executive Power." Article I stated: "The Emperor is sacred, inviolable, and cannot be held accountable," and Article V gave the emperor "supreme command of the armed forces" and the right to "declare war, and conclude peace."[64] Germany and Russia also placed the power to declare war solely in their emperors' hands.

In deciding whether to go to war, of course, the emperors consulted a small coterie of advisors—eight to ten people—according to Hamilton and Herwig. In Austria-Hungary's case, "This coterie consisted of the emperor, Franz Josef, the political leaders, the senior diplomats, and the top military leaders—collectively, the Council of Ministers."[65]

While generals were involved, civilians outweighed them. The 1964 antiwar movie *Dr. Strangelove* contains this dialog involving Georges Clemenceau, Prime Minister of France during World War I:

> GENERAL JACK D. RIPPER: Mandrake, do you recall what Clemenceau once said about war?
> GROUP CAPT. LIONEL MANDRAKE: No, I don't think I do, sir, no.
> GENERAL JACK D. RIPPER: He said war was too important to be left to the generals.[66]

General Ripper admitted that Clemenceau might have been right during World War I, but he concluded that World War III, which he thought was inevitable, was too important to be left to the politicians. So Air Force General Jack D. Ripper decided to launch his own nuclear strike against the communist Soviet Union. The film ends with a B-52 pilot riding a thermonuclear bomb dropping on Russia.

During Clemenceau's time, all three emperors were empowered to declare war, but they were little more suited to the responsibility than General Ripper. Redlich noted that Franz Josef "had not been gifted by nature with the powers of brain and foreign policy." But, he continued, "Most of the monarchs of his day were in no better case."[67] In one way, they were very much like the Air Force general in their readiness to use military power to defend "national interests" and in their willingness "to take enormous chances, or more precisely, willing to pay enormous costs for the sake of that aim."[68]

Unlike General Ripper, however, their view of "national interests" was more personal than ideological. Whether or not King Louis XIV actually said *"L'État, c'est moi"* (The State is me), the emperor, the kaiser, and the tsar actually conflated the state with themselves, or at least with their respective Habsburg, Hohenzollern, and Romanov dynasties. "Their policies sought, in one way or another, to demonstrate that nation's prestige and power. In their view, a threatening or competing 'upstart' must be put down."[69]

In keeping with their 19th-century mentality and their divine choice and guidance, Franz Josef, Wilhelm, and Nicholas all figured in the tragedy of affairs ending in World War I. Otte concluded: "What is remarkable about the July crisis was the poor intellectual quality of the decision-making, and the haphazard policy-making processes with their endless capacity for unreality. This problem was particularly acute in the three eastern military monarchies."[70] Concerning the decision to go to war, the three emperors were—in President George W. Bush's terminology—"the deciders."

During America's war in Iraq, President Bush defended his Secretary of State, Donald Rumsfeld, against criticism that he was ignoring advice of military commanders. The president said, "I listen to all voices, but mine is the final decision," he said. "And Don Rumsfeld is doing a fine job.... I hear the voices, and I read the front page, and I know the speculation. But I'm the decider, and I decide what is best."[71] President Bush demonstrated what Christopher Clark suggested, that it is too simplistic to draw a line between "democratic" and "autocratic" methods for deciding to engage in warfare.[72] Nevertheless, the emperors of Austria-Hungary, Germany, and Russia enjoyed greater latitude in their roles as "deciders" concerning whether their nations went to war.

6

Peasants in Passage

Blissfully unaware of world events, the newlyweds worked hard after their marriage, Samko mainly as a laborer and Anna most likely as a cleaning lady. They had moved from 23 E. 165th Street to 1026 E. 165th Street (further east in the Bronx), managed to save money (as did most immigrants), and surely like most Slovak immigrants, sent money back to their families with glowing reports about living in America.

Their marriage greatly benefited their economic situation, for they became an economic unit. Chapter 2, "The Peasant's Voyage," estimated Samko's annual income when single as $400. Now he and Anna formed a family with alternative sources of income. Robert Chapin's book, *The Standard of Living Among Workingmen's Families in New York City*,[1] explains how that benefitted them. In 1907, Chapin supervised the collection and analysis of data for 391 families in New York, breaking down the numbers by income levels *and* by the families' nationalities: "American" (88 families), Russian (78), Italian (69), Teutonic [northern European] nations (46), Austro-Hungarian (39), "Colored" (29), Irish (26), Bohemian (14), and other (2).[2]

Chapin wrote, "A comparison of the different nationalities with reference to the sources of income shows that the greatest dependence on other resources than the father's wages is found among the Bohemians, Austrians and Russians"[3]—an omnibus category for Slovak immigrants. Those "other resources" came from working wives, or from working children, or from taking in lodgers. Wives with children typically could not work, so instead took in lodgers. Wives without children could work fulltime or part-time and also house lodgers, which often meant cooking for them and washing their laundry. Having no children, Anna could work and accept boarders. Her likely work as a cleaning lady—which Chapin called a "janitress"—added to the family income, and their move to a different address in the Bronx may have been to allow boarders. They certainly were planning to make as much money as possible.

Whatever Anna's contribution was to Samko's income, Chapin's analysis suggests that it was probably less than half his estimated $400 annually.[4] Nevertheless, let us assume that their combined total pushed them just above Chapin's threshold of $600 for the 318 families earning between $600 and $1,100. That would place them at the bottom 15 percent of the 39 Austro-Hungarian families he studied.[5] They would still be poor. How could they save anything?

Chapin's study tracked amounts and types of family expenditures as well as amounts and types of income. He tallied income and expenses over specified periods and reported the results in three categories: computations ending in a *balance* (± $25), in a *surplus*, or in a *deficit*. Over all 318 families with income over $600 yet under $1,100, 36.5 percent reported a balance, 36.5 percent a surplus, and 27 percent a deficit.[6] Fully half of the Austro-Hungarian families enjoyed a surplus compared with only 23 percent of the American and Teutonic families.[7] Only 9 percent of Austro-Hungarian families ran a deficit, compared with 37 percent of the Americans.

Like other immigrant families, Samko and Anna scrimped on virtually everything in order to save money. Chapin explains how families with little income could actually save some:

> Considered from the view-point of the content of a standard compelled to resort to the supplementary sources of income, they are either content with a lower standard of comforts than families of the other class, or are able to attain it at a lower expense....
>
> This indicates that on the lower incomes, where most of these cases with sub-normal standard are found, an even balance or a surplus can be attained only by curtailing expenditures for necessaries below the point of meeting the requirements of healthy existence.[8]

Determined to return home with money they made in America, Samko and Anna were busy trying to make a living and had no time to keep up with European politics.

People at the bottom of the social and political ladder usually have little idea of what is going on at the top of the ladder. In the decade before World War I, Slovak peasants in Hungary were generally ignorant of the ins and outs of international relations. Back home, they might have read censored accounts in Magyar newspapers, such as *Pesti Hírlap*, *Pesti Napló*, and *Népszava*, but few did. They could have read one of several Slovak newspapers, such as *Národné noviny* (National News), published in Turčiansky Sv. Martin, but these had tiny circulations. In America, Konštantín Čulen said that Slovaks also "did not readily embrace" the newspaper: "It had to be pushed into their hands."[9] Nevertheless, in some years, the 30,000 subscribers to New York's Slovak newspaper, *Amerikánsko-slovenské noviny*, exceeded all domestic papers in Slovakia.[10]

Perhaps Samko and Anna read the *Amerikánsko-slovenské noviny*, but the Pittsburgh paper sold in New York certainly lacked the international coverage of the *New York Times*, which they were unlikely to read. So they probably missed this front-page story published in the *Times* on May 30, 1905, exactly one month after their wedding.

"CZAR'S SEAPOWER IS ANNIHILATED" reported that the Japanese had destroyed Russia's powerful Baltic fleet, sent to avenge Russia's defeat in the Battle of the Yellow Sea. After the humiliating loss, pressure mounted on the Tsar as sailors mutinied, most notably on June 14, 1905, as dramatized in the famous 1925 Russian movie *Battleship Potemkin*.

About the time of the *Potemkin* mutiny, Samko and Anna got a different sort of news: they learned that Anna was pregnant, which altered their plans. They had intended to work for a few years, return to Slovakia with enough money to buy land, and live happily ever after—the common dream of Slovak immigrants to America. Their dream could be realized only if both were earning money. They could not do that while caring for a child. Anna would certainly have to cut down on her hours at work, and a child would take up space that could be used for boarders.

Of course, they wrote to Slovakia about Anna's pregnancy. By return mail, and to their surprise, they learned that Samko's older brother Ján and his younger brother Martin were planning to come to America! The brothers were not doing nearly as well economically in Krajné as Samko and Anna were in New York. Perhaps they could swap countries: Ján and Martin could come to New York to work while Samko and Anna returned to Slovakia with their child and tend to the farm. Of course, much remained to be worked out, but it was a plan.

Burdened with these immediate concerns, Samko and Anna certainly missed the lengthy commentary in the *Times* later that June by foreign correspondent Walter Littlefield. His "INSIDE STORY OF THE MOROCCO IMBROGLIO" summarized months of diplomatic intrigue and gunboat diplomacy involving the European powers and poor Morocco.[11] The inchoate Moroccan government was beset by European powers eager to help their citizens make money while their governments accumulated colonial possessions.

In seven columns spread over the top of the paper, Littlefield brought readers up to speed concerning an international crisis in 1905 that involved the key western European powers, Spain, Britain, and even the United States. All recognized France's "special interests" in Morocco, but Germany claimed commercial interests in Morocco and challenged France's position as gatekeeper to the vulnerable kingdom. The crisis became significant because it ultimately increased the diplomatic status of Kaiser Wilhelm II at the expense of France, already suffering from its defeat in the 1870 Franco-German War. The crisis in Morocco was one of the earliest and sharpest international disputes that formed the backdrop for World War I.

When Ján and Martin Mozolák decided sometime in 1905 to join their brother in America, they did so with little thought about, and less knowledge of,

CZAR'S·SEAPOWER·IS·ANNIHILATED

13·Ships·Known·to·Be·Sunk·and·7·Captured.

BIG·BATTLESHIPS·PRIZES

Admiral·Rojestvensky's·Fate·Is·Unknown.

NEBOGATOFF·A·CAPTIVE

Japanese·Take·3,000·Russians·Prisoners.

CHASING·THE·REMNANTS

Togo·Following·up·His·Victory—One·Russian·Ship·Reaches·a·Japanese·Port·and·Surrenders.

New·York·Times
May·30,·1905,·p.·1

troubles brewing in Russia and Germany's growing aggressiveness. As their plans to cross the ocean crystallized, they wrote Samko that they hoped to arrive early in 1906, perhaps before the baby was born. What's more, they had persuaded some others from Krajné to seek their fortunes in America!

On January 15, 1906, Samko got mixed news from the midwife attending Anna at their housing on 165th Street in the Bronx. Anna gave birth to a healthy boy, *and* to a healthy girl. Their twins were named John and Susanna "Mosolak" on the birth certificate in Figure 6.1. The document certified John and Susanna as United States citizens—real *Američany*. But now Samko and Anna had not one child to care for, but two!

On January 17, just two days after the twins were born, Samko went dockside to greet the arrivals on the *Kaiser Wilhelm II*, which had left Bremen on January 9. List 22 of the ship's manifest identified not two, but *six* passengers from Krajné:

Name	Age	Destination	Whom will you be joining?
Ján Mozolák	32	New York	Brother, Samuel Mozolák, No. 1026 E. 165
Martin Mozolák	32	"	Brother, Samuel Mozolák, No. 1026 E. 165
Martin Tomašovič	26	"	Br in law, Samuel Mozolák, No. 1026 E. 165
Martin Slezak	45	"	Friend, Samuel Mozolák, No. 1026 E. 165
Martin Kolník	23	"	Friend, Samuel Mozolák, No. 1026 E. 165
Samuel Nebesky	32	Newark	Sister: Kelli Mike Nebesky; Newark, N.J.

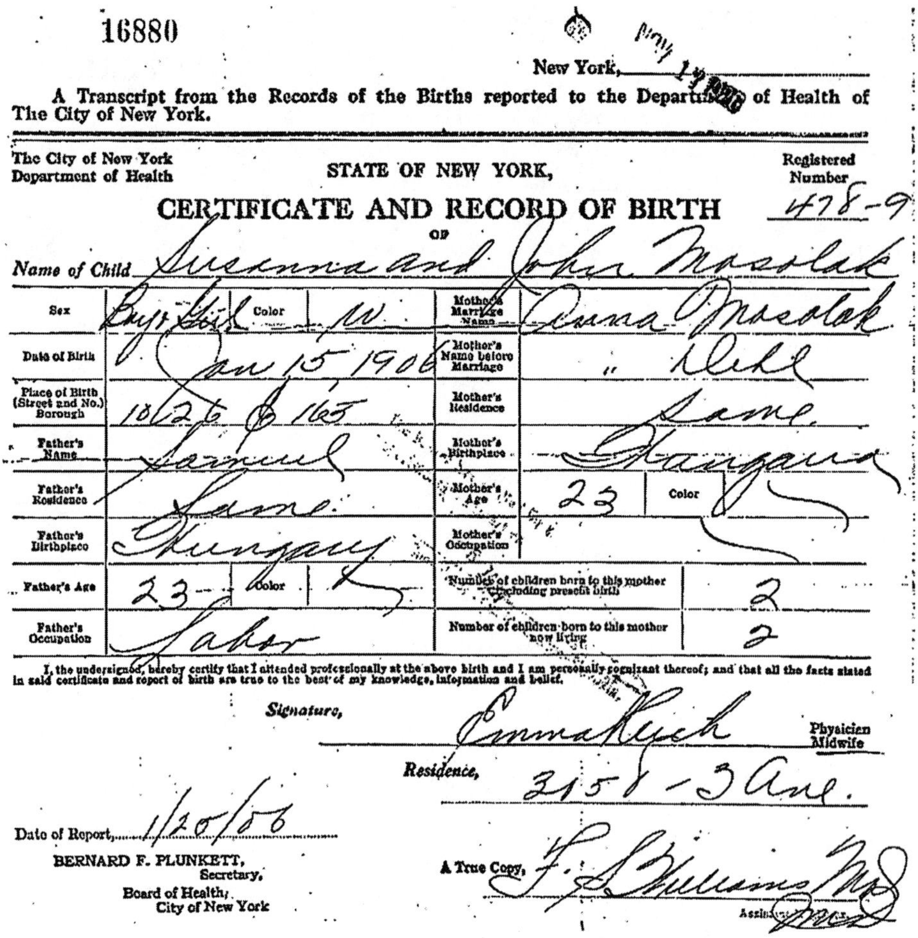

16880

New York, Nov 14 19..

A Transcript from the Records of the Births reported to the Department of Health of The City of New York.

The City of New York
Department of Health

STATE OF NEW YORK,

Registered Number 478-9

CERTIFICATE AND RECORD OF BIRTH OF

Name of Child	Susanna and John Mosolak		
Sex	Boy, Girl — Color W	Mother's Name	Anna Mosolak
Date of Birth	Jan 15, 1906	Mother's Name before Marriage	" Dell
Place of Birth (Street and No.) Borough	1612 E 165	Mother's Residence	Same
Father's Name	Samuel	Mother's Birthplace	Hungary
Father's Residence	Same	Mother's Age	23 — Color
Father's Birthplace	Hungary	Mother's Occupation	
Father's Age	23 — Color	Number of children born to this mother (including present birth)	2
Father's Occupation	Labor	Number of children born to this mother now living	2

I, the undersigned, hereby certify that I attended professionally at the above birth and I am personally cognizant thereof; and that all the facts stated in said certificate and report of birth are true to the best of my knowledge, information and belief.

Signature, Emma Reich — Physician / Midwife

Residence, 2158 - 3 Ave.

Date of Report, 1/20/06

BERNARD F. PLUNKETT,
Secretary,
Board of Health,
City of New York

A True Copy, F. S. Williams MD

Figure 6.1: Mozolák Twins' 1906 Birth Certificates. John and Susanna "Mosolak" (incorrect spelling) were born on January 15, 1906. The birth certificate reported both parents' ages as 23. Samko apparently aged two years since their marriage the previous year while Anna remained 23. (Midwife Emma merely wrote down what she heard.) Credit: Family document.

The very day the twins were born, the ominous item on page 5 of the *Times*, "RUSSIANS EXPECT A BAD YEAR," noted that Russian newspapers "almost unanimously predict a continuance of the revolutionary struggle in 1906." Even if they had seen this item, Samko and Anna would once again see no connection between the revolutionary struggle in Russia and their future life.

Oblivious of the troubles in Europe, Samko and Anna had their own problems in New York, caring for newly-born twins and now responsible for an influx of six Krajné countrymen. We can only speculate how Samko and Anna reacted to the situation. Anna, from a different but nearby village, may have known Samko's brothers. More importantly, all were fellow Slovaks, eager to help and anxious to make money. One left for Newark, New Jersey. The Slovak superintendent of Samko's apartment house would help the other five find lodging. Then they would look for work in New York.

Samko's Krajné visitors probably heard that they could make more money by moving inland to work in the mines or mills, but heartened by his well-being, they stayed in the area. While working for less pay, they faced less hazardous conditions—excluding occasional fights with the Irish, with whom they competed for unskilled work. Because the great wave of Irish immigration had occurred earlier, the Irish knew how to operate in the city. Surprisingly, employers did not always value their experience and their ability to speak English. Čulen wrote:

> RUSSIANS·EXPECT·A·BAD·
> YEAR ¶
> ——¶
> Czar·Honors·Reactionaries ¶
> ——¶
> Talks·to·Meyer·at·New·Year·
> Reception. ¶
> ¶
> *New·York·Times* ¶
> January·15,·1906,·p.·5 ¶

> Hardworking and diligent Slovaks, who willingly accepted any kind of job for any kind of wage, represented serious competition for the more demanding and selective Irish. Employers also preferred the Slovaks for their inability to speak English and a certain reticence that prevented them from aggressively asserting their demands. That made it easier tor the employers to withhold some of the workers' deserved reward. Where a Slovak would only shrug his shoulders over some issue, an energetic Irishman would vehemently demand what he thought was his. The employers also knew that the Slovaks could not go back to their country unless they earned enough money for the trip, and that this money had to be earned in their factory. This, no doubt, lowered the wages.[12]

The Irish gained a reputation for drinking and fighting, and they suffered social and economic discrimination (e.g., "No Irish need apply" signs). Slovaks acquired a negative reputation of a different type: They were thought inferior to Czechs. Popularly called Bohemians, the Czechs had come earlier and were better known—linked to beautiful Prague, Antonín Dvořák's 1893 inspiring *New World Symphony*, and lovely crystal vases. Slovaks were regarded as slower and less talented. Consider how Maurice Davie, a distinguished professor of sociology at Yale University, described Slovaks in his 1936 book, *World Immigration*: "The Slovaks … are closely related to the Czechs though less culturally advanced and with a much higher rate of illiteracy…. They have no independent history. They are essentially an agricultural people, slow in mind, peaceful in character, fond of music and song, wandering often as tinkers and farm laborers all over Austria-Hungary."[13] Davie probably reflected Americans' prevailing opinion of Slovaks in the early decades of the 20th century.

The learned professor's personal opinion about the scourge of immigration by "darker-skinned races" also probably reflected public opinion at the time for "keeping the United States as far as possible a white man's country": "Our own history, as well as the history of other countries, affords many examples of the serious difficulties that arise when members of very diverse races come into intimate contact. Experience shows that the yellow, brown, and black races are unassimilable, at any rate by us, and the United States would only be inviting trouble and adding to her already large and serious race problems by admitting members of such races. Their exclusion is indispensable to the welfare of the United States."[14] To many white American citizens, immigrants from Eastern Europe, and especially from Southern Europe, were only a shade above the "darker-skinned races" and equally "unassimilable," to use Professor's Davie's term. Nevertheless, Samko's brothers, brother-in-law, and friends all found work in New York and eventually returned to Krajné, presumably wealthier than they had been when they left.

By late spring in 1906, the twins were almost six months old. Samko and Anna decided that they could take them to Krajné. Then they would replace Ján and Martin on the farm during the summer. Veterans of one Atlantic crossing, Samko and Anna knew what to experience during their twelve days onboard during the return voyage. Their twins were still young enough to breast-feed, so that handled the feeding problem. They gambled that John and Susanna, still babies, could survive the voyage. Back in Krajné, Samko would look after the farm during the summer and through the harvest. Sometime in the fall, the twins would be weaned and could be left with Samko's mother, who was nearing sixty. She would care for them while Samko and Anna returned to New York to work for a few more years. By the time Samko and Anna would depart—according to the plan—her sons Ján or Martin or both would be back from America, with money in their pockets.

We do not know exactly when Samko, Anna, and their four-month-old twins sailed from New York, because the U.S. government recorded only immigrant arrivals, not departures. Other family records indicate that Samko and Anna left the country in May 1906.[15] They presumably traveled again in steerage, or perhaps in third class, which some steamship companies had introduced. If in steerage, they probably enjoyed more living space, for ships carried fewer passengers to Europe than from Europe. Given that John and Susanna were still in diapers, Samko and Anna (of course Anna) had to wash, dry, and change diapers on ship. We can assume that their family attracted affection and assistance from fellow Slovaks on their own travels back to their homeland.

Some immigrants from the "old country" made the crossing enough times that they became known as "birds of passage." In his 1912 book *The New Immigration*, Roberts said, "They come as pilgrims—for a season, work here and there, accumulate a few hundred dollars, and then return."[16] (Ján and Martin were examples.) Čulen estimates that 20 percent of all Slovak immigrants to America had made the voyage at least twice.[17] One source claimed that only 67 percent of all immigrants at that time settled permanently in the United States.[18] That figure matches well to a detailed study of Hungarians who immigrated into the U.S. and emigrated out of the U.S. from 1908 to 1913, which claimed a net immigration of 62.1 percent.[19]

If prior to leaving in the spring of 1906, Samko and Anna saw the item on page 5 of the *Times* titled "WILLIAM'S VISIT TO VIENNA," they would not have thought much about it. Bearing a Vienna dateline, the article said that Kaiser Wilhelm appreciated Emperor Franz Josef's support during the Moroccan crisis. It continued, "The newspapers here discuss the political importance of the approaching meeting of the two Emperors at considerable length, referring to probable changes in the relations between the various powers and the isolation of Germany."

WILLIAM'S·VISIT·TO· VIENNA.

German·Emperor·Striving· to·Strengthen·Austrian· Alliance.

New·York·Times ·May·9,·1906;·p.·5

Germany had few friends among the major European powers. After losing the 1870 Franco-Prussian War, France became its sworn enemy. Britain, then the dominant power in the world, saw in Germany a rising power whose economic output would soon eclipse Britain's. Russia, which believed that German officialdom viewed Slavs as inferior, was no friend. Austria-Hungary and Germany had formed the Dual Alliance in 1879, which Italy joined in 1882 to create the Triple Alliance. But Italy was not regarded as a

Great Power, and its commitment was suspect anyway. Germany also doubted whether Austria-Hungary itself was still a Great Power, but it was the only adjacent country whose military was of any significance. A strengthened alliance with Austria-Hungary was the best among the limited options.

Samko and Anna likely understood none of this as they sailed to surrender their twins temporarily to family in Slovakia. Issues of foreign affairs and international relations were the provinces of ruling heads of states. European monarchs, presumably, were prepared by education and training to handle disputes among nations. Monarchs and their foreign ministers had successfully used diplomacy to avoid debilitating wars within Europe since the 1815 Conference of Vienna. Surely they would do so again.

Although crossing the ocean with two infants must have been an ordeal, Samko and Anna managed to arrive safely in Krajné early in the summer of 1906, with the children in good health. Returning to his home village, Samko, his new wife Anna, and their twins (the *Americany*) were treated like explorers returning from a hazardous trek. Not only had they sailed across the ocean, but they had done it twice. Here they were, back in Krajné, and rich! In truth, the family was just getting by. Much of what they made in New York had been mailed back to Slovakia, most to Samko's mother in Krajné, but perhaps some to Anna's parents in the nearby village of Hrachovište. Then there was the cost of the return voyage and the train ride from Bremen to Slovakia. And they had to have money for returning to New York to resume working.

Samko and Anna planned to go back as soon as possible after the twins were weaned, but that would take several months. During their stay in Krajné, neighbors certainly peppered Samko with questions about America. How much money did he make, and what did he do to earn it? Did people really live better there? How much English did he learn? What about the Krajné men who left in January to join them? How were his brothers, Ján and Martin Mozolák; his brother-in-law, Martin Tomašovič; Martin Hizak; and Martin Kolník doing? And what does he know about Samuel Nebesky, who traveled to New Jersey?

Everyone enjoys a certain amount of celebrity, and Samko was probably no different. He had good reason to be satisfied with his accomplishments since leaving Krajné just four years earlier. He had crossed the ocean; managed to live and work in a foreign land; got married to a pretty girl; sired twins; welcomed his older brothers to his American turf; and recrossed the ocean—all by the age of 24.

After Samko and Anna settled temporarily in Krajné, they were even less likely to follow political news. Moreover, international relations were not a major topic of village discussion. Krajné villagers, like so many others, failed to see the gathering storm clouds. Similarly, Samko's brothers and other Slovaks back in New York probably missed articles in the *New York Times* about European politics.

The outcome of the international Conference on Moroccan Reforms, held in Algeciras, Spain, was particularly noteworthy. It ended on March 31, 1906, exactly one year after Kaiser Wilhelm II had landed at Tangiers and challenged France's influence in Morocco. On April 1, 1906, the *New York Times* carried four different stories on pages 4 and 10, and a long commentary on page SM7, about the conclusion of the conference and its implications for international politics. The amount of space and diversity of attention that the *Times* gave to the conference reflects its political importance.

A story on page 4, "MOROCCO CONFERENCE ENDS WITH AGREEMENT," optimistically said, "The manner of the settlement is satisfactory both to France and Germany.

It removes the causes for friction and restores international relations to a normal condition." Immediately following that article was one titled "ROW LASTED JUST A YEAR," referring to the Kaiser's visit to Tangiers on March 31, 1905, and saying: "Since that visit the dispute between Germany and France has more than once seriously threatened the peace of Europe." Also on page 4, a short item titled "A VICTORY FOR FRANCE" warned, "It is not believed that Germany will give up her effort to obtain a footing in the Mediterranean." The long commentary on page SM7, "A GERMAN BOMB WHICH MAY NOT EXPLODE," reported dark financial dealings between monarchs underlying the controversy.

> MOROCCO·CONFERENCE ¶
> ENDS·WITH·AGREEMENT ¶
> ———¶
> Accord·on·All·Points—Protocol·to ¶
> be·Drawn·Up·at·Once. ¶
> ———¶
> POLICE·PLAN·IS·TEMPORARY ¶
> ———¶
> To·be·Operated·for·Five·Years· ¶
> France·Gets·Three·Shares·of·Bank¶
> ——Delegates·Praise·Our ¶
> Mediation. ¶
> ———¶
> *New·York·Times* ¶
> April·1,·1906,·p.·4 ¶

But the most revealing report, "ALGECIRAS AND AFTER," appeared on page 10. It contended that Germany lost prestige in isolation, as only Austria stood with Germany in the dispute, and it said about Germany: "Moreover, it is hardly to be questioned that she brought all Europe into the quarrel with France with the hope that the understanding between France and Great Britain would be weakened by the terrible strain. It has been strengthened, and in the process the relations between Russia, the ally of France, and Great Britain, for half a century jealous and apprehensive of Russia, have been improved. These are the losses of Germany, and they are very considerable." So by the spring of 1906, journalists saw an isolated Germany, befriended only by Austria, jousting with France backed by Russia and Britain. This view presaged the combatants' alignment in World War I.

Sam and Anna remained in Krajné through the rest of 1906. They took in the harvest, waited until the twins were weaned, and planned to return to New York soon after the Atlantic Ocean was cleared of ice. The year-old twins would stay in Krajné to be raised by Grandma while their parents worked in New York. Arrangements were made with brothers Ján and Martin to return to Krajné early in the spring, when passenger ships could sail safely. Samko and Anna arrived in New York on April 12, 1907, on SS *Gera* of the North German Lloyd Line.[20] About that time, Ján and Martin presumably arrived back in Krajné.

No documents exist concerning the life that Samko and Anna lived in New York after 1907. We presume that they continued to write their family in Krajné and to send money buried in clothing. Once again, husband and wife were consumed by their labors, living simply to maximize their savings. And once again, they paid no attention to international relations and monarchical politics. In any event, few readers of the *New York Times* on September 1, 1907, saw the untitled news item buried in page C3 that announced "the formal conclusion of the Anglo-Russian Convention," which was "welcomed in Great Britain as putting an end to the long years of misunderstanding, and ill feeling between the two powers, particularly in respect to the near Far East." This insignificant news item signaled a significant political event.

For years, Britain and Russia had clashed over their commercial exploitations of weaker territories: Persia, Afghanistan, and India. The Anglo-Russian Convention settled most of these disputes. In conjunction with the Anglo-French Entente Cordiale of 1904, which ended centuries of antagonism between Britain and France, all three nations—Britain, France, and Russia—were linked together in a relationship called the "Triple Entente." It was not a formal alliance, but an understanding that the nations would cooperate if attacked by a common enemy.[21]

Signing of the Anglo-Russian Convention in 1907 and the emergence of the Triple Entente alarmed Kaiser Wilhelm II, who felt surrounded by potential enemies. Britain—Germany's economic rival—ruled the seas and boxed in Germany on its northern coast. Russia—Europe's largest country by far in size and population—walled in Germany on the east. France—defeated in the 1870 Franco-Prussian War and stripped of the Alsace-Lorraine territory—was Germany's implacable foe to the west. Already feeling isolated by the outcome of the 1906 Moroccan Conference that favored France, Wilhelm and his military advisors felt encircled. Germany could count on support only from Austria-Hungary on the south. Although Italy in 1882 had joined with Germany and Austria-Hungary in the Triple Alliance, Italy was a weak power and unreliable partner.

While monarchs, foreign ministers, and general staffs were aligning their countries on the European chessboard in 1907, Samko and Anna, among many thousands of Slovaks in America, lived their lives unaware of these diplomatic maneuvers. In fact, they were no less knowledgeable than millions of peasants of all nationalities back in the homeland. That was especially true in Hungary, where politics was the province of the ruling Magyars. At that time, Magyars held all but a handful of the 413 seats in the Hungarian parliament.[22] So far, there was no actual danger of war, certainly no threat issuing from their peace-loving 78-year-old Emperor Franz Josef. But that was about to change.

To explain how events from 1907 ratcheted towards war in 1914, one must refer to the 1878 Congress of Berlin, held to settle the status of Ottoman territories in the Balkans after the Russo-Turkish War. Victorious Russia reclaimed territories and authority around the Black Sea, while the helpless Ottoman Empire (known as "the sick man of Europe") lost control of territories in the Balkans to the dictates of Russia and the European powers. The Congress created the new entity, Bulgaria, as an independent principality inside the Ottoman Empire. Romania, Serbia, and Montenegro gained their independence. In a particularly peculiar arrangement, Austria-Hungary was allowed to occupy Bosnia-Herzegovina while it remained within the Ottoman Empire.

Then suddenly in early October 1908, Bulgaria and Austria-Hungary broke the 1878 Treaty of Berlin in coordinated actions that upset the balance of power among nations and threatened war. The *New York Times* reported the developments in a flurry of articles over October 6–10. Although the story reporting Bulgaria's independence from Turkey appeared first, Austria-Hungary's annexation of Bosnia-Herzegovina occurred almost simultaneously.

Given that Bulgaria violated the Berlin Treaty, the first paragraph in "POWERS SEEK TO AVOID WAR" cut to the core: "The question which has been stirring the whole of Europe more deeply than any similar question in the memory of the present generation is this, Does it mean war?" Both Britain and France reportedly advised Turkey not to go to war over the issue, but the article warned of a greater threat: Serbia (written "Servia" then) might go to war over Austria-Hungary's expected annexation of Bosnia-Herzegovina: "Reports from Belgrade indicate that Servia has been aroused to the danger point, bands of Servians marching in the streets of Belgrade and shouting for war with Austria, rather than annexation."

For thirty years, 1878–1908, Austria-Hungary kept troops in Bosnia-Herzegovina and governed it as its own province. Why didn't Austria-Hungary just annex it? One answer came from the Hungarian half of the government, which feared that adding about a million Slavs would further dilute its Magyar minority.[23] Another came from Serbia, the Balkan Slavic champion, which resented Austria-Hungary's repression of Slavs and coveted the neighboring lands for itself. But probably the biggest barrier to annexation was Russia, which backed Serbia, and regarded itself as defender of all Slavs in Europe. Emperor Franz Josef, according to a writer at the time, understood that Austria-Hungary only occupied and did not *own* Bosnia-Herzegovina, so never once set foot there throughout the time it was formally in the Ottoman Empire.[24]

Then on October 7, 1908, the *Times* reported in "AUSTRIA TAKES TWO PROVINCES" that "Emperor Francis Joseph formally proclaimed the practical annexation of Bosnia and Herzegovina to the dual monarchy." What caused the change? On September 15–17, the Austrian foreign minister, Alois von Aehrenthal, and the Russian foreign minister, Alexander Izvolski, met in Bohemia and struck a bargain: Russia would accept annexation in return for Austria-Hungary's support for open access to the Black Sea.[25]

According to Izvolski, the two countries were to coordinate the announcement of this bargain, so he did not immediately notify the Tsar of the ministers' agreement. However, Aehrenthal promptly told Franz Josef that the deal was done, and on September 29 the Emperor signed letters for presentation to fellow monarchs on October 5 announcing the annexation.[26] All recipients were surprised by the news, some were angry, and Izvolski was furious at what he regarded as a betrayal.

"AUSTRIA TAKES TWO PROVINCES" charged that both Austria-Hungary's annexation and Bulgaria's independence violated the 1878 Treaty of Berlin, and said: "The present situation is as follows: Turkey calls upon the powers to preserve to her what they guaranteed by that treaty; Austria and Bulgaria strongly declare their determination to keep what they have taken. Servia is protesting belligerently against being hemmed in more strongly between two unpopular neighbors and against having the Servians in Bosnia absorbed into the Austro-Hungarian nationality."

POWERS·SEEK·TO·AVOID·WAR

———

Conference·Expected·to·Revise·Berlin·Treaty·in·View·of·Bulgaria's·Action.

———

TURKEY·SU5PECTS·GERMANY

———

Proclamation·of·Bulgarian·Independence·Takes·Place·at·Tirnovo·Amid·Cheers.

———

MINISTERS·BLAME·AUSTRIA

———

England,·France,·and·Russia·Are·Busy·Working·in·the·Interest·of·Peace.

———

New·York·Times
October·6,·1908,·p.·1

AUSTRIA·TAKES·TWO·PROVINCES

———

Bosnia·and·Herzegovina·Are·Annexed·and·a·Liberal·Constitution·Granted

———

SERVIAN·ARMY·MOBILIZED

———

Leaders·of·All·Parties·Angered·by·Austria·and·War·Talk·Is·Popular

———

CONFERENCE·ON·BULGARIA

———

Britain,·France,·and·Russia·Acting·Together—Bulgarian·Minister·Explains·the·Declaration·of·Independence

———

New·York·Times
October·7,·1908,·p.·1

A burst of reports followed in the *Times*. "RUSSIA AND ENGLAND CLASH" on October 8 was about the conference to address the major powers' different interests. Russia felt that its interests were most harmed by the actions, particularly by Austria-Hungary's annexation: "M. Isvolsky, the Russian Minister of Foreign Affairs this afternoon made public an interview in which he proclaims the Treaty of Berlin to have been directed against Russia.... M. Isvolsky explained that when Baron Aehrenthal, the Austro-Hungarian Minister of Foreign Affairs, broached the

RUSSIA·AND·ENGLAND· CLASH ¶
——— ¶
First·Treaty·Revised-Second· Wants·the·Status·Quo ¶
——— ¶
New·York·Times ¶ October·8,·1908,·p.·2 ¶

subject of the annexation of Bosnia and Herzegovina he informed him that Russia considered impossible any modification of the treaty of Berlin without the assent of the signatories."

Two days later, on October 10, 1908, the *Times* ran a front-page story, "AUSTRIA FEARS A SERVIAN WAR," about war between Austria-Hungary and Serbia over the annexation of Bosnia-Herzegovina, and between Bulgaria and Turkey over Bulgaria's declaration of independence: "That war in the Balkans was a possibility was admitted in Vienna last night. Servia has been so stirred by the annexation of Bosnia and Herzegovina by

AUSTRIA·FEARS ¶ A·SERVIAN·WAR ¶
——— ¶
King·Peter,·Threatened·with·Loss·of· Crown,·May·Be·Forced·to·Fight. ¶
——— ¶
BULGARIA·PRESSES·TURKEY ¶
——— ¶
Demands·by·Wire·the·Recognition· of·Her·Independence·Austria· Supports·Her. ¶
——— ¶
TURKEY·TO·GATHER·ARMY ¶
——— ¶
Fears·Conference·of·the·Powers· Would·Lead·to·Dismemberment·of· the·Empire. ¶
——— ¶
FRANCE·IS·SEEKING·PEACE ¶
——— ¶
Hopes·Still·That·Powers·Will·Settle· Differences·in·Congress-Russia's· Position·Explained. ¶
¶
New·York·Times ¶ October·10,·1908,·p.·1 ¶

Austria-Hungary that the people unitedly are demanding war. King Peter, who is threatened with the loss of his crown if he holds back, may choose to fight. Montenegro may join forces with Servia in a clash. Austria is concentrating her forces to meet this situation.

Bulgaria meanwhile is pressing Turkey for recognition of her independence, and the country is deeply stirred."

Also on October 10 the *Times* ran two front-page stories about impending war: "AUSTRIA'S ARMY IS READY" and "SERVIANS STILL EAGER TO FIGHT," which said:

Renewed demonstrations were made, in Belgrade, Servia, yesterday, the people demanding the resignation of the cabinet and also the abdication of King Peter unless he declares war against Austria-Hungary. It is said that 150,000 Austrian troops can be thrown into Servian territory in twenty-four hours.

Vienna has a report that a fatal clash has occurred on the Servian Frontier.

A British fleet of two battleships, two cruisers, and two torpedo-boat destroyers is to-day well on its way from Malta to the Aegean Sea to stop the agitation in Turkey.

The forts on the Bosphorus yesterday fired blank shots across the bows of a steamer flying the new Bulgarian royal flag as it attempted to pass them.

By this time, international events that preoccupied European monarchs had progressed far enough and were serious enough that talk of war may have penetrated into Slovak villages in Hungary—the villages that would provide the soldiers to fight for the Emperor and for the glory of the Empire.

Both Ján at 38 and Martin at 34 were in the military reserves, old enough to have escaped the first call-ups. Had Samko at age 26 been in Krajné instead of New York, he would probably have been among the first to go. But if Ján and Martin had indeed heard about the conflict with Serbia over Bosnia-Herzegovina, a land that they may never have known about, they still must have been nervous. It would have been ironic if they were forced to fight fellow Slavs in Serbia to fulfill the territorial aspirations of a country they had recently fled to find work abroad.

As it happened, war did not occur over these matters in October 1908, although the controversies and threats dragged on into the first quarter of 1909. At the end, Turkey did not attack Bulgaria. Bulgaria was allowed to become independent without major repercussion from Turkey, which eventually received 125 million francs in compensation.[27] Serbia did not attempt to take Bosnia-Herzegovina, allowing

> **SERVIANS·STILL
> EAGER·TO·FIGHT**
> ————
> Parliament·Will·Meet·Today—
> Clash·on·the·Frontier·Is·Reported·
> in·Vienna
> ————
> 150,000·AUSTRIANS·READY
> ————
> British·Fleet·Leaves·Malta·for·the·
> Aegean·to·Still·the·Agitation·in·
> Turkey
> ————
> ISVOLSKY·GOES·TO·LONDON
> ————
> Russia's·Foreign·Minister·Seeks·
> Aid·of·Britain·in·Calling·
> Conference·of·the·Powers
> ————
> *New·York·Times*
> October·10,·1908,·p.·1

Austria-Hungary to incorporate it into its empire. Although Serbia was inclined to fight Austria-Hungary, Serbia lost the backing from Russia—still smarting after its humiliating defeat by Japan in 1905. Especially after Germany announced that it would back Austria-Hungary, Russia chose not to join the fight. Brook-Shepherd wrote: "Indeed, it was German pressure on Russia, transmitted downward from St Petersburg to Belgrade, which finally led Serbia, on 31 March 1909, to recognize the annexation and even to pledge 'good neighborly relations' with Austria."[28] Franz Josef's bold action and military resolve, with German support, faced down Serbia and Russia. Turkey later recognized the annexation of Bosnia-Herzegovina and received 2.2 million pounds in compensation.[29]

By avoiding war in the Balkans in 1908–1909, the diplomatic system of alliances, communications between monarchs, and international conferences, once again, seemed to have worked. It was a complicated process, but it avoided war in this instance. Although the diplomatic system failed to avoid war in two other instances—1912 and 1913—it did contain their scope. Neither the First Balkan War in 1912 nor the second in 1913 involved Austria-Hungary as a combatant, but both affected its relations with the Balkan nations. Given the intricacies and general messiness of Balkan politics, these conflicts—which virtually ousted the Ottoman Empire from Europe—will only be summarized here.

The First Balkan War in 1912 war essentially pitted a newly formed Balkan League—Serbia, Bulgaria, Greece, and Montenegro—against what remained of the Ottoman Empire. Backed by Russia, the League was formed to wrest Macedonia from Turkey. The First Balkan War was short, beginning on October 8, halting temporarily with an armistice on December 3, and resuming briefly in January 1913, after a *coup d'état* in Turkey. Within a few months, the League had achieved most of its objectives, as one source states: "Under a peace treaty signed in London on May 30, 1913, the Ottoman

Empire lost almost all of its remaining European territory, including all of Macedonia and Albania. Albanian independence was insisted upon by the European powers, and Macedonia was to be divided among the Balkan allies."[30] Peace in the Balkans did not follow the end of the war, however, as the victors quarreled over the spoils. Although Bulgaria gained substantial territory under the treaty, it did not get what it wanted in Macedonia, while Serbia and Greece felt that Bulgaria got more than it deserved. Romania, not a combatant in the war, coveted territory of an enlarged Bulgaria on its border.

The Second Balkan War in 1913 was fueled by envious Serbians, Greeks, and Romanians, who formed an alliance against Bulgaria on June 1. At the end of the month, King Ferdinand of Bulgaria sought to gain lands in Macedonia and attacked Serbian and Greek forces in the area, only to be promptly defeated. Eschewing another international conference among European powers, the combatants signed a treaty on August 10 that divided most of Macedonia between Serbia and Greece and ceded some Bulgarian territory to Romania, leaving Bulgaria much smaller than before the war. The results of the two Balkan Wars are portrayed in Map 6.1.

The two Balkan wars stoked the hatred, not too strong a word, between Serbia and Austria-Hungary. Its roots lay in Hungary's treatment of its three percent Serbian minority, and in Austria-Hungary's fear that fiery Serbs in Hungary and in Serbia would ignite its other substantial Slavic minorities. Margaret MacMillan wrote: "Austria-Hungary feared that it was going to disappear as a power unless it did something about South Slav nationalism within its own borders and that meant doing something about the magnet of a South Slav and independent Serbia."[31] The wars confirmed Austria-Hungary's perception: "Serbia had become for Austria-Hungary's leaders both its most dangerous neighbor in the Balkans and an existential threat."[32]

Additionally, neither the ruling Germans in Austria nor the ruling Magyars in Hungary liked Slavs as a people, and the dislike was reciprocated. Piled on top of these historic enmities were Austria-Hungary's annexation of Bosnia-Herzegovina and its support for Bulgaria over Serbia in both of the Balkan wars. Austria-Hungary favored Bulgaria for several reasons. One was that Bulgaria did not border on Hungary, as Serbia did, and another was that few Bulgarians lived in Hungary, and so did not challenge the monarchy by clamoring for their rights.

Another reason for Austria-Hungary's implacable opposition to Serbia was that it was Russia's client. Russia used Serbia to project Russia's authority as defender of Slavs in the Balkans, and as Serbia's patron, Russia's government protected Serbia as best it could from one thousand miles away. In 1909, Russia knew that it was in no position to back up a Serbian war with Austria-Hungary over Bosnia-Herzegovina, and Serbia then was not strong to take on the fight alone.

While Serbia on its southern border threatened Austria-Hungary's unity, Russia on its eastern border threatened Austria-Hungary's existence. Poles and Ruthenes (Rusyns), both Slavic people, constituted almost 20 percent of the Empire's population and lived in territories bordering Slavic Russia. Czechs and Slovaks, also Slavic people, lived close by and totaled another 15 percent of the Empire's inhabitants. Franz Josef feared that his Slavic subjects, linguistically and perhaps culturally similar to Russians, could not be relied on if push came to war with Russia.

Slavic emigrants in the United States did not usually follow European politics very closely, if at all. But information and stories about the old country inevitably crept into conversation at the tavern or workplace. Mark Wansa's *The Linden and the Oak*, a powerful

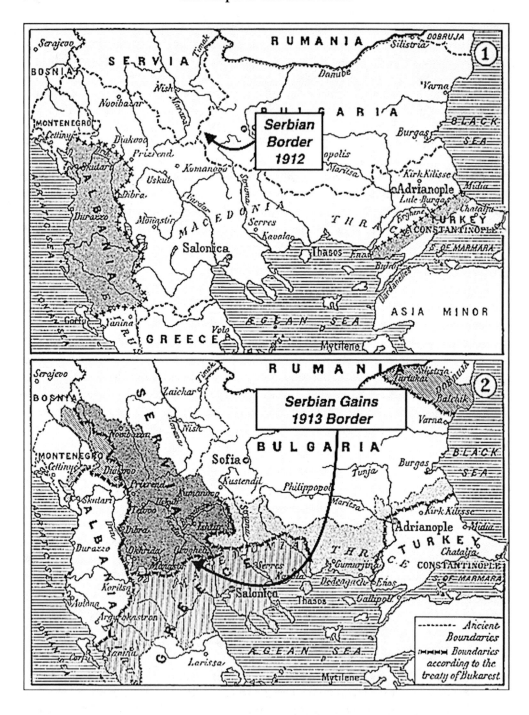

Map 6.1: THE BALKAN NATIONS AFTER THE 1912 AND 1913 BALKAN WARS. Treaties pressed by the major European powers confined the Balkan Wars of 1912 (1) and 1913 (2) to the Balkans, but Austria-Hungary feared that Serbia's successes in 1913 would encourage her to champion Serb dissension within Austria-Hungary. Serbia was spelled "Servia" then. Credit: "Report of the International Commission to Inquire into the Causes and Conduct of the Balkan Wars" 1914; at https://www.lib.utexas.edu/maps/historical/history_balkans.html. In the public domain.

novel about the Eastern Front, imagined a prewar conversation between Vasyl, a Rusyn from Galicia on the Russian border, and a Slovak at their workplace in New Jersey: "In Ameryka there had been much talk about Serbia and Bulgaria and Russia and Austria-Hungary and the possibility of war. It was all very confusing. One man, a Slovak co-worker at the carpet factory, had said to Vasyl, 'Why you want to go back to the Austrian Empire, eh? There will be war, you know? And you, a Russian, living in the Hungarian half of the Austrian Empire!' When Vasyl told the man he was not a Russian, the Slovak responded, 'You talk like a Russian!' Vasyl did not know how to respond."[33] In the novel, as in real life, some Rusyns did defect to the Russian army when war came—as did some Czechs and Slovaks.

The Second Balkan War in 1913 did not itself produce a broader European war. Norman Angell's 1910 book *The Great Illusion* argued that industrialized countries had recognized the futility of war.[34] Angell cogently reasoned that war had become futile because war was too costly. Such countries had become so economically interdependent that war would be economically harmful to both sides. Prominent statesmen and business leaders endorsed Angell's thesis. Diplomatic successes in avoiding war in 1905–06 and 1908–09 were cited, as were the quick settlements of the Balkan Wars in 1912 and 1913.

Certainly Samko and Anna were not fearful of war in Europe as they planned their return to Slovakia in January 1914. They had made enough money, and Anna was pregnant again. It was time to return. Their twins John and Susanna, now 8 years old, had already started school in Krajné. We do not know exactly when Samko and Anna embarked from New York, but it was probably in April or May. We do know that Samuel Mozolák, Jr., was born in Krajné on June 3, 1914.

7

Imperial Deciders

In the middle of the 19th century, monarchs reigned over every European nation except Switzerland. Their royal courts were as pompous and ostentatious as they had been in the 18th century. Miranda Carter, a historian of the era's dynasties, wrote that royalty was obsessed with "the tiniest details."[1] She noted, "The intricacies of dress were an expression of the pointless arbitrariness and the leisurely emptiness of court life, which had been invented in the eighteenth century by absolutist monarchs to keep control over their most senior subjects."[2]

Chapter 1, "The Emperor in Vienna," described Americans' amusement over the operetta-like aspects of the Austro-Hungarian Empire in the 19th century. As war historian Christopher Clark wrote, "The effete rituals and gaudy uniforms, the 'ornamentalism' of a world still largely organized around hereditary monarchy, had a distancing effect on present-day recollection. They seemed to signal that the protagonists were people from another, vanished world. The presumption stealthily asserted itself that if the actors' hats had gaudy green ostrich feathers on them, then their thoughts and motivations probably did too."[3] Royal courts early in the 20th century reflected the past century's ornamental glitter, but their monarchs operated in a society that relied on electricity, telephone, telegraph, subways, and railroads—technology introduced decades earlier (and described in Chapter 1). Automobiles and airplanes were soon added to the list. So monarchs in the major powers governed in a more modern era than suggested by the stuffy and quaint social conventions that governed their royal machinery for making foreign policy.

In fact, Clark regarded the "Crisis of 1914 as a modern event, the most complex of modern times, perhaps of any time so far." He says, "The key decision-makers—kings, emperors, foreign ministers, ambassadors, military commanders and a host of lesser officials—walked towards danger in watchful, calculated steps."[4] Although other governmental officials had key roles in shaping foreign policy decisions, only the monarchs themselves could decide on going to war. The emperors were the deciders. Only they could "push the button," and they were ill-equipped to make that decision.

After Germany defeated Emperor Napoleon III in 1870, France joined small and famously neutral Switzerland in the tiny two-nation club of European republics. By 1914, every major European military power but France was a monarchy. In that fateful year, Emperor Franz Josef at 84 years of age had already ruled Austria-Hungary for 66 years. Wilhelm II (age 55) had been kaiser for 26 years, and Nicholas II (age 46) was tsar for almost 20 years. They certainly had experience in government, and yet, as Carter wrote: "They were all three anachronisms, ill-equipped by education and personality to deal with the modern world, marooned by history in positions increasingly out of kilter with their era. The system within which they existed was dying, and the courts of Europe had turned from energetic centres of patronage into stagnant ponds of tradition and conservatism. The world was leaving them behind."[5] Chapter 5, "Imperial Ignorance," inventoried the monarchs' various shortcomings—modest intellectual abilities (shared by all three), lack of international experience (Franz Josef and Nicholas), limited capacity for sustained attention (Wilhelm and Nicholas), unfamiliarity with their own subjects' lives (shared by all three), inability to make decisions (Franz Josef and Nicholas), tendency to make too many decisions, make them too quickly, and change them too often (Wilhelm). Franz Josef also suffered under the irredeemable handicap of being a tired old man.

Nevertheless, each of the three monarchs defended his right to divine right to rule autocratically. None faced the brutal truth that their authority had ebbed, both *de facto* and *de jure*. Franz Josef, Wilhelm, and Nicholas deluded themselves in thinking that they were still autocrats, attempting to govern as they did when they assumed the throne in the 19th century. Liberal and democratic forces had whittled down their powers over the decades so that their authority had been significantly constrained by the second decade of the 20th century. The whittling process had a common element in each empire—pressure from liberals to participate in government through a functioning parliament.

In England, the monarch's divine right to rule had ended nearly three hundred years earlier with the execution of Charles I in 1649, followed by the "Glorious Revolution" of 1688–1689, which divided governmental power between the king and parliament. However glorious that revolution may have been, it was certainly not democratic, for most citizens had no representation in parliament. Nevertheless, it did replace England's autocratic monarchy with a constitutional monarchy. Enlightened by three centuries of liberal political thought, democratizing forces in Germany, Austria-Hungary, and Russia not only sought to participate in government through functioning parliaments but through *elected* parliaments, even if they were not broadly representative bodies. Over decades, these liberal forces chipped away some autocratic powers of the three ruling monarchs. Let us consider each in turn.

Kaiser Wilhelm II of Germany suffered the earliest and the most from liberal and democratizing pressures. The great Prussian statesman Otto von Bismarck had engineered the formation of the German nation in 1871 under a constitution that invested sweeping executive power in an emperor (kaiser) governing with a parliament (Reichstag), which the kaiser could dissolve and call for new elections. Bismarck also arranged for then Wilhelm I, King of Prussia, to hold the title of kaiser and to govern through a chancellor responsible only to the kaiser. Bismarck, of course, became chancellor.

In keeping with the times, Bismarck also allowed the formation of parliamentary parties. So in theory, as MacMillan argued, Germany had been created as a constitutional monarchy: "It had a federal parliament, the Reichstag, elected by universal male suffrage, with responsibility for approving federal budgets. It had a federal council, the Bundesrat, made up of representatives from the states, with the right to oversee such crucial areas as foreign affairs and the army and navy."[6] But she continued: "Theory was one thing, reality another. The council never became important; Bismarck never had the slightest intention of sharing his power or that of Prussia. He combined the offices of German Chancellor and Prussian Minister-President and the practice continued until the end of the Great War. He was also Foreign Minister and ran foreign affairs largely out of the Prussian Foreign Ministry. With overlapping jurisdictions it was never clear where responsibility really lay."[7] Also in theory, Kaiser Wilhelm I had supreme power, but Bismarck actually wielded power on behalf of the kaiser. When they differed, Bismarck would threaten to resign, and the kaiser would cave in to his powerful chancellor.

Wilhelm I died in 1888 and was succeeded by his son, Frederick III, who died of throat cancer after reigning only 99 days. Before the year ended, Wilhelm II succeeded his father as kaiser. Young, headstrong, mercurial Wilhelm II soon clashed with old Chancellor Bismarck. Given that Wilhelm had said, "We Hohenzollerns receive our crown only from Heaven and in the duties connected to it we are responsible only to Heaven," he was not inclined to delegate his responsibilities.[8] In March 1890, Wilhelm did something that his grandfather could not. He dismissed Bismarck, ostensibly for not keeping him informed on all policies—domestic and foreign.

Kaiser Wilhelm may have rid himself of Bismarck, but not Bismarck's constitutional legacy. Unwilling and unable to govern by himself, he appointed Leo von Caprivi as chancellor to push his policies through a Reichstag already divided by party politics. Caprivi encountered opposition to the crown's proposals concerning tariffs, educational reforms, and "anti-revolutionary" activity, among other topics.[9] What particularly vexed Wilhelm was the Reichstag's reluctance to fund his desired and expensive shipbuilding program of Admiral Alfred von Tirplitz, who envisioned a fleet strong enough to destroy England's Royal Navy.[10] Chancellor Bernard von Bülow, who succeeded Caprivi in 1900, had the task of persuading the Reichstag to fund the program. Despite some successes, he failed to raise the desired funds and resigned in 1909.[11] The new chancellor was Theobald von Bethmann Hollweg, who served into World War I.

Detailing this parade of chancellors—from Bismarck to Caprivi to Bülow to Bethman Hollweg—demonstrates that Kaiser Wilhelm often failed to compel the German government to do his bidding. Autocracy had its limits in Germany, especially in raising funds. Nevertheless, Wilhelm, who proclaimed often and loudly that he was the "Supreme War Lord," enjoyed more power concerning military and foreign affairs. His biographer, John Röhl, claimed that he "could not and would not be bypassed." The kaiser "had the final say on all significant matters, most notably on all appointments to high office and in decisions affecting war and peace."[12]

Other historians concur. One described how the kaiser isolated the civilian government from military affairs: "In Germany, where the army and the Kaiser had succeeded by 1889 in excluding both the War Ministry and parliament from military policy-making, war planning belonged exclusively to the Great General Staff; the navy's admirals were fed crumbs and even the Prime Minister, Bethmann Hollweg, was not told of the central war plan [the Schlieffen plan] until December 1912, though it had been in preparation since 1905."[13] Another historian credited the kaiser for being in charge throughout the month preceding the outbreak of the war: "Though the German generals played a major role in the last phase of the crisis (and gradually took over completely once the fighting began), it was the Emperor and Supreme War Lord William II who was in undisputed command throughout the fateful month which followed. That is why German policy zigzagged and even somersaulted during these weeks."[14]

German generals (privately) faulted the kaiser for his lack of military knowledge, his unwillingness to study relevant papers and documents, and what one might call today his attention deficit disorder. Nevertheless, Kaiser Wilhelm II, His Imperial Majesty, was in charge. In 21st century terminology as uttered by United States President George W. Bush, Kaiser Wilhelm was Germany's "decider" concerning war and peace.[15] He alone could push the "war" button.

Tsar Nicholas II of Russia began his rule with virtually no constraints on his power. Few members of the imperial family after Catherine the Great entertained western European ideas about liberal government, and the Russian Orthodox Church supported the tsar's autocratic rule. Nicholas himself subscribed to the popular myth that the common people were devoted to him and that he best knew his people's needs and how to care for them. As stated in a major biography, "Nicholas believed in the personal, patriarchal rule of the monarch."[16] Another biographer stated: "Theoretically the tsar's power was unlimited—the Romanovs liked to think of Russia and its empire as one enormous feudal estate in which everything derived from them. They were tenacious in their determination not to let go of a single drop of power."[17]

Eventually, liberal ideas of government crept into the top and bottom of Russian society. Educated professionals on the margins of the government pressed for greater political participation, while those outside the circle—both educated and uneducated—plotted for more drastic changes. Military defeats by the Japanese in 1904 and 1905 fed social unrest, forcing Nicholas to allow a national representative assembly in February 1905. Even then, he justified his action, according to one account, "not as the acceptance of a constitutional limitation on his personal autocratic power but as the revival of a custom and as a means to better hear the voice of the *narod*"—the people.[18]

In practice, the tsar neither listened to nor even heard peoples' voices in the new assembly, the Duma. He dissolved the first Duma in 1906 and the second in 1907, each after having served only three months. The third and fourth Dumas, which lasted their five-year terms, had somewhat more impact. In 1909, the Duma attempted but failed to assert control over defense policy.[19] In 1912, it had to be courted for an increase in the military budget.[20] Although Nicholas largely ignored the Duma and dissolved it when sufficiently irritated, it did limit his freedom of action in domestic policy.

Nicholas's rule was constrained more by his nature than by his Duma. During his twenties, when a future tsar should be thinking about governing his empire, Nicholas showed his laziness and boredom with government routine. After a ten-month tour of his empire from west to east, which should have heightened his sense of responsibility, he wearied of receiving government documents: "I am simply unable to understand how one can possibly read this mass of papers in one week. I always restrict myself to one or two more interesting files while others go directly into the fire."[21]

Lacking the discipline to do the work required of a tsar, Nicholas could be said to be unwilling to govern. Lacking the ability to make firm decisions and to direct his ministers, he was also unable to govern. Ministers pitched their proposals to the tsar, who usually agreed (or at least did not disagree) without written records of oral decisions. Ministers schemed for his attention, eliciting support for contradictory plans. Rather than dominating his ministers like a proper autocrat, Nicholas worked around them. Clark wrote, "Confronted with a ministerial bloc that threatened to confine his freedom of action, Nicholas withdrew his support and intrigued against the men he had himself placed in power."[22]

In foreign and military affairs, however, the tsar enjoyed wide powers. Especially around 1900, Nicholas cranked up Russia's commercial and military activities in the Far East.[23] And Nicholas fiercely defended his authority, saying, as MacMillan reported, "Military doctrine consists of doing everything which I order."[24] From 1911 to 1914, the tsar reasserted his autocratic power in foreign affairs.[25] When it came to the crucial matter of mobilizing the army for war, the tsar was Russia's decider.[26] He owned the button to start war.

Emperor Franz Josef of Austria-Hungary ascended the throne in 1848 during a revolution against Habsburg rule. Guided by his advisors, the young monarch imposed absolute rule. After his ignominious 1859 military defeat while commanding his army in Italy, Franz Josef responded differently. In 1860 he resurrected a defunct parliament with the power, on paper, to reject or approve taxation, and to "cooperate" on framing legislation. While such concessions to liberal and democratic pressures had little effect on his autocratic rule, parliament did not simply rubber stamp his budgets.[27] Nevertheless, Brook-Shepherd said, "The Emperor's personal control over his army and foreign policy remained, however, beyond the law."[28]

After Austria-Hungary's second ignominious defeat—this time by Bismarck's Prussian army in 1866—Franz Josef agreed to the historic Compromise with Hungary in 1867 that established the Dual Monarchy. As argued earlier, magnates controlled the Hungarian government, ruling on behalf of a Magyar plurality. The 1867 Compromise did not merely constrain Franz Josef's rule within Hungary. It virtually ended his rule in Hungary.

However, Franz Josef continued to command the army, navy, and foreign affairs of Austria-Hungary as emperor and king respectively in the Dual Monarchy. To fund these activities, the two countries shared defense and finance ministries, whose common budget was to be negotiated between the countries every ten years, beginning in 1867. The Austrian and Hungarian delegations always defended their countries' special interests.[29] Franz Josef and the Austrians favored spending on the military more than the Hungarians. Great War historian Geoffrey Wawro described the dynamic: "Since Austro-Hungarian budgets had to be approved by both parliaments, the Hungarians got in the habit of slashing or vetoing army bills that would expand or modernize the regular army, which they viewed as a threat: German-drilled 'Mamelukes' [militaristic slaves] who might invade Hungary and tear up the Ausgleich."[30] Every ten years, the Hungarians balked at funding the military and at paying their assessment. The consequence was that military spending was held below what Franz Josef wanted and far below that being spent by other powers.[31]

At the beginning of the 20th century, the once-powerful Austro-Hungarian Empire was on the skids. People began referring to it—instead of Turkey—as the "sick man" of Europe. Wawro said: "Austria—by then part of a Dual Monarchy with neighboring Hungary—had been reduced to a Balkan power, vying with Italy for the epithet 'Least of the Great Powers,' and, like the Ottoman Empire, in danger of slipping out of the great-power club altogether."[32] So with the 1867 Compromise, Emperor Franz Josef compromised his own rule, granting to a component part of his empire a veto on what was to him the most important attribute of his empire, its status as a Great Power among European nations.[33] In today's parlance, he was in denial about the bad marriage he had entered into with Hungary.

Nevertheless, the old emperor—who reached 80 years of age in 1910—remained in command of his empire's foreign and military affairs. Franz Josef, however, was not a war hawk. He had commanded the army only once, at the Battle of Solferino in 1859, and had lost to French and Sardinian forces. Seven years later Austria lost again at the decisive Battle of Königgrätz in 1866 and was expelled from the German confederation. Alan Palmer reported that during a Balkan controversy in 1912 he told his ministers, "I don't want war," banging his fist on the table, "I have always been unlucky in wars."[34] Nevertheless, only Emperor Franz Josef could declare war. In that respect, he was Austria-Hungary's decider, and he was eventually persuaded to push the button.

It is easier to fix the responsibility for starting World War I than to determine its cause. It is also easy to miss the distinction between starting and causing a war.[35] Many Americans today would finger Kaiser Wilhelm's Germany—if not the kaiser himself—as the Great War's instigator, a term that merges the ideas of cause and start. That Germany instigated the war is how a U.S. government agency saw it in 1918. Its official *Handbook of Diplomatic History of Europe, Asia, and Africa 1870–1914* concluded:

> In 1914 the situation in Europe seemed to be favorable to an aggressive policy on the part of Germany. The situation appeared even to demand it, if she hoped to realize her ambitious plans. To Germany it appeared that delay would improve the military situation of Russia, would solidify the situation in the Balkans unfavorable to Austria-Hungary and Germany, and would bar the route to the East. An immediate war, Germany believed, would find France filled with political dissension and in the midst of her army reorganization; it could probably be undertaken without the interference of England, weakened by civil war in Ireland and by a widespread pacifist sentiment. Germany was ready, "the day" seemed to have dawned, and *Germany plunged the world into war*.[36] [Emphasis added.]

The *Handbook of Diplomatic History*'s conclusion was explicitly reflected in Part VIII on "Reparations" in Article 231 of the 1919 Versailles Peace Treaty, the infamous "War Guilt Clause": "The Allied and Associated Governments affirm, and Germany accepts, the responsibility of *Germany and her allies for causing all the loss and damage* to which the Allied and Associated Governments and their nationals have been subjected as a consequence of the war imposed upon them by the aggression of Germany and her allies."[37] [Emphasis added.] Germany's "allies" in the war were Austria-Hungary, Bulgaria, and the Ottoman Empire. Austria-Hungary and the Ottoman Empire had already been dismantled, and poor, small Bulgaria commanded no resources with which to compensate the Allied and Associated Governments.

There were no opinion polls at the time, so one cannot accurately estimate the public's view of who started or caused the war. Before the war, Americans liked Germans. Writing his 1914 book *American Public Opinion*, James Whelpley relied on readings and observations to estimate public perceptions. Concerning Germany, Whelpley concluded just before the war: "Relations between Germany and the United States are excellent and always have been. America has been the objective point of millions of German emigrants for the past fifty years. No questions of diplomacy have arisen to cast a shadow upon the intentions of either Government towards the other."[38]

In 1928, a decade after the war's end, Sidney Bradshaw Fay published two volumes titled *The Origins of the World War*. He distinguished between "the underlying causes of the war before Sarajevo" (Volume I)[39] and "the immediate causes of the war after Sarajevo" (Volume II).[40] Each volume ran over 500 pages. Fay despaired of treating the "underlying causes" in a single volume of only 500 pages. He said, "These are so complex and reach so far back into the past that any attempt to describe them adequately would involve nothing less than the writing of the whole diplomatic history of Europe since 1870, or rather from 1789; some questions go back to the age of Louis XIV, and even to that of Charlemagne."[41]

Fay was more sanguine about ascertaining the immediate causes of the war after Sarajevo. He emphatically dismissed "the verdict of the Versailles Treaty that Germany and her allies were responsible for the War," which Fay regarded as "historically unsound" in view of available evidence.[42] Instead, Fay concluded, "Austria was more responsible for the immediate origin of the war than any other Power."[43] While urging a revision of prevailing thought about culpability for the war, he recognized that "widespread popular feeling" against Germany in 1928 made revision "doubtful."

Revising the belief that Germany caused World War I became even more doubtful after Germany indisputably caused the European portion of World War II. Opinion surveys near the end of World War II suggested that most Americans blamed Germany for both wars. A 1944 Gallup poll asked, "As soon as Germany is defeated, do you think she will start making plans for another world war?"[44] Sixty percent said yes against only 21 percent saying no. In 1961, just 16 years after the end of World War II, German historian Fritz Fischer also blamed Germany for World War I, charging that its leaders planned the aggression.[45] Historians Hamilton and Herwig wrote that Fischer's "thesis" was "so radical, so powerful, and so devastating to German conservative historians, that attention was riveted almost exclusively on Germany. Austria-Hungary's part in starting the 'great seminal catastrophe' of the twentieth century was glossed over."[46]

Hamilton and Herwig edited their own 500-page book, *The Origins of World War I*, in 2003.[47] In 2004, they authored a more concise and analytical book on its origins.[48] Its bibliography listed a score of other books on the topic. European historian Sheehan noted that the causes of World War I "remain the subject of intense debate."[49] MacMillan said that we remember the Great War "because it is such a puzzle. How could Europe have done this to itself and to the world? There are many possible explanations; indeed, so many that it is difficult to choose among them."[50] Clark's book *The Sleepwalkers* avoided looking for the war's causes—"imperialism, nationalism, armaments, alliances, high finance, ideas of national honour"—and instead investigated *how* the war occurred, looking for "the sequences of interactions that produced certain outcomes."[51]

Clark contended that "the events of July 1914 make sense only when we illuminate the journeys travelled by the key decision-makers."[52] By describing those journeys over more than 500 pages, Clark detailed how the war occurred. In the process, he shifted attention away from the enduring enmity between the Germans and the French in northern Europe to the later but smoldering hostility between Austria and Serbia in southeastern Europe. His conclusion: There can be no dispute that the Great War started in southeastern Europe.

On June 28, 1914, Archduke Franz Ferdinand of Austria-Hungary—heir to the throne—and his wife, Sophie, Duchess of Hohenberg, were assassinated during a visit to Sarajevo in Bosnia, which Franz Josef had annexed to his empire in 1908. The next day, aware of the ramifications of this event, the *New York Times* ran 18 different stories on the assassination, on warnings against the archduke going to Sarajevo, on his bravery after the initial attempt on his life, on Emperor Franz Josef's reactions, on Kaiser Wilhelm's reaction, and so on. The main headline, "HEIR TO AUSTRIA'S THRONE IS SLAIN WITH HIS WIFE BY A BOSNIAN YOUTH TO AVENGE SEIZURE OF HIS COUNTRY," ran across the top of page 1.

In 1999, the celebrated Dutch author Geert Mak spent untold hours reading, one after the other, daily issues of Vienna's leading newspaper, *Neue Freie Presse*, published in the summer of 1914.[53] Mak said that the paper issued a special edition on the assassination in the evening of June 28, reporting all the gory details. Although the killings were the talk of the town, financial trading remained calm. On July 2, the paper wrote, "The political consequences of this act are being greatly exaggerated.'"

Mak said that *Neue Freie Presse* did not report on growing tension with Serbia until July 13, more than two weeks after the attack. Not until July 20 did the paper discuss unrest in its pages, referring to Russian interference and ultimatums. The word "mobilization" did not appear until July 24, and not until July 26 did an editorial warn against "total" war with Serbia. On July 29, it reprinted Franz Josef's declaration of war, issued the previous day.

On Saturday, August 1, the headline was *"Die Monarchie und das verbündete Deutschland in Waffen* [The monarchy and its ally Germany in arms]." The text read, "Germany, along with Austria, is mobilising against the Russians. France receives a German ultimatum: the country must declare its neutrality within eighteen hours. A French mobilisation will mean 'immediate war.'"[54]

Today we know a great deal about Gavrilo Princip, the 19-year-old Bosnian Serb who fired the shots, the six Bosnian terrorists in the assassination plot, and the tragedy of errors that somehow culminated in their success.[55] At that time, Franz Josef and his government only knew that most were ethnic Serbians. They suspected that government figures in adjacent Serbia were involved in the plot, but lacked proof. Nevertheless, Franz Josef's army chief of staff, General Conrad von Hötzendorf, and his foreign minister, Count Leopold Berchtold, urged an immediate declaration of war.[56] While genuinely outraged at the assassination, they also saw it as a convenient pretext to "do something" about troublesome Serbia, which had been stirring up trouble among Austria-Hungary's Slavic subjects.

Chapter 3, "The Emperor's Subjects," describes how Hungary's policy of Magyarization victimized its Slavic nationalities—Slovaks, Ruthenians, Serbs, and Croats. In truth, the Austrians also mistreated their Czech, Polish, and Slovenian nationalities. Hilde Spiel reported on their status in Austria: "True, the German-speaking 'master-race' in Vienna treated them [their Slavs] considerably better than the Magyar 'master-race' in Budapest treated the Slovaks and Romanians under their jurisdiction. Yet the Slavs in the Dual Monarchy were on the whole considered inferior to the other member nations—'a people without a history,' as the German socialist Friedrich Engles [*sic*] slightingly called them—and mainly fit to serve as tailors, cobblers and domestic servants, as, indeed,

> **HEIR·TO·AUSTRIA'S· THRONE·IS·SLAIN·WITH·HIS· WIFE·BY·A·BOSNIAN· YOUTH·TO·AVENGE· SEIZURE·OF·HIS·COUNTRY** ¶
>
> ——— ¶
>
> Francis·Ferdinand·Shot·During· State·Visit·to·Sarajevo ¶
>
> ——— ¶
>
> TWO·ATTACKS·IN·A·DAY ¶
>
> ——— ¶
>
> Archduke·Saves·His·Life·First·Time· by·Knocking·Aside·a·Bomb·Hurled· at·Auto ¶
>
> ——— ¶
>
> SLAIN·IN·SECOND·ATTEMPT ¶
>
> ——— ¶
>
> Lad·Dashes·at·Car·as·the·Royal· Couple·Return·from·Town·Hall· and·Kills·Both·of·Them. ¶
>
> ——— ¶
>
> LAID·TO·A·SERVIAN·PLOT ¶
>
> ——— ¶
>
> Heir·Warned·Not·to·Go·to·Bosnia,· Where·Populace·Met·Him·with· Servian·Flags. ¶
>
> ——— ¶
>
> AGED·EMPEROR·IS·STRICKEN ¶
>
> ——— ¶
>
> Shock·of·Tragedy·Prostrates· Francis·Joseph ¶
>
> ——— ¶
>
> Young·Assassin·Proud·of·His· Crime. ¶
>
> ——— ¶
>
> *New·York·Times* ¶ June·29,·1914,·p.·1 ¶

did many of those Czechs who made up thirty percent of the citizens of Vienna."[57] Serbia by itself posed a significant threat to Austria-Hungary, for Serbia was backed by Russia, a self-proclaimed champion of fellow Slavs. As MacMillan wrote, "Austria-Hungary feared that it was going to disappear as a power unless it did something about South Slav nationalism within its own borders and that meant doing something about the magnet of a South Slav and independent Serbia."[58] She said, "Serbia had become for Austria-Hungary's leaders both its most dangerous neighbor in the Balkans and an existential threat."[59] Already, people were speaking about a "Yugoslavia." In Slavic languages, "yugo" and its variants translates as "south."

Since Austria-Hungary's humiliating defeat by Prussia in 1866, Franz Josef had tried to avoid war, and he was not inclined to declare war now out of grief for his disliked nephew. Moreover, many troops were on summer leave, helping on Hungarians farms, and would not return until July 25. And as reflected above in Mak's reporting of the Vienna press, there was no public clamor for retaliation for weeks after the assassinations. Although the honor of his empire demanded that Franz Josef do something, he had to consult first with the Hungarian Prime Minister István Tisza, whose support was needed to commit the empire to war.[60] Initially, Tisza opposed waging war on Serbia, fearing Russia would intervene to protect their Slavic brothers. After weeks of debate, Tisza came around to support a harsh ultimatum that Serbia grant Austria-Hungary certain rights to intervene in its government. Germany's promise of support against Russia apparently decided the issue. Austria-Hungary's ultimatum was issued on July 23. Serbia was given just forty-eight hours to answer.

Swallowing hard, Serbia replied within the deadline on July 25, accepting all conditions except one—to allow foreign investigators on its territory. Instead of considering Serbia's humble reply a diplomatic victory, an old and tired Franz Josef succumbed to the war fever around him and decided on July 28 to sign a war manifesto against Serbia, which—issued in ten languages[61]—said in part:

> A series of murderous attacks, an organized, carefully prepared, and well carried out conspiracy, whose fruitful success wounded me and my loyal peoples to the heart, forms a visible bloody track of those secret machinations which were operated and directed in Serbia.
>
> The honor and dignity of my monarchy must be preserved unimpaired, and its political, economic, and military development must be guarded from these continual shocks…. Serbia has rejected the just and moderate demands of my Government and refused to conform to those obligations the fulfillment of which forms the natural and necessary foundation of peace in the life of peoples and States. I must therefore proceed by force of arms to secure those indispensable pledges which alone can insure [sic] tranquility to my States within and lasting peace without.[62]

Franz Josef's invocation of "the honor and dignity of my monarchy" is significant. Avner Offer's perceptive essay on honor and the 1914 war said, "Honor was a quality that every member of the aristocracy, the gentry, the higher professions, and the military possessed by virtue of their occupation and social station."[63]

To preserve honor was an end in itself. When honor was joined to the kingdom, individual lives mattered little. In her 1889 antiwar novel *Lay Down Your Arms*, Bertha von Suttner—winner of the 1905 Nobel Peace Prize—expressed the ideas' importance to an Austrian general speaking to the book's heroine: "My dear, a kingdom, a state, lives a longer and more important life than individuals do. They disappear, generation after generation, while the state expands still farther, grows into glory, greatness and power, or sinks and crumples up and disappears, if it allows itself to be overcome by other kingdoms. Therefore the most important and the highest aim for which any individual has to struggle, and for which he ought to be glad to die, is the existence, the greatness and the well-being of the kingdom."[64]

Today, "honor" has relatively little importance in public opinion as a social value. A computer search for the terms "important" and "honor" in 600,000 polling questions asked in the United States since the 1930s turned up only five using both terms and only one question that was remotely relevant. It was in a 1980 survey about the occupation of the American Embassy in Teheran and asked: "If it comes down to it and we had to choose, which do you think is more important in settling the hostage situation in Iran— to preserve the lives of the 52 hostages or to preserve the honor of the United States?"[65] A majority of respondents (52 percent) thought that preserving hostages' lives was more important than preserving the nation's honor (35 percent). A separate search for "values" found an open-ended question in a Gallup 2012 survey that asked, "In your view, what is the most important problem with the state of moral values in the country today?"[66] Gallup grouped responses into 21 categories, none mentioning honor. Only 4 percent of respondents chose the closest category, "Dishonesty-Integrity-Deception." That "honor" is rarely mentioned in sample surveys suggests that people no longer regard it as an important moral value.

That was not the case in the late 19th and early 20th centuries in the Habsburg dynasty, which still practiced a chivalric code of conduct from medieval times. István Deák's book on the Habsburg officer corps, 1848–1918, devotes a chapter to its "Latter-Day Knights," which stated, "Behavior of Habsburg army officers, like that of officers of other dynastic armies, was regulated by a code of honor."[67] He quoted a "basic principle" from a military commentary—"the officer's honor must be protected at all costs"—that was ingrained in military officers, which included the emperors of all Great Powers in Europe. And no emperor behaved more like a military officer than Franz Josef. Regardless of cost, honor had to be maintained.

Consider this telling example: The chief of Serbia's general staff, General Radomir Putnik, happened to be in Budapest when Franz Josef declared war on Serbia at the end of July 1914. Austria-Hungary's high command wanted to intern its top enemy general. Franz Josef would have none of it. He ordered a special train to take Putnik back to Serbia, where he later commanded the force that defeated the invading Austro-Hungarian army.[68] Conrad, Austria-Hungary's chief of staff, quoted Franz Josef in his memoirs as saying, "If the Monarchy must die, then it must at least die with honor."[69]

Franz Josef had been warned that declaring war with Serbia would risk war with Serbia's protector, Russia. If Russia attacked Austria-Hungary, Germany would declare war on Russia—which would certainly bring France to the aid of Russia, her ally, and possibly invite Britain to support France and Russia against Germany. Even journalists outside of Europe anticipated that sequence of events. Figure 7.1, "The Chain of Friendships," reprints an American 1914 political cartoon of uncertain origin that succinctly captured the anticipated dynamics.[70] Despite such widespread expectation, the old Emperor hoped that his war with Serbia would be contained within the Balkans. That was not to be.

On July 29, the day after Emperor Franz Josef made his fateful decision, the Russian Tsar and his cousin, the German Kaiser, exchanged ten telegrams in English, their preferred common language.[71] John Röhl's exhaustive biography of Kaiser Wilhelm stated that his chancellor, Bethmann Hollweg, proposed telegramming the tsar to bolster the Kaiser's position in the crisis. The kaiser's telegram would shed guilt on Serbia and portray him as a man of peace.[72] Röhl's claim may be true, but the tsar actually sent the first telegram. Excerpts from this remarkable exchange between monarchs and relatives facing war testify to how they agonized over the decisions they alone could make. Here are excerpts by date and time of receipt:

Figure 7.1: THE CHAIN OF FRIENDSHIP. **"If Austria attacks Serbia, Russia will fall upon Austria, Germany upon Russia, and France and England upon Germany." That was the reasoning behind this prescient 1914 political cartoon, which succinctly captured the subsequent events. Credit: commons.wikipedia.org; in the public domain. Reportedly published by the *Brooklyn Eagle*, the cartoon was not found when searching the newspaper for June-August 1914.**

    1. Tsar to Kaiser: *29 July, 1 a.m.*—In this serious moment, I appeal to you to help me. An ignoble war has been declared to a weak country. The indignation in Russia shared fully by me is enormous. I foresee that very soon I shall be overwhelmed by the pressure forced upon me and be forced to take extreme measures which will lead to war.

    2. Kaiser to Tsar: *29 July, 1:45 a.m.* [sent 28 July; the Kaiser sent this telegram, intended to paint Serbia as the villain, before getting the previous one]—It is with the gravest concern that I hear of the impression which the action of Austria against Serbia is creating in your country. The unscrupulous agitation that has been going on in Serbia for years has resulted in the outrageous crime, to which Archduke Francis Ferdinand fell a victim. The spirit that led Serbians to murder their own king and his wife still dominates the country.... On the other hand, I fully understand how difficult it is for you and your government to face the drift of your public opinion.... I am exerting my utmost influence to induce the Austrians to deal honestly to arrive to a satisfactory understanding with you.

    3. Kaiser to Tsar: *29 July, 6:30 p.m.* [After receiving Nicholas's telegram #1, Wilhelm wrote again]—I received your telegram and share your wish that peace should be maintained. But as I told you in my first telegram, I cannot consider Austria's action against Serbia an ignoble war. Austria knows by experience that Serbian promises on paper are wholly unreliable.... I therefore suggest that it would be quite possible for Russia to remain a spectator of the Austro-Serbian conflict without involving Europe in the most horrible war she ever witnessed.

4. Tsar to Kaiser: *29 July, 8:20 p.m.*—Thanks for your telegram, conciliatory and friendly. Whereas official message presented today by your ambassador to my minister was conveyed in a very different tone. Beg you to explain this difference! It would be right to give over the Austro-Serbian problem to the Hague conference. I trust in your wisdom and friendship.

5. Tsar to Kaiser: *30 July, 1:20 a.m.*—Thank you heartily for your quick answer. Am sending [General] Tatischev this evening with instructions. The military measures which have now come into force were decided five days ago for reasons of defence on account of Austria's preparations. I hope from all my heart that these measures won't in any way interfere with your part as mediator which I greatly value. We need your strong pressure on Austria to come to an understanding with us.

6. Kaiser to Tsar: *30 July, 1:20 a.m.*—Best thanks for telegram. It is quite out of the question that my ambassadors language could have been in contradiction with the tenor of my telegram…. Austria has only mobilised against Servia & only a part of her army. If, as it is now the case, according to the communication by you & your Government, Russia mobilises against Austria, my rôle as mediator you kindly intrusted me with, & which I accepted at you[r] express prayer, will be endangered if not ruined. The whole weight of the decision lies solely on you[r] shoulders now, who have to bear the responsibility for Peace or War.

7. Kaiser to Tsar: *31 July*—On your appeal to my friendship and your call for assistance began to mediate between your and the Austro-Hungarian Government. While this action was proceeding your troops were mobilised against Austro-Hungary, my ally. Thereby, as I have already pointed out to you, my mediation has been made almost illusory…. I now receive authentic news of serious preparations for war on my Eastern frontier. Responsibility for the safety of my empire forces preventive measures of defence upon me…. The responsibility for the disaster which is now threatening the whole civilized world will not be laid at my door. In this moment it still lies in your power to avert it…. The peace of Europe may still be maintained by you, if Russia will agree to stop the milit. measures which must threaten Germany and Austro-Hungary.

8. Tsar to Kaiser: *31 July* [this one and the previous telegram crossed]—I thank you heartily for your mediation which begins to give one hope that all may yet end peacefully. It is technically impossible to stop our military preparations which were obligatory owing to Austria's mobilisation. We are far from wishing war. As long as the negotiations with Austria on Servia's account are taking place my troops shall not make any provocative action. I give you my solemn word for this. I put all my trust in Gods mercy and hope in your successful mediation in Vienna for the welfare of our countries and for the peace of Europe.

9. Tsar to Kaiser: *1 August*—I received your telegram. Understand you are obliged to mobilise but wish to have the same guarantee from you as I gave you, that these measures do not mean war and that we shall continue negotiating for the benefit of our countries and universal peace dear to all our hearts. Our long proved friendship must succeed, with God's help, in avoiding bloodshed. Anxiously, full of confidence await your answer.

10. Kaiser to Tsar: *1 August*—Thanks for your telegram. I yesterday pointed out to your government the way by which alone war may be avoided. Although I requested an answer for noon today, no telegram from my ambassador conveying an answer from your Government has reached me as yet. I therefore have been obliged to mobilise my army. Immediate affirmative clear and unmistakable answer from your government is the only way to avoid endless misery. Until I have received this answer alas, I am unable to discuss the subject of your telegram…. I must request you to immediatly [*sic*] order your troops on no account to commit the slightest act of trespassing over our frontiers.

Given that events had already spiraled out of the emperors' control, most histories of the Great War attach little importance to this exchange of telegrams.[73] For example, Dominic Lieven's 400-page book, *The End of Tsarist Russia*, ignored it completely. Lieven did cite a July 29 telegram from the Kaiser that said, "Everything possible must be done to save the peace," but that passage was not in the ten telegrams exchanged.[74] Nevertheless, these highly personal messages between cousins as monarchs of countries verging on war display their anguish better than the writings of any historian or journalist. The telegrams began warmly with salutations and were signed either "Nicky" or "Willy." Stripped of diplomatic language, they also stated—literally in plain English—their concerns after learning that Emperor Franz Josef declared war against Serbia on July 28.

One cannot read this exchange without sensing the anguish of both monarchs at the prospect of war between their countries. True, Kaiser Wilhelm previously had made bellicose remarks, but people characterized him as "big in words and weak in deeds."[75] These telegrams reveal a genuine desire to avoid war. Nicholas, a shy, quiet man so unlike his cousin, had experienced humiliating defeats by Japan. He too wished to avoid war. Both were pathetically unable to do so.

Faced with deciding whether to commit their nations to war, both monarchs carried burdens from past decisions. The kaiser was thought to have "given in" during the 1905–06 Morocco crisis.[76] Recalling that criticism, Wilhelm told the industrialist Krupp in early July, "This time I shall not give in."[77] The tsar, in turn, was painfully aware of his failure to support Serbia in 1908 when it threatened war over Franz Josef's annexation of Bosnia-Herzegovina. When Nicholas considered his options in 1914, his aide General Tatistchev said, "Yes, it is hard to decide," but the tsar vowed, "I will decide."[78]

In fact, both monarchs had already made decisions toward war. On July 26, the same day that Franz Josef assented to partial mobilization prior to declaring war on Serbia, the tsar consented to placing frontier fortresses on the Austrian and German borders in a "state of war."[79] On July 28, Russia announced a partial mobilization,[80] and on July 30, as he vowed, the tsar ordered general mobilization. On July 31, the kaiser ordered general mobilization too.[81] Winston Churchill explained that to generals, especially German generals, mobilization "spelt war."[82]

Within a week, all major European powers were at war.[83] On August 1, Germany declared war against Russia, and on August 3 against both France and Belgium. On August 4, England declared war against Germany. Before the end of August, the war spread to the Far East, as Japan declared war against Germany and Austria-Hungary. In October, war broke out in the near east, as Turkey declared war against Russia, France, and Britain. The year 1914 ended with Italy being the only European power not at war.

Italy, which had been allied with German and Austria-Hungary, soon turned on her former allies and declared war against Austria-Hungary in May 1915. Tiny San Marino quickly followed Italy and declared war against Austria-Hungary. Before the end of the year, Bulgaria was at war with Serbia and Montenegro with Bulgaria. By the end of 1916, Portugal and Romania became embroiled in the conflict. The United States declared war against Germany on April 6, 1917, but not against Austria-Hungary until December 7. By then, numerous Latin American countries joined the fray. Cuba, Panama, Brazil, Nicaragua, Costa Rica, Haiti, and Honduras declared war against Germany, Austria-Hungary, or both. For good measure, Greece, Siam, Liberia, and China also decided it was good politics to declare war against Germany, Austria-Hungary, or both. The Great War was indeed a world war.[84]

Living through the months when the war hideously unfolded throughout the world, Stefan Zweig wrote about "man's helplessness against world events" decided by "a dozen other persons whom one had not ever known or seen." He lamented, "They made decisions in which one had no part and the details of which one never heard and yet made final dispositions about my own life and every other life in Europe. My destiny lay in their hands, no longer permitted freedom or compelled slavery, and for millions like everybody else, defenseless as a fly, helpless as a snail, while life and death, my innermost ego, and my future were at stake, the forming thoughts in my brain, plans born and unborn, my waking and my sleep, my will, my possessions, my whole being."[85] Historians concur that Zweig's "dozen unseen persons" made many errors of judgment while deciding their way into World War I. To T.G. Otte, "The degree of professional incompetence displayed at St Petersburg, Berlin and Vienna during July 1914 was striking."[86] Winston Churchill viewed the matter somewhat differently, writing: "A situation had been created where hundreds of officials had only to do their prescribed duty to their respective countries to wreck the world. They did their duty." The emperors "felt themselves morally gripped by firm seconds who led them remorselessly to the duelling-ground, cautioned them against betraying weakness or nervousness on the field of honour, handed them the pistols and gave the signal to fire upon each other to their mutual destruction."[87]

Virtually all observers now—and most observers just after the outbreak of war—spread incompetence liberally across the relatively few persons who plunged their countries into a global war. But only three people—the emperor, the kaiser, and the tsar—had the power to choose between war and another course of action. The deciders decided for war. Having exercised their unique powers to start the war, all three divine authorities became irrelevant to waging it.

8

Peasants Under Arms

Anna Mozolák was pregnant in the spring of 1914 when she and Samko sailed from New York for Krajné. On June 3, she gave birth to a son, named Samuel, after his father. Mother and father were happy to be reunited with their twins, Ján and Zuzanna (no longer called John and Susanna, as named on their New York birth certificates). Thanks to working in New York for seven years, Samko and Anna were now sufficiently prosperous to provide for a more comfortable living in Slovakia.

For nearly a month after Samuel Junior was born, life was good. Then on June 28, 1914, his father's life was threatened by something that happened 500 miles away. Archduke Franz Ferdinand—whom Samko did not know and would not even have been entitled to meet—was assassinated in Sarajevo, Bosnia, the territory annexed by Emperor Franz Josef some years earlier. Given that Samko had left Austria-Hungary a young peasant with minimal education and was gone for seven years, he quite possibly did not even know who Franz Ferdinand was—that he was heir to the emperor's throne.

Samko may have responded the way Švejk did in the postwar Czech novel *The Good Soldier Švejk*, when hearing the charwoman say, "And so they've killed our Ferdinand."

"Which Ferdinand, Mrs. Müller?" he asked, going on with the massaging. "I know two Ferdinands. One is a messenger at Průša's, the chemist's, and once by mistake he drank a bottle of hair oil there. And the other is Ferdinand Kokoška who collects dog manure. Neither of them is any loss."

"Oh no, sir, it's his Imperial highness, the Archduke Ferdinand, from Konopiště, the fat churchy one."

"Jesus Maria!" exclaimed Švejk. "What a grand job! And where did it happen to His Imperial Highness?"

"They bumped him off at Sarajevo, sir, with a revolver, you know. He drove there in a car with his Archduchess."[1]

When Samko learned of the assassination, he probably did not consider that it would affect his life. Many Americans also must have had a hard time grasping the significance of killing an archduke in an obscure city, Sarajevo, over 4,000 miles away in a operetta-sounding place called Bosnia-Herzegovina. What was an archduke anyway? Why was one so important that his assassination should draw eighteen stories the next day in the June 29 *New York Times*? Unfamiliar with royal titles, most Americans today don't know that a British duke outranks an earl. (Or is it the other way around?) Some know that the Prince of Wales is next in line to be King of England, but the title, "archduke," is not used for British royalty and is uncommon even for European royalty.

Back then, archduke was a Habsburg title granted to royals who elsewhere would be princes. In fact, the title itself did not signify that Franz Ferdinand was heir to the

Austro-Hungarian throne. Austria had several archdukes—just as other monarchies had several princes. One needed to know something about Austro-Hungarian politics to understand that this particular archduke, Franz Ferdinand, was next in line to be Emperor of Austria and King of Hungary. Few who knew Franz Ferdinand liked him very much, and some disliked him intensely. Still, the honor of the Austro-Hungarian Empire required that someone pay dearly for his assassination.

Reactions to the archduke's assassination varied across countries and across peoples within countries. Great War historian Sean McMeekin wrote, "Franz Ferdinand had been unloved at court and not better liked in Viennese society. His murder was not so much mourned in the city as appreciated for its titillating shock value."[2] Historian Christopher Clark too reported "no outpouring of collective grief" in Vienna, where "[t]he meaning of the assassination was for most people essentially political rather than sentimental."

In Budapest, knowledgeable Magyars smiled at news of the assassination. They knew that Franz Ferdinand disliked Magyars and detested Hungary's power within the Dual Monarchy. In that city, Clark said, "many greeted with a sense of furtive relief the news that the nemesis of Magyardom had perished. But even here, the bourgeois press framed the event as a world-historical moment and fulminated against the suspected authors of the outrage."[3] Slavs in Hungary, however, regarded the archduke as an ally, one who would curtail Magyar rule. Upon assuming the throne, Franz Ferdinand (they hoped) might create a "Triple" Monarchy, with the empire's Slavs forming one part of the triad. Then the Austrian Germans and the Slavs in the new territory could together outvote the Magyars, thus avoiding the German-Magyar deadlock in the Dual Monarchy. Milan Hodža, one of only two Slovak members of the Hungarian parliament and later prime minister of Czechoslovakia, had consulted with the Archduke on such plans.[4] His laudatory obituary of Ferdinand in *Slovenský týždenník* [*Slovak Weekly*] began, "Unheard-of sorrow gripped the hearts and stunned the senses of the oppressed of Hungary....[5]

The possibility of war to avenge the assassination excited elements of the general population. One source said, "Hungary, too, like the other countries which became belligerents, was caught up in this war fever, while in Slovak villages fanatics ran about crying out in Magyar, '*Eljen a haboru!*" (Long live war!)"[6] No doubt, some young men, even young Slovaks, eagerly anticipated the glories of war, but many of the emperor's subjects feared that war meant personal hardships at home—in addition to fighting and dying on the battlefield. Because the government censored publications, the press in Austria-Hungary did not reflect popular opinion about going to war with Serbia over the assassination.

World War I historian A.J.P. Taylor wrote, "The war has been blamed on the peoples of Europe. The cheering crowds, it is said, gave the statesmen no choice and drove them into war." But, he says, that claim does not stand: "The crowds cheered only after the decisions had been made. There were none of the demonstrations, intended to make statesmen do something or not do something, that there were later in the 1930s and often are at the present day. In Austria-Hungary, for instance, the crowds cried 'Death to the Serbian dogs' only after war had been declared."[7]

One reading of Slovak opinion at the time comes from the 650,000 living in the United States by 1914, constituting "about one-quarter of all the world's Slovaks."[8] Konštantín Čulen wrote, "Slovaks in America immediately recognized that this was the final settlement of old accounts, and that the time was nearing at which the final solution of the most serious problem of Slovak life had to be solved."[9] Čulen did not present any hard evidence about Slovak opinion, but history professor Gregory Ference later analyzed the content of three different Slovak newspapers published in Pennsylvania from July to October 1914.[10] The papers were *Jednota* (Union) of the First Catholic Slovak Union; its chief rival, the secularist *Národné noviny* (National News) of the National Slovak Society, and the unofficial paper of the Slovak League; and *Slovenský hlásnik* (Slovak Herald) of the Lutheran Slovak Evangelical Union. These excerpts from Ference's study outline the shape of Slovak thought then.

- The assassination of the archduke shocked the American Slovaks. Prior to the death, some Slovaks believed that when Francis Ferdinand ascended the throne, he would become a foe to the concept of Austria-Hungary and the supremacy of the Magyars in Hungary. [pp. 1–2]
- By July 9, views toward the heir apparent began to change. Although the Slovak American press saw Francis Ferdinand as a potential benefactor of the Slovaks in Hungary, as it became evident that the Austro-Hungarian government started pursuing an anti–Serbian [line] which meant for the Slovaks an anti–Slavic policy, views changed on the late heir. Now he became a German of the Habsburg dynasty who with the Magyars had oppressed the Slovaks for centuries. [p. 2]
- The three newspapers quickly came to view the war and its causes as one of Slavdom versus Germanism. *Národné noviny* summed up the Slovak feeling: "The homeland did not attack anyone, but yes, it was driven by Berlin, threatening the life of all Slavdom. This is not a war of Austria-Hungary against Serbia, but this is a war of Germans against Slavs, therefore against us." [p. 5]
- The three weeklies at various times all predicted that the map of Europe would be altered by the partition or destruction of the Dual Monarchy upon the victory of the Allies, which the papers all believed would occur. [p. 8]
- *Národné noviny* concluded the possibility of an independent Slovakia whether under Russian protection or, in an intriguing proposal, united with the Czech Lands. It remarked that it did not consider the latter a good idea since it believed that the Slovak language and culture would then be assimilated in time by the immensely richer Czech culture. [p. 9]
- Lastly, as all fighting countries, the Habsburg Empire needed manpower and looked to its citizens abroad. The three newspapers warned their readers not to comply with the notifications of the Austro-Hungarian consulates, which appealed to reservists to return to fight. Shortly after the war began, *Jednota* advised Slovaks not to report for duty. [p. 15]
- *Národné noviny* urged its readers not to listen to the consulates: "Remember, that when you are here in America no one can force you to go home…. Do not go, although you would receive a hundred summons for this…. You are in America and Hungary cannot send gendarmes here after you." [p. 16]

Ference's analysis of contemporary Slovak newspapers in Pennsylvania echoed the July 28, 1914, demonstration organized by the Czech National Alliance on behalf of the Slavic community in Chicago on the day that Franz Josef declared war on Serbia. Leaders urged the crowd to write home to their friends and relatives, urging them "to resist conscription and, if resistance was not possible, to turn sides and fight with their Serbian brothers."[11]

Outside of Serbia, European governments (if not always their citizens) were repulsed by the Sarajevo assassinations on June 28 and were prepared to accept military retaliation by Franz Josef on Serbia. But Austria-Hungary took weeks to frame an official response. It finally came on July 25 in a humiliating ultimatum to Serbia that its framers intended to be unacceptable. By then, the sense of revulsion had lessened, and Austria-Hungary had lost its psychological advantage. Historian Geoffrey Wawro wrote: "Had the ultimatum been delivered a month earlier, on the heels of the assassination, it would have been greeted with international sympathy, but by now—several weeks after the murder—the slow march of this demarche was such that Austria had lost its early edge in the crisis. Moral outrage had faded."[12]

If the feeling of moral outrage had faded among European governments after a month, it probably vanished among those segments of Hungary's population expected to fight for the honor of the Empire. Indeed, few Magyars shed any tears initially over the death of Archduke Franz Ferdinand. If he had succeeded his old uncle as emperor, they fully expected him to curb Hungary's influence in the Dual Monarchy. In contrast to the Magyars in Hungary stood the Germans in Austria, who lost both a countryman and their future emperor. They were most likely to harbor thoughts of revenge.

In between the Magyar and German extremes stood the empire's nine other nationalities—the Czechs, Slovaks, Poles, Ruthenians, Romanians, Serbs, Croats, Slovenians, and Italians—who suffered political, economic, and social discrimination from their Austrian and Hungarian rulers. The general staff of the Austria-Hungarian army was not certain that new recruits would flock to the empire's cause in a battle against Slavic Serbia, given that most conscripts would be Slavs themselves.

Historians Richard Hamilton and Holger Herwig noted the ironic twist of events. The assassinated Archduke Franz Ferdinand was the most outspoken *opponent* of war with Serbia. He urged the Monarchy to "stay clear of Balkan entanglements" and regarded war with Serbia as "nonsense."[13] Hamilton and Herwig said, "A rash, impetuous act of murder committed by a teenager at Sarajevo on 28 June 1914 removed the Dual Monarchy's most influential and outspoken opponent of war with Serbia and, consequently, of war with Russia."[14]

For decades, the Austro-Hungarian army had been groomed to defend the crown against internal enemies, not foreign ones. Until the mid–19th century, other European countries also used their militaries to police disorderly public gatherings,[15] but the purpose of Austria-Hungary's army was far broader than policing. Hungarian scholar István Deák said that it was "to project the image of the throne and the army as the supreme guardians of citizens' peace, security, and prosperity," which "could be achieved much better by a traditional force, preferably on horseback in spectacular uniforms, with drawn sabers gleaming, than by a democratic mass army dressed in grey or khaki and armed with modern weapons. The Habsburg army's fabled brass bands and its officers in dazzling operetta costumes were worth many a modern division when it came to safeguarding domestic peace."[16]

Unthreatened with actually going to war, peasant lads regarded compulsory military service either as an unwelcome interference with their lives or as a welcome break from farm work, depending on their personal circumstances and spirit. Pieter Judson described some benefits of military service to the potential peasant: "Three years of regular pay, medical care, food and accommodation, some technical training that could prove useful for a later civilian career, exposure to other languages of the monarchy, and often the experience of serving in several regions of the monarchy."[17]

Few imagined they might actually *die* in the service of the emperor. Certainly Samko did not leave Krajné for New York in 1902 to avoid the possibility of being killed in battle when fulfilling his military service. True, he lied about his age in applying for permission to emigrate, saying that he was 17 when he was really 19 and thus soon eligible for service. But fear of dying was not the reason he sailed to America.

Twelve years later, Samko was back in Krajné in time for Emperor Franz Josef's declaration of war against Serbia on July 28, 1914.[18] Perhaps his village learned what was in store for its young males as the Slavic village in Timrava's novel *That Alluring Land* got the news:

> Just after midnight, the town drummer began to beat out his summons for a solemn proclamation.... He shifted around on his crooked legs, coughed, and began to roar like a lion.
> "It is hereby proclaimed that a telegram from the highest Royal and Imperial military authority announces that we have declared war on the Kingdom of Serbia! Therefore, every conscript between the ages of twenty and forty years must appear in the morning at the notary's office and go off at once to battle!"[19]

The next morning, several older gentlemen had already gathered at the notary's office:

> They were also affected by news of the war, but of course none of them had to go and fight. Their hearts beat with aroused manliness, their eyes burned with fervor, their faces flushed. Nothing was better than this war! Every man was overjoyed, it was what every patriot had longed for!
> "It had to come," said Mr. Baláň, a tall, still youngish, dark-haired man, as he raised his round chin victoriously. He was the notary of the county and the most enthusiastic of all. "Anything else is out of the question. This war is the salvation of our country!"[20]

Baláň was just over forty, so he felt protected by age—less certain by his position as notary—as he proclaimed: "'Everyone joyfully and proudly, yes, proudly, has to take up the sword. I'll go myself—we'll all go!' Baláň waved his hand like a valiant warrior and tossed his head. 'We'll beat Serbia in a day—they're a toy for us. It'll be magnificent to return home as victors!'"[21]

Among those in Austria-Hungary who knew about the impending war and who would be fighting whom, Baláň's prediction of quick victory was the prevailing opinion in the summer of 1914. After all, Austria-Hungary was historically one of Europe's Great Powers—along with Britain, France, Russia, and Germany. Indeed, Austria-Hungary had 51 million people versus Serbia's 4.5 million. Begun in the summer, the war would surely be over by Christmas. That was the widespread view across nations.[22] At age 32, Samko was too old to be called to duty immediately, but not having completed his military service may have put him at risk.

Ironically, many peasants who sailed to America hoping to avoid military service in their home countries found themselves subject to the military draft in the United States after it declared war on Germany, April 6, 1917. In *The Long Way Home*, David Laskin traced the lives and military contributions of twelve immigrants from Europe who served in the American armed forces during World War I.[23] As he noted, they were not isolated cases: "Some half a million other immigrants from forty-six different nations did the same. At the height of the nation's involvement in the worldwide conflict that became known as the Great War, fully 18 percent—nearly one in five—of the 4.7 million Americans in uniform had been born overseas."[24] Most who served in the U.S. military were conscripts, not volunteers, but that was not true of Matej Kocak, one of the twelve men featured in Laskin's book.

Matej Kocak was a Slovak from the village of Gbely, fewer than 40 miles due west of Krajné. Like Samko, Matej was born in 1882. Matej immigrated to the United States in 1907 five years after Samko, and settled in Binghamton, New York. Unlike Samko, who sought employment, Matej enlisted in the Marine Corps during peacetime the same year he arrived and reenlisted twice, eventually serving with great distinction in World War I.

After the U.S. declared war on Germany, Matej's cousin, Paul Kocak, whose family had also immigrated to Binghamton, was drafted into the army. Although the United States had declared war only on Germany, the Slovak emigrants understood that the U.S. was fighting the Central Powers, which included their homeland, Austria-Hungary. That inspired rather than worried them. Laskin wrote: "American Slovaks had been praying for months that the United States would enter the battle against Germany and the hated Austrian Empire, and after the declaration in April, support for the war became practically an article of faith. Slovak priests and community leaders stood shoulder to shoulder exhorting local boys to do their duty to their homeland and their adopted country, now joined in a single glorious cause. The Binghamton Slovak paper proudly printed the names of the twenty local Slovak boys who had volunteered to serve with the U.S. Army."[25]

Although Paul had not volunteered, he was still on track to fight for his new country. Laskin said:

> Binghamton's Slovak families, Kocaks among them, turned out en masse at Slovak Hall for a farewell banquet honoring the boys going to war. "Slovak men!" local luminary Imrich Mažár addressed the assembled. "Please keep in mind that you are sons of the great and oppressed Slovak nation…. We were not even allowed to say that we were oppressed in the old country, in the Austro-Hungarian Empire. It was only when we arrived in our new home, the free America which accepted us as its sons, that we started to yell aloud for the whole world to hear about our persecution." Mažár went on to remind the men that they would be fighting not only for their "new country, which accepted you as its sons" but also for the liberation and rights of "the Czecho-Slovak nation" that would emerge from the ashes of war. A Catholic priest blessed the new soldiers; their mothers wept; their fathers beamed with pride."[26]

Paul went off with a secret burden. His father, still in the old country, had been conscripted into the Austrian-Hungarian army, allied to Germany. After the United States declared war on Austria-Hungary on December 7, 1917, he might face his father in battle. Somehow the secret of his father's service came out after Paul completed boot camp. Private Kocak was then declared an enemy alien and received a general discharge from the army in September 1918, a year after he had entered it.

Paul's cousin, now Corporal Matej Kocak, had already shipped out for France on December 8, 1917, the day after the declaration of war against Austria-Hungary. On December 31, 1917—having turned 35 the day before—he began his service in France with 66th (C) Company, 5th Marine Regiment, 2nd Division. Chapter 14, "Peasant Gains," will tell how Matej became another datum, but an illustrious one, in the deadly statistics of World War I.

Samko had eluded military service twelve years earlier as a young man just prior to his 20th birthday. Now at age 32 with a wife and three young children, he was immune to the five factors that historian Niall Ferguson said motivated British men (and presumably men in other countries) to volunteer for the war in great numbers:

1. *Successful recruitment techniques:* Speeches exhorting national defense; posters, leaflets; military bands

2. *Female pressure:* Women shunning men not in uniform, even accusing them of cowardice.

3. *Peer-group pressure:* Friends, neighbors, and colleagues pledging to join up together.

4. *Economic motives:* Unemployed men welcomed the food, clothing, and shelter.

5. *Impulse:* Volunteering with little thought of the consequences—or causes—of the war.[27]

Even Stefan Zweig, the Viennese writer and intellectual who abhorred violence, wrote of the city's prewar atmosphere:

> And to be truthful, I must acknowledge that there was majestic, rapturous, and even seductive something in this first outbreak of the people from which one could escape only with difficulty. And in spite of all my hatred and aversion for war, I should not like to have missed the memory of those first days. As never before, thousands and hundreds of thousands felt what they should have felt in peacetime, that they belonged together. A city of two million, a country of nearly fifty million, in that hour felt they were participating in world history, in a moment which would never recur, and that each one was called upon to cast his infinitesimal self into the glowing mass, there to be purified of all selfishness. All differences of class, rank, and language were flooded over at that moment by the rushing feeling of fraternity.[28]

Of course, Zweig was reporting the cheers in Vienna, Austria's capital city. In the countryside, reactions were muted. Max Hastings wrote, "Rural communities of all nationalities were stunned if not profoundly dismayed; most of those who cheered in the streets were the urban young, without responsibilities."[29] Niall Ferguson referred to photographic evidence of celebrations in European cities that showed mostly middle class demonstrators.[30] Nevertheless, Hungarian Dániel Szabó claimed that war support "increased with the isolation of the village and the consequent lack of information."[31] Joy at the prospect of defending the empire was undoubtedly less in non–Magyar farms and villages, especially among Slovak peasants who would have to fight on behalf of their oppressive rulers. Szabó also said that "the sentiment was much weaker or entirely absent among the peasant farmers who had returned from America." Of course, Samko had just returned.

In a trivial sense, Samko had actually reduced his required military service by sailing to New York in 1902. Back then, the term of active duty was three years. In 1912, the Austria-Hungary government reduced active duty to two years, but it extended the reserve obligation from seven to as much as twenty-seven years. The changes were calculated to increase the army's size in case of war. Depending on their ages during their active duty, men could be recalled up to age 50.[32] While men that age could be recalled in *theory*, people never thought they would actually *be* called given Austria-Hungary's strength, Serbia's weakness, and the inevitability of the war's concluding by Christmas.

Unfortunately, the war was not going according to Austria-Hungary's plans—or rather, according to its hopes. Franz Josef had hoped that the war could be localized: Austria-Hungary v. Serbia—a *mano-a-mano* contest between his mighty army and a weak one fighting for Alexander, Regent of Serbia. If the war were not localized—Russia entering to defend Serbia—his generals hoped that Germany would furnish enough forces to help defeat the Russian hordes. Both hopes were crushed. The war was not localized, and Germany did not provide enough troops to prevent Austria-Hungary from being engaged in bitter battles against Russian troops.

Within weeks, reports of casualties filtered back to the countryside. Back in the Slavic village in Timrava's novel, many of the same older men gathered in the house of Stepka, one of the village's wealthier residents.

They were all grave. Their enthusiasm for the war had cooled off, and the fire in their eyes had died out. Old Stepka, with his long nose, still hated and wanted to destroy the enemy, as was proper, but in his own mind it was already "Devil take the war!" His own son was there.... He had left enthusiastically enough, and his letters came often, but now he was writing not of the glories of fighting for the fatherland but of the suffering, and he praised the comforts of home.

Baláň also no longer burned with such fervor for the war as before. It was true he still sometimes cried out, "We'll all go off to war, bravely ahead!"—but now it sounded somehow forced. In his mind was rising the fear whether he himself might in fact go off. Older and older men were being drafted, even those who had been classified unfit. The doctors were choosing, sorting over, but in the end taking everyone, so it really could happen that we'll all go off.[33]

Days later, another telegram arrived and Baláň asked:

> "What's in it?"
> "All men between the ages of twenty-five and forty-five have to report for examination," said Siricky. His words were scarcely out when Baláň slid flat onto the floor.[34]

Timrava's fiction faithfully reflected the facts, which were detailed by historian István Deák: "Early losses were staggering. Within a few months, approximately 80 percent of the original standing army had become casualties; in the first year of the war, 2,738,500 men were lost to death in battle, epidemics, frostbite, wounds, or captivity. This was more than six times the number of men in the peacetime army of 450,000. The effect on the army and the population can be easily imagined. As active-service soldiers and reservists gradually disappeared, their places were taken by youngsters and older men or men formerly considered unfit for service, all of them trained in haste."[35]

Everyone expected the war would be over by Christmas, but it was not. Samko was called sometime in 1914[36] and reported to the 15th Hungarian *Honvéd* regiment headquartered in Trenčín, thirty miles away. Most of the conscripts in Samko's *Honvéd* regiment were Slovak peasants from the land surrounding Trenčín. Military historian J.S. Lucas listed Trenčín's 15th *Honvéd* as the only predominantly Slovak regiment out of the 32 original regiments in 1914.[37] Four others were identified as Magyar-Slovak, but only the 15th *Honvéd* was Slovak. Indeed, most of the 32 regiments represented mixes of nationalities. Samko's Slovak regiment was combined with its sister regiments, the 13th at Pozsony and the 14th at Nitra (both Slovak-Magyar) to form the 37th *Honvéd* Infantry Division (HID) with headquarters in Pozsony. It was the only division in the Austro-Hungarian army with a Slovak majority.[38]

Austro-Hungarian authorities initiated an enormous increase in the size of their army. Existing law before July 1914 anticipated an army of 240,000 by 1918.[39] After the outbreak of war against Serbia, authorities planned for an army of over 3,000,000.[40] At that time, Austria-Hungary had a population of about 50 million. Given that half of the population was women, more than ten percent of all males would need to serve to create an army of 3 million. Virtually every male between 20 and 45 was at peril of fighting in the war.

The Austro-Hungarian military was pleasantly surprised that their ill-treated minorities gave little resistance to conscription. As Zweig wrote: "Then the people had unqualified confidence in their leaders; no one in Austria would have ventured the thought that the all-high ruler Emperor Franz Josef, in his eighty-third year, would have called his people to war unless from direct necessity, would have demanded such a sacrifice of blood unless evil, sinister, and criminal foes were threatening the peace of the Empire."[41] Unfortunately, few Austro-Hungarian officers gave minority recruits reason to give their all for their emperor. Writing about the Eastern Front, Norman Stone said: "But 'equality before supreme sacrifice' had a way of becoming equality before supreme incompetence. Czech soldiers, largely urban, literate and questioning, were bewildered at the army's treatment of them as half-witted peasants; at the other end of the scale, Ruthene peasants resented having to fight Russians whose language they understood and whose religion they shared."[42]

Like recruits in every army, the Slovak peasants got prescribed haircuts (to 7 cm on top and 3 cm in back), and each was assigned barrack space (4.5 meters).[43] That was their introduction to army discipline. Like his new comrades, Samko got the standard military issue, which at the beginning of the war (when the empire still had abundant resources) was 60 pounds of clothing and equipment as itemized by Lucas[44]:

1	cap	1	cartridge box with fittings
1	jacket	1	Infantry style leather waist belt & buckle
1	overcoat	1	bayonet scabbard
1	pair trousers	2	Infantry pattern leather cartridge pouches
1	pair gaiters or puttees	1	leather rifle sling
1	shoulder roll	2	overcoat straps
2	sets of underclothing	2	pack straps
1	vest (cotton)	1	haversack (known as a bread bag)
1	(ditto) pair pants	1	aluminum water bottle
1	neck cloth	1	identity document in brass case
2	pairs of boots (light, heavy)	1	set eating utensils
1	pair woolen gloves	1	part of a tent
1	hide knapsack	1	set cleaning brushes.

Concerning firearms, Lucas stated: "Arms carried were normally the M95 magazine rifle, issued for all ranks from Corporal downwards, although in some cases the older rifle 88/90 was distributed, 1 bayonet. Each man carried 120 rounds of ammunition (40 of which were kept in the cartridge pouches, 80 in the cartridge box, under the knapsack). In every section there were 6 men equipped with a spade, two men with picks and one man with a wire cutter. Two pairs of flat pliers were also carried."

Simply listing a soldier's standard equipment illustrates the complexity of equipping an army, even a hundred years ago. Multiply this list by three million—the size of Austria-Hungary's army at all ranks when war came[45]—and it underscores the enormousness of the task. Most conscripts were unfamiliar with rifles and cartridges, and many never owned clothing that matched—much less two sets of underclothing and two pairs of boots. Before billeting in their barracks, they may never have lived in buildings with electric lights and running water. Having a personal aluminum water bottle was both a novelty and a luxury.

Also, these Slovak recruits probably had little knowledge about whom they would be fighting and why. As they marched away in the summer of 1914, soldiers of the 2nd battalion of the Prague-based 28th Infantry Regiment pasted a slogan on their wagons, "*Jdem na Srby a nevime proč*" ("Off to fight the Serbs, we don't know why!").[46] Watson said that other Czech soldiers sported a similar slogan, "We are marching against the Russians and we do not know why."[47]

Samko was probably like other Slovak recruits in not understanding whom he was fighting and why, but in other respects, he was not like the Slovak peasants in his regiment. He was certainly older than most. He had lived and flourished in New York, the new world's greatest and most modern city. He had ridden New York's subway, shopped its stores, experienced electric lighting, and enjoyed the benefits of running water and flushing toilets. He also understood and spoke some English, which was an ability shared by less than 2 percent of infantry officers and by less than 20 percent of officers on the general staff in 1904.[48]

Perhaps Samko's worldly accomplishments only made him an outcast; they certainly made him different from others in his outfit, but he was just as ignorant about the war. He also was like them in that he spoke Slovak. Since it was designated a Slovak unit, the 15th *Honvéd*'s language of command was Slovak—although its commander was almost certainly Magyar. That was convenient for life in Samko's regiment while it was in its barracks, but it was not functional for the regiment when it mixed with other Austro-Hungarian troops in the field, who most likely spoke a different language and whose officers were apt to give commands in German.

An army's performance depends in a major way on the effectiveness of communication among its components—troops must communicate effectively with one another, as well as officers, who must communicate effectively with their troops. Communication is aided when troops and officers speak a common language. Germany's army was composed mainly of German soldiers and nearly all spoke German. Russia's army was composed mainly of Russians and nearly all spoke Russian or related Slavic languages like Polish or Ukrainian. France's army was composed mainly of Frenchmen and nearly all spoke French. Britain's army of English, Scottish, and Welsh soldiers virtually all spoke English—so too did most of the two million volunteers from its territories, including the one million–plus from India. Serbia's army was composed mainly of Serbians and nearly all spoke Serbian or a related Slavic language like Croatian.

The Austrian-Hungarian army was different. It was composed of troops who spoke eleven different languages and officers who spoke different languages from their troops. War historian John Keegan estimates that its troops were "44 percent … Slav (Czech, Slovak, Croatian, Serb, Slovene, Ruthenian, Polish and Bosnian Muslim), 28 percent German, 18 percent Hungarian, 8 percent Romanian and 2 percent Italian."[49] The ethnic composition of the army's troops reveals only part of its nationalities problem. The other part is the overwhelmingly German composition of its officers. Prior to the war, Gunther Rothenberg, historian of Franz Josef's army, said: "Although Germans comprised only 24 percent of the total population and 25 percent of all ranks in the armed forces, they provided over 70 percent of all regular and 60 percent of all reserve officers. In the reserves Magyars constituted 24 percent and Czechs 10 percent. The rural nationalities—Galicians, Ukrainians, and Rumanians—contributed only insignificant numbers statistically."[50]

One suspects that the German and Magyar officers in 1914 regarded their non–German and non–Magyar charges as inferior—as did the military historian, J.S. Lucas, writing 40 years ago: "There were pronounced differences between the mental levels of the races within the Dual Monarchy and a higher proportion of the more intelligent Hungarian, Czech and German peoples was to be found in the cavalry, the artillery and the technical branches of the Army than in the infantry, 67 percent of whose total strength was made up of Slavs."[51] A charitable interpretation of Lucas's rating Slavs at a different "mental level" would be that he intended to say that the Slavs—especially the Slovaks, Serbs, and others living in Hungary—had inferior education, largely as a result of its Magyarization policy described in Chapter 2. Indeed, Lucas specifically acknowledged "Magyar hatred and oppression of its Slav minorities." He also noted that the infantry was composed of rural folk having little contact with modern society:

Most of them were peasants, accustomed from birth to early rising and to long hours of hard toil for a small wage. Their endurance was incredible and their demands small. Banded together in regiments they moved, during their period of service, from the Depot in which they received their basic training, to a battalion in some part of the vast Empire. In many cases the Regimental Depot was not in the regimental recruiting area. This was done to discourage desertion and to ensure that the loyalty of the soldiers was not undermined by fraternisation with civilians. The soldiers were, therefore, stationed among people whose language they did not speak. In their regiment, possibly even in their battalion, would be men of other nations and the presence of these aliens acted as a spur to encourage the men to compete, militarily, against each other.[52]

As serious as the language problem was, military historian Lucas believed that the more critical problem was an outgrowth of the 1867 Compromise that created the Dual Monarchy.[53] Austria-Hungary was saddled with not two but three armies. As will be described at length in the next chapter, "Imperial Armies," there was the joint or common army, under personal command of Emperor Franz Josef. There was also an Austrian army, the *Landwehr,* and a parallel Hungarian army, the *Honvéd,* in which Samko Mozolák served. All three armies were funded by agreement by the Austrian and Hungarian parliaments. In theory, all were ostensibly under the emperor's ultimate command. In practice, the Hungarian *Honvéd* charted a separate course. For example, Norman Stone said that Hungarian landowners commandeered troops to help with the harvest, occupying the efforts of a half a million troops in 1915, as the war raged.[54]

Erich Maria Remarque was neither a Slovak nor a peasant. He was a German university student who was drafted into World War I at age 18, wounded in battle, and survived to write *All Quiet on the Western Front* (*Im Westen nichts Neues*). His 1929 novel quickly became a best-seller. It was translated into twenty-five languages, sold over thirty million copies, and made into a movie, which won the Academy Award for Best Picture in 1930. Although Remarque wrote about the Western Front from a German soldier's perspective, his observations bear upon the experiences of peasants forced to take up arms in defense of Austria-Hungary.

Remarque classified his fellow troops by age groups: "All the older men are linked up with their previous life. They have wives, children, occupations, and interests, they have a background which is so strong that the war cannot obliterate it. We young men of twenty, however, have only our parents, and some, perhaps, a girl—that is not much, for at our age the influence of parents is at its weakest and girls have not yet got a hold over us. Besides this there was little else—some enthusiasm, a few hobbies, and our school. Beyond this our life did not extend."[55] Remarque acknowledged that young men like him "had no definite plans for the future."[56]

Samko Mozolák at 32 had definite plans for his future. He and his wife Anna had just returned to his home village of Krajné with money earned from working seven years in New York City. They had recently been reunited with their eight-year-old twin U.S. citizens, Ján and Zuzanna, and they had an infant son, Samuel, born that June in Krajné. They planned to improve the Mozolák family's land holdings and live a prosperous life in their village before he was drafted into Hungary's *Honvéd.* He knew far more about the world than other troops, including his officers, and yet he did not really know what the war was about, why he had been pulled from his home village to fight for the honor of the Habsburgs.

Samko must have had thoughts similar to Jozef Vinich, a Slovak soldier in Andrew Krivak's novel, *The Sojourn.* Vinich was born and raised in Colorado. A family tragedy forced him to return with his father to rural Austria-Hungary prior to the Great War.

After war started, he was in the Habsburg army on the Italian Front and wondering if he, a Slovak, was fighting on the right side: "What was a Czecho-Slovak to me, though, a boy raised among Carpathian peasants in a Magyar culture, professing loyalty in a poor school to a Habsburg, and speaking a language in secret they spoke in a land called America? What could those Czech propagandists tell me about nationality? Yet, on and on they went, the Bohemian officers of the legionnaires, telling us that the Hungarian king had kept us in his pocket for centuries, that our own nation was a right to us, and that a Czecho-Slovak division was already being trained to fight against the Austrians in the mountains."[57]

Vinich was not alone in his confusion. Arthur May reported this entry in the diary of a Hungarian officer: "They abuse me for not being a patriot. I was born a Slovak. I passed my infancy in Vienna, my early youth in Bohemia, two years at Budapest, three years in Switzerland and then Paris—and after that a poor devil is expected to know what he really is and actually to be an Austrian patriot."[58]

Soldiers on both sides wondered what the war was about. In Alexander Solzhenitsyn's novel *August 1914*, a hospitalized ensign asked why Russia sought to defend Serbia: "'War of liberation'! They call it that just to work on people's emotions. 'Save our brothers the Serbs from the hands of Austria!' So they're sorry for the Serbs, are they? We oppress all the non–Russian people in the empire but we don't seem to feel sorry for them."[59]

German soldiers in *All Quiet on the Western Front* also questioned why they were fighting the French. On the occasion of a visit from Kaiser Wilhelm, soldiers wondered whether there would have been a war if the Kaiser had said, "No." Remarque answered:

> "I'm sure there would," I interject, "he was against it from the first."
> "Well, if not him alone, then perhaps if twenty or thirty people in the world had said No."
> "That's probable," I agree, "but they damned well said Yes."
> "It's queer, when one thinks about it," goes on Kropp, "we are here to protect our fatherland. And the French are over there to protect their fatherland. Now who's in the right?"[60]

Later, their conversation again turned to the origin of the war:

> "…almost all of us are simple folk. And in France, too, the majority of men are labourers, work-men, or poor clerks. Now just why would a French blacksmith or a French shoemaker want to attack us? No, it is merely the rulers. I had never seen a Frenchman before I came here, and it will be just the same with the majority of Frenchmen as regards us."
> "They weren't asked about it any more than were."[61]

Rulers in any country—then or now—never ask "simple folk" whether they want war. But at least today rulers have reliable ways to estimate public opinion. At that time—before sample surveys—there was no reliable way to do so. Public opinion was defined by national newspapers, which also shaped it according to business interests, political inclinations, newsstand sales, and governmental dictates. If "the people" were enraged by Archduke Ferdinand's assassination in Sarajevo, the Vienna press did not capitalize on their ire. According to Geert Mak in Chapter 7, "Imperial Deciders," the *Neue Freie Presse* carried no stories clamoring for war with Serbia in the weeks following the event.

Christopher Clark wrote, "It remained unclear how the public opinion within artic-ulate elites with direct access to the press related to the attitudes prevailing among the masses of the population. War scares and jingo campaigns made good newspaper copy, but how socially deep were they?"[62] Later, Clark noted that politicians realized that "the press was the instrument of foreign policy"; however, "this did not prevent policy-makers from taking the press seriously as an index of opinion."[63]

In her biographical survey of the cousin emperors—George, Wilhelm, and Nicholas—Miranda Carter contended that by the mid–1890s, European newspapers were "more politicized, more engaged by international affairs, more aware of themselves as organs of public opinion, and much more aggressive." All three emperors began to think "that what foreign newspapers said about one was an accurate measure of how one was regarded abroad."[64] That was in spite of the symbiotic relationship that existed between their own government and their own press.[65] Clark went further, saying, "Some monarchs and statesmen were positively obsessive about the press and spent hours each day poring through cuttings."[66]

Sizable portions of simple folk in Central Europe, illiterate or unschooled, did not follow or understand international politics. Historian Stephen Fischer Galati held that the common people "had little if any knowledge of the maneuvers and deals made by politicians with the European powers as the price of participation in the war."[67] Although peasants and workers were not asked whether they wanted to go to war with their neighbors, Galati said that they went obediently and fought well: "The most remarkable feature of the military actions of World War I in East Central Europe was the dedication of the rank and file to the causes for which they fought. Whether the soldiers fought for the kaiser, the tsar, or the various kings of the countries of southeastern Europe, they did so with courage and tenacity."[68] Men went most obediently and fought best in the early stages of the war, when everyone believed that it would be short—over by Christmas, they predicted. When people realized that the war, which started in the summer, would last through the winter, enthusiasm began to wane.

9

Imperial Armies

Austro-Hungarian Emperor Franz Josef, German Kaiser Wilhelm II, and Russian Tsar Nicholas II considered themselves soldiers. They were by law their armies' supreme commanders and viewed their armies as *imperial* armies—their personal domains. Of the three, Franz Josef had the most personal impact on the functioning of his army—one-quarter German, one-fifth Hungarian, and the rest (a majority) composed of subjects from more than nine nationality groups, all subject to varying degrees of political oppression.

Echoing other historians of the era, J.S. Lucas rationalized how a polyglot collection of antipathetic groups could form a cohesive fighting force. He says that they did it for Emperor Franz Josef:

> The inability or the unwillingness of the various national groups to tolerate each other would, perhaps, have been almost impossible of resolution under any other form of government than a Monarchy, and the Austrian solution to this problem had been a simple, almost feudal, but very effective one: direct and personal loyalty to the Emperor who, as Head of the Army, was himself a soldier. The loyalty of the Army was focussed upon and centered around the person of the Monarch, representing the traditional Dynasty, and all ranks of the Armed Forces were deeply aware of the affection in which the ruling family held them. This two-way loyalty, from the Army to the military structure and the Sovereign and from him back to them, this paternalism, permeated the whole military structure and was reflected in the officers' treatment of their men.[1]

Writer Gordon Brook-Shepherd said, "At the turn of the century, citizens could not imagine life without Franz Josef, who had reigned for 52 years. Indeed, economic times were good. Not as good as in Germany, but good."[2] Joseph Redlich, Franz Josef's political contemporary, concurred: "Nor can any Austrian who lived through the period of his latter age deny that, with the years, the aged Emperor enjoyed great personal popularity and genuine respect among the mass of the population."[3] Gunther Rothenberg, who studied Franz Josef's army in great detail, summed up the situation at his death in 1916: "While the old emperor had lived, he had constituted a strong cohesive force almost by sheer habit. When Francis Josef passed away, one of he basic foundations of the unity of the realm, affection for the venerable old emperor rather than for the supranational principle he symbolized, also passed and long pent-up forces were released."[4]

The theme of loyalty to Emperor Franz Josef is often cited to explain why soldiers from oppressed nationalities led by officers from ruling minorities did not rebel more often and earlier. Nevertheless, Slavic and Italian soldiers rebelled often enough and early enough to affect the army's performance in the war. Franz Josef's Austrian commanders were not confident of their Slavic troops' loyalty in campaigns against Russians on the

Russian Front and against Serbians on the Balkan Front, and they doubted their Italian troops' loyalty against Italy on the Italian Front. Postwar analyses portrayed a mixed picture of the military performance of the different nationalities. Keegan wrote:

> [T]he Germans were always dependable, if some never wholly enthusiastic; the Hungarians, non–Slavs and privileged co-equals, remained reliable until defeat stared them in the face at the end; the Catholic Croats had a long record of loyalty to the empire, which many of them maintained; the Poles, hating the Russians, distrusting the Germans and enjoying large electoral and social privileges under the Habsburgs, were *Kaisertreu*; the Bosnian Muslims, sequestered in special, semi-sepoy [native] regiments, were dependable; the Italians and the rest of the Slavs, particularly the Czechs and Serbs, lost the enthusiasm of mobilisation quickly. Once war ceased to be a brief adventure, the army became for them "a prison of the nations," with the ubiquitous German superiors acting as gaolers.[5]

And dark days of defection and defeat were to come. When war began at the end of July 1914, Austria-Hungary was assembling an army of three million men. Unfortunately, its army was encased in a tripartite military structure designed to serve the bifurcated political structure of the Dual Monarchy. The military picture was further confused by using two official languages and nine or so other languages spoken by the troops who would serve. Using German and Magyar terms to describe the structure helps illustrate its complexity.

First, as Austrian war historian Peter Jung explained, there was the common army and navy, institutions representing the military power of both components of the Dual Monarchy. Their titles were usually expressed in German because they were under the direct command of Emperor Franz Josef. They were the *kaiserliches und königliches gemeinsames Heer* and the *kaiserliches und königliches Kriegsmarine* (in English, the Imperial and Royal Common Army, and the Imperial and Royal Navy). The German phrase *kaiserliches und königliches* was often written as *k.u.k.—kaiser* for Franz Josef as Emperor of Austria and *könig* for King of Hungary. The common or joint army was called the *k.u.k.*[6]

Then there were separate military institutions within each country. The *k.k. Landwehr* (Imperial Royal Territorial Force) operated on the Austrian side, and the *Imagyar király Honvédseg* (Royal Hungarian Army) on the Hungarian side. It was usually called simply the *Honvéd* (army). The common army had far more troops than the territorial forces, and enlistees preferred the more professional and better-equipped common army. In theory, men who presented themselves for the draft were assigned by ballot to the common army or—depending on their residence—to either the Austrian or Hungarian territorial forces.[7] Jung said, "To make it even more complicated, the administration was shared by three ministries. The *k.u.k. Kriegsministerium*, with a special Naval Section, was responsible for the Common Army, and ministries for 'home defence' for the *Landwehr* and the *Honvéd* existed simultaneously in Vienna and Budapest; naturally, each of the home defence and territorial forces and ministries used its own principal language."[8]

According to Holger Herwig, "The language of command was German for the *k.u.k.* Joint Army and the *Landwehr*; Magyar for the *Honvéd*; and Croatian for the reserves of Bosnia and Herzegovina." Army regulations "stipulated formal command, service, and regimental languages to be used by each of the eleven ethnic nationalities."[9] German officers communicated among themselves in German, and (in theory) they were to command any non–Germanic troops (i.e., most of their troops) in their native languages. So the language of instruction depended on the ethnic composition of the regiment, "any unit having more than 20 percent of its total strength in one racial group was permitted to have instruction in that language."[10]

Unfortunately, most of the units used more than one language, according to military historian Gunther Rothenberg: "In 1901 out of 256 units of the common army, 94 employed but one language, 133 used two languages, and 28 authorized the use of three or even four languages. And in Hungary, except for the purely Magyar units, there were 20 regiments employing their various national languages: 2 Slovak, 3 Rumanian, 6 German-Magyar, 1 German-Slovak, 3 German-Rumanian, 5 Magyar-Slovak, 6 Magyar-Rumanian, and even 1 Magyar-Rumanian-Ruthene regiment."[11] Geoffrey Wawro's study of the Habsburg Empire in the Great War underscored the problem of communication within the army. There was a huge difference between prescription and practice:

> In Hungary, languages other than Magyar were simply banned. In Austria, foreign military attaches noticed that the multilingual ideal was rarely attained in practice; theoretically, the men in a Slovenian regiment, for example, would speak Slovenian among themselves but be commanded in German. The troops therefore learned a few dozen phrases in German, but officers in such a regiment were expected to be fluent in Slovenian in order to explain complicated matters and build esprit de corps with their men. In reality, the largely German officer corps would lean hard on cheat sheets like *Military Slovenian: A Handbook*, which contained useful phrases including "Shut your mouth," "Don't speak unless spoken to," "No smoking in the stables," and "Do you still not understand?"[12]

The longstanding language problem showed up in many ways. Rothenberg, who specialized in the history of Franz Josef's army, related an incident in 1897: "Czech nationalists started a campaign asking that recruits called up for muster but not yet in uniform should answer roll call with *Zde* instead of *hier*. Though trivial, at the time it was considered a serious attack on the German language of command. As usual, the military authorities overreacted and the emperor too was adamant. During a state dinner he told a Czech delegate that 'on the *Zde* issue I can see no compromise. If necessary I will proclaim martial law to settle this business, because I am very strict in military matters.'"[13]

Because of these language problems, Austro-Hungarian military leaders feared resistance, if not revolt, by the non–German and non–Magyar population—which comprised half the empire—to increased conscription at the start of the war. They were surprised to find little opposition. To the contrary, wrote historian Norman Stone: "In reality, the peoples' enthusiasm for the Monarchy, when war broke out, took the authorities themselves by surprise. IV Army command reported of its journey through Bohemia in August 1914 that 'the behaviour of the populace, of all nationalities, was the best conceivable throughout our journey. Patriotic feeling was everywhere in evidence, and at the larger stations the troops were given bread tea cigarettes etc. by women of all classes.' Men of all nationalities hoped—in accordance with official pronouncements—that now at last they would be regarded as equals by the German and Hungarian establishment, not just as tolerable minorities."[14]

According to István Deák, distribution of nationalities in the Emperor's Joint Army, the *k.u.k.*, closely matched the population distribution. Slovaks represented 3.8 percent of people in Austria-Hungary in 1910, and they were 3.6 percent of the rank-and-file in the *k.u.k.*[15] Hungarian observers saw a "big difference" between Emperor Franz Josef's *k.u.k.* and King Franz Josef's Hungarian *Honvéd*. In Jozef Cíger-Hronský's novel *Jozef Mak*, recruit Mak learned that the Emperor had "an old army with a polished name, but the King has only raw honveds."[16] The *k.u.k.* also was more tolerant toward Slovaks and other Slavs than the Magyar *honvéd*. Yet even the *k.u.k.* had no measurable percentage of Slovak officers; even Ruthene officers computed to 0.2 percent.[17]

The history of the *Landwehr* and the *Honvédseg* is also significant. Formed after the 1867 Compromise that created the Dual Monarchy, these institutions were supposed to reflect the duality in the empire's military forces. From a military standpoint, political duality works against military cohesion. Writing on military culture, Peter Wilson stated, "Centralisation and military cohesion are clearly linked. Decentralised states generally have similarly decentralised armed forces, often loosely organised without clear institutional identities."[18] So even if the two halves of the monarchy agreed in their political views, decentralization would have impaired military effectiveness. That their political views did not agree compounded the military problem.

From the beginning, according to Tibor Hajdu, the *Honvéd* harbored two conflicting political negatives.[19] One was that the first generation of Hungarian officers still hated Franz Josef for suppressing their 1848 uprising. The other was that Austrian leaders distrusted their fellow Hungarian citizens, fearing that they might employ the *Honvéd* and rise again against Austria. Hence, the Austrians allowed the Hungarian *Honvéd* to have only infantry and cavalry—not artillery. (The Austrian *Landwehr* also lacked artillery, but the Austrians controlled the Common army, which had all the big guns).

By the turn of the century, Magyars came to value their *Honvéd* as a Hungarian institution, and it won some use of Hungarian as a language of command in addition to German. On the other side of the Dual Monarchy, prominent Austrian military and governmental officials still distrusted the *Honvéd*. Éva Somogyi quoted the Austrian prime minister, Ernest Köber, as believing "that the Dual Monarchy was not yet strong enough to survive the 'independent Hungarian army' that would be the 'inevitable consequence of the creation of a *Honvéd* artillery.'"[20] Nevertheless, Franz Josef eventually approved giving the *Honvéd* its heavy guns, saying, "The *Honvéd* artillery was not granted at the time of its creation because of the lack of trust…. Since that time the *Honvéd* has evolved in such a way that there is no longer any reason to entertain this sort of distrust."[21]

Although some Austrians allowed that the *Honvéd* deserved their trust, few Hungarians reciprocated the feeling. Somogyi wrote:

> In Hungary the joint army was in itself an object of opposition attacks, being an institution that all strata of Hungarian society considered the symbol of an alien and hostile power. This army, German in language of command and imbued with loyalty to the emperor, was seen as an impediment to Hungarian aspirations for full self-government and independent Great Power status and an obstacle to the social advancement of the country's gentry-minded middle class.
>
> …
>
> The joint army, moreover, was an institution in which Hungarians became just one among many nations, where Romanian and Slovak peasants from Hungary learned that there could be and were limits to Hungarian influence. The joint army—complained Count Albert Apponyi, who was to organize an opposition party on a platform of military reform—did not see to it that military education stressed Hungarian patriotism, national spirit, and attachment to the Hungarian state.[22]

The Austrian half of the Dual Monarchy valued the joint army for integrating recruits of different nationalities into the empire. Pieter Judson said that military service provided the "most influential point of contact between the Habsburg state and its male citizens" and "played a major role in inculcating male citizens from every region with a defined set of common practices and imperial ideologies."[23] Fearing that the joint army would accomplish precisely what the Austrians valued, the Hungarian parliament kept the joint army weak. Under the terms of the Dual Monarchy, both parliaments had to agree on its funding. István Deák wrote, "Many explanations could be offered for Austria-Hungary's failure to prepare even semiadequately for the war. To my mind, the primary one lies in the very nature of the Monarchy...." He continued, "Convinced, not without justification, that the officer corps was hostile to the Compromise of 1867 and viewing the army as an alien institution, Hungary's political leaders did their best, at least until 1912, to limit military expenditure. Because the Hungarians never achieved the same parity in military matters that they had obtained in foreign policy, they consistently voted against the expansion of the armed forces and against massive rearmament."[24]

Franz Josef's special problem was getting cooperation from the Hungarian half of his empire.[25] Under the 1867 Compromise, a common budget for both halves of the empire (which included military expenditures) had to be renegotiated every ten years. Typically, the Hungarian delegation resisted spending, at least any spending that would increase their own contributions. For example, the Hungarians in 1897 refused to pay 42 percent of the common budget as proposed by the Emperor's ministers, finally agreeing to raise their contribution from 31.5 to 34.4 percent.[26] The 1907 decennial negotiation threatened the defense of the empire, as the Hungarian team refused to support increased military spending.

Deák's assessment supports the claim that Emperor Franz Josef was in a state of denial about the merits of his Dual Monarchy, which concerning military affairs was more a "Dual Anarchy."[27] While the emperor persisted in defending the 1867 compromise as bolstering Austria-Hungary, Deák and others blamed the terms of the Dual Monarchy for undercutting its Great Power status. For example, historian Geoffrey Wawro wrote: "The Hungarians, determined to curb the power of Vienna, had kept the army so small since 1866 that it was ludicrously over-officered; with 20,000 officers for an army of 335,000 in 1913, it had the highest ratio of officers to troops of any great power, and these officers were changing in the first place, they were graying, which meant senescent commanders and a huge apparatus of well-paid retirees who drained funds from the active duty army."[28]

Fellow scholar Christopher Clark concurred in assessing the Dual Monarchy problems:

> In Austria-Hungary, the tumultuous domestic politics of dualism virtually paralysed the monarchy's military development after the turn of the century, as autonomist groups within the Hungarian parliament fought to starve the monarchy's joint army of Hungarian tax revenues and recruits. In this environment, proposals for increased military allocations were worn down in endless legislative feuding, and the Habsburg military languished in a condition, as the Austrian staff chief put it, of "persistent stagnation." This was one reason why, as late as 1912, Austria-Hungary spent only 2.6 percent of its net national product on defence—a smaller proportion than any other European power and certainly far below what its economy could afford (the figures for Russia, France and Germany in that year were 4.5, 4.0 and 3.8 percent respectively).[29]

Scholars vie in describing how poorly Austria-Hungary was prepared for war. Gunther Rothenberg's succinct summary should suffice: "In 1914 the Habsburg Army was weak in trained manpower and low in firepower. Even when units of the Austrian *Landwehr* and the Hungarian *Honvéd* were included, and since 1912 these second line units were considered as first line, Austria-Hungary could muster only 48 infantry divisions, compared to 93 for Russia, 88 for France, and 11 for Serbia."[30]

Sources differ on the sizes of the Austro-Hungarian joint army and its components prior to the war.[31] János Decsy said that the effective force numbered approximately 1.4 million men, which, after mobilization, soon reached 2.3 million.[32] His estimate of 2.3 million is lower than the 3.3 million given by J.S. Lucas in *Austro-Hungarian Infantry, 1914–1918*, but Lucas said, "The actual figure of fighting men on active service was 1,421,000. All the rest were rear echelon, supply and medical personnel."[33] Of course, all nations' standing armies counted more than just fighting troops, and—depending on the source—army size differed for every country.

One source reported the comparative data on the sizes of standing armies (and reserves) for August 1914 and all forces mobilized in 1914–1918 for sixteen belligerent nations.[34] It estimated the standing army of the Austro-Hungarian Empire, including the *k.u.k.*, *Landwehr*, and *Honvéd*, at three million, lying between Decsy's and Lucas's numbers. Its data on standing armies and reserves for eight prominent belligerents in 1914 are portrayed in Figure 9.1. At three million men, the Austria-Hungarian army on paper seems formidable. Although its army ranked behind the other Great Powers—Russia, Germany, and France—it was more than twice that of Italy, which was 70 percent as populous. Great Britain's defense did not depend on her small army but on her large navy, twice the size of any other. Serbia's small 200,000-man army encouraged Austria-Hungary's hope for a quick victory after declaring war.

Quantitatively speaking, an army of three million seems like a lot, but quality was also important. And the quality of Austria-Hungary's army was suspect because of its multiplicity of languages, its archaic leadership, and its obsolete equipment. Its language problem—inability of officers talking to troops and troops talking among themselves—was discussed in Chapter 8, "Peasants Under Arms." Its archaic leadership was reflected

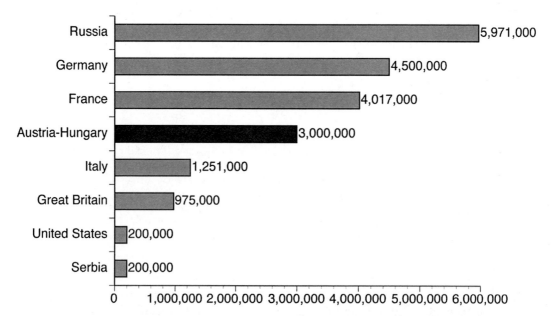

Figure 9.1: STANDING ARMIES AND RESERVES IN 1914. Historically, Austria-Hungary ranked as one of Europe's Great Powers, but its reputation exceeded its capabilities by the 20th century. On paper, it still had Europe's fourth-largest standing army prior to World War I, but it was stronger on paper than in practice. Data: *Spartacus Educational,* http://spartacus-educational.com/FWWarmies1914.htm.

in its beplumed officers dangling useless swords that they often ditched in battle. Ensign Béla Zombory-Moldován, holding the lowest officer rank in the Austro-Hungarian army, was entitled to wear a sword and was required to draw it on certain occasions. He described in his memoir what happened once when he delivered his platoon report to his battalion commander:

> He roars at me.
> "Ensign! You will present your sword when you report! Perhaps you're not aware that you're in the field of battle?"
> I yank my sword out, and endeavor to comply sufficiently with regulations to stop us from losing the war.[35]

War historian Max Hastings said, "The Hapsburg Empire's generals waltzed better than they fought, and lacked the slightest awareness of what man-management meant."[36] The army's equipment and weaponry lagged behind new standards. In János Decsy's judgment:

> Above all, in 1914, the army was short of firepower. It was weak in artillery, which was in the process of reorganization at the time war broke out. Most of its field pieces were obsolete, with steel-bronze barrels. The Austro-Hungarian infantry division was supported by fewer pieces than that of any other major army except the Italian…. Moreover, the firing range of the Austro-Hungarian 15-cm heavy howitzer was only 5,000 m, compared with the 8,000 m of the 12-cm Serbian gun. Furthermore, prior to the war, each artillery battery had had 250 shells for training purposes, compared with 650 and 730 in Germany and France, respectively, and between 500 and 600 in Russia.[37]

Engaged in battle, Ensign Zombory-Moldován fumed about his army's poor equipment: "Damn them! They blocked legislation for the sake of these stupid national-language commands, and held up modernization of the army. Now here we are, unprepared and outnumbered three to one. The whole brigade has a total of four 7.5-centimeter field guns. The Russians have twelve."[38] János Decsy quoted a German observer attached to Austria-Hungary's high command who said that the Dual Monarchy's army was "adequate for a campaign against Serbia, but inadequate for a major European war."[39]

Although Austria-Hungary declared war only against Serbia, it expected and planned to fight with its ally Germany against Russia too. Anticipating a two-front war, Austria-Hungary counted on subduing Serbia quickly. Then it would fight only on the Russian Front. Unfortunately for Franz Josef, the conflict exploded beyond expectations. Austria found itself simultaneously fighting against Serbia on its southeast and against Russia on its northeast. Then it unexpectedly fought against its former ally Italy on its south and— for good measure—against Romania on the east. Austria-Hungary found itself embroiled in a major European war, for which it was poorly prepared.

Warfare between national armies is enormously complex. Ordinary readers have little appreciation of how complex it is. Take the phrase "order of battle." In its broad sense, it defines the hierarchical organization, command structure, strength, disposition of personnel, and equipment of units and formations of the armed force. In its narrow sense, it refers to the army's table of organization. According to Decsy: "At the outbreak of the war, the Austro-Hungarian army, including the *Honvédseg* and the *Landwehr*, could field only 48 infantry, 2 territorial, and 11 cavalry divisions and 36 brigades, organized into 17 corps and 6 armies."[40] The previous chapter, "Peasants Under Arms," mentioned that most Americans don't know whether a duke outranks an earl (he does). They also probably do not know the relative sizes of these military units: army, corps, division, and brigade. The specific sizes of these units vary with each country's military, but their relative sizes tend to hold across countries and range roughly as in Figure 9.2, which shows the relative sizes in the Habsburg army after 1908.

Figure 9.2 prompts several observations. First, a nation's "army"—e.g., Austria-Hungary's 3-million-man national army—consisted of distinct units themselves called Armies. In August 1914, Austria-Hungary's standing army had six separate Armies numbered from 1st through 6th, each army commanded by a different general. Over the course of the war, the number of men under arms shrunk substantially through deaths, casualties, and desertions, and by October 1918 Austria-Hungary's final order of battle listed only three Armies, reconstituted as the 6th, 10th, and 11th.[41] Those numbered 1 to 5 had been decimated.

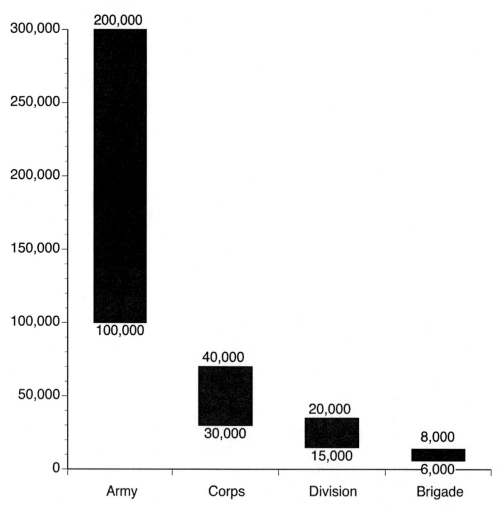

Figure 9.2: RELATIVE SIZES OF HABSBURG ARMY UNITS. **A military's "Order of Battle" includes the relative sizes and terms of units in its hierarchical structure. A nation's "army" is usually composed of several Armies with designated numbers or names. These distinct Armies usually consist of 100,000 or more troops divided into two or more corps. Corps are made up of divisions, which are usually divided into brigades, sometimes called regiments or battalions. Data from Table 1.3 in István Deák, *Beyond Nationalism: A Social and Political History of the Habsburg Officer Corps, 1848–1918* (New York: Oxford University Press, 1990), p. 15.**

Second, each Army was typically composed of one or more corps, identified by Roman numerals and typically commanded by a lieutenant general. Each corps in Austria-Hungary's army represented one of its sixteen Army Corp Districts plus a seventeenth formed at the war's outbreak.[42] For example, the 1st Army in 1914 consisted of three corps: I Corps (Cracow), V Corps (Pressburg), and X Corps (Przemyśl).

Third, corps are composed of several divisions, each commanded by a major general, and of numerous brigades, each commanded by a lieutenant colonel/colonel/brigadier. In the Austro-Hungarian army, a division usually had two infantry brigades, each having two infantry regiments of 3,000 to 4,000; each regiment was divided into battalions of about 1,000 each. Losses over time cut Austria-Hungary's divisions' size almost in half by 1917, but other nations also suffered comparable decreases.[43]

This information about Austria-Hungary's order of battle helps us to understand the course of World War I, by considering how divisions were deployed over time. Although nations' army divisions varied from 15,000 to 20,000 troops, they were similar enough in size across national armies to allow rough comparisons of military strength. Individually, they also represented major components of engagement on battlefields. Crudely speaking, victory usually went to the side that maintained supremacy in the number of divisions on the front.

Military historian Albert Nofi compiled data on the number of infantry and dismounted cavalry divisions for each of the belligerents at quarterly intervals during the war.[44] His data are graphed in Figure 9.3, which portrays how the opposing sides—the Central Powers and the Allied Powers—allocated their divisions from the start of the war to the end in the Eastern Theater on three major fronts: the Balkan, Russian, and Italian.[45]

Three observations emerge from the graphs:

1. Allied nations fighting on the side of the original Entente—France, Russia, and Britain—fielded many more divisions than the Central Powers.

2. Russia alone supplied most of the Entente's divisions in the Eastern Theater until it signed the Brest-Litovsk Treaty on March 3, 1918, and withdrew from the war.

3. When Russia left the war, the Entente evolved into the Allied Powers, gaining more national allies during the war than the Central Powers:

- The Allies attracted troops from Serbia after its defeat; from Italy, which declared war on Austria-Hungary on May 23, 1915; from Romania, declaring war on August 27, 1916; and from Greece, joining the war on July 2, 1917. The Allies also created Polish and Czech divisions from Poles living in Russia and from Czech defectors.
- The Central Powers did entice Bulgaria to join them in 1915, and—despite the fact there was no Poland at the time—they fielded a Polish division, created by the Habsburg monarchy from Poles living in its Galicia territory.
- Aligned with the Central Powers from the beginning, Turkey's many divisions are not included here because most fought against Russia further east.

Perhaps a fourth observation from Figure 9.3 is that the number of German divisions on the eastern fronts plummeted in 1917 after the Russian revolution and the Treaty of Brest-Litovsk. Ending the war with Russia allowed Germany to transfer divisions from the Russian, Balkan, and Italian fronts to the Western front. Figure 9.4 plots the *percentages* of German, British, and French divisions deployed over the course of the war on these fronts rather than the *number* of divisions. The French never deployed more than 11 percent of their divisions to those eastern fronts and the British never more than 28 percent. After the war began, the Germans were forced to allocate increasingly more of

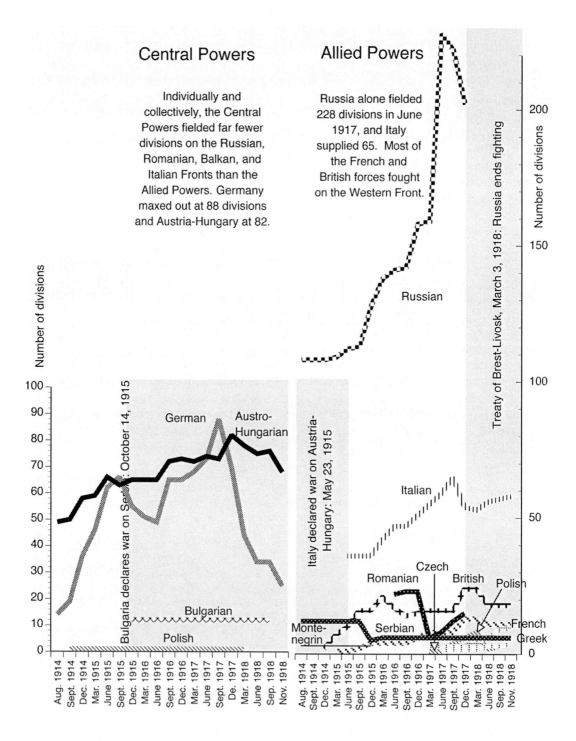

Central Powers

Individually and collectively, the Central Powers fielded far fewer divisions on the Russian, Romanian, Balkan, and Italian Fronts than the Allied Powers. Germany maxed out at 88 divisions and Austria-Hungary at 82.

Allied Powers

Russia alone fielded 228 divisions in June 1917, and Italy supplied 65. Most of the French and British forces fought on the Western Front.

Figure 9.3: Divisional Strength in Eastern Theaters, World War I. The Entente nations fielded many more divisions than the Central Powers in the Eastern Theater but lost troop superiority after Russia withdrew from the war. That allowed Germany to shift divisions to the Western Front. Other countries joined to fight against the Central Powers in the east, transforming the Entente into the Allied Powers. Data: Alfred Nofi, "Comparative Divisional Strengths During World War I: European Belligerents and Theaters," in Király and Dreisziger, *East Central European Society in World War I*, Tables 1 and 2.

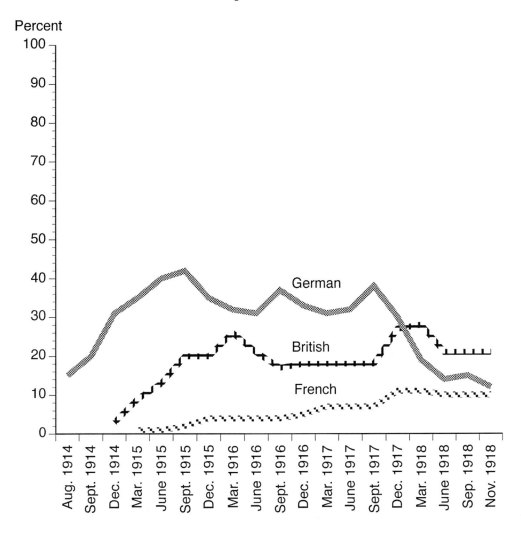

Figure 9.4: PERCENTAGES OF GERMAN, BRITISH, AND FRENCH TROOPS ON EASTERN FRONTS. In September 1915, one year after the war began, Germany had deployed more than 40 percent of its divisions to the Eastern Front—not what it had anticipated according to the Schlieffen Plan. After Russia withdrew from fighting in 1917, Germany shifted its troops back to the Western Front, in line with the Schlieffen Plan, but about two years later than anticipated. Both Britain and France had to send troops east after Russia left the war. Data: Alfred Nofi, "Comparative Divisional Strengths During World War I: European Belligerents and Theaters," in Király and Dreisziger, *East Central European Society in World War I*, Tables 1 and 2.

their divisions to the east, primarily to fight the Russians. By September 1915, almost half of their divisions (42 percent) were fighting in the Eastern Theater, not on the Western Front against the French and the British.

In a sense, sending increasing numbers of their divisions to fight against Russians in the east was exactly what German generals had planned. Expecting Russia to flood the eastern battlefield with troops, they planned to transfer troops from the Western Front to the Russian Front after knocking out France early in the war. Germany counted on Austria-Hungary to hold its own against Russia for a few weeks while it was vanquishing

France. Germany assumed that Russia would need time to fully mobilize its troops. War historian Max Hastings said that all "operational plans in 1914 were complex, that of the Russians most of all, because of the huge distances involved." He adds, "Each mobilised soldier of the Tsar must travel an average of seven hundred miles to reach his regiment, against a German's average of two hundred. The strategic rail network required twelve days' warning of a call to arms, and troop concentrations would anyway be much slower than Germany's."[46] All Germany's expectations failed to materialize. Germany did not quickly vanquish France; Austro-Hungarian troops were unable to hold their own against the Russians early in the war; and Russia proved its ability to transport its divisions to the battlefield more quickly than anticipated. That was largely due to unexpected improvements in Russia's railways.

Railroads were employed in war not long after public railways began operating in Britain in the 1830s, as documented in Edwin Pratt's *The Rise of Rail-Power in War and Conquest, 1833–1914*.[47] Pratt stated that in 1833, a German entrepreneur wrote about "the military value" of a railroad between German cities. "With the help of such a railway, he argued, it would be possible to concentrate large bodies of troops at a given point much more speedily than if they marched by road."[48] Pratt then mentioned several instances of railroad usage in important 19th-century European battles. Few standard political histories mentioned them:

- Who knew, for example, that the railroad figured at all in crushing the 1848–49 Hungarian rebellion against Austria? But Pratt stated: "In 1849 a Russian corps of 30,000 men, with all its equipment, was taken by rail from its cantonments in Poland to Goding, Moravia, whence it effected a junction with the Austrian army."[49]
- Who knew that "railways first played a conspicuous part in actual warfare, both strategically and tactically" in Franz Josef's defeat in the 1859 Italian campaign? Pratt said: "In eighty-six days—from April 19 to July 15—they transported an aggregate of 604,000 men and over 129,000 horses."[50]
- Who knew that railways contributed to the Prussians' 1866 victory over Austria? Pratt wrote: "Movements of troops by rail were certainly effected in one-third of the time they would have taken by road, while the Prussians, gaining a great advantage, by the rapidity of such movements, over Austria, routed her combined forces within seven days of crossing the frontier, and dictated terms of peace to her within a month."[51]

Admittedly, railways were used only in limited ways in these battles, and problems occurred, but each usage taught lessons, and no one learned better than the Germans. Pratt wrote that immediately after Prussia's 1866 defeat of Austria, "a mixed committee of Staff officers and railway authorities was appointed, under the supervision of [General] von Moltke, to inquire what steps should be taken to organise the Prussian military transport services on such a basis as would avoid a repetition of the faults already experienced, and give a greater guarantee of efficiency on the occasion of the next war in which Prussia might be engaged.[52]

The Germans periodically updated their railway regulations prior to their 1870–71 war against France, such that the Germans had "in 1870, nine lines of concentration available, namely, six for the Northern and three for the Southern Army; and between July 24 and August 3, there were dispatched by these different routes 1,200 trains, conveying 350,000 men, 87,000 horses, and 8,400 guns or road vehicles."[53] France, in contrast, "embarked on her tremendous conflict with no organisation for military transport apart from the out-of-date and wholly defective regulations" from 1859.[54]

War historian Christopher Clark wrote, "Railways (like hydroelectric dams in the 1930s–50s, or space travel in the 1960s) held a special place in the imperial imaginary [*sic*] at the turn of the twentieth century."[55] Military use of railroads was complex and exacting work. It required collecting information and preparing calculations concerning

(1) the number of vehicles required for a given number of men, with horses, guns, munitions, stores, road vehicles, etc., so that rolling stock can be used to the best advantage and according as to whether the troops carried belong to the Infantry, Cavalry or the Artillery; (2) the number of vehicles that can be made up into a train going by any one route; (3) the length of time likely to be taken for the entraining and detraining respectively of a given unit; (4) the time intervals at which a succession of troop trains can follow one another on the same line; (5) the speed of troop trains; and (6) the further intervals to be allowed in the arrival at one and the same station, or centre, of a number of trains starting from different points, so as to avoid the risk of congestion and of consequent delays.[56]

The information and calculations were incorporated into detailed military timetables for each deployment of troops. Germans were good at such tasks, and Germany had a half century of experience with military use of railways before the outbreak of World War I.

Colette Hooper's *Railways of the Great War* stated, "In 1870, there were some 64,000 miles of tracks in Europe. By 1914, that figure had almost tripled to 180,000 miles."[57] Her book included a map of Central Europe depicting a spaghetti-like maze of railways.[58] She described the First World War as a "railroad war like no other": "It was different from previous European conflicts, because by 1914 the railways had reached such a high degree of development that all war planning on the Continent depended on efficient mobilization by rail—in a process that, once launched, was evidently unstoppable. A generation later, at the time of the Second World War, the lorry, jeep and tank were advanced enough to reduce somewhat armies' reliance on trains."

Germany in particular built its railways with military purposes in mind. Germany saw herself surrounded by potential enemies to the west (France) and east (Russia) that had entered into a military alliance in 1892. Strategic use of railways offered a way to fight a war against them on both fronts. Hooper wrote: "First dreamt up at the turn of the twentieth century by Chief of the Imperial German General Staff, Alfred von Schlieffen, it was based on the premise that Russia, with a sparse railway network and vast distances to cover, could not mobilize troops as quickly as Germany. Schlieffen thus proposed that in the event of war, the bulk of Germany's men could initially be deployed westwards to rapidly overwhelm France. They would then turn back in time to meet the Russians."[59] Hooper described Germany's extensive railway preparations: building new lines toward its western borders, double-tracking existing lines, expanding key junctions, adding new yards, and extending platforms to accommodate loading and unloading of military trains.[60] Historian Clark reported on France's railway improvements following its defeat in the 1870 Franco-Prussian war. Whereas Germany had built thirteen railway lines to its borders, "France had sixteen, all of which were double-tracked, with junction lines to bypass loops, stations and intersections."[61]

Because France counted on Russia in a future fight against Germany, France needed its ally Russia to have a militarily efficient railway. In 1842, Russia had established a

Department of Railways to link St. Petersburg with Moscow.[62] However, Russia lagged behind the other continental powers in its railroad network because its vast land area soaked up track. According to League of Nations statistics, Russia in 1913 had 68,006 kilometers of track, more than Germany's 63,687 kilometers and France's 39,389 kilometers.[63] Unfortunately for Russia, its railways were spread over 21,745,000 square kilometers—much more than Germany's 541,000 square kilometers and France's 536,000.[64] True, much of Russia's territory was sparsely populated; nevertheless, Russia in 1913 had only 3 kilometers of railroad track per square kilometer versus Germany's 118 and France's 73. Aware of the problem, France stepped in to finance Russia's railway construction.[65]

On paper, Austria-Hungary had more kilometers of railroads (45,222) than France, but the larger Austria-Hungary had almost the same proportional amount of railway (72 kilometers per square kilometer). Map 9.1 depicts only the thousands of miles of principal railways in the belligerents by 1914, and Hooper's detailed map of Central Europe (mentioned above) showed that these trunk lines had many branches.[66] Military historian Rothenberg found that Austria and Hungary "were spending large sums mounting to

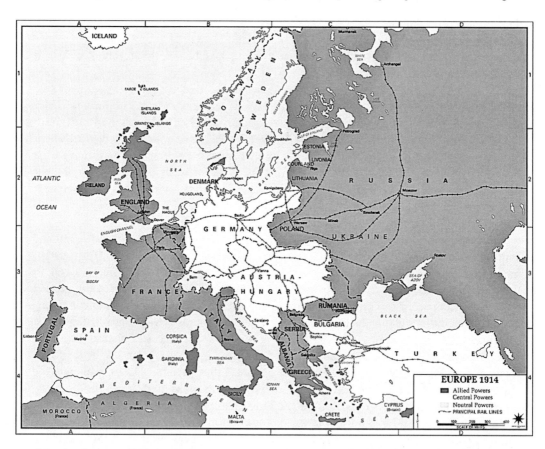

Map 9.1: PRINCIPAL RAILWAYS OF THE WARRING NATIONS IN 1914. **Thousands of miles of railroads crisscrossed Europe at the outset of war. Having developed its railways with attention to military usage, Germany had a more extensive and effective network of railroads than Austria-Hungary. Railroad construction continued furiously during the war. Credit: Department of History, U.S. Military Academy at West Point, available at http://www.emersonkent.com/map_archive/europe_1914.htm. In the public domain.**

over 20 percent of their total budget on railroads."[67] However, "the new lines did not always conform with the strategic priorities of the general staff." This was especially true in Hungary, "which was trying to promote economic autonomy." The German general staff concluded, "The railway network [of Austria-Hungary] was entirely inadequate for the necessary movements of troops."[68]

According to Geoffrey Wawro, by 1914 Russian railways were better than those in Austria-Hungary: "Russia had four single-tracked lines (which meant that traffic could flow in only one direction at a time) and five double-tracked lines (permitting two-way traffic). Austria had just seven single-track railways, and two of these had to stagger through the high Carpathians. By the grim arithmetic of the time, this meant that Russia could send 260 trains a day into the Polish-Ukrainian theater of war, versus Austria's 153."[69]

Troop movement by railway concerned military leaders at the highest levels. A short quotation from David Stevenson's article on "war by timetable" indicates the depths of the concerns expressed by German Chief of Staff Helmuth von Moltke and Major General Wilhelm Groener, head of the staff's railway division: "According to Moltke and Groener, Germany had fifteen Rhine bridges and thirteen double-tracked concentration lines in the west, as well as four double-tracked transverse routes, two on each side of the Rhine. And yet, they now alleged, France could concentrate as much as five days faster if both sides proclaimed mobilization at the same time. In the east, four double-tracked lines ran to the Vistula, but only two double-tracked lines beyond it into East Prussia, one of which was dangerously close to the border."[70] Stevenson suggests that unfavorable railway circumstances may have altered the staff's plans for an eastern offensive.

Most civilians have no inkling of the vast sizes of national armies and of what was required to supply the troops and even to move them from one location to another. Peter Englund claimed that "forty trains a month" were needed to "supply a division of 16,000"—more than a train a day.[71] Herwig reported, "The Military Telegraph Section of the German General Staff mobilized 3,822,450 men and 119,754 officers as well as 600,000 horses. This gigantic force transported to the front in 312 hours by 11,000 trains. More than 2,150 54-car trains crossed the Rhine River over the Hohenzollern Bridge at Cologne in 10-minute intervals between 2 and 18 August.[72]

Indeed, A.J.P. Taylor argued in his book *War by Time-Table* that military leaders in 1914 were prisoners of railway timetable logic for troop mobilization. Victory depended on transporting vast numbers of troops to battle positions before the opponents' troops materialized. Barbara Tuchman described General Moltke's reaction to Kaiser Wilhelm's eleventh-hour attempt to halt mobilization on August 1: "'Your Majesty,' Moltke said to him now, 'it cannot be done. The deployment of millions cannot be improvised. If Your Majesty insists on leading the whole army to the East it will not be an army ready for battle but a disorganized mob of armed men with no arrangements for supply. Those arrangements took a whole year of intricate labor to complete'—and Moltke closed upon that rigid phrase—… 'and once settled, it cannot be altered.'"[73] Moltke's statement notwithstanding, Tuchman wrote that the plans could have been altered. Stevenson raised the more general question: "whether possessing the capability to launch offensive blows also constituted an incentive to do so: whether railway capacity was not simply a passive precondition for hostilities but actively promoted them."[74] In other words, did the railroads play a role in causing the war or simply facilitate fighting the war?

Stevenson (and others) contended that rapid transport of troops by rail served as the basis of Germany's Schlieffen Plan for a two-front war. Only rapid troop movements would enable a quick defeat of France in the west followed by a crushing of Russia on the east. Stevenson also noted that Germany had not finalized its railway plans and Austria-Hungary had an inadequate infrastructure for aggression against Serbia. Yet both countries plunged into war in 1914.

Before the Great War, thousands of peasants had been employed in clearing land, cutting timbers, and laying track for railroads running through their lands. Few who toiled on the railways thought they would be privileged to travel on a train, but they were mistaken. Soon they would be hurtling toward battles on troop trains running on the very tracks they had laid, traveling perhaps ten times as swiftly as by foot and horse.[75]

10

Peasants in Peril

Support for the war in Austria-Hungary fell just weeks after it began, especially in rural areas of Slovakia, which included Samko's village of Krajné. In his study of the social bases of the opposition in Hungary, Dániel Szabó analyzed popular songs of the times to detect how attitudes toward the war changed:

> In the beginning, songs combined loyalty to the monarch ("Francis Josef is my father") with motifs of Hungarian nationality—the national tricolor and the three-colored cap button. The larger social unit ("My fatherland, you beautiful Hungary") as a unifying force, however, figured only in variants of songs written by known authors.
>
> ...
>
> With time, the motifs gradually turned to grief and resignation: "a sad Saturday evening ... they'll take me to Doberdo [a bloody Serbian battlefield]"; "They'll take me away to war / I won't be your daughter's beloved"; "I'm going to Serbia to fight for my country / My heart aches for my sweetheart."[1]

Szabó found that soldiers' "marching songs" also treated "themes of death, relationships, the loss of relationships, the causes of the war." The songs did not curse their enemies as much as the battlefields, such as Doberdo above. Later in the war, "songs turned up referring to the Burg at Vienna or to the Germans, indicating the foreignness, the irrelevance of the war, to Hungarians."[2] The initial spurt of villagers' identification with Austria-Hungary soon faded: "During the protracted war, great emotions were evoked not by the successes or defeats of the Monarchy but rather by the immediate surroundings, the village and the family. As older and older age groups were called up, they were less enthusiastic from the start."[3]

Decades later, a Krajné historian reconstructed how the war impacted Samuel Mozolák's home village: "Meanwhile at home the army began to commandeer animals, especially horses, for its needs. The second wave of mobilization included all men to 50 years. Only women, old men and children remained in Krajné. Women and children had to shoulder the burdens of the farm. Food was lacking. Rationing was introduced for kerosene and flour. Everything was decided by the notary Nozdrovický and his wife, the 'almighty' lady. Crushing blow for local believers was the requisitioning of the church bells for the needs of the army."[4]

From an economic standpoint, the war imposed more hardships on people living in cities than in farming areas, which produced food for both civilians and soldiers. A substantial body of writing arose on problems of "food and war" in Europe then.[5] Szabó cited data from Budapest: "In Budapest, food prices had begun to climb by July 29, 1914; in January 1915 it became compulsory to use 50 percent ersatz flour in baking bread; in March 1915 the government set a ceiling on the price of flour and corn equaling a price rise of 9–10 percent. That November milk rationing was introduced. In December, a law was passed against profiteers. In January 1916 bread was also rationed: urban consumers received 210 grams of flour or the equivalent in bread. In August 1916 the price of milk and in October the price of sugar were increased."[6] Because Hungary was the empire's agricultural food basket, economic hardships were even greater in Austria.[7] In Vienna, German and Czech scientists developed substitutes for conventional foods. Bread, for example, could be made from corn or chestnuts. At the extreme, a kind of bread could even be made from straw, hay, or ground birch tree bark.[8]

Civilians suffered from shortages because of their military's enormous need for food, coal, and other goods. Gary Shanafelt noted that in 1914 none of the European powers, including Germany, had stored up provisions for a protracted war, and Austria-Hungary was particularly ill-prepared:

> In both halves of the Monarchy, there were laws providing for the exercise of emergency powers by the governments in the case of war, but little had been done in practice to anticipate the economic demands of a major conflict. There were no stockpiles of either military supplies or foodstuffs, no plans for maintaining adequate reserves of raw materials.
>
> …
>
> Agriculture had already faced problems before the war, but under the initial dislocations of the conflict the 1914 grain harvest in Hungary actually fell from 60 million quintals to 40 million [one quintal=100 kilograms]. Moreover, the Monarchy's institutional conflicts made it more difficult to mobilize effectively what it had. The war had scarcely begun when the Hungarians closed the border with Austria to a free flow of commodities, refusing to release their grain to Cisleithania except at the price of political and economic concessions.[9]

Alexander Watson wrote, "Even more important, any tampering with agriculture or the food supply risked antagonizing the landed aristocracy and gentry who dominated Hungarian politics."[10] István Tisza, the Hungarian prime minister and himself a large landowner, defended agricultural interests, "even at the expense of the wider imperial war effort."

On the home front as on the battle front, the Dual Monarchy functioned increasingly like the Dual Anarchy, its dismal nickname.[11] Writing about "everyday life" in Vienna during the war, social historian Maureen Healy commented on the food situation: "Hungary had the right to sell to Austria, but was under no formal obligation to do so."[12] Consequently, "Austria-Hungary was at war with itself" over food.[13] Healy cited a woman who heard that residents of Bratislava, 75 miles from Vienna, could buy "poppy seed and nut strudel made with white flour." Writing to a local official, she asked, "Is the other half of the empire (*die andere Reichshälfte*) in cahoots with the enemies trying to starve us?"[14] The food situation was sufficiently grim at "the level of high politics" that "Austrians cited the Hungarian food policy as a key factor in the eventual collapse of the Habsburg state."[15]

While Austria-Hungary's civilians were finding it difficult to live with food shortages, its soldiers were finding it hard to fight on an empty stomach. One might expect some supply gaps to arise as the war progressed, but the Monarchy's troops experienced all sorts of supply deficiencies during the war's first year. A British journalist, Max Hastings, described the situation in his book written decades later: "Franz Josef's soldiers suffered infinite hardship and grief in the winter of 1914 because their commanders refused responsibly to address their feeding and welfare. Lt. Aleksandr Trushnovich, a Slovenian, described the miserable rations issued to his soldiers—black bread, meatless stew, black coffee substitute—'they were almost starving.' Meanwhile he and his fellow officers 'received more calories than the entire company, wine and cake, also cigarettes and cigars which I gave to the men.'"[16]

Officers in every army had, and still have, perquisites. But high-level officers in the Austro-Hungarian army lived extraordinarily well compared to their troops. A Hungarian soldier, Pál Kelemen, described the situation in his journal entry written on a day in February 1916, when military headquarters in Montenegro was being moved: "In spite of the very inadequate facilities for transporting the general supply, all the vehicles have been requisitioned to help move Headquarters. Columns of trucks wind over the mountains, packed with cases of champagne, wire-spring beds, floor lamps, special kitchen equipment, and various crates of delicacies. The troops receive a third of their normal rations. The infantry at the front has had only a morsel of bread for four days, but the staff officers' mess serves the usual four course dinners."[17]

That level of comfort was just for the field headquarters. The Austrian High Command lived even better in Teschen, a pleasant town in Austrian Silesia. Holger Herwig stated that officers there enjoyed Court table service, tennis, horseback riding, and visits to local coffee houses.[18] Teschen was hundreds of miles from fighting on the Eastern Fronts. In contrast, the main German Headquarters for most of the war was in Spa, Belgium, closer to the Western Front. On these matters, Herwig recounted Austro-Hungarian General Arz von Straussenburg's defense, made in August 1918 at the end of the war: "Arz staunchly defended the right of officers to preferential rations and accommodation, and declined to follow what he called the 'German example,' whereby officers and men ate the same food at the front. Such an egalitarian turn was out of the question due to the 'differences in educational levels' between officers and men. How could one expect Austrian-German officers to consume food from kitchens staffed by different nationalities? The General found the prospect 'insufferable.' And what Austrian-German officer, Arz wished to know, would agree to serve in an army where officers and men ate from the same menu?"[19]

Whereas Austria-Hungary made sure that its officers ate much better than their troops, Germany's policy, according to Peter Lummel, tried "to ensure that no soldier experienced the hunger felt by German civilians," making "investment in modern ovens and field kitchens" to deliver good food to the men.[20] Military historians agree that the German command was far more efficient and effective than the Austro-Hungarian command in supplying its troops. Their judgments were reflected in war novels. In *The Linden and the Oak*, set on the Russian Front, Mark Mansa told about Rusyn soldiers who ran out of lime to cover their comrades' corpses. A sergeant said: "Our German friends have offered us some of their lime. The Germans never run out of it. They plan ahead. They always have plenty of what an army needs. They know before any offensive that they will need many men and many guns and many shovels and many bags of lime. Our army never plans as well as the German army."[21]

Austro-Hungarian soldiers were also awed by how well the German solders were equipped. Andrew Krivak's protagonist, Jozef Vinich, described the *Sturmtruppen* of the *Armeeoberkomando*, who "carried with them what seemed like the crucial elements of an entire supply truck on their belts and backs—double rations of food, water, gas masks, filters, hand grenades, flashlights, spades, pickaxes, wire cutters, medical kits, compasses, whistles, trench daggers, bayonets, pistols, carbines, and on and on."[22]

Of course, novelists exaggerated these differences, as in this passage from *The Good*

Soldier Švejk about a meeting between Austro-Hungarian soldiers and their German allies: "Like an elite among them all Reich Germans were oiling about and aristocratically offering the Austrians cigarettes from their lavish supplies. In the Reich German field-kitchens in the square there were even whole barrels from which they tapped beer for the men, who fetched rations of it for their lunch and supper. The neglected Austrian soldiers with their bellies distended by filthy concoctions of sweet chicory hung around them like greedy cats."[23]

Novelists may have exaggerated the plight of the Monarchy's troops, but their food situation was truly dire. Writing on the mobilization of food supplies in Austria-Hungary, Horst Haselsteiner found a calamitous situation in 1917–18, citing army needs for that year "as 7 million quintals of flour and 14 million of cereal fodder. The army actually received 5,084,200 quintals of flour and only 2,273,900 quintals of cereal fodder (1,727,200 from Hungary and 546,700 from Austria).... Whereas upon mobilization in 1914 each soldier had received 400 grams of meat per day, the ration was later cut by half, and by the beginning of 1918 scarcely 100 grams per man per day were available."[24]

All belligerents faced staggering tasks in feeding and equipping their troops. The scales of operation were enormous, even given the railways' great capacities for transport. Joe Kirchberger detailed the supply problems, which only started with delivering supplies to the railheads for distribution:

> While some of the major railheads were not particularly far from the front, actually moving the supplies to where they were needed created many problems, and these rose dramatically when a major offensive was being prepared, simply because of the sheer volume of items required. Goods had to be unloaded from the trains, possibly stored, and then divided into the smaller loads that were needed for the various sectors of the front. The large depots and smaller ones nearer the front were often camouflaged to prevent the enemy from attacking them with artillery and aircraft and to disguise any increase in supply activity, which was a sure sign of a forthcoming offensive.[25]

To appreciate how huge these depots could be, see Photo 10.1, which reproduces a photo of "stacks of food" on the Western front. Despite all this effort at supply, troops at the various fronts suffered from shortages of provisions.

Everyone in the infantry—peasants and non-peasants alike—had to learn how to march to their battles. As Austro-Hungarian military historian J.S. Lucas wrote: "Despite the vast and efficient network of railways which covered the Empire, once outside the railway area then all movement was on foot."[26] Troops movements were calculated according to the standard of 100 paces to the minute, 24 minutes to the mile: "The normal day's march for small units was 12 miles (20 kms) and just under 9 miles (15 kms) for Corps or larger formations. The maximum length of a day's march was never to exceed 31 miles (50 kms) and this special effort could not be demanded for more than a few days in succession. This was not surprising for the soldiers carried most of their equipment and clothing upon their backs."[27] The equipment and clothing on a soldier's back typically weighted 60 pounds, as itemized and described in Chapter 8, "Peasants Under Arms."

How fast and how far troops could march in a given amount of time was critical to military planning. Lucas said, "Like all armies of the period its fastest pace was that of the horse but mainly it was the Infantry's 100 paces to the minute, 24 minutes to the mile which regulated the marching columns."[28] Military writer John Keegan said, "Such calculations were the groundwork of staff-college training."

> Students, transferring from prepared tables the length of a marching column—twenty-nine kilometres for a corps, for example—to a road map, could determine how many troops could be pushed

Photo 10.1: STACKS OF FOOD FOR ALLIED FORCES ON THE WESTERN FRONT. **This photo, labeled "Stacks of food, etc." shows the staggering amount of food and other materiel stashed at just one supply depot in France. The military forces on both sides required many hundreds of trainloads of supplies. Credit: The photo was taken by British photographer Ernest Brooks and made available by the National Library of Scotland at http://digital.nls.uk/first-world-war-official-photographs/pageturner.cfm?id=74545992. Source attribution permits usage.**

through a given sector at what speed. Since thirty-two kilometres was the limit of a forced march, that would be the advance of a corps on a single road; but the tail of a column twenty-nine kilometres long would remain near or at the marching-off point at the day's end. If there were twin parallel roads, the tails would advance half the distance, if four three quarters, and so on. Ideally, the units of a corps would advance not in column but in line abreast, allowing all of it to arrive at the day's end thirty-two kilometres further on.[29]

Keegan noted that a forced march was limited to 32 kilometers; military writer Lucas said that Austro-Hungarian troops should never march more than 50 kilometers. Nevertheless, they did. After a long forced march, Hungarian ensign Béla Zombory-Moldován wrote in his memoir: "This idiotic seventy-five kilometer march had been ordered by the regimental commander, former staff officer Bél Sérsits, who was from Kissár. By the time we reached our destination, half the regiment had been rendered unfit for action from damage to their feet and general exhaustion."[30] His entry helps understand the significance of Holger Herwig's criticism of Austro-Hungarian military leadership: "Austro-Hungarian troops paid the price in physical exhaustion as they marched to the front on foot. It is estimated that the four Habsburg armies in Galicia undertook daily forced marches of almost 20 miles [32 kilometers] between 19 and 26 August [in six days] just to reach the Russian border. A weary army confronted the Russians at Lemberg early in September 1914."[31]

Disciplined marching was necessary to transport large numbers of troops from one location to another, but it—like other practices—was not well suited to battle. "In 1914," István Deák wrote, "it was expected that platoon and company commanders would march into battle ahead of their men, and that cavalry officers would ride in front of the line, all the while conspicuously displaying their insignia of rank."[32] Austria-Hungary was not the only army to make this mistake early in the war. Winston Churchill colorfully described how "The French infantry marched to battle conspicuous on the landscape in blue breeches and red coats. "Their artillery officers in black and gold were even more specially defined targets. Their cavalry gloried in ludicrous armour. The doctrine of the offensive raised to the height of a religious frenzy animated all ranks, and in no rank was restricted by the foreknowledge of the modern rifle and machine gun. A cruel surprise lay before them."[33] The net effect was to generate significantly higher death rates among officers than among the rank-and-file. As battles took their toll in lives, the reality of kill or be killed sunk in among the troops. Remarque's novel captured the mood: "We march up, moody or good-tempered soldiers—we reach the zone where the front begins and become on the instant human animals."[34]

Early in the war, all European armies emphasized bayonet drills in the infantry and sabre and lance use in the cavalry. These weapons "complemented traditional military ideas of honor and glory."[35] Officers taught troops the beauty and power of cold steel and made "appeals to their patriotism to attack and to die."[36] Earlier, Barbara Tuchman described the romantic but outdated notion of battle that captured the thinking of French generals: "Her will to win, her *élan*, would enable France to defeat her enemy. Her genius was in her spirit, the spirit of *la gloire*, of 1792."[37] Only offense, not defense, brought glory!

In his study of "the cult of the offensive," Stephen van Evera agreed that France was "obsessed with the virtues of the offensive," but all other belligerents also belonged to the cult.[38] Austria-Hungary's chief of staff Conrad believed that "infantry remained the queen of battle and that *élan* could overcome superior numbers as well as defensive fire."[39] If proper *élan* demanded theatrical charges into battle, then the actors must be suitably costumed for their parts. Before the war, the French parliament allowed—to the cry *"Le pantalon rouge, c'est la France!"*—its infantry to continue wearing their traditional red trousers instead of camouflage dress.[40]

As noted in Chapter 1, "The Emperor in Vienna," Austria-Hungary had the most dashing uniforms of all the major European nations. Two books on the Austro-Hungarian forces by author Peter Jung and illustrator Darko Pavlovic documented their fancy uniforms, insignias, and markings.[41] The cavalry had the most splendid outfits. Pál Kelemen wrote how he looked on August 25, 1914, as he arrived in Galicia by train from Budapest, "dressed in his hussar's uniform of red trousers, blue tunic, pale-blue embroidered *attila* [shortcoat] and high leather boots.[42] The infantry had recently been given pike-grey uniforms, but the cavalry won an exception from Emperor Franz Josef to forego the infantry's uniforms and to keep its blue blouses and red pants.[43]

As it turned out, 19th-century military *élan* and *haute couture* proved of little value in offensive charges against 20th-century weapons. Peter Englund described the special case of the Austro-Hungarian cavalry, "the pride of that army, the jewel in its military crown, the men with the finest uniforms." He points out, "It no longer has any meaningful function and can hardly ever be sent into action. They have tried, and whole regiments have been mown down by a couple of machine guns. On the whole, the cavalry have done little more than herd prisoners of war, patrol behind the lines and put on splendidly colourful parades. Their horses, moreover, demand huge quantities of fodder which, like everything else nowadays, is in short supply."[44] Fancy uniforms also proved hazardous to officers, who typically drew fire while leading charges in their brightest uniforms.[45] When not leading charges, they were often picked off by snipers. After waves of French infantry in red pantaloons were slaughtered in 1914, their battle dress was changed to a grayish blue. As it turned out, Austria-Hungary's pike-grey infantry uniforms, a kind of blue that offered camouflage in the Alps, made soldiers stand out on the Galicia plains. Field-grey uniforms replaced them in 1915 to reduce casualties.[46]

Winston Churchill castigated the "attack" philosophy that dominated thinking on both sides of the conflict: "Each was sure that he had only to gather a few more army corps and a few more cannon to break the opposing line and march triumphantly, as the case might be, to Paris or the Rhine. They were of course, as we now know, absolutely out of touch with the true facts and values. Neither of them, nor their expert advisers, had ever sufficiently realized the blunt truth—quite obvious to common soldiers—that bullets kill men."[47]

Writing of his experiences in the German army on Western Front, Remarque said that soldiers needed two things for contentment: "good food and rest."[48] They usually got neither. Instead, they got plenty of experiences that generated discontent and misery. The troops' food shortages have already been mentioned. Rest and particularly sleep were also in short supply. In his book on "life in the trenches," Stephen Currie wrote that men "almost invariably suffered from sleep deprivation." "'My average of sleep has been 2½ hours in the twenty-four,' wrote one soldier, and his experience was common enough among enlisted men on both sides. Sleep was difficult for several reasons. For one, nearly every minute of active frontline duty was already taken up with some assigned task or other. Another reason was the noise created by shelling and gunfire. Finally, sleep was difficult because of the conditions in the trenches. Lack of physical comfort and constant mental and emotional stress did not lend themselves to lengthy, deep, or untroubled sleep."[49]

Norman Gladden, a British soldier who had fought on the Western Front before being transferred to the Italian Front, found the change "a much more pleasant experience than similar occasions in Flanders had been. Italy produced little shelling, and the head-quarter billets were usually unshattered houses, often standing nakedly above the trenches."[50] Later, Gladden rhapsodized about his Italian adventure: "We bivouacked in Italian tents in a meadow on the bank of a stream, and enjoyed the sylvan tranquillity of the place in brilliant sunshine. We seemed to be at least a hundred miles away from the battle line along the top of that steep green wall reaching far above us. We had our refreshing bath and made a visit to the over-flowing divisional canteen set up in the neighbouring village of Fara. The contrast between our two worlds was hardly credible."[51] Gladden's paean to serving in Italy invokes Hemingway's fictionalized account of his own military service in *A Farewell to Arms*, a romantic tale of love on the Italian Front.

Hemingway's fiction was certainly not matched by fact for most of the Austro-Hungarian forces on the Russian, Balkan, Romanian, and Italian fronts. Although those troops sometimes fought from trenches, they mainly fought on open lands and in mountains on these fronts. Photo 10.2 shows how fighting on the mountains differed from fighting from trenches. These troops were often on the move. Wherever they fought, they sought untroubled sleep.

Much of their problem was finding a safe place to sleep—or any place to sleep. Consider the Alpine units in Photo 10.2. Problems existed even on flat land. Imagine a regiment from 3,000 to 5,000 exhausted troops on the march looking for a safe place to bed down for the night. Sometimes they looked for patches of dirt to pitch tents, more likely they looked for a bit of shelter to lie under blankets, and occasionally they occupied a village and commandeered halls, houses, or barns. Hašek's novel *The Good Soldier Švejk* describes such a find: "The company had to be billeted in a small devastated distillery at the other end of the village, where half a company could be put into the fermenting room. The rest were billeted by tens in various farms where the rich nobility had refused to shelter the miserable riff-raff who had lost their homes and land and been reduced to beggary."[52] Almost always, troops slept at the opportunity, not at bedtime. Even peasant soldiers from primitive hovels slept more comfortably at home than in the field, and infinitely more securely.

Biology requires that soldiers get food and sleep; it also dictates that soldiers generate waste. Political and military historians of World War I talk little about latrines; novelists discuss them a lot. Urination and defecation may not be important in the outcome of battles, but they are important in soldiers' lives. As adults back home, they performed these functions privately. Few recruits came from homes with indoor toilets, so they were familiar with an outhouse or a "privy," politely defined as "a private place of easement," like a latrine.[53] In the army, however, latrines were public places, and using them was difficult for new troops. Remarque wrote about his experience:

Photo 10.2: AUSTRO-HUNGARIANS TROOPS IN ITALIAN CAMPAIGN. On the Western Front, most troops fought from trenches spread over flat land. On the Balkan Front, and especially in Italy (here), troops often fought on mountainous battlefields. Credit: *Harper's Pictorial Library of the World War, Volume III: Battles, Sieges and Campaigns* (New York: Harper & Brothers, 1920), p. 225. In the public domain.

I well remember how embarrassed we were as recruits in barracks when we had to use the general latrine. There were no doors and twenty men sat side by side as in a railway carriage, so that they could be reviewed all at one glance, for soldiers must always be under supervision.

Since then we have learned better than to be shy about such trifling immodesties. The soldier is on friendlier terms than other men with his stomach and intestines. Three-quarters of his vocabulary is derived from these regions, and they give an intimate flavour to expressions of his greatest joy as well as of his deepest indignation.[54]

Away from camps, soldiers had to evacuate their bowels however they could, and battle fright sometimes caused them to do so involuntarily. In Remarque's, novel, one terrified recruit was consoled by a veteran: "Many's the man before you has had his pants full after the first bombardment. Go behind that bush there and throw your underpants away."[55] Other novelists wrote about feces in the fields, as in Hašek's *The Good Soldier Švejk*: "And as the troops passed through and camped in the neighbourhood there could be seen everywhere little heaps of human excrement of international extraction belonging to all peoples of Austria, Germany and Russia. The excrement of soldiers of all nation-alities and of confessions lay side by side or heaped on top of one another without quar-relling among themselves."[56]

Inabilities to control the generation and disposition of human waste in the field had health consequences. Men went for days, even weeks, wearing soiled clothing. They lived cheek by jowl in filthy conditions, spreading diseases, often through body lice.[57] Certainly these were not the conditions imagined by those marching off at the start of the war. Author Stefan Zweig recalls what it was like in Vienna: "There were parades in the street, flags, ribbons, and music burst forth everywhere, young recruits were marching tri-umphantly, their faces lighting up at the cheering."[58] Now those still alive at the front were hungry, dirty, exhausted, and often sick.

While good food and rest were important to the troops' comfort, adequate military equipment, primarily rifles, machine guns, and ammunition—especially artillery shells—were important to their survival. Hew Strachan summarized the situation concerning the shells: "Shell shortage was a phenomenon common to all the armies by the winter of 1914–15. Most had built up stocks which they thought would be sufficient for a minimum of three months' fighting, and in some cases six months.' But they ran out of shells much faster than that. The French were short of shells by mid–September, and the Germans, British, and Russians by late October. Thus the cause of shell shortage was not that the war was longer than they had expected but that its nature was different."[59] A new type of warfare arose in which entrenched armies bombarded each other with millions of shells. Strachan explained that the "fixed positions" of trench warfare "enabled the guns to identify more targets. This not only increased shell consumption, it also generated a demand for a different type of shell from that with which most field artillery batteries were equipped in 1914. Shrapnel, which burst in the air scattering fragments in a forward projection, was the preferred munition against dispersed infantrymen advancing over open ground. But high explosive was deemed more appropriate against men who had dug in."[60]

Currie cited staggering artillery statistics: "On one day in September 1917 alone, the British fired off nearly a million rounds of ammunition from their heavy guns. A two-week period of heavy fire outside Ypres, Belgium, cost the British another 4 million rounds or more."[61] Winston Churchill, who served as Britain's munitions minister for a time, reported: "Russia had entered the war with about 5,000 guns and 5,000,000 shells. During the first three months of fighting she fired on an average about *45,000 shells day*. The output of her factories in Russia did not exceed *35,000 shells a month*. By the begin-ning of December, 1914, scarcely 300,000 shells, or barely a week's requirement, remained out of the initial reserve."[62] Photo 10.3 proves that a single picture outweighs a thousand words on the consumption of artillery shells in World War I.[63]

Leonard Smith offered a sobering observation on the devastation wrought by such bombardments: "The British fired some 1.5 million shells in the seven days preceding their attack along the Somme in July 1916, or some 30 shells per thousand square yards of front—all for a strategically insignificant advance. By the time the French were successfully advancing in the summer of 1918 they were firing some three shells per meter of front."[64]

Although all warring nations struggled to keep their troops supplied with rifles, machine guns, and ammunition, Austria-Hungary had "embarrassingly small quantities" of such weaponry and little capacity for producing it.[65] In September 1916, according to Norman Stone's research, Germany could produce 7 million shells per month, Russia 4.5 million, and Austria-Hungary 1 million.[66] Fortunately for Austria-Hungary, it did not engage primarily in trench warfare, but was hampered by shortage of artillery shells nonetheless.[67]

Photo 10.3: SHELL CASING ALONG ROADWAY IN FRANCE, 1918. **The phrase, "the contents of which have been dispatched over into the German lines," tagged this photo of shell casings along a roadway in France, which suggests the staggering number of cannon rounds fired in just one engagement. Credit: The photo was taken by British photographer Tom Aitken and made available by the National Library of Scotland at http://deriv.nls.uk/dcn30/7440/74407448.30. jpg. Source attribution permits usage.**

Austria-Hungary struggled to supply its troops with nearly all types of military hardware. Ian Beckett said: "Austro-Hungarian industry never produced more than limited numbers of trench mortars, flame-throwers and light machine guns. Austria-Hungary was also short of rail transport with which to carry war production or, indeed, anything else. The situation was exacerbated by coal shortages, which further reduced not only production of engines and rolling stock, but the ability to keep the rail system running."[68]

Machine guns were the new and efficient troop-killing weapon. Hew Strachan said that two machine guns per battalion was standard across all armies at the beginning of the war. By 1918, each German battalion had six machine guns, with comparable increases in the French, British, and Austro-Hungarian armies.[69] In contrast to rifles, which were relatively easy for peasants to use, machine guns were complex *machinery* that required training to use and maintain properly. Slovak, Ruthenian, Serbian, Romanian, and even Magyar conscripts were challenged to learn war skills that had little to do with farm work or peaceful pursuits of any type.

Austria opened a War Exhibition in 1916 to entertain the public and educate citizens about its newfangled weapons, their soldiers' heroic deeds, and the people's determined will to hold out for a victory. Unfortunately, Hungary—the other half of the empire at war—decided not to participate. Healy said that Hungary demurred, citing "the exclusively Austrian direction of the project, the fact that proceeds would benefit only Austrian charities and the inadvisability of publicly displaying new war technology."[70]

As the war progressed, old people and women left in the troops' home villages suffered from the absence of their sons and husbands. The Slovak novelist writing under the pen name Timrava wrote: "Each day brought new pain to the villagers. The women in black never even paused in their wailing, and always had swollen eyes. Their work didn't go right because their thoughts flew to their husbands and sons. And each day brought new fears, doubts, and rumors that someone else had fallen in battle. This one was mutilated, that one was torn apart by a shell, another had his head blown off, others their hand or foot torn apart. There was no end to the weeping, lamentation, wailing."[71] After more bad news, an old man Demak moaned to an old woman:

"My God, why are we suffering, what are we fighting for?" But he found no reply, no explanation.
"What for?" sighed the old woman sitting in bed, made helpless by her anguish. "Who knows? Probably not even those who started it!"
"For sure they won't tell us, and they'll never ask us whether we want a war," said Anča as she was kneading the dough.[72]

Many Austro-Hungarian troops—especially many non–Germans and non–Magyars—also began to ask why they were fighting. Slavic troops—Slovaks, Czechs, Poles, Ruthenians, Slovenes, Croats, and Serbs—were especially perplexed. Max Hasting recited a conversation between a Russian casualty and a wounded Habsburg prisoner on the same cart:

"Hungarian?"
"No—Slovak."
"Have a lot of you surrendered?"
"Oh yes, a lot, and a lot are killed…. We had fun in the first days, but after that not at all. There was no food…. Bread had run out and tins as well, they only gave us coffee twice."
The Slovak told the Russian that he had left a wife and two children in the Carpathians. In the usual placatory fashion of prisoners, he praised the Russians and called them a kind, good people.
"Tell me, sirs, what have we been fighting for? I don't know why they sent us to fight our own people."[73]

In 1930, American Dorothy Giles published a travel book, *The Road Through Czecho-slovakia*, that contained this conversation about the Great War with a man in Bohemia. He registered his confusion in his reply: "For seven years I fought. Four times I was wounded. When the War came, the Mayor stood up in the square. He said we Bohemians were of Austria, and we must defend our fatherland against the Italians…. My company was with the Hungarians. They are not like us, the Hungarians. But they were good fellows in their way. When things were very bad, Kaiser Karl came to visit us. He said that we were all Austrians and soon the War would be over, and we would go back to our homes and all would be well."

Although World War I only spanned five calendar years, the villager said he fought for seven years. The other two years came after the 1918 armistice and the founding of Czechoslovakia, which sparked localized conflict with Hungary. "Then there was peace. An officer came from Prague. He said that we Czechs were not Austrians any more. He said we must defend our fatherland against the Hungarians. They sent us away to Slovakia, to the Carpathians, to fight the Hungarians. For three years there I fought the men who had been my comrades. It is hard to understand…."[74]

Samko Mozolák too had to wonder what the war was about, and why he was in it. Given his unhappy experience in a Magyar school in his Slovak village, he certainly did not wish to sustain Magyar rule in Hungary. He was also not devoted to Emperor Franz Josef, a Habsburg of German extraction who had ignored Magyar repression of his fellow Slovaks. With a wife, three young children, and money in the mattress, Samko was not in the army to get girls and see the world. He had already lived in the new world and left it to return to the old. No, Samko was in the army because Franz Josef had declared war on Serbia. The emperor had commanded his subject's service, and Samko was compelled to serve.

11

Imperial Irrelevance

Chapter 7, "Imperial Deciders," described Emperor Franz Josef, Kaiser Wilhelm II, and Tsar Nicholas II as their nations' "deciders" concerning the question of war or peace. They alone were empowered to "push the button" to start a war. Franz Josef was the first to push it on July 28, 1914, by declaring war against Serbia; followed by Tsar Nicholas II, who ordered general mobilization of troops (tantamount to declaring war) on July 31; and by Wilhelm II, who declared war on Russia on August 1. After they decided to start the Great War, they were largely bypassed by their generals in waging it. Their Imperial Majesties became irrelevant to the war's eventual outcome.

Once upon a time, emperors, kaisers, tsars, and kings actually and effectively commanded their forces. In the first two decades of the 18th century, Russian Tsar Peter the Great devised military campaigns and personally led his forces into battle. He famously fought against Swedish King Charles XII, described as "the most daring and aggressive soldier of the age."[1] King Charles's soldierly predecessor, King Gustavus Adolphus, who died leading a cavalry charge, had standardized field artillery and later attached cannons to cavalry units. Despite these developments in warfare during the era, Peter the Great's biographer, Robert Massie, wrote: "The decisive arm, however, was not the artillery or the cavalry but the infantry, and the great battles of the age were won by infantry battalions advancing or standing in line, fighting each other with muskets, flintlocks, pikes and, later, bayonets."[2] Even then, Massie said, "The organization of a battle—keeping thousands of men in ranks, arriving in proper formations at the proper moment, under enemy fire—was in itself a stupendous task."

Infantry dominated battle to the middle of the 19th century. By the American Civil War of 1861–1865, soldiers no longer relied on pikes and flintlocks. Cannons became far more powerful; railroads transported troops and supplies; and the telegraph sent messages. But troops still used horses and bayonets, and military campaigns were planned and fought similarly to the way they were in the age of Peter the Great and King Charles XII. Monarchs in the middle of the 19th century could still personally command their armies in battle. In fact, they did in the 1859 Battle of Solferino in present-day Italy. That was the last major battle "in which all the armies were under personal command of their monarchs"—Franz Josef, France's Napoleon III, and Victor Emmanuel II, leading the Sardinian Army.[3] After Austria-Hungary lost, Franz Josef never again took direct command of his forces in battle.

By the beginning of the 20th century—as weapons of war became more mechanized, along with the means of transporting weapons, troops, and supplies—the task of running a war outstripped monarchs' knowledge and capabilities. War was entrusted to professionals. Margaret MacMillan succinctly illustrated the new situation: "When Germany called up over 2 million men, with their tons of materials and some 118,000 horses, in the summer of 1914, it took 20,800 trains just to get them ready to be moved toward the frontiers."[4] As professionals planned for the next war, they relied on technical experts—scores of them. Of the German preparations for war, MacMillan says, "Underlying the war plans, and one of the most important parts of the work of the general staff, were hundreds of pages of detailed mobilization and railway plans."[5] A.J.P. Taylor even suggested that military experts planned "war by timetable."[6] Despite the increasing complexity of warfare, European monarchs were loath to relinquish control of their armies.

As discussed in Chapter 5, "Imperial Ignorance," the Austro-Hungarian Emperor, the German Kaiser, and the Russian Tsar headed their nations' armies and navies as Supreme Commanders or "War Lords." Each treated the military as an extension of his personal rule. The sovereigns installed and uninstalled generals, proposed and opposed changes in military operations, drew up potential battle plans, and designed military uniforms. Kaiser Wilhelm II was especially keen on building a German navy greater than Britain's.

Years before conflict broke out, key generals anticipated a major European war and worked feverishly to gain military advantage. Gordon Brook-Shepherd wrote: "In every major continental capital it was the generals who now hotted that pace up beyond containment. Each step they urged upon their sovereigns was intended to place their armies in the best position to fight that European war which, by 28 July, had appeared on the horizon."[7] In times of peace, the real generals prudently allowed their Imperial War Lords to play war games. Their monarchs gleefully commanded real soldiers—and predictably won the games. When real fighting occurred, the generals took over the war, and the three divine commanders—to different degrees—became irrelevant.

Of the three sovereigns, Kaiser Wilhelm's impact on the start and conduct of the war "remains the most controversial," according to Christopher Clark, who said, "The extent of his power within the German executive is still hotly disputed." (Chapter 7, "Imperial Deciders," offers some conflicting claims.) Clark wrote that Wilhelm claimed to be in charge: "The Kaiser certainly came to the throne intending to be the author of his country's foreign policy. "The Foreign Office? Why, I am the Foreign Office!" he once exclaimed. "I am the sole master of German policy," he remarked in a letter to the Prince of Wales (the future Edward VII), "and my country must follow me wherever I go."[8] Also, John Röhl said in his exhaustive biography of Wilhelm II: "As Kaiser, King, and Supreme War Lord, Wilhelm II was simply bound to be central to the decision-making process in July 1914, and a heavy responsibility rests on his shoulders for the terrible catastrophe that befell the world that summer."[9]

For years Wilhelm claimed that in case of war, he would be his own chief of staff. When war actually broke out, he turned command over to the German General Staff and gave Field Marshal von Moltke permission to issue orders in his name.[10] Röhl notes that even in the early weeks, "the Kaiser played a less active role than might be supposed." Röhl identified the "actual wire-pullers" at the start of the July crisis as "the Chancellor [Theobald von Bethmann Hollweg] and the Foreign Secretary [Gottlieb von Jagow], together with the Under Secretary in the Auswärtiges Amt [Ministry of Foreign Affairs], Arthur Zimmermann, and the Director of its Political Department Wilhelm von Stumm." The week before the outbreak of the war: "[T]he generals Erich von Falkenhayn and Helmuth von Moltke then took control. The Chancellor sent Wilhelm off on his annual cruise along the coast of Norway, partly in order to create the impression that Germany had no foreknowledge of the bomb about to explode in the Balkans, but partly also to prevent the unpredictable monarch from interfering with the *circulos* of the Wilhelm-strasse [home of the foreign office]."[11]

Another of Wilhelm's biographers, Giles MacDonogh, reported Wilhelm's complaints to a visitor: "The Kaiser says he was treated as a nonentity by his General Staff; that they made a point of contradicting every order or command that he gave; that he was turned out of the room whenever the telephone rang at Headquarters, so as not to hear the commands and the real facts."[12] According to Röhl, war-hawk politicians and generals felt that the unpredictable kaiser needed to be "managed" so that he would not upset their plans: "There is evidence that the Kaiser was to some extent manipulated, and at times even misled, both by Bethmann and by the military leaders, particularly when, after his return to the capital at the end of July, he sought to prevent Britain's entry into the war."[13]

Once the war started, German military and political leaders relegated the kaiser to the sidelines and took over. Winston Churchill said that Wilhelm might be asked to decide between competing battle plans, "as one might spin a coin," but he was irrelevant otherwise.[14] General Helmuth von Moltke commanded the General Staff from the start of the war until he was dismissed after Germany's defeat in the battle of the Marne. Moltke was replaced by General Erich von Falkenhayn, who served until August 1916. Falkenhayn was replaced by General Paul von Hindenburg and General Erich Ludendorff—formally Hindenburg's deputy but regarded as more creative and dominant. After July 1917, when Theobald von Bethmann Hollweg was dismissed as Chancellor, Hindenburg and Ludendorff wielded enormous power. Churchill said that they "had usurped, or at least acquired, the main control over policy. The Emperor, inwardly appalled by the tide of events, suspected of being a pacifist at heart, failed increasingly to play his part. Thus on definite trials of strength the military power proved repeatedly to be predominant."[15]

Other observers provided sharper judgments of the joint rule of Hindenburg and Ludendorff. Miranda Carter said, "Germany had become essentially a military dictatorship; Wilhelm was the flimsy fig leaf."[16] Gary Shanafelt reported an Austrian leader's conclusion that "Germany had become a 'pure military dictatorship,'"[17] while Holger Herwig wrote, "Few checks, if any, existed to curb the near-absolute 'silent dictatorship' of the Supreme Command. The Kaiser had long been relegated to the background, a pathetic figurehead."[18]

Having become irrelevant for running the war long earlier, Wilhelm was stripped of his prize title, "Supreme War Lord," in September 1917, when the military awarded it to Hindenburg. A dejected Wilhelm moaned, "I may as well abdicate."[19] Abdication came later, after the war's outcome had been decided. On November 10, 1918, the former Kaiser Wilhelm II of Germany and King of Prussia crossed the border into the Netherlands, where he lived until June 1941.

If, to Germany's generals, their Supreme War Lord was unpredictable and needed managing before becoming irrelevant to their war plans, Russia's Supreme Commander from the beginning was notably indecisive and generally incompetent to command. (One historian said a royal observer described Tsar Nicholas II's rule as "an autocracy without an autocrat."[20]) At the beginning, the tsar—enthralled by his military—gave free rein to his generals and became "a reviewer of troops, a pinner-on of medals, a visitor to munitions factories and hospitals."[21]

In true imperial tradition, the tsar had named his uncle, Grand Duke Nicholas Niko-laevich and grandson of Tsar Nicholas I, as commander in chief of the Russian Imperial Army. Appointed in August 1914 (the month war began), Nikolai Nikolaevich had not participated in its planning and was not allowed to choose his own staff to replace the tsar's cronies. Nevertheless, he accepted the command. In his novel *August 1914*, Alexan-der Solzhenitsyn explained: "Nikolai Nikolaevich had always regarded the will of the Lord's Anointed as sacred. He had been brought up to regard his nephew as his ruler; otherwise, the monarchical principle was meaningless."[22] The tsar also saddled Grand Duke Nicholas with General Nikolai Nikolaevich Yanushkevich as his chief of staff. Gen-eral Yanushkevich was described as "an office-bound pen-pusher" who himself had never commanded troops in the field.[23] Solzenitsyn's novel depicted the Russian military staff's incompetence leading to the destruction of the Russian Second Army in the Battle of Tannenberg during the first month of the war.

Within months of its start, the war effort became a disaster, according to historian Miranda Carter:

> Vast sums had been poured into the army, but it was still run by courtiers. War planning had been minimal. No one had expected a prolonged conflict and the state's creaking mechanisms simply weren't up to running a long war. Several devastating defeats—the result both of German effective-ness and the hopelessly archaic ideas of the Russian top brass—were followed by the call-up of barely trained reserves, and a supply crisis. The Ministry of War had made no provision for winter uniforms and boots; ammunition began to run out. By early 1915 soldiers were told to limit themselves to ten bullets a day. Losses were huge and pointless. One British observer saw 1,800 new recruits arrive at the front without a single rifle. They waited until casualties made guns available. He then watched as 1,600 of them died.[24]

As military defeats mounted, Nicholas II suddenly fantasized that he, as Tsar of Rus-sia, could change the fortunes of war by taking personal command. Miranda Carter imag-ined him wishfully thinking, "if he took charge God would save Russia, and the devoted peasants would fight all the harder." In September 1915, Nicholas replaced the Grand Duke and his chief of staff and assumed supreme command of the army, with General Mikhail Alekseyev as his chief of staff. Carter described his government's reaction: "It was so clearly a bad idea that when Nicholas announced it his entire Council of Ministers fell silent. 'This is so terrible,' Saxonov wrote in his diary, 'that my mind is in chaos.' It was a decision, another minister noted drily, "fully in tune with his spiritual frame of mind and his mystical understanding of his imperial calling."[25] Having the tsar assume personal command proved to be as bad as his ministers feared. Although General Alek-seyev made the important military decisions, the tsar became personally responsible for Russia's numerous military defeats. The tsar moved from the capital, Petrograd (St. Peters-burg sounded German, so it was renamed) to military headquarters (*Stavka*) in Mogilev, almost 500 miles south of Petrograd. Away from the seat of government, he was unable to appreciate Russia's political deterioration. By early 1917, popular revolts had spread across Russia.

Even during the March revolution, Tsar Nicholas II never seemed to grasp the sit-uation—that he was not only irrelevant to the war effort but also that he was the source of Russia's social unrest. Winston Churchill stated that Mikhail Rodzianko, Chairman of the State Duma, on March 11, 1917, cabled a frantic message to the tsar, which said in part: "POSITION SERIOUS. ANARCHY IN THE CAPITAL. GOVERNMENT PARALYZED. ARRANGEMENTS FOR TRANSPORT, SUPPLY AND FUEL IN COMPLETE DISORDER.

GENERAL DISCONTENT IS INCREASING. DISORDERLY FIRING ON THE STREETS. PART OF THE TROOPS ARE FIRING ON ONE ANOTHER."[26] Miranda Carter described the tsar's reaction: "Nicholas told his senior commander Alekseev, 'Fat Rodzianko has sent me some nonsense which I shall not even bother to answer,' and suspended the Duma."[27]

En route to Petrograd days later, Nicholas was confronted by his generals, who advised him, begged him, to abdicate. Churchill said the tsar faced "a patriotic revolt against the misfortunes and mismanagement of the War. Defeats and disasters, want of food and prohibition of alcohol, the slaughter of millions of men, joined with inefficiency and corruption to produce a state of exasperation among all classes which had no outlet but revolt, could find no scapegoat but the Sovereign."[28] Finally alerted to reality, Tsar Nicholas II abdicated on March 15, 1917. However, the tsar and his family did not—like Kaiser Wilhelm—enjoy a life of abdication in a friendly country. After living for months under house arrest, Tsar Nicholas II, Tsarina Alexandra, and their five children were murdered by Bolsheviks in July 1918.

Octogenarian emperor Franz Josef attempted to keep up with domestic political affairs and geopolitical strategy, but government had become too complex for direct monarchical rule.[29] World War I historian Christopher Clark wrote:

> An overview of the early twentieth-century monarchs suggests a fluctuating and ultimately relatively modest impact on actual policy outcomes. Emperor Franz Josef of Austria-Hungary read vast quantities of dispatches and met with his foreign ministers regularly. Yet for all his stupendous work as the "first bureaucrat" of his empire, Franz Josef, like Nicholas II, found it impossible to master the oceans of information that came to his desk. Little effort was made to ensure that he apportioned his time in accordance with the relative importance of the issues arising. Austro-Hungarian foreign policy was shaped not by the executive fiats of the Emperor, but by the interaction of factions and lobbies within and around the ministry.[30]

Russian historian Dominic Lieven's observation about tsarist Russia—"No human being can be head of a modern state and government for the whole course of an adult life"[31]— applied perfectly to Franz Josef. Unlike his performance when he was young, octogenarian Franz Josef absented himself from key meetings prior to the Great War. Alan Palmer wrote: "In the critical weeks of the Franco-Prussian War of 1870 the Emperor had presided over five ministerial conferences in twelve days, but he never attended any of the thirty-nine meetings of the Council of Ministers for Common Affairs convened during the last three and a half years before the First World War."[32]

By 1913 Franz Josef had already ceded considerable military authority to his dynastic heir, Archduke Franz Ferdinand—despite regarding him as aggressive, impetuous, and of questionable judgment. Nevertheless, he named Franz Ferdinand Inspector General of the armed forces, making him second only to the emperor in defense matters.[33] Franz Ferdinand's appointment did not signal any change in policy. The emperor had long pursued peace in international politics, and Ferdinand had been quoted as warning, "A war between Austria and Russia would end either with the overthrow of the Romanovs or with that of the Habsburgs, perhaps with both."[34] Niall Ferguson, among many historians, viewed Archduke Ferdinand as "restraining the recklessly bellicose" chief of staff, Franz Conrad von Hötzendorf.[35]

Conrad, however, itched to go to war with Serbia, or with Italy, or with one or two other countries. Max Hastings cited a passage from Franz Ferdinand to Leopold von Berchtold, Austria-Hungary's foreign minister: "Excellency! Don't let yourself be influenced by Conrad—ever! Not an iota of support for any of his yappings at the Emperor!

Naturally he wants every possible war, every kind of hooray! rashness that will conquer Serbia and God knows what else…. Through war he wants to make up for the mess that's his responsibility at least in part. Therefore: let's not play Balkan warriors ourselves. Let's not stoop to this hooliganism. Let's stay aloof and watch scum bash in each other's skulls. It'd be unforgivable, insane, to start something that would pit us against Russia."[36]

One historian reported that Franz Josef was already so feeble that "that whenever Archduke Franz Ferdinand repaired to his Bohemian country house or to his Adriatic palace, a special tram was kept waiting to rush him back to Vienna in case the emperor was stricken."[37] Ironically, the emperor's heir died first. While acting in his capacity as Inspector General, Franz Ferdinand was assassinated in Sarajevo, where he went to observe military maneuvers in Bosnia-Herzegovina. An article evaluating his influence stated, "Alive, Franz Ferdinand had acted as a brake upon the pressures for military action; dead, he became the pretext for war."[38]

In spite of being almost 84 years old when he declared war on Serbia to defend Austria-Hungary's honor after the assassination, Franz Josef certainly had more initial impact on the Great War than the kaiser and the tsar. Emperor Franz Josef started it. Afterward, however, Franz Josef played no operational role in the war's conduct. Sean McMeekin wrote, "Emperor Franz Josef I, as ultimate arbiter and signator of all key decisions, … did not design the policies—he merely confirmed them."[39] His biographer, contemporary, and occasional advisor, Joseph Redlich, gave this account of the emperor's distance from the war he started: "He never took any part in the strategic decisions of Headquarters, located, during his lifetime, at Teschen in eastern Silesia. His loyal old head of the military chancellery, General von Bolfras, kept him regularly informed on everything to do with the conduct and policy of the war. He was deeply incensed by the confidential reports that began to reach him rather early, of desertions from Czech, Ruthenian and Italian regiments, but does not seem to have realized anything like their full political significance."[40]

Already old when he declared war against Serbia on July 28, 1914, Franz Josef did his best to monitor its developments without involving his heir apparent, 27-year-old Archduke Karl. Although young Karl was isolated from military affairs, he was placed at the disposition of the high command—in accordance with dynastic tradition. Formally, the emperor was the army's supreme commander, but he delegated his military authority to Habsburg Archduke Friedrich, who in turn entrusted his powers to chief of staff Conrad von Hötzendorf. Already irrelevant to the conduct of the war, the old emperor's role became more passive than ever. Arthur May said, "Emperor Francis Josef stamped his approval upon what the officials had decided."[41] Gary Shanafelt relates a story told by Austrian staff officer Edmund Glaise von Horstenau after an audience with Franz Josef toward the end of 1915: "The Emperor complained that Conrad did not keep him properly informed, then momentarily dozed off in the middle of Glaise's report. Franz Josef occasionally presided at meetings of the Common Ministers Council and continued his habitual routine, reading and approving dispatches, almost to the day of his death. But he was clearly no longer able to muster the energy to make major decisions or directly supervise the war effort."[42]

Until his death on November 21, 1916, Franz Josef plugged away reading and signing routine reports and documents. Joseph Redlich sympathetically wrote: "On November 20, Franz Josef exerted his last strength in a vain effort to deal with the papers that had that morning been brought to him. He was not to leave his bed again. An agonizing cough robbed him of sleep and he sank hour by hour. On November 21, at 9 o'clock in the evening, he was released from his suffering."[43] Redlich continued to say, "The Emperor's death did not make any great difference to the people, the less that, since the beginning of the war, Francis Josef had personally disappeared altogether from their vision."[44] Nevertheless, a vast crowd stood in reverent silence along the route of the funeral procession.

Redlich, who attended Franz Josef's funeral on that cold November day, wrote that despite "frightful losses in the war, that still raged, suffering and the permanent under-feeding of millions in the capital," many thousands of Viennese lined the street to pay respect to the only monarch they had ever known. The emperor's funeral cortege through the streets of Vienna is documented in film footage on YouTube.[45] Certainly many fewer viewed their emperor lying in state (Photo 11.1).

Arthur May respectfully described the funeral over ten pages in *The Passing of the Hapsburg Monarchy 1914–1918*.[46] Here is his touching description of the emperor's entombment:

> At the Church of the Capuchins, Montenuovo [a court official], obedient to ancient ritual, advanced to the door and, after banging on it with a staff, demanded admission. From within the Guardian Father, as though taken unawares, inquired in deep, sepulchral tones:
> "Who is there?"

Photo 11.1: EMPEROR FRANZ JOSEF, LYING IN STATE. **Emperor Franz Josef of Austria-Hungary died on November 21, 1916, at age 86. Appointed emperor on December 2, 1848, he ruled his empire for eleven days short of 68 years. Credit: Albert Margutti, *The Emperor Francis Joseph and His Times* (New York: George H. Dooran Company, 1921). In the public domain.**

"His Majesty, the most sovereign Emperor, Francis Joseph."
"I know him not."
"The Emperor of Austria and the Apostolic King of Hungary."
"I know him not."
After a third knock on the church door, the Guardian Father asked,
"Who demands to enter?"
"A man of sin, our brother Francis Joseph."
Thereupon the door was gently opened and the coffin was carried to the subterranean crypt.[47]

"Respect" was perhaps the best description of public feeling toward their emperor. Not particularly friendly to anyone, he was courteous to virtually everyone. Unlike the isolated Nicholas II or the imperious Wilhelm II, Franz Josef made himself formally accessible to the public. The contemporary Hungarian author István Deák wrote admiringly: "He granted over a hundred audiences weekly, receiving all visitors, be they archdukes, cabinet members, or the poorest of the poor, in the same atmosphere of dignity and carefully orchestrated ritual. Standing at attention, the emperor-king caused his visitors to adopt the same military posture and to report to him briefly and precisely."[48] Unlike many Austrian officials, including and especially the assassinated Archduke Ferdinand, Franz Josef did not overtly dislike Magyars, or any of the nationalities under his rule. The emperor learned to speak a decent Magyar to go along with Czech and Italian (in addition to his native German and the international diplomatic language, French). In contrast, his assassinated heir Franz Ferdinand knew no Magyar, was incensed when Hungarian officers spoke it in his presence, and reportedly closed the curtains on his personal train when traveling through Hungary.[49]

Of special note in that infamously anti–Semitic region and era, Franz Josef showed no hostility to Jews. He consulted often and was friendly to the Jewish statesman Joseph Redlich. More significantly, he protested when "certain Viennese circles" refused shelter to Jewish refugees from Galicia and offered to accommodate them himself in his summer palace at Schönbrunn.[50]

Pieter Judson offered a revised view of Franz Josef as a ruler who "watched over the progressive transformations of society, moderating social radicalism of the politicians when necessary."[51] Similarly, John Deak claimed, "The monarchy was drastically transformed under Emperor Franz Josef (reigned 1848–1916) into a complex, multinational polity."[52] However, both authors focused on progress only in the Austrian half of the empire. Judson himself said, "If in Austria a centralized system was devolving, increasing power of the communes and crownland governments, in Hungary the opposite took place."[53] Deak mentioned Hungary only twice in his long essay, and that only in passing.[54]

Franz Josef had ruled Austria-Hungary as emperor and king for eleven days short of sixty-eight years. Under his long rule, his Dual Monarchy suffered increased domestic strife. Austria experienced conflicts from Czechs who demanded political rights on a par with those enjoyed by Germans, tensions with Italy over Austrian lands populated with Italians, and pressures from Serbs and Slovenians to fulfill their own national interests. Meanwhile, Hungary smothered claims from Slovaks, Ruthenians, Serbs, and Romanians who sought political rights commensurate with those given to Magyars.

Internationally, Austria-Hungary was no longer widely regarded as one of Europe's Great Powers. Geoffrey Wawro wrote that in 1913 a Vienna newspaper referred to Austria as "the *Schlemihl* of Europe": "'No one likes us and every disaster befalls us.' Only the

'Sick Man of Europe,' the decrepit Ottoman Empire, which had just lost provinces in North Africa and the Balkans to hungry new powers, could compete with Austria for the title of 'world's biggest loser.'"[55] The emperor was aware of the domestic problems and the international decline in stature, but he was stuck in the past and unable to meet the governing challenge. He denied that the 1867 Compromise with Hungary—which gave Magyars control over their minorities—lay at the root of his inability to address minorities' problems in Austria. He also denied that the Compromise—which allowed Hungary to veto the army's expansion and improvement—pushed Austria-Hungary toward *Schlemihl* status. Franz Josef deserved his people's respect as a person and perhaps even their admiration. However, he did not govern his empire well, and he eventually destroyed it by declaring war on Serbia in a horribly misguided attempt to restore its honor.

As related in Chapter 1, "The Emperor in Vienna," Franz Josef suffered through three tragedies in his personal life before the 1914 assassinations in Sarajevo. In 1861 his younger brother Maximilian was executed by firing squad in Mexico after an aborted attempt to become its emperor. In 1889, his son and heir, the psychologically troubled Crown Prince Rudolph, shot his mistress and committed suicide. In 1898, his wife Empress Elisabeth was assassinated in a random act of anarchism. After his wife's murder, according to Alan Palmer, Franz Josef cried, *"Mir bleibt doch gar nichts erspart auf dieser Welt!"* ["So I am to be spared nothing in this world!"].[56]

But he was spared something. Redlich, at the end of Franz Josef's biography, summed up the emperor's life: "Thus it seems that tragedy in the full sense belongs not so much to Francis Joseph as to the imperial idea, in the old Austrian sense, as embodied in him. If he himself once voiced the complaint, 'Nothing in this world has been spared me,' his biographer must reply that the last blow was spared him—the downfall of his realm." That tragedy—the collapse of Austria-Hungary and the end of Habsburg rule in Europe—remained to be endured by his grandnephew and successor, Archduke Karl.

Archduke Karl, also known as Charles,[57] became emperor at age 29 immediately after Franz Josef's death on November 21. He was crowned Karl I, Emperor of Austria, and Karl IV, King of Hungary, on December 30. Despite his youth and political inexperience, Karl vowed to govern the country over which he reigned. Gary Shanafelt wrote: "Where Franz Joseph had little more than passively approved his advisers' policies in the last years of his reign, Karl intended to take an active part in decision-making, and, despite his inexperience, to alter both the domestic and the foreign policy basis of the Monarchy."[58] Karl assumed the title of Supreme Commander of the whole army from Archduke Frederick on December 2, but—for the time—he kept Conrad von Hötzendorf as Chief of Staff. In so doing, Karl retained someone as committed to continuing the war as Karl was to ending it.

To the new emperor, and to contemporary observers, the war had devastated Austria-Hungary at the end of 1916. Karl determined to end it quickly and peacefully. According to Holger Herwig, the new emperor had a lot to learn: "Unfortunately, Karl brought to the throne a strange combination of idealism, inexperience, obstinacy, and personal prejudices; he was 'volatile, lacking in balance and experience, and strangely unable to make and stick with decisions.' Karl's overall programme was to seek an end to the war, to consolidate the Monarchy by way of internal reforms, and to shake off German suzerainty."[59] In late January 1917, a month following his coronation, Karl secretly sought peace separately from Germany. His wife Zita's brothers, Sixtus and Xavier, both princes of Bourbon-Parma (an Italian branch of the Spanish House of Bourbon), were officers in the opposing

Belgian army. They met in Switzerland with their mother, Maria Antonia, Duchess of Bourbon-Parma. She gave them a letter from Karl stating terms for a negotiated peace between Austria-Hungary and the Entente. Sixtus met secretly with Karl later, but they could not convince French and British leaders to accept their peace terms.

Their clandestine meetings were publicly exposed in April 1918, and Karl suffered severely from what became known as the Sixtus Affair. Shanafelt wrote: "The result of the crisis was to discredit the dynasty among the Austrian Germans and the Magyars, previously its strongest supporters, while Karl's efforts to ingratiate himself with the Germans after it broke had the same effect on the other nationalities. The Emperor was rumored to be completely under the influence of the Empress Zita and her shady if not treasonable Parma family connections. The throne lost its moral authority among its subjects, perhaps the last means of countering the political and economic disintegration around it."[60]

As the war turned sharply against the Central Powers in the summer of 1918, Karl renewed his efforts to seek a separate peace. In September and October he appealed to United States' President Woodrow Wilson for peace on the basis of Wilson's Fourteen Points, which had caught European politicians' imagination, even if it eluded their understanding. In keeping with the spirit of Wilson's "Points," Karl issued an Imperial Manifesto transforming the Austrian half of the country into a federal state with autonomous Romanian and Ruthene national councils.[61]

The nationality groups paid little attention to his efforts, and President Wilson paid none—refusing to deal at all with the Habsburg monarchy. Herwig reported on Joseph Redlich's last meeting with Emperor Karl I of Austria and King Karl IV on Hungary at Schönbrunn Palace on November 8: "Pity overcame Redlich, though he was no monarchist. He found the 'poor young Kaiser' stripped of all authority and power, a solitary and pathetic figure amidst the baroque splendour of the Habsburg palace built by Karl VI and Maria Theresa, and once occupied by Napoleon I. The Army had been 'split into a million atoms.' Not a 'trace of the power' of the old Habsburg dynasty remained, 'neither in Vienna nor in Prague, neither in Budapest nor in Agram' [the German name for Zagreb, Croatia]. The dichotomy between Karl's current powerlessness and the grandeur of Schönbrunn 'symbolizes the deepest tragedy of earthly fame and human power.'" Sunday, November 10, 1918, when he attended mass in Schönbrunn's imperial chapel, marked Karl's final public appearance as emperor. His cabinet begged him to abdicate the next day. C.L. Sulzberger reported his wife Zita's retort: "A king can never abdicate; he can only be deposed. I would rather die with you here. Then Otto [their son] would succeed us, and if he were deposed there will always be enough Habsburgs left."[62]

Karl did issue a statement on November 11, but it was more a renouncement than an abdication.[63] The ex-imperial family traveled by train to take up residence in Switzerland. Stefan Zweig happened to be at the Austrian border station, Feldkirch, when he witnessed the arrival of a special sort of train: it was "not the customary, shabby, weather-beaten kind, but with spacious black cars, a train de luxe. The locomotive stopped. There was a perceptible stir among the lines of those waiting but I was still in the dark. Then I recognized behind the plate glass window of the car Emperor Karl, the last emperor of Austria standing with his black-clad wife, Empress Zita. I was startled; the last emperor of Austria, heir of the Habsburg dynasty which had ruled for seven hundred years, was forsaking his realm!"[64] The Hapsburgs joined the Russian Romanovs and the German Hohenzollerns among the politically displaced dynasties. As dramatized in the impressive 1974 BBC TV miniseries *The Fall of Eagles*,[65] all three imperial eagles had fallen.

The dynastic eagles had become irrelevant militarily long before they fell. Austria-Hungary's generals had planned for war against Serbia for years, so the country had adequate time to prepare for the war when it finally began. Indeed, *all* the Great Powers had battle plans for wars against likely enemies, usually their neighbors. French generals had formulated a series of plans (designated with Roman numerals) for recovering the Alsace and Lorraine territories lost to Germany in the 1870 Franco-Prussian war. War historian Ian Beckett said, "Plans VIII and IX in 1887 and 1888 had been offensive but then Plans X to XVI between 1889 and 1909 had reverted to what might be termed a defensive-offensive strategy."[66]

Russian generals also had contemplated fighting Germany on its west, as well as the Ottoman Empire to the south, but Russia's objectives in the two cases were different. Russia by 1910 had "Plan 19" for a two-front war against Germany and its ally, Austria-Hungary.[67] Russia would invade East Prussia on the northwest and Galicia, the Habsburg province, on the southwest.[68] Concerning the Ottoman Empire, Geoffrey Wawro summarized the tsar's dream: "Tsar Nicholas II vowed to push into the Balkan space, nurture Slavic kingdoms like Serbia, and annex a land bridge to Constantinople and the Dardanelles, reclaiming the old Eastern Orthodox capital and linking the Black Sea and the Mediterranean through the Turkish Straits."[69] Russian generals' Plan 19 against Germany and Austria-Hungary was conceived as a defensive measure, to counter Germany's expected aggression. Russia had no desire to "digest large populations of disgruntled Germans" or Poles who (through past experience) were "implacably hostile to Russian rule." Therefore, according to William Fuller, "plans to exact territorial gains from either Germany or Austria-Hungary had considerable drawbacks."[70] To the south, however, Russia definitely coveted the two straits in Turkey, the Dardanelles and Bosphorus, that controlled access to the Black Sea.

As the largest empire in the world, Britain planned simply to keep the status quo. Winston Churchill wrote, "The Cabinet was overwhelmingly pacific": "At least three-quarters of its members were determined not to be drawn into a European quarrel, unless Great Britain were herself attacked, which was not likely. Those who were in this mood were inclined to believe first of all that Austria and Serbia would not come to blows; secondly, that if they did, Russia would not intervene; thirdly, if Russia intervened, that Germany would not strike; fourthly, they hoped that if Germany struck at Russia, it ought to be possible for France and Germany mutually to neutralize each other without fighting."[71] Historically, Britain had regarded France as its mortal enemy, but began to see Germany as the greater threat, especially if she controlled the continent by conquering France. Although Britain had fewer than a million soldiers—by far the smallest army of the Great Powers—its navy was twice as strong as Germany's, and it was determined to exceed Germany's plans to enlarge its navy to challenge Britain. Moreover, according to Churchill, navies (unlike armies) were inherently mobilized. "The British Navy had all its best ships fully and permanently manned with whole-time men…. Measured by quality nearly the whole of its power was therefore constantly available."[72] Britain's army posed no threat to Germany, but Britain's navy did.

Thus, Germany had some basis for thinking that all of the Great Powers save Austria-Hungary were potential enemies. Historians say that Germany had an "encirclement complex."[73] Although recent writers have questioned the importance and even the existence of the fabled Schlieffen Plan,[74] most historians contend that Germany based its military strategy on a 1905–06 memorandum by chief of staff Count von Schlieffen, who

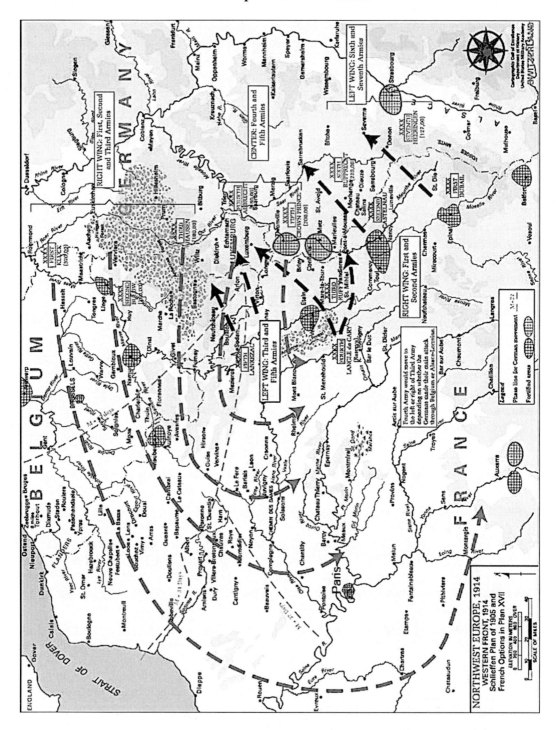

Map 11.1: THE SCHLIEFFEN PLAN. Before retiring in 1906, Germany's Chief of Staff Count von Schlieffen (who died in 1913) envisioned a novel plan for a Franco-German war. He proposed to conquer France by sweeping through Belgium and attacking from the north. Credit: Department of History, United States Military Academy at West Point, from http://alphahistory.com/worldwar1/world-war-i-maps/nggallery/page/1. In the public domain.

retired in 1906 and died in 1913.[75] Schlieffen envisioned a novel plan for a Franco-German war. Dismissing Russia as too weak to fight after its disastrous 1905 defeat by Japan, Schlieffen proposed to conquer France by sweeping through Belgium and attacking from the north, as diagrammed in Figure 11.1.

His successor, Helmuth von Moltke, adapted Schlieffen's plan for a two-front war against both France and Russia, which by 1914 had recovered from its Japanese debacle. Like Schlieffen, Moltke would attack France from the north, expecting a quick victory. Germany would merely hold Russia at bay on the east until it could bolster its troops with those that had just crushed France. Some critics contend that Moltke's adaptations—fewer troops sweeping through Belgium—weakened the plan.[76] Others defended his changes.[77] Like Schlieffen, Moltke counted on support from Austria-Hungary, its partner since 1870 in their Dual Alliance. Unlike Schlieffen, he did not count on help from Italy, their partner since 1882 in the shaky Triple Alliance.

As early as 1909, Austria-Hungary's chief of staff, Franz Conrad von Hötzendorf, had formulated his own plans for fighting a major war. The plural term, "major *wars*," is more appropriate, for Conrad at different times conjured up alternative targets: Serbia, Italy, Montenegro, Albania, and even Russian Poland. Conrad seemed to regard war as a cure-all for Austria-Hungary's declining stature. Holger Herwig quoted Austria-Hungary's Foreign Minister as saying that Conrad's counsel was simply, "war, war, war."[78]

Beginning in 1909, for example, Conrad had alternative plans for fighting three wars, designated as Case "I" for Italy or Case "R" for Russia, and a minor war against Serbia and Montenegro, Case "B."[79] After the Archduke Franz Ferdinand's assassination on June 28, 1914, Conrad saw the chance to punish Serbia ("Dog Serbia") for the dastardly deed by ethnic Serbs.[80] He would activate Case B.

According to Wilhelm II's biographer, John Röhl, German generals and some politicians also saw the assassination "as a welcome opportunity to launch the so-called preventive war against Russia and France [following the Schlieffen plan] under what they thought would be favourable circumstances: neither Russia nor France was militarily 'ready,' and England, faced with the Irish problem, the militant suffragette movement and other difficulties, could not go to war...."[81]

Although military and political leaders expected Russia to defend Serbia from any attack, Conrad's original battle plans were aimed only at Serbia.[82]

Under pressure from Germans and Hungarians fearful of Russian retaliation, Conrad returned to his 1909 plan for a possible war against Russia in Hungary's northeast region of Galicia and against Serbia to the southeast: "Minimal forces were assigned to the south (*Minimalgruppe Balkan*, with 12 divisions) and to Galicia (*A-Staffel*, with 30 divisions), and either of these could be brought up to offensive strength by the addition of a "swing force," *B-Staffel*, with 12 infantry divisions and 1 of cavalry."[83] D.E. Showalter described Conrad's 1914 version of his plan: "Eight divisions were to deploy against Serbia, twenty-eight against Russia. The remaining twelve might be considered either a swing force or a strategic reserve, to be deployed where the need was greatest."[84]

Characterizing Conrad's action as "a masterpiece of Habsburg bumbling," Niall Ferguson said, "Conrad initially sent four of his reserve of twelve divisions to Serbia, then had to recall them to Galicia when it became clear that the German 8th Army was not going to assist him against the Russians." As Showalter observed, "They would spend the war's crucial first weeks shuttling from one theatre to the other, and being nowhere at the right time." In Winston Churchill's oft-cited assessment of Conrad's actions: he removed his army "before it could win him a victory" and swung his strategic reserve to Galicia "in time to participate in its defeat."[85]

Assessing the importance of strategic plans, war historian John Keegan said, "Plans do not determine outcomes. The happenings set in motion by a particular scheme of action will rarely be those narrowly intended, are intrinsically unpredictable and will ramify beyond the anticipation of the instigator."[86] That was true of Moltke's two-front plan for war against France and Russia and of Conrad's two-front plan against Serbia and Russia. Realizing that Russia—whose population was 1.5 times the combined populations of Germany and Austria-Hungary—could mobilize overwhelming numbers of troops, each plan *depended* on quick victories against their smaller opponents, France and Serbia. If the first phase failed, so did the strategy for victory. In fact, nothing went as planned for the Central Powers. Germany did not defeat France quickly and was soon bogged down in a two-front war. Austria-Hungary did not dispatch Serbia promptly and was soon bogged down in its own two-front war.

To complicate their situation, the two Central Power allies did not work closely together and had different primary targets. Germany's primary target was France, but attacking France meant fighting Russia, France's ally. Austria-Hungary's primary target was Serbia, but attacking Serbia meant fighting Russia, Serbia's Slavic champion. Only through their military alliance did France and Serbia become Germany's and Austria-Hungary's common enemies. Otherwise, Austria-Hungary had no quarrel with France, nor Germany with Serbia. Only at the very end of the war did Austria-Hungary send troops to fight in France, and they arrived too late to help. In contrast, Germany was forced to rescue Austria-Hungary's military from defeats on every front in the Eastern Theater—the Balkan, Russian, Romanian, and Italian.

Prior to the war, Germany's chief of staff Moltke and Austria-Hungary's chief of staff Franz Conrad von Hötzendorf discussed their joint responsibilities for war with Russia.[87] According to war historian Ian Beckett, Moltke—who "had had no great faith in Austro-Hungarian military prowess"—did not commit anything definite; neither did a wary Conrad: "Conrad formed the impression that Germany would support Austria-Hungary in any future war and that Moltke had promised an early offensive by the German Eighth Army in the east. In turn, Moltke formed the impression that there would be Austro-Hungarian help in defending east Prussia against the Russians through an immediate Austro-Hungarian offensive."[88] As it happened, "neither the Austro-Hungarians nor the Germans were to honor what the other believed had been promised."

Gary Shanafelt's book *Secret Enemy* explores Austria-Hungary's uneasy relationship with its ostensible ally, Germany. Although Germany in early July 1914 assured Austria-Hungary of its backing in a campaign against Serbia, July ended "with Germany demanding that the Monarchy direct its forces against Russia so that Germany could launch its own campaign against France."[89] In the process, Germany took the initiative in the alliance: "The Germans declared war on Russia on August 1; Austria-Hungary did not follow suit until the 6th and only after considerable prodding from Berlin. It continued to be at peace with France and Britain, both now engaged in hostilities with Germany, for another week. The initiative for the final declaration of war came from London and Paris, not Vienna. The Austrians had finally secured German backing—but not for a localized war against Belgrade, rather a world war against the Entente; and thus ultimately not for the Austrian interests but for German ones."[90] By the time Austria-Hungary invaded Serbia in early August, Germany was encountering delays in its offensive on the

Western Front. Not only was Germany unable to mount its promised offensive on the Eastern Front, but it demanded that Conrad supply more Austro-Hungarian troops to fight the Russians.

In his novel *To the Last Man*, Jeff Shaara reported an apocryphal conversation between the top German generals, Paul von Hindenburg and Erich Ludendorff, that reflected the German staff's poor opinion of their Austro-Hungarian allies. Ludendorff was reported to say,

> "I have been recently asked why Germany has allowed herself to be allied with an Austrian corpse. I admit, I still have no good answer."
>
> "Politics, General. Simple as that. Emperor Franz-Josef is a relic, a tired old man who bends to the will of anyone he fears. He fears the kaiser, and so, he obeys. Kaiser Wilhelm sees Austria-Hungary as a land of opportunity. He probably believes that one day he might unite the two empires, if not by a military alliance, then perhaps by marriage. It is, after all, what monarchs do."
>
> "But Austria cannot fight."
>
> "Do not exaggerate, General. The Austrians can certainly fight. What they cannot do is *win*."[91]

12

Peasants in War

Samko Mozolák's military experience is not extensively documented. He was conscripted too late for Austria-Hungary's August 1914 invasion of Serbia on the Balkan
Front. However, the Vienna war archives documented his service on the other three Eastern Fronts—the Russian, Romanian, and Italian.[1] Together, these four fronts constituted
the Eastern Theater of World War I. Austria-Hungary and its German ally fought together
across the Eastern Theater, while Germany fought alone on the Western Front. Austria-
Hungary played no part in Germany's invasions of Luxembourg, Belgium, and France,
and the empire did not send any troops to the Western Front until the summer of 1918,
when its two divisions arrived too late to engage in combat.[2]

Before considering the plight of soldiers and civilians in the Eastern Theater during
World War I, we should briefly review the situation on the Western Front. Germany had
marched its army into Luxembourg on August 2, 1914, and invaded Belgium on August
4. Intending to invade France from the north through Belgium and win a quick victory,
Germany encountered fierce resistance from Belgian troops, slowing its invasion of
France. The French army was supported by a small British Expeditionary Force (BEF),
by expeditionary forces from several British dominions, and—beginning in June 1917—
by the American Expeditionary Forces (AEF). France, Britain, and the United States
became known as the "Allied" forces, to differentiate them from the Entente alliance of
France, Britain, and Russia.

The German chief of staff, Helmuth von Moltke, had adapted a plan to invade France
drawn up by his predecessor, Alfred Graf von Schlieffen, in 1905–06. As described by
Winston Churchill, Schlieffen's plan envisioned "the advance of Germany from the north
into the heart of France, and the consequent destruction of the French armies, together
with the incidental capture of Paris and the final total defeat of France within six weeks."[3]
Belgium's strong resistance had already delayed Germany's northern march through
France by at least two weeks. A month after Germany invaded Belgium, the Allies stalled
the German invasion on September 5–12, at the first Battle of the Marne River northeast
of Paris. Instead of defeating France within six weeks, German troops were mired in
trenches fighting French and British troops five months after the invasion. So began the
trench warfare on the Western Front, which readers know from movies about World
War I.

On Christmas Eve and Christmas Day 1914, weary and homesick troops on both
sides stopped fighting, sang carols, shared food, and even exchanged gifts. The *London
Daily News* published a British officer's account of his experience:

On Christmas morning two British soldiers, after signalling truce and good-fellowship from the perilous crown of their trench, walked across to the German line with a plate of mince pies and garniture and seasonable messages. They were most cordially received, had a good "feed," washed down by a choice bottle of Liebfraumilch, and were sent back with packets of Christmas cards—quite sentimental—wreathed with mistletoe and holly, for distribution among their fellows.

Later in the day the Germans returned the compliment and sent a couple of gayly caparisoned heralds, apparently Landsturm men, across to the evergreen embowered dugouts of the British.[4]

Stanley Weintraub's book *Silent Night*[5] recounted celebrations of the 1914 Christmas truce in magazine stories, books, plays, and films. The truce was also reenacted in an opera, *Silent Night*, which won a Pulitzer Prize for the Minnesota Opera in 2012.

Despite a Christmas truce's humanitarian appeal, military high commands on both sides at the time were aghast at the unwarlike behavior of their soldiers. Weintraub wrote: "For the rival governments, for which war was politics conducted by persuasive force, it was imperative to make even temporary peace unappealing and unworkable, only an impulsive interval in a necessarily hostile and competitive world."[6] In fact, the *New York Times*, in reprinting the *London Daily News* British officer's account, accompanied the item by quoting a French officer who had witnessed such a Christmas truce: "From a military point of view, be said, such truces were deplorable. For, as he put it, not more than two or three of them would be required to make the soldiers on both sides ask, 'Why are we killing each other?' Then there might well follow, 'There has been enough of this foolishness! Let's go home!' And if enough of them did it, that would be the end of the war. The chance that they will do any such thing is, indeed, the remotest of possibilities. That amazing coercion, 'discipline,' in all except the rarest instances, overcomes all the ordinary 'resistances,' including even the instinct of self-preservation."[7] In short, soldiers on one side needed motivation to kill soldiers on the other side. Fraternization reduced that motivation; any friendly contact among troops was unacceptable. Consequently, military authorities disciplined the offending officers. Great Britain conducted at least one court-martial in 1915 involving the commander of the Scots Guard and a company officer.[8]

Max Hastings said that "spontaneous truces" also occurred in the Eastern Theater on all fronts except along Serbia.[9] He reported an incident on Christmas Day in Galicia, when Russian besiegers of Przemyśl (an Austro-Hungarian fortress) "deposited three Christmas trees in no man's land with a polite accompanying note addressed to the enemy: 'We wish you, the heroes of Przemyśl, a Merry Christmas and hope that we can come to a peaceful agreement as soon as possible.'"[10] Hastings also said, "In no man's land, soldiers met and exchanged Austrian tobacco and schnapps for Russian bread and meat. When the Tsar's soldiers held their own seasonal festivities a few days later [according to Russian Orthodox tradition], Habsburg troops reciprocated."[11]

Kevin McNamara's book on Russia's Czecho-Slovak Legion described another incident on the Russian Front on Christmas Day 1915. He wrote that legionnaires in Russian trenches "began singing 'Stille Nacht,' the German 'Silent Night'" to those in the Austrian trenches. One enemy replied, "'Wir danken' ('We thank you')." Then the legionnaires "began singing 'Silent Night' in Czech, after which Czechs on both sides yelled greetings to one another."[12] In addition to Christmas, Arthur May documented "an Easter Celebration" involving Russian, Austrian, and Polish troops in the Eastern Theater in 1916.[13]

Excepting the isolated Christmas truce in 1914, warfare on the Western Front featured industrial-scale killing with little exchange of territory. By late 1916, according to Herwig,

"The French maintained about 3,250 miles of trenches, the British another 6,000, and the Central Powers just under 12,000—an underground labyrinth sufficient to girdle the globe."[14] Herwig said, "The German campaign of 1914 [the Schlieffen Plan] was predicated on a swift and decisive victory in the west by the 40th day of mobilization; when it did not materialize, the great gamble had failed."[15] Germany became locked in a two-front war against France and Russia.

While Germany was failing to conquer France as planned, Conrad was failing to subdue Serbia according to schedule. Austria-Hungary invaded Serbia in mid–August 1914 but could not hold the scant territory it captured. By December 1914, Serbia had humiliated Austria-Hungary, ten times larger in population, by repelling Austro-Hungarian troops back across the border. Sources estimated Serbian losses (killed, wounded, or missing) at about 170,000 but Austro-Hungarian losses at over 210,000.[16] As David Fromkin pointedly summed up Conrad's adventure: "His armies invaded Serbia. They brought the Serbians to battle. And—crushingly, overwhelmingly—the Austrians lost!"[17] In truth, Austria-Hungary lost at the time only in the sense that it did not win a quick victory. Nevertheless, its "loss" stung.

Victory in Serbia was important to Germany, the Habsburgs' Central Powers ally. It needed control of Serbian railways to supply Turkey, which had recently joined the Central Powers. So in 1915, Germany took over the Serbian campaign. The conflict expanded into the Balkan Front when Bulgaria—which secretly joined the Central Powers in late September—declared war against Serbia, hoping to regain former territory. As German and Austro-Hungarian troops attacked Serbia from the north, Bulgarians attacked from the east. The Central Powers conquered Serbia by the middle of December 1915, driving its forces beyond its southern border with Greece.[18] To Franz Josef, the victory tasted bittersweet. It was won by the Germans and Bulgarians, not by his Austro-Hungarian army.[19]

Many defeated Serbian troops fled south of the Serbian border to join a multinational force of French, British, Italians, Greeks, and Russians assembled in the Greek port city of Salonika. Mobilized too late to prevent Serbia's defeat, these Entente forces were also unable to dislodge Bulgarian troops across the border. Dug into defensive positions in Salonika throughout most of 1916 and 1917, they were derisively dubbed the "forgotten army,"[20] or, more picturesquely, "the gardeners of Salonika."[21]

If not by then forgotten, the act that started World War I—Franz Josef's decision to preserve Habsburg honor by punishing Serbia for Archduke Franz Ferdinand's assassination—became eclipsed by events. Fearing that war with Serbia might cause war with Russia, Austria-Hungary sent troops to its northeastern province of Galicia. When Germany declared war against Russia on August 1, Russia responded by simultaneously invading Prussia and Galicia. Within the first three weeks of the month, Russian troops pushed deep into German and Habsburg territory as shown in Map 12.1.

In the battle of Tannenberg at the end of August 1914, Germany turned back Russia's invasion of Prussia. Early that month, Austro-Hungarian forces also advanced from the fortress city of Lemberg (Lwów in Polish; Lviv in Ukrainian) in Galicia. Jan Slomka, mayor of Dzikow, a Galician village, recalled watching the emperor's troops pass by on August 20: "Never had the village seen such a sight. There were regiments from Cieszyn, Biala, Cracow, Bochnia, Sancz, etc., and with them went their bands, cavalry, field artillery, sappers, medical troop and field kitchens. Lastly came the motor-trucks and a mighty stretch of farm wagons from points west. It looked as though a nation was migrating,

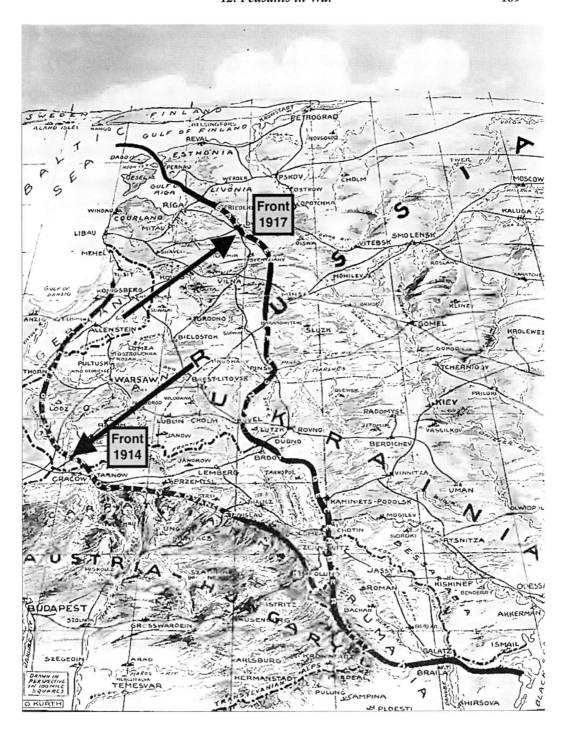

Map 12.1: EASTERN FRONT IN 1914 AND 1917. Early in the war, Russian troops pushed deep into German and Habsburg territory, as marked by the black arrow. Three years later, the Central Powers pushed far into Russian lands, shown by the other arrow. Credit: Adapted from a map in *The War of the Nations: Portfolio in Rotogravure Etchings* (New York: The New York Times, 1919), p. 215. In the public domain.

and all to the north and east—toward Lublin."[22] By mid–September, however, the Russians had routed the Austro-Hungarian army, and thousands of the empire's Slavic troops surrendered or offered to switch sides. On September 14, Mayor Slomka wrote: "It became clear that the whole Austrian army was in flight from Lublin. Many who had seen that splendid array as it advanced into Russian Poland to the very last would not believe that it had not dealt with the enemy, but was in retreat before him."[23]

The Russians captured Lemberg and laid siege to the garrison at Przemyśl, which fell in March 1915. Ian Beckett reported that Austria-Hungary lost 750,000 men in the first six months of war in the Carpathian Mountains, "in effect ending the Austro-Hungarian army as a significant military force."[24] Gunther Rothenberg quoted from the Austrian official war history: "The old professional army died in 1914."[25]

So by the end of 1914, the once respected Austro-Hungarian army had been twice trounced: once by Serbia and once by Russia. In the case of Serbia on the Balkan Front, the Germans and Bulgarians preserved Franz Josef's honor by snatching victory from the jaws of defeat. In the case of Galicia on the Russian Front, Germany rode to the rescue whenever defeat seemed imminent, but otherwise the Austro-Hungarians were left on their own. Austria-Hungary found itself everywhere subservient to a Germany that was fighting its own battles in the west. Gary Shanafelt described the situation: "Rather than a short, victorious campaign, Austria-Hungary found itself locked into a grueling war of attrition with the apparently inexhaustible forces of Czarist Russia while its German ally expended its chief energies elsewhere."[26] Austria-Hungary geared up to engage Russian troops on the plains and foothills northeast of the Carpathian Mountains. The *World History of Warfare* said that battles on the Eastern Front ranged over "wide plains, rivers, swamps, and forests" with "almost limitless perspectives" producing a different kind of war from the Western Front. "Thus, there was much greater scope for maneuver, large scale victories, and for massive disasters, unknown in the west."[27]

The more mobile warfare on the Russian Front resulted in repeated territorial exchanges, as opposing forces won and lost land and villages. Mayor Slomka reported on how the fighting wrenched his village and its surrounding area: "Less than a year of war, and our neighbourhood had seen nine big advances of armed troops: five times had the Austrian army passed through, and four times the enemy. Twice the county was occupied by the Russians, the first time for three weeks, the second for nearly eight months—from November 5, 1914, to June 22, 1915. Three great battles were fought there: the first for three days, the second during the whole of October along the San [River], and the third for six weeks in May and June 1915."[28]

Austro-Hungarian soldiers sometimes fought from trenches, but battle lines in the Eastern theater were too fluid for extended trench warfare. Troops often fought over two mountain ranges and their foothills, where the terrain discouraged digging. Most readers know more about the Alpines than the Carpathians. The Alpine Mountain system stretches about 750 miles in an arc from the present-day countries of Monaco on the southwest, north through France, Switzerland, Austria, and south to Slovenia, Bosnia, Serbia, and Albania on the southeast. Nearly all of the Italian and some of the Balkan campaigns occurred in the Alps.

The Carpathian Mountain system has lower peaks than the Alps, but the Carpathian system covers more territory. As depicted in Map 12.2, it stretches over 900 miles in a semicircle from the present-day Czech Republic on the west, through Slovakia and southern Poland on the east, south through Ukraine and Romania (where most of the range

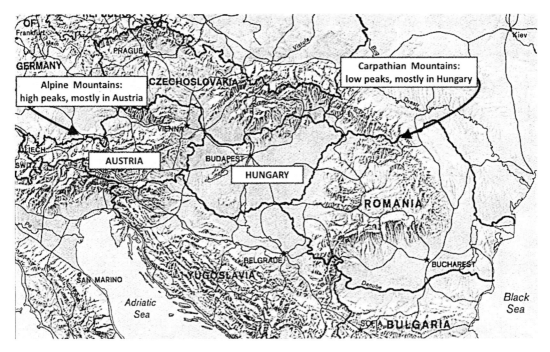

Map 12.2: Central European Mountain Ranges. Battles occurred in the Alps on the border with Italy and along the Carpathian range in Hungary. The Carpathians arched down from Hungary's northern and eastern borders with the Austrian provinces of Galicia and Bukovina to its southern border with Romania. Russian forces that swept through the plains of Galicia and Bukovina faced fierce fighting against Austro-Hungarians and Germans in the eastern Carpathians. Battles occurred further south in the Carpathians after Romania entered the war against the Central Powers. Credit: Adapted from a map at https://commons.wikimedia. org/wiki/File%3ACarpathians_dem.jpg and attributed to Ibarka, who released the work into the public domain.

is located), and juts slightly westward into Serbia. North of the Carpathians, German troops fought Russian troops, usually unaided by Austria-Hungary. In the Carpathian foothills, Austro-Hungarians—often aided by German troops—fought Russians in Galicia, Bukovina, and Romania.

Soldiers on all sides during World War I committed atrocities on opposing soldiers and on civilians in enemy territories. Germans and Russians perpetrated plenty of crimes against each other's soldiers and citizens, but historians contend that Austro-Hungarian troops behaved even worse during the 1914 battles in Galicia and Serbia. After the emperor's forces drove the Russians from Dzikow in Galicia, Mayor Slomka wrote of his ethnically Polish inhabitants: "The village greeted the Austrians warmly, offered what they had, and called them their deliverers. But no such comfort came of it all as folks hoped for, and the general joy was soon broken by grief. The troops acted very harshly toward the civilians. For the most part we had Hungarian regiments."[29] Alexander Watson said that the Habsburg army in Galicia "far exceeded its German ally and enemies in murderousness" and massacred "between 25,000 and 30,000 of its own Ruthene (Ukrainian) population for largely imaginary acts of treason in 1914–15."[30]

Concerning Habsburg outrages in Galicia, Watson attributed them to racism: Magyars took out after Slavs and Jews: "First, the most brutal part of the Habsburg army was, significantly, also its most nationalistic: the Hungarian *Honvéd*. Within days of its arrival in Galicia, the force acquired an ugly reputation.... The Magyars came from a society that had long regarded Slavs with contempt and pursued obtrusive assimilationist policies. Anti-Semitism was on the rise and the political disputes in the decade before hostilities had sharpened Hungarian nationalism. *Honvéd* troops were thus likely to look down on Poles, Ruthenes and Jews. Exacerbating the violence was the force's poor discipline."[31]

Watson theorized that Magyar troops "were ill-equipped to communicate with the population."[32] Their Magyar language was very different from the Slavic languages of Poles, Ruthenes, and Serbs. While Watson's "failure to communicate" explanation would also apply to Magyar treatment of Serbs in Serbia, it would not account for the atrocities he described by Russian troops against Poles and Jews, even those who spoke Slavic languages.[33] Ruthenes, whom Russians condescendingly regarded as "little Russians," mostly suffered a different fate: the smothering of their distinct language and religion.[34]

Concerning Habsburg atrocities in Serbia, R.A. Reiss, professor of forensic science at the University of Lausanne, compiled a detailed 190-page report with statistics and photographs based on his firsthand observations in Serbia in late 1914.[35] Writers Audoin-Rouzeau and Becker summarized his findings concerning the Serbian district of Breziak, saying, "In this district the Austrians killed 54 persons in various ways. Most of them were disembowelled with the large sabres that were carried by four prisoners [*sic*]."[36] Serbia commissioned Reiss's report for propaganda purposes, fulfilled when it was published in Britain in 1916, and historian Arthur May referred to Reiss as "a slick journalist endowed with a fertile imagination."[37] Nevertheless, other sources corroborated Reiss's findings and provided photographs of Serbian civilians executed under orders of Austro-Hungarian General Oskar Potiorek. Photo 12.1 reproduces one of several photographs of hangings and atrocities that appeared in *1914/1918*, a Czech publication of war photographs.[38]

John Reed, the American journalist who later wrote firsthand about the Russian revolution, was in Serbia at the time and filed a similar report of Austro-Hungarian atrocities: "The soldiers were loosed like wild beasts in the city, burning, pillaging, raping. We saw the gutted Hotel d'Europe and the blackened and mutilated church where three thousand men, women and children were penned together without food or water for four days, and then divided into two groups—one sent back to Austria as prisoners of war, the others driven ahead of the army as it marched south against the Serbians."[39]

The truth is that warfare elicited soldiers' dark sides in all belligerent nations. Men who were normal peasants and workers in peacetime killed as they were instructed. In *All Quiet on the Western Front*, novelist and former soldier Erich Remarque wrote, "We have become wild beasts. We do not fight, we defend ourselves against annihilation."[40] They also went beyond killing enemy soldiers. Novelist and Rusyn historian Mark Wansa conceived of a conversation between two Ruthenes in the Habsburg army torching the landscape in front of Russians advancing in Galicia:

"Vasyl, the farmers around here look and talk just like us. Why must we burn their homes? Where will they go?"

"I don't know. They have nowhere to go. You have seen the roads—there are almost as many refugees as soldiers on the roads."

"But, Vasyl, it makes no sense. Why must we burn their homes? These people have done nothing wrong—how is it that they are our enemy?"

"We do what we are told to do because that is what the army wishes."[41]

Photo 12.1: SERBIAN CIVILIANS HANGED BY AUSTRO-HUNGARIAN SOLDIERS. Serbian civilians executed under Austro-Hungarian General Oskar Potiorek's order in 1916. Credit: Photo by an unknown photographer published before 1923; in the public domain: https://en.wikipedia.org/wiki/File:Hromadná_poprava_srbského_obyvatelstva.jpg.

Wansa is a 21st-century writer, but Timrava in 1918 told a similar story about the Slovak soldier Siricky in "Great War Heroes":

"Up north there's some kind of big battle. They're pushing through the lines again. Burning villages and beating everyone they can catch. People are fleeing, leaving everything they have behind, and only old people who can't run are left. Good God, does it have to come to this?"

"Yeah, yeah—why, ours are doing the same thing down south. The Lord's punishing us," sighed the pious Koska.

Burning out villages, taking their homes from peaceful people, making beggars of men and women who aren't guilty in any way…. That's being done, and I'm supposed to do it too. I don't have any strength or will for it. I don't want to, even though 1 love my native land. I just can't, thought Siricky, tormented. To take away the roofs over old people and children, to become an animal instead of a human—ah, I can't endure it.[42]

Conscripted too late to fight against Serbia, Samuel Mozolák was recorded on active duty on May 25, 1915. He had passed his 33rd birthday, and his American twins Ján and Zuzanna were nine years old. He was at the Russian Front with the 37th *Honvéd* Infantry Division of the 1st Army, which fought in Galicia. Early battles in Galicia had already cost Austria 420,000 casualties (killed, wounded or captured), around one-third of the army's effective field strength.[43] Historian Timothy Snyder concluded: "The monarchy's peacetime army had been destroyed by the Russians and the Serbs in the first months of the war. By Christmas 1914, some 82 percent of the original infantry complement of the Habsburg armed forces were casualties. About a million men were dead, wounded, or sick. The rest of the war would be fought by reserves, civilians, and officers just completing their training."[44] Samko probably was among the poorly trained recruits rushed into battle with just a few weeks of "rudimentary soldiering."[45] He soon became one of the many thousands of Austro-Hungarian soldiers wounded in Galicia. Entering active duty in the spring of 1915, Samko was wounded for the first time on September 26. By that date, his new son and namesake was just one year old. We presume that Samko was not treated for simple first aid in the field but sent to a military hospital, for he did not return to active duty until December 25.

Samko's available military record does not state the nature of his wound. He did not die, so his wound probably was not especially serious. Medical care on the battle lines in World War I was not good. Joe Kirchberger said this about the medical services: "Those beyond hope were recognized as such and allowed to die; where possible, their pain was masked with powerful drugs. For the rest, those who had a chance of surviving, the medical staff assessed their wounds, and those with minor or not immediately life-threatening injuries were put to one side, and the more serious but survivable cases were attended to as priority dictated. The key factor was rapid and effective medical care. If a soldier's wounds could be dealt with quickly and effectively, he had a far greater chance of survival."[46]

Germany could boast that its soldiers had the best medical care in World War I. Holger Herwig wrote that "the German Army's medical corps was probably the best prepared among the major combatants."

> By 1900 surgery had reached legitimacy as a scientific revolution transformed the Army's erstwhile barbers and bloodletters into modern practitioners of medicine. Ether and chloroform for anaesthesia had been introduced in 1847, surgical antisepsis followed in 1867, steam sterilization of surgical instruments was practised by 1886, and X-rays came on the scene in 1895. Further strides in medicine were achieved during the Great War: sterilized gauze, rubber gloves, motor ambulances, mobile laboratories featuring diagnostic bacteriology, lighter X-ray machines, intravenous saline transfusions, blood transfusions, clinical thermometers, improved retractors and hemostatic forceps, surgical lighting, and the hypodermic syringe. In short, the Prussian-German Army pioneered in applying medical breakthroughs on the battlefield.[47]

In contrast, the Austro-Hungarian army arguably provided the war's worst medical care. Herwig said that Austria-Hungary was "utterly unprepared for the Great War." He noted, "In August 1914 the Army drafted medical students to assist surgeons in the field. While this brought its complement of doctors to 1,500—or two for every 1,000 soldiers—it also meant that there was no resupply of doctors on the way after 1914."[48]

Leo van Bergen's book on military medicine in World War I focused on the Western Front, where "medicine became an integral feature of military planning."[49] Years of trench warfare permitted the development of a hospital system to augment first-aid stations at the front. There were field hospitals removed from the fighting, larger evacuation hospitals further in the rear, and major base hospitals in safe cities. Medical services were less developed in the Eastern Theater, yet they probably were needed more there; because of "the racial aspect the battles were often even more merciless and barbaric than in France and Belgium," and because "the Eastern Front was the most lethal in percentage terms, certainly in the first year of fighting."[50]

According to data pieced together by van Bergen, most nonfatal wounds were attributed to artillery shells (about 80 percent) and to bullets (about 20 percent, mainly from machine guns).[51] Bayonet wounds were difficult to tally, but they were far less than anticipated, probably because there was less hand-to-hand combat than expected.[52] If the wounded were fortunate enough to reach a field or base hospital, their chances of survival were good. Even in the Austro-Hungarian army, "the surgical recovery rate was 78 percent in field hospitals and 77 in evacuation hospitals," and fewer than four out of one hundred died on the operating table.[53]

Military hospitals' success in patching up the wounded and returning them to battle led a French doctor and writer to refer to his field hospital as the "repair shop."[54] An American nurse with the French army bitterly characterized her hospital unit as a "laundry" embedded in a war conspiracy: "It is all carefully arranged. It is arranged that men should be broken and that they should be mended. Just as you send your clothes to the laundry and mend them when they come back, so we send our men to the trenches and mend them when they come back again. You send your socks and your shirts again and again to the laundry, and you sew up the tears and clip the raveled edges again and again just as many times as they will stand it. And then you throw them away. And we send our men the war again and again, just as long as they will stand it; just until they are dead, and then we throw them back into the ground."[55]

Of soldiers on the Western Front who survived to hospital admission, more were wounded in the arms or legs (51 percent) than in the torso (21 percent) or the head (17 percent). The worst place to be hit was in the abdomen, even worse than wounds to the head. According to van Bergen: "Of one British sample of a thousand soldiers with stomach wounds, 510 died on the battlefield, 460 on their way to hospital and 22 following surgery. Only 8 survived, or 0.8 percent."[56]

Applying these statistics to Samko Mozolák's hospitalization in 1915, one might infer that he caught shrapnel from an artillery shell in an arm or leg. In any event, he managed to escape death, almost certainly more to luck than to proper military training or to good medical care. If he were indeed hit by shell shrapnel, he escaped the major source of battlefield deaths in World War I. Most of the millions of soldiers who died were killed by the millions and millions of rounds of explosives fired during the war.[57] Van Bergen described the destructive power of such explosives: "Huge shells churned the earth, uprooting trees and throwing them into the air along with mud, chunks of rock and human corpses. Some craters were as big as swimming pools. A medical officer with the 2nd Royal Welch Fusiliers gave a vivid description of the power of shellfire: 'Two men suddenly rose into the air vertically, fifteen feet perhaps, amid a spout of soil 150 yards ahead. They rose and fell with the easy, graceful poise of acrobats. A rifle, revolving slowly, rose high above them before, still revolving, it fell.'"[58]

Despite his study of the war's threats to life and limb, van Bergen found that most soldiers entering any battle on the Western Front had a much greater chance of living than dying. He wrote, "In some particularly ferocious confrontations up to 30 percent died, but the figure was generally far lower."[59] Of course, those figures applied to individual battles. An individual's chances of dying increased with each battle he fought.

Fear of dying itself often increased with each battle. In Gabriel Chevallier's 1930 novel/memoir *Fear*, the decorated French soldier described his feeling toward the end of the war huddled in a trench during bombardment: "I have fallen to the bottom of the abyss of my self, to the bottom of those dungeons where the soul's greatest secrets lie hidden, and it is a vile cesspit, a place of viscous darkness. Here is what I have been without knowing it, what I am: a fellow who is afraid, with an insurmountable fear, a cringing fear, that is crushing him…. It would take brute force to drive me out of there. But I think I would rather die here than climb up those steps…."[60]

After recovering from his wounds, Samko Mozolák was assigned to the 314th *Honvéd* Infantry Regiment (HIR) in the 70th *Honvéd* Infantry Division (HID) on December 25, 1915. Like his old regiment and division, the 314th HIR and 70th HID were serving in Galicia against the Russians. For the first six months after he arrived, according to William Philpott, "the Galician front had been quiet … the Austrian defences had proved strong, and their defenders well-equipped with artillery and machine guns."[61] Then on June 4, 1916, the Galician front erupted as Russian General Aleksei Brusilov began what became known as "Brusilov's offensive." Philpott said, "In the offensive's first week the Russians captured 216 guns and 190,000 prisoners and inflicted at least 100,000 casualties."[62]

Brusilov's offensive occurred across a broad line. Samko's 70th HID was in the Olyka area, about 225 miles west of Kiev. One report described the onslaught in the area:

> Artillery shells fall on Hapsburg positions all night. On the morning of the fifth, the barrage becomes very heavy creating a haze over the battlefield. Around 9 a.m. Russian assault troops from the 2nd ID and the 4th ID appearing out of the haze fell upon the Austrian 2nd ID; troops of the 14th and 15th ID's attacked the 70th Honved (Hungarian) ID in the first trench line. The Austrians are routed, panic sets in, and they run for the rear—in many cases officers in front of men, although the 10th Honved did put up resistance.[63] Austrian troops in reserve suddenly found themselves in heavy combat and were unable to be used to restore the line. Group Szurmay (70th Honved ID 2 ID) is decimated, and masses of its troops surrender. 70th Honved loses 7,000 men out of 12,200.[64]

Watson gave a similar account, saying that the 70th *Honvéd* lost 40 to 50 percent of its men: "By mid-afternoon, what was left of the 70 [HID] had broken and was streaming back to the Styr River. Units became mixed up, panic spread and exhausted troops ceased to obey orders to form defensive lines and instead flooded rearwards. The army's main supply base, the town of Lutsk, was abandoned on 7 June."[65]

Samko was lucky to be among the 5,000 survivors, and fortunate that Brusilov's offensive outran its supply lines and stalled. After July 4, the Germans and Austro-Hungarians took defensive positions in the area. Philpott said, "Thus the pattern was set for Russian operations over the summer: a heavy slogging fight between Russia's masses and a fairly solid Austrian defence stiffened 'like stays in a corset' by German reserve formations doled out sparingly by [German chief of staff Erich von] Falkenhayn, who by then had taken effective control of the Austrian front in Galicia as well."[66]

Nevertheless, battles still occurred on that portion of the Russian Front during the summer, and Samko was wounded for the second time on August 10, 1916. This time, his wounds were judged to be sufficiently serious to evacuate him to the military base hospital at Ružomberok in Slovakia. He almost certainly went by hospital train carrying hundreds of other wounded soldiers. Stefan Zweig described these hospital trains as "ordinary freight cars without real windows, with only one narrow opening for air, lighted within by sooty oil lamps. One crude stretcher stood next to the other, and all were occupied by moaning, sweating, deathly pale men, who were gasping for breath in the thick atmosphere of excrement and iodoform [an antiseptic]. The hospital orderlies staggered rather than walked, for they were terribly tired; nothing was to be seen of the gleaming bed linen of the photographs. Covered with blood-stained rags, the men lay on straw on the hard wood of the stretchers, and in each one of the cars there lay at least two or three dead among the dying and groaning."[67]

Mozolák oral family history holds that Samko had two wounds when he reached the hospital. He had been bayoneted in the shoulder and shot in the foot, according to Samko's son, Ján. At age ten, Ján had accompanied his mother to visit his hospitalized father in Ružomberok, 120 miles northeast of their home village of Krajné.[68] Ján recalled little else from his visit except his father's wounds.[69]

The first time Samko had been wounded, in 1915, only three months passed—from September 26 to December 25—before he returned to the field. His 1916 wounds took six months to heal. Samko did not return to action until February 8, 1917. By then, Ján and his twin sister Zuzanna were eleven years old.

When wounded in Galicia, Samko had been engaged on the Russian Front. Two weeks later on August 27, 1916, Romania declared war on Austria-Hungary. So when he returned to combat six months later in 1917, Samko fought Russians and Romanians in Austria-Hungary's Bukovina region on the Romanian Front, southeast of Galicia and not very far from the old Russian Front in Galicia.

Romania had vacillated over entering the war, and on which side. Weighing promised gains from both the Entente and the Central Powers, Romania finally decided to enter on the side of the Entente, expecting to wrest from Austria-Hungary three territories: Transylvania, Bukovina, and the Banat—a western region in present-day Romania.[70] All had substantial Romanian-speaking populations. Indeed, Hungary's population itself was almost 15 percent ethnic Romanian.[71] The multinational nature of the Habsburg armies presented problems when they fought nations on their borders. The Habsburg monarchy feared that troops' loyalty would waver, depending on whom they fought. It tried to avoid sending Slavic troops to the Russian Front, sending Italian troops to the Italian Front, and sending Romanian troops to the Romanian Front. However, such deft allocation of forces was not always possible.

Romanian novelist Liviu Rebreneau told a story about a general who had just decorated an Austro-Hungarian soldier, Apostol Bologa, for extreme bravery. The general personally invited Bologa to join him on his next campaign on the Romanian Front. Despite being greatly honored by the general's invitation, Bologa asked instead to continue at the Italian Front.

> Suddenly General Karg stopped short as if a ray of light had entered his brain. He again took a few steps backwards and glued his gaze on Bologa, trying to read his innermost thoughts. For several seconds there reigned a grave-like silence in the room, while outside could be heard the grinding of cart wheels and the noisy chirping of the sparrows in a tree under the office window. Apostol unconsciously closed his eyes to protect himself from the general's scrutiny.
>
> "You are a Romanian?' the latter jerked out abruptly, his voice almost hoarse.
>
> "Yes, Excellency; answered the lieutenant quickly.
>
> "Romanian!' repeated the general, surprised and irritated, in a tone as if expecting a denial.
>
> "Romanian!" repeated Bologa more firmly, drawing himself up and puffing out his chest slightly.
>
> "Yes, very well, of course…" stammered Karg presently, suspicious and scrutinizing. "Yes, certainly…. But then your request surprises me … very much…. It would seem to me that you differentiate between the enemies of your country."[72]

Romania invaded Transylvania when it declared war on Austria-Hungary, causing the monarchy to suspect its ethnically Romanian citizens of conflicting loyalties. Viewed as sympathetic to the invaders, local Romanians suffered from the Hungarian authorities and army.[73] Other nationalities, especially Ruthenes and Serbs, were also mistreated by the Habsburg military, especially if they lived in a war zone.

Unluckily, Romania joined the losing side in August 1916. Although Austria-Hungary seemed weak and ready to be plucked, Germany immediately came to its ally's aid. Herwig wrote, "Within 3 weeks of Romania's declaration of war the OHL [Supreme Army Command] assembled 200,000 soldiers, half of them German, in Transylvania."[74] The campaign was over by the end of November, and Bucharest was occupied in early December.

Fighting still continued into 1917, with German and Austro-Hungarian troops facing Romanians and Russians. Samko Mozolák distinguished himself on the battlefield during the August 1917 Battle of Oituz.[75] On November 11, 1917, he was one of seven members in the 3rd Company of the 314th HIR recommended for bravery in the face of the enemy. The action occurred between September 25 and November 10, 1917, around Transylvania's Nemira Mountains, north of Oituz on Map 12.3 of the Romanian Front in 1916–1917. Oituz is about 60 miles northeast of Brasov (formerly Kronstadt) in today's Romania.

According to Romanian military historian Glenn Torrey, major battles in mid–September 1917 marked the end of offensive operations by the Central Powers on the Romanian Front.[76] Battles afterward defended against Romanian and Russian forces on Romania's eastern border with Moldavia and Russia. Samko may have fought against either Roma-

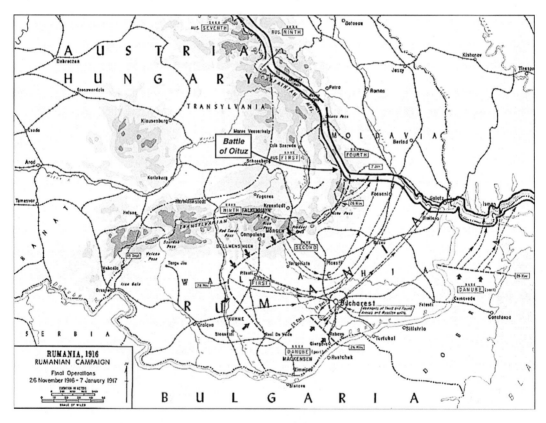

Map 12.3: ROMANIAN FRONT IN 1916–1917. Although the Central Powers occupied Bucharest by the end of 1916, Romanian forces, joined with Russian troops, continued to fight in the mountains to the north through the summer of 1917. Samko won recognition for bravery under fire during the August 1917 Battle of Oituz, which was one of the last major encounters in the Romanian conflict. Credit: Website of the Department of History, United States Military Academy at West Point at http://www.westpoint.edu/history/SitePages/WWI.aspx. In the public domain.

nians or Russians. Either way, the fighting came weeks before an armistice was reached on December 9 between Romania and the Central Powers.[77]

His military commendation, reproduced in Figure 12.1, was approved by the Commandant of the Infantry Division Brigade (*Honvéd gyalog dandár hadosztály*) on December 13, 1917. It is not known whether Samko actually received *Der Tapferkeitsmedaille* (the Medal for Bravery). He may not have returned to Krajné to entrust it to his family before being hustled off to his next campaign on the Italian Front in early 1918. By then, twins Ján and Zuzanna were twelve years old, and Samuel, their little brother, was going on four.

Italy—formerly allied with Germany and Austria-Hungary—had declared war against Austria-Hungary on May 23, 1915. Like Romania, Italy schemed to gain disputed territories from Habsburg rule, mainly the Tyrol and the Austrian Littoral, which included the port of Trieste.[78] Austria-Hungary generally controlled the high ground in this mountainous region, and so had the military advantage in defense. Italy focused on attacking up the sixty-mile-long valley of the Isonzo River, which emptied into the Adriatic Sea roughly 15 miles west of Trieste. In the summer of 1915, Italy began a series of "eleven battles of the Isonzo." Samko must have participated in some or all of these battles, for his 314th HIR served in the 208th infantry brigade of the 70th HID in the IV Corps of the Isonzo Army.[79]

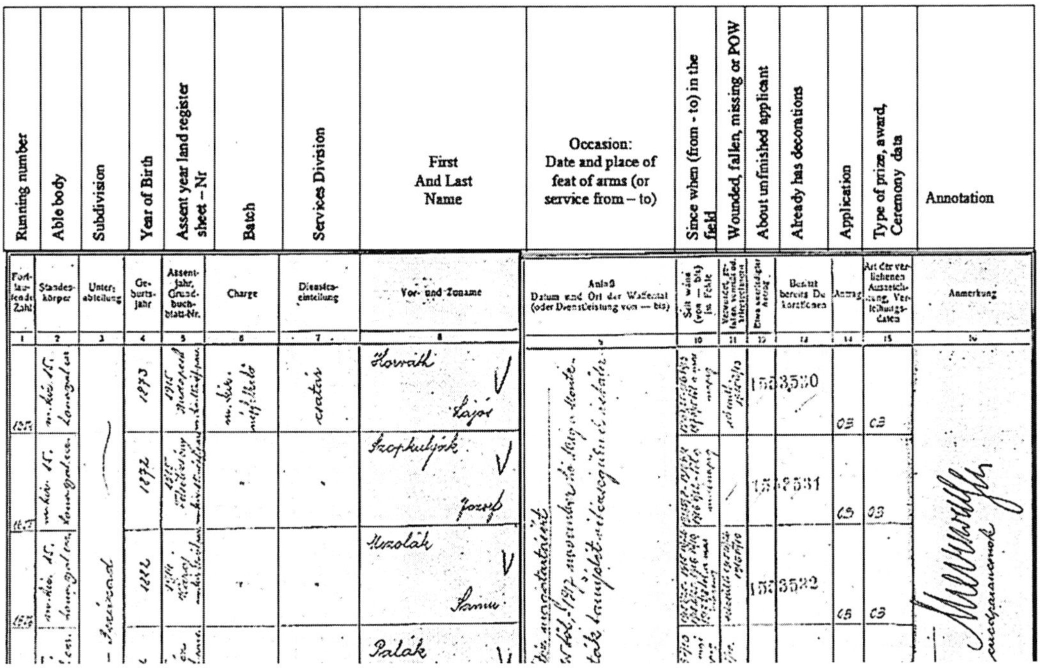

Figure 12.1: AUSTRO-HUNGARIAN MILITARY COMMENDATION FOR BRAVERY. **Partial list of military commendation approved on December 13, 1917, naming seven members in the 3rd Company of the 314th HIR to be recommended for bravery in the face of the enemy during the period of September 25 to November 10, 1917, serving at Mount Nemira in Transylvania. Samuel Mozolák's name is third on the list, tagged with English translations above the columns. Credit: "Verzeichnis über beantragte (verliehene) Auszeichnungen" [Registry of requested (awarded) commendations], December 13, 1917. Family document.**

The first five battles occurred over almost a year and produced little for Italy except massive casualties. A sixth battle in August 1916 won Italy a bridgehead across the river, but the next four battles changed little until Italy made gains in the eleventh battle of September 1917. Perhaps Italy was inspired by 50-year-old Arturo Toscanini, who was conducting martial music near the battlefield.[80] The Italian gains were sufficient to bring Germans to aid the faltering Austro-Hungarian army. Just a month later, in the Battle of Caporetto (also called the twelfth battle of Isonzo), the Germans routed the Italians, sending them fleeing westward toward the Tagliamento River about 20 miles to the west.[81]

Ernest Hemingway, a Red Cross volunteer on the Italian side who suffered leg wounds from a mortar shell, wrote about that battle in *A Farewell to Arms*:

> I asked about the break through and he said that he had heard at the Brigade that the Austrians had broken through the twenty-seventh army corps up toward Caporetto. There had been a great battle in the north all day.
>
> "If those bastards let them through we are cooked," he said.
>
> "It's Germans that are attacking," one of the medical officers said. The word Germans was something to be frightened of. We did not want to have anything to do with the Germans.
>
> "There are fifteen divisions of Germans," the medical officer said. "They have broken through and we will be cut off."[82]

Hemingway described the terrified flight of citizens from the expected enemy advance: "In the night many peasants had joined the column from the roads of the country and in the column there were carts loaded with household goods; there were mirrors projecting up between mattresses, and chickens and ducks tied to carts. There was a sewing-machine on the cart ahead of us in the rain. They had saved the most valuable things. On some carts the women sat huddled from the rain and others walked beside the carts keeping as close to them as they could. There were dogs now in the column, keeping under the wagons as they moved along."

Fortunately for the Italians, their exhausted opponents did not continue their pursuit, and what was left of the Italian army eventually regrouped along the Piave River, west of the Tagliamento and roughly 50 miles west of the Isonzo.[83] Diary notes of November 1, 1917, by Pál Kelemen, an Austro-Hungarian soldier at Caporetto, help us understand why the victorious forces did not continue their pursuit.

> As they start forward or stand still, blocked by those ahead, or lie down at the roadside, it seems impossible that these are the fighting troops with which the statesmen and the generals are defending the Monarchy. That this tattered ravaged band with their shaggy beards, their crumpled, soaked, and dirty uniforms, their dilapidated footgear, and the exhaustion in their faces constitutes "our brave infantry."
>
> Now there is a halt. The whole battalion sinks down on the slope. Some of the soldiers take ration cans out of their knapsacks and with the long blades of their claspknives they lift out the food and shove it raw into their mouths. Their hands are black with dirt, horny, heavy moving. On their faces the wrinkles stretch and fold again as they chew. They sit on the wet stones and stare into the open tin cans without expression.[84]

Sources report that by the end of December 1917, Italy had lost 450,000 men, killed, wounded, missing, or taken prisoner at Caporetto.[85] One historian called it "one of the Great War's most spectacular operational successes."[86] It ended what István Deák called "a miraculous year for Austria-Hungary," when "not a single enemy soldier stood on Habsburg territory. On the contrary, Austro-Hungarian armies were everywhere deep inside enemy territory."[87] Shanafelt found that "Austrian units occupied Serbia, Montenegro, northern Albania, and Southern Poland."[88]

Meanwhile—and despite their army's successes—civilians in Austria and Hungary in 1918 were desperately short of food, thousands of workers in Vienna and other cities went out on strike, and troops fought to maintain order among restless inhabitants across the country. Ironically, the military situation against its foreign foes was the best since the start of the war. Watson summed up the situation: "The Habsburg Empire should have stood triumphant in the early summer of 1918. It had outlasted the autocratic regime of the Tsar that in peacetime had so publicly hoped for its collapse and dismemberment. Moreover, the external irredentist threats that had so frightened Austro-Hungarian leaders before the war had been eliminated. Serbia and the south of Poland were under occupation, a favourable treaty had been signed with Romania in May 1918 and the Italians were in abeyance after their heavy losses the previous autumn in their rout at Caporetto. There was no reason to continue fighting."[89] Emperor Karl and his foreign minister, Count von Czernin, also thought that it was time to end the war, but Germany still wanted to continue fighting. And Germany controlled Emperor Karl.

In the Sixtus affair (described in Chapter 11, "Imperial Irrelevance"), Karl had secretly tried to arrange a separate peace from France and then lied about doing so. The revelation, which became public in April 1918, dishonored the emperor before his citizens and emasculated him before the German government. Too weak to defy German demands, Karl agreed to mount a major offensive in southern Italy in the late spring to support a German offensive on the Western Front.

Many Austro-Hungarian generals thought that their army was ill prepared in every way—by numbers, health, weapons, and supplies—for an offensive against the Italian troops who had dug in for months along the Piave River. Nevertheless, Karl ordered them to attack. Historian István Deák described the condition of the troops: "On June 15, 1918, when the army mounted its last great offensive on the Piave, some troops were sent forward with a daily ration of only eight ounces of almost inedible bread and three ounces of meat. The soldiers weighed an average of 50 kilograms (about 120 pounds); they had no underwear, no decent boots, and, just as often, insufficient ammunition. It is no exaggeration to say that the men went forward at the Piave mainly because they hoped to reach the Entente trenches, with their fabulously rich stores of food, tobacco, and liquor."[90] One might think that Deák went too far in stressing food as a motivation, but Emperor Karl's "inspirational order of the day" to his troops also appealed to their stomachs, saying, "We shall strike a final blow at the perfidious enemy, and bring about peace…. Glory and honor await you beyond the Piave River, and abundant spoils and good food."[91]

Virtually all German forces on the Italian Front had been shifted to the Western Front by the summer of 1918, leaving the Habsburg command to fight on its own. Emperor Karl unwisely allowed rival generals Conrad and Boroević to divide the weakened, undernourished Austro-Hungarian army, each leading separate attacks when many thought it could not mount even one serious offensive.[92] Map 12.4 lays out the terrain over which the Austro-Hungarian armies fought against Italian and Allied forces in 1917 and 1918. One army (Conrad's) would attack from the mountains in the Trentino region on the west, and the other (Boroević's) across the Piave River on the east. Both attacks began on June 15, and both needed to succeed. Unfortunately for Austria-Hungary the Italians had learned their battle plans.

The Italians quickly checked Conrad's attack from the mountains. The headline of a June 18 dispatch to the *New York Times* read, "FOE'S DEAD BLOCK DEFILES: MOUNTAIN

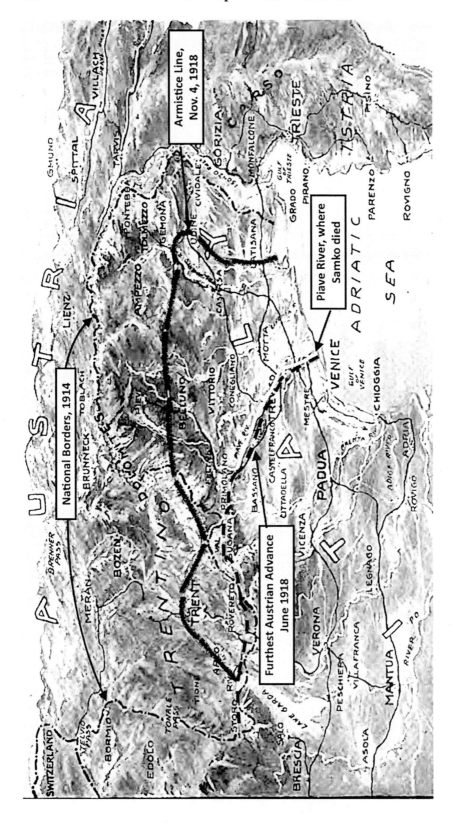

Map 12.4: Terrain in Italy for the 1918 Battle of the Piave River. One Austro-Hungarian force (Conrad's) attacked from the mountains in Trentino on the north, while the other force (Boroevič's) plunged across lowlands from the east, pushing across the Piave River. Conrad's troops were slaughtered in the mountains, while Boroevič's were trapped across a rising river. Credit: Adapted from color map facing page 246 of *Harper's Pictorial Library of the World War, Volume III: Battles, Sieges and Campaigns* (New York: Harper & Brothers, 1920). In the public domain.

SLOPES BLACK WITH BODIES OF AUSTRIAN STORMING TROOPS."[93] As a result, wrote David Raab in *The Battle of the Piave*, "half the battle was lost." Nevertheless, general Arthur Artz von Straussenburg, commanding the Isonzo Army under Boroević, "issued orders for the troops to cross the Piave at any cost."[94] Under murderous artillery fire, his troops built pontoon bridges.[95] "On the 16th, the 70th *Honvéd* made progress and even managed to get some artillery across the river," Bennighof wrote,[96] and Artz's forces managed to occupy some territory before being stopped by a counterattack. Soon, the Italians pinned the Austro-Hungarians back against the river.

During the fighting that June, each day melted more snow in the mountains. Each day more water flowed into the rising and now turbulent Piave River. Describing the troops' situation just three years later, one book stated that the troops' "condition became critical when the Piave suddenly rose in flood on June 18, swept away the temporary bridges and boats used for the crossings and even barges loaded with men and materials of war."[97] Samko's 70th *Honvéd* division and other units were stranded across a raging river and away from supplies.

With Conrad's mountain offensive stalled, the Italians concentrated their forces against the hapless Habsburg army. Bennighof said that Emperor Karl's officers advised withdrawal, and "on the evening of 20 June Karl ordered the offensive halted and the *Isonzo Army Group* back over the Piave. The wounded, support troops and artillery units crossed over on the night of 21–22 June, with the infantry following on the next night."[98]

Recrossing the Piave was more dangerous, both because the river had risen and because the Italians and their Entente allies were pounding them as they fled. Raab's factual statement, "The bridge builders tried to work quickly against the rising tide, even as their work was being bombed by the swooping airplanes,"[99] was reflected in Andrew Krivak's novel, *The Sojourn*. Krivak's protagonist, the Slovak soldier Jozef Vinich, described his unit's retreat from the Piave: "Horses, trucks, artillery caissons, and men poured over the Piave under even greater danger from aircraft and machine guns now, because our supporting guns had gone silent from ever more accurate Italian fire and the continuous, lethal presence of British planes."[100] According to Bennighof, "*The Isonzo Army Group* had lost nearly 96,000 men in just five days of fighting, and its assault battalions had been nearly wiped out."[101]

Samko's 70th HID was in the assault group that crossed the Piave River on June 16. Vienna's military records state that he was reported missing on June 19. His grandson, John Mozolák, Jr., provided this account: "A friend of the Mozolák family, who returned from the campaign, said that he saw Samko lying in a shell hole, his left arm blown off at the shoulder. Samko said that he was not going home in that condition. From that day, he was listed as missing in action. His body may be lying unidentified in an Italian cemetery or have been washed away by the heavy rains flooding the Piave River." That family story matches Raab's claim that "the Piave River spewed dead bodies, broken bridges, boats, and other debris of war into the sea."[102] It also fits newspaper stories of the day at home and abroad. One in *The Advertiser* of Adelaide, South Australia, had a Washington dateline of June 24 and this headline: THE ITALIAN VICTORY; ALL GROUND REGAINED; GREAT AUSTRIAN LOSS. Its text stated, "The flooded Piave washed away the bridge and the river soon contained 1.000 [1,000] Austrian corpses. The enemy divisions on the Italian side of the Piave were decimated."[103] Photo 12.2 shows some of the lucky Austro-Hungarian troops who managed to live and be captured. Samko was not among them.

Photo 12.2: Austro-Hungarian Troops Who Survived the Piave River Battle. According to *The Literary Digest History of the World War*, the total Austrian losses (killed, wounded, or captured) were over 200,000 compared with 40,000 Italians. Credit: Underwood & Underwood photo in Francis Whiting Halsey, ed., *The Literary Digest History of the World War, Volume IX* (New York: Funk & Wagnalls, 1919), p. 125. In the public domain.

Following the battle of the Piave River, Samko was officially reported as missing along with thousands of others. Many recorded as "missing" in the Austro-Hungarian army were in fact deserters. This was true especially on the Russian Front, where whole regiments sometimes mutinied or deserted—especially Czechs and Ruthenes.[104] As described in Chapter 8, the same 28th Czech regiment that left Prague with its wagons bearing the slogan, "*Jdem na Srby a nevíme proč*" ("Off to fight the Serbs, we don't know why!"), surrendered almost *en masse*, causing the emperor to disband it.[105]

Desertion of Austro-Hungarian troops was also a serious problem on the Italian Front in 1918 that was exacerbated by "front propaganda." The propaganda campaign was organized by the Inter-Allied Propaganda Commission and supported by British experts, notably R.W. Seton-Watson and Henry Wickham Steed. As stated in Chapter 3, "The Emperor's Subjects," Seton-Watson seared the monarchy in his book, *Racial Problems in Hungary*; so did Steed as author of *The Hapsburg Monarchy* and as foreign editor of the *London Times*. Both men were attached to Britain's Department of Propaganda for Enemy Countries, which was organized in February 1918 and operated out of a mansion called "Crewe House."[106] Seton-Watson and Steed were sent to Italy in April 1918 to help create what became known as the Padua Commission, which ran the propaganda campaign on the Italian Front.

Crewe House took credit for various efforts to encourage Austro-Hungarian defections, especially from Czechs and other Slavs. Campbell Stuart, Crewe House's Deputy Director, wrote: "Gramophone records of Czecho-Slovak and Southern Slav songs were secured by the British Commissioner and effectively used for the awakening of the nationalist sentiment among the troops of these races in the Austrian armies. The instruments were placed in 'No Man's Land,' and so close to each other were the front trenches of the opposing armies that the words and music could easily be heard."[107] Stuart also reproduced as "Leaflet No. 18" a four-paragraph "Message of Professor Masaryk to the Czechoslovak Army in Italy." Printed in the Czech language, thousands of leaflets were dropped by planes and balloons over the Austro-Hungarian lines.[108] Figure 12.1 reproduces the original Czech and an English translation. The leaflet aimed at persuading Czechs and Slovaks to defect to a Czecho-Slovak "Legion," composed of about 20,000 captured or defected countrymen and under Italian command.[109] After the war, Crewe House considered its operations against Austria-Hungary" its most "striking success."[110]

Mark Cornwall, an expert on World War I propaganda, vouched for the value of the 1918 Allied propaganda campaign against Austria-Hungary in Italy, but said, "[It] was the Italians who were engaged in the most sophisticated example of front propaganda, a campaign which may have been given focus by British advisers but always retained a solid Italian base and outlook."[111] The Padua Commission targeted Magyars among the Austro-Hungarian troops with over nine million leaflets, such as Manifesto 109 telling Hungarian troops that they were fighting not for Hungary but for Germany, Austria, and Turkey.[112]

Desertions did increase after the disastrous Piave campaign. Military historian Gunther Rothenberg found that "refusals to go into action, and mass desertions became

Poselství prof. Masaryka československému vojsku v Italii.

Prof. *T. G. Masaryk* poslal z Washingtonu prostřednictvím král. italského velvyslanectví československému autonomnímu vojsku v Italii tento vzkaz:

"Bratři! Rakousko-Uhersko, chtějíc zlomiti ve vlasti oposici československou, tvrdilo, že naše vojsko je sebranka, jež nemá ani politického ani vojenského významu. Vypustilo dokonce lež, že naše vojsko se skládá z Rusů a jiných národností a že nezlává vojska československého. Náš národ neuvěřil tomuto klamu a zůstal nesmiřitelným a hrdým na své vojsko. Tehdy Rakousko-Uhersko pokusilo se zasaditi rozhodnou ránu našemu národu tím, že by zničíc vás zničilo vojsko jeho. Chtělo zmocniti se naší vlajky odboje a samostatnosti, symbolu víry a aspirací našeho národa.

"Bratři! Vaše vůle, váš dalekozraký hled překazily plány nepřítele. Náš prapor vlaje ještě hrdě na posici svěřené vaší ochraně. Náš národ pozná vaše hrdinské činy a všechno srdce se pohnou hlubokou vděčností k vám. Chloubou nad vámi a hrdou vzpomínkou padlých bratrů.

"Jako váš vrchní velitel posílám vám svůj nejsrdečnější dík za udatnost, kterouž jste znova přispěli k vítězství našeho národa, Italie, Spojenců a celého lidstva.

Nazdar!"

T. G. Masaryk.

Nutkalo nás pochlubiti se vám uznáním našeho milovaného vůdce, jenž nás i národ náš dovede k vítěznému cíli.

Jsme přesvědčeni, že i vy, ve shodě s celým národem, vidíte spásu Vlasti a uskutečnění našich svatých práv jen v rozbití Rakouska.

Až poženou vás, abyste nastavili prsa za proradnou dynastii, k níž národ nemá závazků, najdete jistě příležitost odpověděti vhodně na staleté útisky a zachrániti se pro lepší budoucnost!

Nazdar!

Vojáci-dobrovolci československé armády v Italii.

V Italii 2. října 1918 — 420.

Message of Professor Masaryk to the Czechoslovak Army in Italy.

Through the agency of the Italian Legation, Professor T. G. Masaryk has sent the following message from Washington to the autonomous Czecho-Slovak army in Italy:

"Brothers! Austria-Hungary, desiring to break the opposition at home, has asserted that our army is a rabble which has no political or military significance. She has even uttered the lie that our army is composed of Russians and other nationalities, and that a Czecho-Slovak army does not exist. Our nation does not believe this dishonesty and has remained obdurate and proud of its army. Then Austria-Hungary endeavoured to deal a decisive blow to our nation by destroying you, and with you its army. She desired to gain possession of our banners of resistance and independence, the symbol of trust and aspiration cherished by our people.

"Brothers! Your will, your far-reaching glance frustrated the enemy's plans. Our flag is still flying proudly upon the position entrusted to you for defence. Our nation recognises your heroic deeds and all hearts are stirred by profound gratitude to you. They extol you and the proud memory of your fallen brothers.

"As your Commander-in-Chief I send you my heartiest thanks for the bravery by which you have contributed to the victory of our nation, of Italy, the Allies and all mankind.

Greetings!"

T. G. Masaryk.

We cannot help telling you how proud we are of the recognition by our beloved leader, who will guide us and our nation to the goal of victory.

We are convinced that you also, in concert with the whole nation, see the salvation of our country and the realisation of our sacred rights only in the destruction of Austria.

When they drive you forward to protect the treacherous dynasty, to which the nation has no obligations, you will certainly find an opportunity of retaliating worthily for centuries of oppression and of saving yourselves for a better future.

Greetings!

Volunteers of the czecho-slovak army in Italy.

October 2nd, 1918.

Figure 12.2: Italian Propaganda Message Intended for Czech Troops in Italy. This propaganda leaflet in Czech is No. 18 among scores prepared in multiple languages that a unit of the Italian military spread widely among Austro-Hungarian troops. Credit: Campbell Stuart, *Secrets of Crewe House* (New York: Hodder and Stoughton, 1921), pp. 176–177 and 250–251. In the public domain.

frequent and were no longer confined to Czechs. Slovene, Ruthene, Polish, Serb, and even Magyar units were also affected."[113] Reliable statistics on deserters are hard to obtain. Mark Cornwall reported a count of 133 deserters from Conrad's 10th and 11th Armies.[114] That tally did not consider the troops' nationality proportions, which determined how many in each nationality were available to defect. Nonetheless, nearly half (55) were Czechs. None were Slovaks.

Slovak Samko Mozolák certainly was not a deserter. He was a veteran soldier who had fought for four years on three fronts, twice suffered wounds that required hospitalization, and had been decorated for bravery in action. He must have been killed in the battle, for his family never saw him again. Samko died at the age of 36 in the service of a Habsburg monarchy that allowed Magyars to dominate his Slovak people. Back in Krajné in the Hungarian half of the Habsburgs' Dual Monarchy, his widow, Anna, was left to raise their three children: twelve-year-old Ján and Zuzanna, and four-year-old Samuel, Jr. Before the year was out—and without moving from Krajné—they would no longer be living in Hungary, but in Slovakia within the new nation of Czechoslovakia.

13

Imperial Losses

Sometimes a war's outcome can be predicted long before it ends. In a sense, the 1918 outcome of the Great War was predictable by December 1914. Barely five months after it began in late July, fighting had already lasted too long for Austria-Hungary and Germany to win—according to their own calculations. Each country had expected to fight different opponents on two fronts. To do so successfully, Austria-Hungary and Germany needed quick victories on one front against their weaker personal enemies—Serbia and France respectively—in order to combine forces on the other front against their stronger common opponent, Russia.

Austria-Hungary thought it would defeat Serbia in a few weeks with one hand tied behind its back. It declared war against Serbia to the south on July 28, bombarded Belgrade on July 29, but did not invade until August 12, using only half its troops. The other half went eastward, augmenting a dozen German divisions to temporarily check Russia, Serbia's champion and France's ally. Germany declared war on Russia on August 1. Its generals thought that Russia needed weeks to fully mobilize and assumed—according to its Schlieffen Plan—that the bulk of Germany's army would sweep swiftly through Luxembourg and Belgium, invading France from the north and defeating her within six weeks. Then Germany would transport its victorious troops by rail to the Eastern Front, joining the rest of Austria-Hungary's victorious troops, fresh from subduing Serbia. Together, the armies of the two Central Powers would defeat the hordes of Russia's untrained and woefully equipped peasants.

Events did not follow according to plan for either country. By December 1914, Austria-Hungary had lost over 200,000 troops in Serbia alone and had been expelled from its soil. The nation's official history of the war branded it as "a serious diminution in the Dual Monarchy's prestige and self-confidence."[1] Habsburg losses to the Russians in Galicia were even greater. Holger Herwig wrote that the empire's war minister calculated all losses by the end of 1914 "at 692,195 soldiers." Herwig concluded, "The Austro-Hungarian Army was nearly eliminated as a fighting force."[2] It repeatedly relied on German troops to rescue it from defeat.[3]

Meanwhile, Germany was having its own troubles. The Allied victory at the Battle of the Marne halted the German advance on September 5–12, just one week before France's predicted defeat. General Erich von Falkenhayn replaced General Moltke, who had planned the Schlieffen campaign. According to Herwig, "The announcement was delayed until 6 November for fear of its negative impact on the home front and to deny Allied claims that Moltke had lost the Battle of the Marne."[4] Some sources say that General Moltke personally told Kaiser Wilhelm, "Your Majesty, we have lost the war."[5] Whether or not he actually said that, Moltke withdrew and died a broken man in 1916.[6] Spoken or not, the assertion was true. Germany had counted on defeating France quickly as the only way to win a two-front war against France and Russia. It also counted on material support against the Russians from a robust Austro-Hungarian army. Germany did not defeat France quickly, and the Austro-Hungarian army was decimated. An impartial observer would have predicted an unfavorable outcome to their war.

Prominent people in both Austria-Hungary and Germany realized soon after Christmas 1914 that the war was not going well, and they sought an early end. Historian Gary Shanafelt reported that the German military rejected various efforts by Habsburg leaders to negotiate peace with France or Russia. He said that Germany was both Austria-Hungary's ally and its "secret enemy," dictating Habsburg foreign policy to serve German interests.[7] "The expectations of the summer, the presuppositions under which the Monarchy's leaders had originally gone to war, had all proven themselves false. How could Austria-Hungary maintain its position as a Great Power and an equal in the alliance under these new circumstances?"[8]

The experienced Habsburg diplomat and minister, Count János Forgách, had decided as early as January 1915 "that the war had to be ended" and prepared a long memorandum for the foreign office. Shanafelt summarized Forgách's report: "The war situation was bleak: Russia had not been defeated, and Italy and Rumania threatened to intervene at any time. The chances of an improvement were 'very slim.' To achieve peace, he was ready to sacrifice the Trentino to Italy to get its mediation and even East Galicia to Russia in exchange for some compensation in Western Poland. But an end to the war could only be gotten with the Germans; hence it was urgently necessary to convince them that a settlement had to be reached."[9] Forgách's recommendation was opposed by Hungarian Minister President István Tisza, who forbade peace negotiations independently of Germany. Although in April 1915 Chief of Staff Conrad "urged peace with Russia in order to contain Italy" and "proposed to give the Russians East Galicia in return for peace and a free hand in the western Balkans," even Conrad "was careful to note that such a step had to be taken in full agreement with Berlin."[10]

Only the emperor had the stature to defy Germany, and Franz Josef was 84 years old, frail, and isolated from military operations. Moreover, he had started the war against Serbia to defend Austria-Hungary's honor. To sue for peace without victory would be dishonorable. Nevertheless, before Franz Josef's death in 1916, historian Arthur May reported that the emperor had lost all hope in the outcome of the war, saying, "Things are going badly with us; perhaps worse than we suspect; the starving people can't stand much more. It remains to be seen whether and how we shall get through next winter. I mean to end the war next spring, whatever happens. I can't let my realm go to hopeless ruin."[11] Unfortunately, Franz Josef died in November, before he could negotiate a peace in the spring of 1917.

However, his 29-year-old successor, Emperor Karl I of Austria and King Karl IV of Hungary, soon proclaimed, "I will do everything to banish in the shortest possible time the horrors and sacrifices of war, to win back for my peoples the sorely-missed blessings of peace."[12] Karl found that ending the war was more easily proclaimed than accomplished. In March 1917, four months after Franz Josef's death, Karl himself tried to negotiate a separate peace with France, as the old man had promised—in the spring.

As described in Chapter 11, "Imperial Irrelevance," Karl's scheme involved his brother-in-law Prince Sixtus, an officer in the (enemy) Belgian army, meeting in secret with French officials in Switzerland and in disguise with Karl in Austria.[13] Sixtus's unsuccessful attempts at negotiating a separate peace were unknown until April 1918—when "the Sixtus affair" was publicized. Because Karl disingenuously disavowed the solid evidence of clandestine negotiations with enemies of the Central Powers, exposing the emperor's secret talks discolored his reputation with his subjects and destroyed any influence he had left with the German military.

Among German civilians, severe food shortages were already sapping support for the war in 1916.[14] Within the military, manpower and supplies were tight. Chief of Staff Erich von Falkenhayn thought that Germany's allies would not last past autumn and reportedly told Bethmann Hollweg in January 1916 that the "Reich's own 'economic and internal political conditions' also made a speedy conclusion to the conflict 'extremely desirable.'"[15] Nevertheless, on February 21 Falkenhayn launched a major attack on the French bastion of Verdun. By the end of April, both sides had lost more than 100,000 men. After Romania declared war on Austria-Hungary on August 28, 1916, Falkenhayn was replaced as Chief of Staff by 68-year-old Paul von Hindenburg. Hindenburg harbored no thoughts of suing for peace. Neither did his younger deputy and tactician, General Erich Ludendorff.

Germany's fortunes rose toward the end of the year. German and Bulgarian troops sprang to Austria-Hungary's defense against Romania, entered Bucharest on December 6, and soon occupied the country. Sensing that Germany could negotiate from a position of strength, Chancellor Theobald von Bethmann-Hollweg on December 12 proposed peace talks between the Central Powers and the Entente nations. He suggested that the talks should be assisted by the good offices of President Woodrow Wilson of the United States, which was not yet in the war. Germany's proposals were vague and certainly did not offer to back down from any territorial gains. Russia, Britain, France, and the United States separately and promptly rejected them within a month.[16] Bethmann-Hollweg was forced to resign in July 1917, and Generals Hindenburg and Ludendorff effectively took dictatorial control of government.

By the middle of 1917, the Central Powers could boast its extensive conquests in a propaganda poster, "*Wer ist Sieger?*" (Who is Winning?), reproduced in Figure 13.1. Using bar graphs, the poster showed that the Mittelmächte (Central Powers), represented by a German soldier, had conquered 548,700 square kilometers of territory compared to a measly 9,400 by the Entente, represented by the likeness of a British soldier. Indeed, throughout most of the war, the Central Powers occupied and fought on lands formerly held by Belgium, Luxembourg, France, Russia, Serbia, and Romania. Except for the first year of the war, relatively few battles in Europe occurred in Germany, Austria-Hungary, or Bulgaria.

Germany's fortunes rose further in 1917 after the Bolsheviks seized power in Russia on November 7 and Lenin instructed Russian troops to elect representatives for armistice talks. Talks began on December 3, an armistice was reached on December 15, and peace negotiations opened soon afterward at the German Eastern Field Army's headquarters in the town of Brest-Litovsk (now Brest, Belarus). All four powers—Germany, Austria-Hungary, Bulgaria and the Ottoman Empire—represented the Central Powers. Only the Russian Bolsheviks, unsupported by their former Entente allies, France and Britain, sat across the table.[17]

Determined to end the war and proceed with the Communist revolution, Lenin on March 3, 1918, signed the draconian Brest-Litovsk Treaty. Holger Herwig summarized

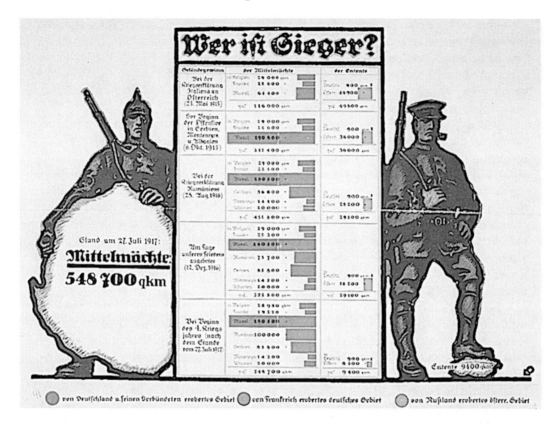

Figure 13.1: "WER IST SIEGER?" (WHO IS WINNING?). This German propaganda poster boasts that as of 27 July 1917 the Central powers occupied 548,700 square kilometers of territory compared with the Entente's measly holdings of 9,400 square kilometers in Germany and Austria-Hungary. Since 23 May 1915, moreover, the Central Powers steadily conquered more land, whereas the Entente steadily surrendered land it had won. Credit: This German propaganda poster, reportedly created by Louis Oppenheim, was published in Berlin by Dr. Selle & Co., 1917. It is available, with no known restrictions on publication, from the Prints & Photographs Online Catalog of the Library of Congress, LC-USZC4-11692.

its harsh terms: "Russia was forced to recognize the 'independence' of Finland and Ukraine; Lithuania, Estonia, Courland, and Livonia were turned over to German 'police forces'; Poland was separated from Russia, awaiting final disposition between Berlin and Vienna; and Russian forces had to evacuate all 'border lands.' Russia lost about 90 percent of its coal mines, 50 percent of its industry, and 30 percent of its population. Under a separate treaty negotiated on 9 February, Germany was to receive 30 percent, Austria-Hungary 50 percent, and Bulgaria and Turkey 20 percent of Ukraine's grain reserves."[18]

With Russia formally out of the war, Romania—defeated and occupied a year earlier—signed the comparably harsh Treaty of Bucharest on May 7. Germany got a ninety-year lease on Romanian oil fields, minerals, and other natural resources; Austria-Hungary gained control of passes in the Carpathian Mountains; and Bulgaria absorbed much of Romania's Black Sea coastline.[19] Both treaties demonstrated what the Central Powers would demand if the Allies lost the war.

Within weeks after they punished Russia and Romania with crushing peace treaties, the fortunes of the Central Powers abruptly turned for the worse from March to May of

1918. In March, Germany launched a huge western offensive, codenamed Operation Michael. Herwig said, "With Russia, Romania, and Serbia defeated, the Supreme Command gambled Germany's future on victory on the Western Front to force Britain and France to their knees before the Americans arrived in strength."[20] Operation Michael failed, and it spawned other failures for the German army. Watson reported, "Between March and the end of July it had suffered 977,555 casualties."[21] As the Germans lost troops, the Allies gained reinforcements, as hundreds of thousands of Americans arrived in Europe. The Germans launched their last major attack on July 15, 1918, pushing toward Rheims and the Marne River, only to be stopped and then repulsed by a major Allied attack a few days later.

Meanwhile on the Italian Front, the war had turned equally badly against Austria-Hungary. Bullied by Germany to support its spring offensive, Emperor Karl approved an attack against the Italians ensconced along the Piave River. It was an ill-advised offensive for which the weakened Habsburg forces were unprepared.[22] The result was a disastrous defeat that shook the army at all levels and "finished off the last Habsburg army in the field."[23] By the end of June, the Habsburg offensive had been crushed, and the Italians prepared for a full assault on Austria-Hungary.

On the Western Front, Allied forces on August 8, 1918, launched a withering artillery bombardment and tank assault against the Germans at the Battle of Amiens, roughly 70 miles north of Paris. General Ludendorff called August 8 "the black day of the Germany army," for it launched the army's virtual expulsion from France.[24] The demoralized German army not only retreated but also collapsed.[25] Germany and Austria-Hungary lost their ally, Bulgaria, on September 29, when Bulgaria arranged for its own armistice with the Allied nations. Even the German military sought an armistice to end the fighting. According to Herwig, General Ludendorff himself laid out the situation on October 1: "The Allies, with the help of nearly 3 million fresh American troops, could soon gain 'a *great* victory, a *breakthrough in grand style.*' One could 'no longer rely on the troops.' The bottom line was that the Army had to be spared a catastrophic defeat at all costs. There was only one solution: the Kaiser and the Chancellor had to 'request an armistice *without any hesitation.*' Lest staff officers not appreciate the full meaning of his words, the First Quartermaster-General repeated that 'prosecution of the war was senseless,' and that only 'a quick end' to the war could save the Army from destruction."[26] Note that the German army had been defeated, but it was not destroyed. Ludendorff sought an armistice to stop fighting so that it would *not* be destroyed.

As wars go, the Great War was particularly ghastly, one seemingly unsuited to a theatrical production. Nevertheless, *Oh! What a Lovely War* was the title of a satirical British stage show in 1961 and a movie musical in 1969. The award-winning antiwar film, directed by Richard Attenborough, savaged the war's origin and conduct through parodies of popular songs of the time, allegorical settings, and fantasy depictions of the countless dead. A remarkably faithful summary of the bizarre folly of World War I, the film merits viewing today.

On January 8, 1918, President Woodrow Wilson addressed the United States Congress and proposed Fourteen Points as the basis of a "program of the world's peace." In summary form, they were:

1. No more secret agreements ("Open covenants openly arrived at").
2. Free navigation of all seas.

3. An end to all economic barriers between countries.

4. Countries to reduce weapon numbers.

5. All decisions regarding the colonies should be impartial.

6. The German Army is to be removed from Russia. Russia should be left to develop on her own.

7. Belgium should be independent as before the war.

8. France should be fully liberated and allowed to recover Alsace-Lorraine.

9. All Italians are to be allowed to live in Italy. Italy's borders are to be "along clearly recognizable lines of nationality."

10. Autonomous development for peoples living in Austria-Hungary.

11. Recognition of historical boundaries for the Balkan states and guarantees of territorial integrity.

12. The Turkish people should be governed by the Turkish government. Non-Turks in the old Turkish Empire should govern themselves.

13. An independent Poland should be created which should have access to the sea.

14. A League of Nations should be set up to guarantee the political and territorial independence of all states.[27]

Wilson's points for peace at the start of 1918 contrasted starkly with the punitive terms of the treaties that the Central Powers imposed on Russia and Romania just months later. The U.S. State Department's Office of Historian website says that "the Fourteen Points still stand as the most powerful expression of the idealist strain in United States diplomacy."[28]

Wilson's idealism captured people's imagination in a war-weary Europe—including politicians who had never conceived of international politics in humanitarian terms. The American president became a hero and his "Fourteen Points" became 1918's mantra.[29] Wilson had declared as early as May 27, 1916, that "every people has a right to choose the sovereignty under which they should live," but he did not use the phrase "self-determination" in presenting his Fourteen Points to Congress on January 8, 1918.[30] Three days before Wilson's address, British Prime Minister Lloyd George had mentioned "the general principle of national self-determination" in a speech to the British Trades Union.[31] Nevertheless, people linked the phase to Wilson and, incorrectly, placed it among his Fourteen Points.

People at all levels of society seemed to grasp the essential meaning of "self-determination," and the concept inspired oppressed subjects in the belligerent nations. Novelist Mark Wansa imagined its impact on two Rusyn (Ruthene) brothers in 1918. Andrii, who trained as a priest, spoke to his brother, who returned from working in New Jersey: "People will listen to us now! There are those in the world—especially among our people in Ameryka—who remember us and wish to see our dreams fulfilled. Prezident Vylson of Ameryka says that all people have the right to self-determination. I once read that he gave a speech that outlined fourteen ways the war could end and how peace could come again to the world. Prezident Vylson of Ameryka is a great man, Vasyl. Was he prezident when you were in Ameryka?"[32] Whereas before, non–German and non–Magyar nationalities might have been content with recognition within a federal system under Habsburg rule, now they were inspired by "self-determination" to seek independence, not just autonomy.[33]

In truth, Wilson's point 10, which specifically referred to Austria-Hungary, stopped short of independence. Its full text said. "The peoples of Austria-Hungary, whose place among the nations we wish to see safeguarded and assured, should be accorded the freest opportunity to autonomous development." Thinking that he might retain his crown by granting nationalities some autonomy, Emperor Karl on September 15 proposed a peace conference to President Wilson. Wilson rejected the proposal the next day.[34]

We should note that some 21st-century observers believed that the monarchy *could have* achieved viable, enlightened government of its nationalities.[35] John Deak's long essay defending Austria as an "evolving constitutional state" contended, "The real tragedy of the First World War, and of the twentieth century itself, may actually be a Habsburg story: the Great War ended the possibilities of multinationalism in Europe."[36] In his recent book, he stated: "We miss the vibrancy of a multinational polity in its attempts to retool itself once again for a new era: in this case, democracy, mass politics, and social welfare."[37] Deak wrote in great detail and even convincingly of the Austrian bureaucracy's mission to serve all of Austria. Yet the Habsburg story also embraced Hungary, where no one could make a creditable case that Habsburg rule advanced "democracy, mass politics, and social welfare."[38]

On October 4, both Austria-Hungary and Germany sent notes to President Wilson requesting an armistice. Wilson ignored Austria-Hungary's note but replied to Germany on October 8, specifying conditions for discussion. The German and American governments exchanged additional notes before President Wilson agreed to propose the armistice to the Allied governments on October 23. Although German General Ludendorff had requested an armistice on the basis of the Fourteen Points, he had to ask his Foreign Office to explain them.[39] By praising points for peace that he neither comprehended nor accepted, Ludendorff hoped to improve Germany's image as being reasonable and cooperative, perhaps even democratic.[40]

From August to October 1918, while the warring nations exchanged notes to end the fighting, battles still occurred. For the most part, the Central Powers were steadily losing to Entente forces. The Central Powers were also losing on the political front. Émigré spokesmen representing Poles, South Slavs, Czechs, and Slovaks undermined Habsburg authority over their peoples—as summarized in Arthur May's chapter, "Entente Cabinets and the Danube Emigrés."[41] The Czech and Slovak leaders, who became active in 1915 and soon formed the Czecho-Slovak National Council, were arguably the most successful.[42] Its three key figures were Tomáš Masaryk, Edvard Beneš, and Milan Štefánik.

Masaryk had been a professor in Prague and member of the Austrian parliament. He had a Slovak father, a Germanized Moravian mother, and an American wife, whom he met in Leipzig. Beneš, born into a peasant family in Bohemia, was also a Prague professor and political activist but thirty years younger. Štefánik, a Slovak who became a French citizen, was an astronomer, aviator, and a general in the French Army, giving him access to political elites. Masaryk went into exile soon after the war's start to work with Entente powers for an independent Czechoslovakia. Beneš followed in 1915. Štefánik was already in Paris. Slovak historian Mark Stolarik detailed the important part played by Slovak-Americans, who often clashed with the European Czecho-Slovak National Council over fear of Slovaks' diminished political status in the new state.[43]

Both Masaryk and Beneš worked to persuade the Allied governments that the Czech and Slovak peoples opposed the war and Habsburg rule, seeking to gain recognition of the Czecho-Slovak National Council. Initially, Masaryk worked mostly in London, while Beneš handled Paris. In 1918, Masaryk focused on winning support in the United States, where he stayed from April 29, 1918, until the end of the war.[44] Historian Z.A.B. Zeman linked the Czech émigrés' activities to the Allies' propaganda program, saying, "The western Allies came to use the exiles from the Habsburg monarchy in the same manner as the Germans had used Lenin and the internationalist movements in Russia" to destabilize the tsarist regime.[45] In fact, Mark Cornwall credited the Central Powers in 1917 as "the first of the belligerents" to launch a coordinated propaganda attack, targeting Russia.[46] Moreover, "On the basis of this experience in the East, Austria-Hungary turned to wield the same weapon against Italy."[47]

Before the war, European governments had looked favorably on Austria-Hungary, despite prewar books (mentioned in Chapter 3) by R.W. Seton-Watson (1908) and Henry Wickham Steed (1913) that denounced the Habsburg's tolerance of Magyarization in Hungary.[48] The 21st-century scholar László Péter said Steed and Seton-Watson helped reverse the British government's "pro–Hungarian" opinion even before the war.[49] After the war began, both worked with Britain's Ministry of Information. Zeman wrote: "Apart from their official activities as experts and propagandists, both men were engaged in journalism as well: Steed was the foreign editor of *The Times*, and Seton-Watson, since October 1916, had spent much of his time and money editing and writing the monthly *New Europe*. They were friends and protectors of Masaryk, Trumbic, and other emigre politicians and they were in complete agreement with the plans of the Czech and South Slav exiles. The Habsburg monarchy was Steed's principal enemy...."[50]

According to documents in Seton-Watson's archives, Slovaks gave a copy of *Racial Problems in Hungary* to Theodore Roosevelt in 1910 when he visited Budapest.[51] By 1918, the propaganda offensive was paying off.[52] Zeman said, "The summer months brought the fulfilment of the dearest wishes of the exiles. On 29 June the French government recognized the right of the Czechoslovaks to independence and the National Council in Paris as the 'first basis of the future government.' On 14 August the British acknowledged the Czechs as an Allied nation and their military units in Russia, France, and Italy as an 'allied and belligerent army waging regular warfare against Austria-Hungary and Germany.' On 3 September the United States government followed suit and recognized the National Council as a 'de facto belligerent government.'"[53]

Sitting in Paris, the Czecho-Slovak National Council, composed of émigrés and claiming action on behalf of the Czech and Slovak peoples, had the audacity to declare war on Germany on August 13. Other political developments occurred at a dizzying rate:

- *September 25:* Italy recognized the Yugo Slav State as independent.
- *October 4:* Bulgaria's King Ferdinand abdicated in favor of his son Boris.
- *October 30:* Turkey arranged its own armistice with the Entente countries.
- *October 31:* former Hungarian Minister President Tisza was assassinated.
- *October 31:* people rebelled in Vienna and Budapest.
- *November 1:* Ukraine and Poland entered a state of war.
- *November 1:* Hungary formed an independent government.
- *November 1:* Bulgarian King Boris abdicated, after less than a month on the throne.
- *November 9:* Germany announced the abdication of Kaiser Wilhelm.

Politics everywhere were in flux. As during the chaotic collapse of communism in Eastern Europe in 1989, the old order was crashing down. Embodying that old order,

Habsburg Emperor Karl desperately tried to salvage his monarchy. After President Wilson snubbed his peace offer based on autonomy for his empire's nationalities, Karl on October 16 published a manifesto to turn Austria-Hungary into a federation of national provinces.[54] His manifesto came too late and its proposal fell too short: Too late because he missed the window when his proposal would have been considered; and too short because non–Magyar nationalities demanded more than autonomy. Hungary refused to agree to his federation idea anyway. On October 18, President Wilson responded by urging nationalities within the Habsburg monarchy to declare their independence.[55] The same day in Paris, the Czecho-Slovak National Council, already recognized by France, Great Britain, and the United States, did just that. They declared the provisional government of a new Czecho-Slovak Republic out of the Habsburg lands.[56]

Historian Holger Herwig concluded that Emperor Karl's manifesto, which he hoped would save the Habsburg Empire, "proved to be its death warrant."[57] On October 24, the Italians began an offensive that defeated the Habsburg troops remaining in the field. On October 28 Habsburg Field Marshal von Boroević demanded an armistice at any price to head off the "anarchy" that would surely spell "catastrophe for Monarchy and Army."[58] The same day, October 28, the Czech National Council in Prague signed a declaration proclaiming the nation of Czechoslovakia. On October 30 the Slovak National Council in Martin, Slovakia, did the same, unaware that the Czechs had signed a similar declaration two days earlier.[59] Echoing Holger, Judson observed, "Had not Vienna deputized the National Councils to reorganize the empire?"[60]

International recognition quickly followed, and the new state of Czechoslovakia was born from adjacent segments in Austrian and Hungarian parts of the collapsing Dual Monarchy. The crumbling Austrian government had already sued for an armistice, which was approved by the Allies' Supreme War Council at Versailles on October 31.[61] Hungarian leaders instructed *Honvéd* soldiers to head home on November 1. Taylor said, "The bulk of the Austro-Hungarian army fell to pieces, each man finding his way back to his national home as best he could amidst confusion and chaos."[62] On November 3, Austria-Hungary signed a separate armistice with the Allied Powers, effective on November 4.

Germany had not yet agreed to an armistice, but its delegates arrived at the Allied General Headquarters on November 8, the day before Germany announced the Kaiser's abdication. French General Ferdinand Foch, Commander-in-Chief of the Allied armies, was eager to stop the fighting as soon as the Germans had agreed to his armistice conditions. Historian Michael Neiberg wrote: "Fighting on to make the symbolic gesture of invading Germany struck him as unnecessary. 'I am not waging war for the sake of waging war,' he told Edward House. 'If I obtain through the armistice the conditions that we wish to impose on Germany, I am satisfied. Once this object is attained, nobody has the right to shed one more drop of blood.'"[63] Foch's armistice terms were harsh, running over thirty-five provisions, and included the surrender of massive amounts of war material, delivery of 5,000 locomotives, 5,000 trucks, 150,000 wagons, and other supplies.[64] German Chief of Staff Hindenburg urged his delegates to soften the terms but said, "You must sign all the same."[65]

Special attention should be given to the text of provision number 2: *"Immediate evacuation of invaded countries: Belgium, France, Alsace-Lorraine, Luxemburg, so ordered as to be completed within fourteen days from the signature of the armistice."* The fact is that the victorious Allies did *not* invade or occupy Germany. It merely held a little German territory west of the Rhine River, the Rhineland. In contrast, the German army—the defeated army—still occupied vast amounts of Allied lands. Hitler historian Laurence Rees wrote that German troops too were "unaware that Germany could scarcely continue to wage" the war. He reported an interview with a fighter on the Western Front, who said: "The front-line troops didn't feel themselves beaten, and we were wondering why the armistice was happening so quickly, and why we had to vacate all our positions in such a hurry, because we were still standing on enemy territory, and we thought all this was strange ... we were angry, because we did not feel that we had come to the end of our strength."[66] Ian Beckett pointed out the irony of the situation: "Since Entente troops only occupied the Rhineland and they did not parade through Berlin as German troops had through Paris in 1871, it was never brought fully home to the German people that they had been defeated, hence the subsequent shock of the terms imposed."[67]

Austria-Hungary could appreciate the irony. Gunther Rothenberg said, "Against all expectations and prognostications, the army had fought for almost four and a half years and when the end came it stood everywhere on foreign soil."[68] Nevertheless, the armistice Austria-Hungary signed confirmed the "verdict on the battlefield." Before renouncing his throne, Emperor Karl wrote (but never delivered) a final message to his troops: "Though our sword is broken, our shield of honor remains untarnished. I have always looked for peace both at home and abroad. As you return home to rebuild, may you rebuild together as you have fought together."[69] Lawrence Rees said that ordinary German soldiers in World War I were bewildered "not only at the swift removal of the Kaiser but at the immediate declaration of an armistice."[70]

Previous armistices on September 29, October 30, and November 4 had ended hostilities between the Allies and Bulgaria, Turkey, and Austria-Hungary respectively. The armistice ending armed conflict between the Allied forces and Germany went into effect at 11:00 a.m. (Paris time) on the 11th day of the 11th month in 1918. Armistices do not end wars. An armistice is merely a formal agreement to stop fighting. In 1953, for example, the war between North Korea and the United Nations ended by armistice. Because no peace treaty was ever signed, North Korea is technically still at war with South Korea, which the United States still defends with troops stationed there. Wars end only when belligerent nations sign peace treaties.

The victorious Central Powers had forced peace treaties on two Allied opponents in 1918—on Russia in the March 3 Treaty of Brest-Litovsk and on Romania in the May 7 Treaty of Bucharest. Serbia, however, was conquered and occupied without a treaty. The German people had reason to be confused by the forthcoming armistice. They knew that their army had defeated Russia, Romania, and Serbia. They also knew that Allied forces had not invaded Germany beyond the Rhine River, 400 miles west of Berlin. Many thought that the November 11 armistice meant that the war had ended in a stalemate. Indeed, no Allied soldiers marched into Berlin. Instead, German soldiers paraded before cheering crowds to hear Germany's new chancellor, Friedrich Ebert, tell them with some justification, "No enemy has vanquished you. As you return unconquered from the field of battle, I salute you!"[71]

The conquering of Germany came in the peace treaties that followed the armistice. Most readers probably know that the Treaty of Versailles ended the war between the Allied Powers and Germany, and they also may know that the treaty created the League of Nations. But unless they are history buffs, readers probably know little more about the lengthy, complex, and monumentally important negotiations, engagingly recounted in Margaret MacMillan's award-winning book, *Paris 1919: Six Months That Changed the*

World.[72] Personal negotiations by the heads of the French, British, Italian, and United States governments generated not one treaty but five individual treaties—one for each of the defeated Central Powers: Germany, Bulgaria, the Ottoman Empire, Austria, and Hungary—which were by then separate countries requiring separate treaties.

Here is an overview and summary of participants, activities, and events in Paris, 1919:

- Invitations to the conference were issued to thirty-two nations; twenty-nine attended. Germany was not invited to participate. The full peace conference met only eight times.[73]
- The three most important actors in the treaty deliberations were Georges Clemenceau, Prime Minster of France; Lloyd George, Prime Minister of Great Britain; and Woodrow Wilson, President of the United States. Wilson fully engaged in the deliberations, returning only twice to the United States and then only for a couple of weeks.
- Along with Vittorio Orlando, Prime Minister of Italy, they constituted the Council of Four, which prioritized and directed the negotiations. They met for the first time on January 12 and met more than one hundred times over six months to late June.[74]
- For the most part, Wilson, Clemenceau, and George worked well together, although they clashed on matters central to their political views.
- Wilson insisted on his Fourteen Points, especially the self-determination of nations and the creation of a League of Nations, whose covenant led off the treaty as Part 1.
- Clemenceau sought to create a weak, heavily indebted Germany that would never again threaten France.
- George sought to protect Britain's worldwide imperial interests as he bargained with both Wilson and Clemenceau on other matters.
- Orlando, handicapped by his limited ability in English, defended Italy's rights to the spoils of war, especially in getting the Tyrol from Austria and Fiume from Hungary, and eventually withdrew from the conference.
- Everyone in the Council of Four was willing to sacrifice self-determination of nations in dividing up the Ottoman Empire.
- Germany did not participate in negotiating the treaty and was not informed of its terms until May 7, which included Article 231 blaming "Germany and her allies for causing all the loss and damage" of the war.
- Germany also had to give up its territorial gains from the Brest-Litovsk Treaty. Germany had until June 23 to accept the terms without material change, which Germany did at the last moment.
- Negotiated mainly in Parisian hotels, the Treaty of Versailles was signed on June 28 in the Hall of Mirrors at the Palace of Versailles, first by two German ministers and then by 65 others representing 32 "original members" of the League of Nations it created.

The Treaty of Versailles only ended the war between the Allies and Germany, but the Paris negotiations outlined terms for subsequent peace treaties with the other Central Powers. For the most part, the treaties were negotiated in Paris hotels but signed in prominent sites in the French countryside that gave the treaties their distinctive names. Briefly, here they are by date, title, and function:

- September 10, 1919, *Treaty of Saint-Germain,* signed in a royal palace in the commune of Saint-Germain-en-Laye, about 19 km west of Paris. Between the Allied Powers and the Republic of Austria, it dissolved the Austro-Hungarian Empire and recognized the independence of Hungary, Czechoslovakia, Poland, and the Kingdom of Serbs, Croats and Slovenes.
- November 27, 1919, *Treaty of Neuilly,* signed in the commune of Neuilly-sur-Seine, 6.8 km from the center of Paris. Between Bulgaria and the Allied Powers, it cost Bulgaria territory on its borders (mainly Western Thrace, ceded to Greece) and cut off Bulgaria from the Aegean Sea.
- June 4, 1920, *Treaty of Trianon,* signed in the Grand Trianon Palace, on the grounds of the Palace of Versailles. Between Hungary and the Allied Powers, it cost Hungary huge portions of its former territory and population.
- August 10, 1920, *Treaty of Sèvres,* signed in the commune of Sèvres, 9.9 km from the center of Paris. Between the Ottoman Empire and Britain, France, and Italy, it ceded all the empire's lands outside of Turkey to the Allied signatories, leading to the creation of Iraq, Syria, Palestine, and Lebanon.

Because the United States Senate failed to ratify the Treaty of Versailles, Wilson failed to realize his cherished idea, the United States' joining the League of Nations. Failure to ratify the treaty also meant that the U.S. had no peace treaty with Germany or any of the belligerents. Consequently, the United States in 1921 negotiated separate treaties with Austria (August 24), Germany (August 25), and Hungary (August 29).[75]

Some conferees who contributed to the draft treaty had second thoughts about the severe terms it imposed on Germany, including reparations of 132 billion marks (about $34 billion in 1921), regarded as beyond its ability to pay.[76] Years later, American relief administrator Herbert Hoover said after seeing the entire treaty for the first time and discussing it with South African delegate Jan Smuts and British adviser John Maynard Keynes, "We agreed that the consequences of the proposed Treaty would ultimately bring destruction."[77] Keynes's widely read 1919 book, *The Economic Consequences of Peace,* warned the same.[78] Decades afterward, many scholars concurred. At the conclusion of *Paris 1919,* historian MacMillan wrote:

> Later it became commonplace to blame everything that went wrong in the 1920s and 1930s on the peacemakers and the settlements they made in Paris in 1919, just as it became easy to despair of democracy. Pointing the finger and shrugging helplessly are effective ways of avoiding responsibility. Eighty years later the old charges about the Paris Peace Conference still have a wide circulation. "The final crime," declared *The Economist* in its special millennium issue, was "the Treaty of Versailles, whose harsh terms would ensure a second war." That is to ignore the actions of everyone—political leaders, diplomats, soldiers, and ordinary voters—for twenty years between 1919 and 1939.[79]

Within the Council of Four, French Prime Minister Clemenceau pressed for the harshest terms on Germany. After all, most of the fighting occurred on French territory, most of the battlefield wastelands spread over French soil, and—except for Russia— France suffered far more casualties than other Allied countries. France was determined to make Germany pay. Winston Churchill said, "The hatred of France for Germany was something more than human."[80]

Even before the Allied Powers gathered in Paris in 1919 to sign the peace treaties ending the war, they planned to create a very different Europe in the future. The future Europe would emerge from a wholesale restructuring of national borders. Most anticipated border changes were inspired by the lofty principle of self-determination of peoples, but many others were motivated by the baser principle of national self-interest. That the Allied leaders raced far ahead in thinking about reshaping Europe is demonstrated by Map 13.1, *The Peace Map of Europe.* It is based on the remarkable 3' by 4' full color map by the celebrated mapmaker Rand McNally, which boldly drew new borders for much of Europe before all the peace treaties were signed.[81]

Untold miseries visited soldiers' families in belligerent countries of World War I. Estimates of battlefield casualties vary somewhat, but all sources tell a dismal story. The United Kingdom's History Learning web site estimated that fifteen belligerent nations in World War I mobilized a total of 65 million men.[82] Of these, 37 million, or 57 percent, were killed, wounded, or missing—perhaps disappearing as prisoners of war, perhaps lying in the ground. Although the Allied nations (originally the Entente) won the war, they suffered more casualties—22 million v. 15 million—than the Central Powers, which lost it. The web site's raw tabulations for both sides were converted into percentages and graphed in Figure 13.2.

Figure 13.3 reports comparable data for selected countries among the Allies and the Entente using the same base scale and legend. It shows that Russia alone had more than 9 million casualties, more than three-fourths of all it mobilized. France, a much smaller country, had over 6 million casualties and a casualty rate almost as high as Russia. Britain had 3.1 million casualties, and Italy—which few Americans recall as being on the Allies' side—had 2.1 million. The United States, whose troops arrived late in 1917, had only about 350,000 casualties.

Figure 13.4 reports data for Germany and Austria-Hungary, the two major countries in the Central Powers, again using the same base and legend. Roughly 1.7 million German and 1.2 million Austro-Hungarian soldiers died in the war.

Although Germany had about 10 million more people than Austria-Hungary, they both had about the same number of total casualties—7.1 and 7.0 million respectively. However, more German soldiers were killed in action (24 v. 17 percent) while Austro-Hungarians were almost twice as likely to become POWs or missing (31 v. 16 percent). Mark Stolarik estimated that of the 400,000 to 450,000 Slovaks mobilized for the war, 69,000 were killed and 62,000 permanently disabled on either the Serbian, Russian or Italian Fronts.[83]

Many Habsburg troops of oppressed nationalities—especially Czechs, Ruthenes, Serbians, and Romanians—defected when they fought against Russia, Serbia, or Romania. Italian defections from Habsburg forces were less problematic, because Italian troops tended not to be sent to the Italian Front. The other two Central Powers—Bulgaria and Turkey—incurred fewer casualties. Bulgaria had fewer than 300,000 and Turkey just short of 1 million, but Turkey's losses were poorly documented. The war cost the Central Powers more than the bulk of its able-bodied male population. Its subsequent peace treaties cost them much of their prewar territory and population. Figure 13.5 graphs the League of Nations' data on European countries' territory, prewar and postwar, as a result of the various Paris peace treaties, which created some new countries out of old ones.[84]

By square kilometers of territory, the new country of Poland was the big winner and Russia (later the USSR) the big loser. Russia, however, lost only 2 percent of its huge landmass, whereas Austria and Hungary each lost over 70 percent of its former territory. Germany, Turkey, and Bulgaria surrendered relatively little land. Little Montenegro and bigger Bosnia were incorporated into the new nation, Yugoslavia, which was dominated

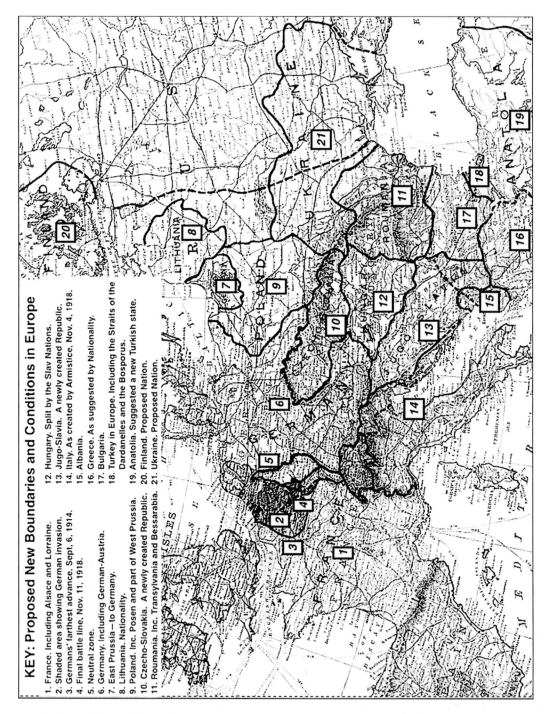

KEY: Proposed New Boundaries and Conditions in Europe

1. France. Including Alsace and Lorraine.
2. Shaded area showing German invasion.
3. Germans' farthest advance, Sept. 6, 1914.
4. Final battle line, Nov. 11, 1918.
5. Neutral zone.
6. Germany. Including German-Austria.
7. East Prussia—to Germany.
8. Lithuania. Nationality.
9. Poland. Inc. Posen and part of West Prussia.
10. Czecho-Slovakia. A newly created Republic.
11. Roumania. Inc. Transylvania and Bessarabia.

12. Hungary. Split by the Slav Nations.
13. Jugo-Slavia. A newly created Republic.
14. Italy. As created by Armistice, Nov. 4, 1918.
15. Albania.
16. Greece. As suggested by Nationality.
17. Bulgaria.
18. Turkey in Europe. Including the Straits of the
   Dardanelles and the Bosporus.
19. Anatolia. Suggested a new Turkish state.
20. Finland. Proposed Nation.
21. Ukraine. Proposed Nation.

Map 13.1: Map of Europe Redrawn by Allied Powers after World War I. Items 2–5 of these 21 "proposed new boundaries" pertained to battle lines. The other items matched fairly well the final borders of 17 countries after the war—except for Austria, which did not even appear. The map showed Austria joining Germany soon after the 1918 armistice, but the victorious Allies did not approve the union, preserving a small, independent Austria. Credit: *Peace Map of Europe: July 4, 1918* (Chicago: Rand McNally, 1919). In the public domain.

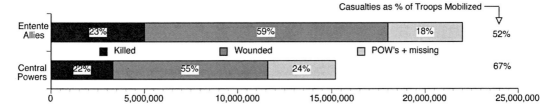

Figure 13.2: WORLD WAR I BATTLEFIELD CASUALTIES FOR OPPOSING ALLIANCES. Fifteen belligerents mobilized about 65 million men in World War I. The Allies (France, Russia, Britain) plus the United States and Italy contributed roughly 39 of the 42 million mobilized in the combined Allied forces. The two original Central powers (Germany and Austria-Hungary) mobilized almost 19 million. Turkey and Bulgaria added another 4 million for a total of almost 23 million. The Allies had more troops and relatively fewer casualties overall—52 to 67 percent. Data: "First World War Casualties" at http://www.historylearningsite.co.uk/world-war-one/world-war-one-and-casualties/first-world-war-casualties/.

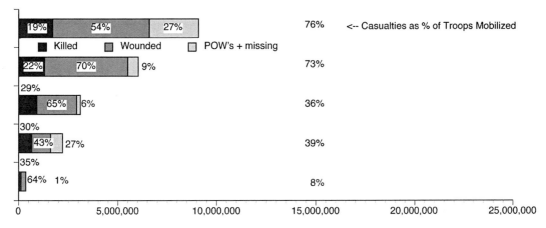

Figure 13.3: WORLD WAR I BATTLEFIELD CASUALTIES FOR SELECTED ALLIED NATIONS. Among the Allied powers, Russia mobilized 12 million men, 76 percent of whom were killed, wounded, or captured. France mobilized almost 8.5 million troops to the British Empire's almost 9 million, and France suffered a much higher casualty rate and a very high death rate. Data: "First World War Casualties" at http://www.historylearningsite.co.uk/world-war-one/world-war-one-and-casualties/first-world-war-casualties/.

by the former Serbia—itself augmented by Hungary's former Croatian territory. Romania was enlarged by Transylvania, taken from Hungary. Czechoslovakia was formed from Hungary's former Slovak counties and Austria's Czech and Moravian lands and a portion of Silesia northeast of Moravia.

The League of Nations' data on European countries' population, prewar and postwar, reveals a similar but more important story concerning new distributions of people. Figure 13.6 graphs the population changes.

On the population change metric, Poland gained the most and Russia lost the most once again. This time, however, Russia's loss amounted to 15 percent of its prewar population, primarily those living in territory that became Poland. The former Austro-Hungarian empire's decreases in population were comparable to those in territory. The peace treaties took away nearly two-thirds of Hungary's 1914 population and nearly 80

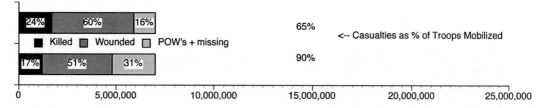

Figure 13.4: WORLD WAR I BATTLEFIELD CASUALTIES FOR TWO MAIN CENTRAL POWERS. Germany mobilized 11 million troops, of whom 65 percent became casualties of the war. Austria-Hungary's 7.8 million troops suffered the highest casualty rate of the war—90 percent. Almost one-third were prisoners or listed as missing, also the highest rate in the war. Data: "First World War Casualties" at http://www.historylearningsite.co.uk/world-war-one/world-war-one-and-casualties/first-world-war-casualties/.

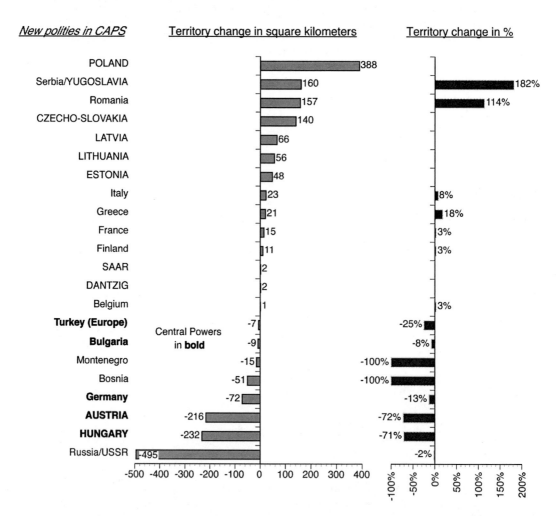

Figure 13.5: TERRITORY CHANGES, PRE- AND POST-WORLD WAR I. From the standpoint of territory, no country gained more square kilometers of land after the war than Poland, which was not a viable nation before the war. Other new nations included Czechoslovakia and the three Baltic states. Although Russia surrendered the most territory, its loss was a small percentage of its total land. The new states of Austria and Hungary replaced Austria-Hungary, and each was greatly reduced in size. Data: League of Nations, *International Statistical Year-Book, 1927*, Table 1, page 14.

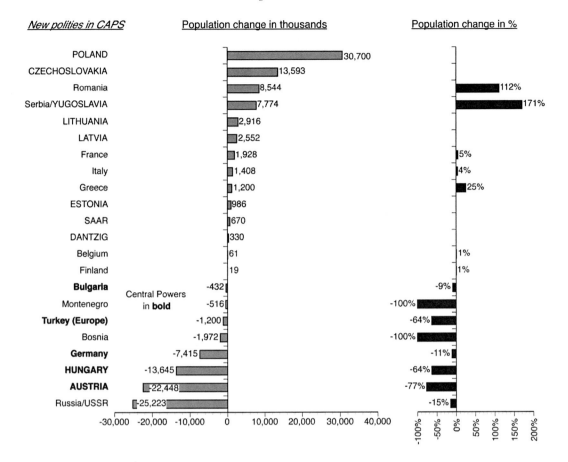

New polities in CAPS   Population change in thousands   Population change in %

Figure 13.6: POPULATION CHANGES, PRE- AND POST-WORLD WAR I. From the standpoint of population, no country gained more people after the war than Poland. Czechoslovakia was the other big winner, while Hungary and Austria were the big losers. Russia again lost the most people, but its loss was a small percentage of its pre-war population. Data: League of Nations, *International Statistical Year-Book, 1927*, Table 1, page 14.

percent of Austria's. All the autocratic imperial governments—Russia, Austria-Hungary, Germany, Turkey, and Bulgaria—lost territory and population because of World War I.

The imperial Habsburg dynasty, which initiated the European disaster by declaring war on Serbia to uphold its stature and the honor of Austria-Hungary, not only lost both stature and honor but dynasty and empire too. When Emperor Franz Josef died in November 1916, the war was not proceeding as he expected. True, Serbia had been vanquished, but Austria-Hungary required help from Germany and Bulgaria to win. Moreover, Austro-Hungarian troops had already suffered more than a million casualties and were still fighting Russians on the northeast, Romanians on the southeast, and Italians on the south. Back home, Austro-Hungarian citizens were suffering severe deprivations from the war. Emperor for almost 68 years that November and widely revered at age 86, Franz Josef had already resolved to seek peace in the spring of 1917. Perhaps he was blessed to die before attempting to negotiate peace against the wishes of his ally, Germany. By dying, Franz Josef retained his illusion of stature and honor. He was also spared witnessing the later loss of his dynasty and empire.

His youthful successor, Emperor Karl I of Austria and King Karl IV of Hungary, vowed to end the war that Franz Josef had begun. Karl encountered implacable opposition from the German military. Untrained in statecraft and inexperienced in politics, Karl not only failed to arrange for a separate peace with the Allied powers, but he managed to discredit himself through the secret Sixtus negotiations with the enemy, to lose authority within his empire, and to place himself and his military more firmly under German control. In late 1918, Karl's last-ditch efforts to save his monarchy were not only unsuccessful; they were ignored. Franz Josef's prized but decrepit Dual Monarchy split into separate Austrian and Hungarian polities.

On November 11, 1918, Karl pointedly "relinquished" his participation in government affairs but—spurred by his wife, Zita—carefully refrained from abdicating his throne.[85] He vainly hoped to be recalled to the throne in one country or the other. Austria—now a republic—would not tolerate the thought, and on April 3, 1919, passed the so-called Habsburg Law, which permanently barred former Emperor Karl and former Empress Zita from returning to Austria.[86]

Historically lagging behind Austria and most of Western Europe in modern political theory, Hungary suffered political turmoil after the war ended. The socialist Count Mihály Károlyi led a revolution and briefly established a democratic republic, which was followed by Béla Kun's short-lived communist government, to be overturned in 1920 by former Austro-Hungarian Admiral Miklós Horthy, ruling as regent in the absence of a king. Royalists, for a time, did tolerate the thought of putting Karl back on the throne. Twice in 1921 Karl attempted to regain his throne but Horthy prevented the restoration. The imperial couple was arrested and turned over to the Allied powers.[87] Later that year, the Hungarian parliament formally dethroned the Habsburg dynasty.[88]

Thus ended 600 years of Habsburg rule in Europe. One might think that ended the Habsburgs' hunt for subjects to rule. But remember what Empress Zita was quoted in Chapter 11 to have told Emperor Karl on renouncing the throne: "There will always be enough Habsburgs left." Moreover, unemployed Habsburgs hungered to rule. Recall Chapter 1's mention of Franz Josef's younger brother, Maximilian, who had no job prospects until the throne of Mexico materialized. Enticed by Mexican monarchists, Emperor Napoleon III had invaded Mexico in 1861 to reestablish the monarchy and to profit from doing so. The local monarchists desired a world-class blue-blood monarch of their own. Unemployed Maximilian's name came to mind, the "Spanish" Habsburgs having ruled the Viceroyalty of New Spain prior to Mexican independence. Maximilian consented to be Emperor of Mexico and sailed there in 1864. Unfortunately for the new emperor, Mexican nationalists ousted the French and executed Maximilian by firing squad in 1867.

Despite that negative precedent for the Habsburg dynasty, family archdukes continued looking for subjects to rule outside of Austria-Hungary. As early as 1907, Archduke Stefan (who stood outside the empire's line of succession) targeted the Polish people to rule with assistance from his sons, Archdukes Albrecht and Wilhelm, whom he steeped in Polish language and culture.[89] Stefan hoped to gain Habsburg consent to rule the Poles in Austria-Hungary's eastern province, Galicia. His rebellious younger son Wilhelm modified the family plan. Wilhelm allowed his father and brother to rule the Poles. Wilhelm chose to rule the Ukrainians.

Historian Timothy Snyder detailed Stefan's and Wilhelm's complex schemes in *The Red Prince: The Secret Lives of a Habsburg Archduke*.[90] The political disruptions brought by the war actually prompted the plan's implementation. Between 1916 and 1918, the Central Powers occupied Russian lands populated by Poles and Ukrainians. They would need new rulers. Snyder said that Stefan agreed to his son's plan in December 1916: "He proposed a Habsburg monarchy composed of Austrian, Bohemian, Hungarian, and Polish kingdoms, as well as a 'Principality of Ukraine.' An archduke would be the regent of each of these kingdoms. The regent of the Polish crownland and the prince of Ukraine would, of course, be Stefan and Wilhelm."[91] Early in 1918, Emperor Karl placed four thousand Ukrainian soldiers and officers in a "Battle Group Archduke Wilhelm."[92] Like protagonists in the television series *Game of Thrones*, Wilhelm now had his own army to impose his rule.

Both Germany and Austria-Hungary, the occupying powers, saw merit in the scheme but differed over which Habsburg should rule which country. Father and son got close to realizing their rule of Poland and Ukraine under the Habsburg banner until 1918, when imperialism succumbed to republicanism. Snyder wrote: "Dynasties suddenly counted for nothing, for less than nothing. Ukrainians in Lviv had founded a republic, whose president informed Wilhelm that his services were not required. In Warsaw, the regency council of the Kingdom of Poland, formed to make Stefan a Polish king, instead transferred its authority to Jozef Pilsudski. He founded a republic."[93] Snyder continued: "For centuries, Christians had regarded the Holy Roman Empire, ruled by the Habsburgs, as the opposite of a sign of the apocalypse: so long as it existed, the world would not end. In the early nineteenth century the Holy Roman Empire had been dissolved, but the Habsburgs, under Franz Josef, had recovered and endured, throwing a grey cloak of timelessness over the shuddering body of a continent changing itself from within. Now, with empires destroyed and dynasties dethroned, progressive time began."[94]

The Allies ended deposed Emperor Karl I's own throne-hunting by banishing him to the small Portuguese island of Madeira in the North Atlantic Ocean, where he died at age 34 on April 1, 1922, survived by his wife Zita and their eldest son, Otto. The former empress referred to their son as Archduke Otto von Habsburg, the legitimate claimant to the dynastic crown. Otto, however, dropped his monarchical claims in 1961, lived in Bavaria, and became a respected member of the European Parliament. Zita died on March 14, 1989, at the age of 96. The *Times* of London began her obituary saying, "End of the Habsburg Empire."[95] Otto died July 4, 2011, at the age of 98. The *Times* of London began his obituary saying, "His death ends a lifetime's attempt to keep alive the memory and political presence of the Austro-Hungarian Habsburg dynasty."[96] The *New York Times* did not take notice of either Habsburg's passing.

14

Peasant Gains

Austria-Hungary had 7 million military casualties in the Great War, which amounted to 90 percent of its mobilized troops. Austro-Hungarian peasants did most of the fighting and suffered most of the war's staggering casualties. If individual Slovak soldiers lost limbs or died, what could they collectively have gained from the war, even if they survived intact? How could the Great War possibly, even remotely, have benefitted Samuel Mozolák or his husbandless and fatherless family? There are no simple answers to questions about what peasants might have gained from the fighting, but the war's consequences produced some gains in return for its priceless cost.

Gunther Rothenberg's comprehensive history *The Army of Francis Joseph* hammered home the morbid message of the war's cost: "When the final tally was made, of the 8 million men mobilized in Austria-Hungary, 1,016,200 had died. In all, 518,000 were killed in action, 1,943,000 were wounded, and 1,691,000 were taken prisoners, of which some 480,000 died."[1] Rothenberg did not estimate the number missing. Most soldiers missing yet alive probably found their way home, but some chose not to return. Samko, officially listed as missing, definitely had reason to return to his family in Krajné. Undoubtedly, he died with thousands of others in the June 1918 Battle of the Piave River, which occurred fewer than six months before the armistice and barely three months before most hostilities ended.

What could Slovak peasants have gained from the war? What could Samko have gained? To frame our answers, let us begin by recalling why Emperor Franz Josef declared war against Serbia. Ostensibly, he sought to uphold his empire's honor by punishing Serbia for complicity in the assassination of Archduke Franz Ferdinand. In reality, his generals favored war to stop Serbia from stirring up Slavic unrest within the empire. Franz Josef and his military conveniently supported Germany's own plans for breaking out of its unfriendly geopolitical box.

Germany's only settled frontier was with its ally, Austria-Hungary, to the south. Boxed in on the north by Britain's command of the sea, on the west by a hostile France, and on the east by a modernizing Russian menace, German generals sought war to break the encirclement and expand. Learning that Russia was mobilizing to support Serbia against Austria-Hungary and knowing that France was bound by treaty to aid Russia, Germany seized the pretext of defending its ally, Austria-Hungary, to attack both France and Russia in August 1914.

Those facts of the war's origin reflect the imperialist mentality of 19th century. Austria-Hungary, Germany, and Russia—all imperial monarchies—defined national interests in terms of territorial acquisitions. Even republican France was obsessed with recovering Alsace-Lorraine, which it ceded to Germany after losing the 1870 Franco-German War. Leaders launched wars to gain territory—usually cloaked in defense of national honor—not to defend humanitarian principles.

Monarchs—and most governments then were monarchies—enticed subjects to fight their wars by invoking love for the motherland/fatherland, hatred of the enemy, devotion to their sovereign, God's will, and, of course, fear of imprisonment for refusing to serve. One or more or all of these factors usually stirred a rush of patriotism among the citizenry who temporarily forgot or redirected their political resentment. In his novel *August 1914*, Alexander Solzhenitsyn analyzed this phenomenon in Russia after the war's start:

> Only a month or three weeks ago, no thinking Russian citizen had doubted the fact that the ruler of Russia was a despicable individual, unworthy of serious mention; no one would have dreamed of quoting him except as a joke. Yet in a matter of days everything had changed. Quite voluntarily, seemingly educated, intelligent people would gather with serious faces around the advertisement pillars, and the Tsar's long string of pompous titles, simply because they were printed on these massive, cylindrical slabs, did not strike them as ridiculous at all. And people of their own accord would read out in loud, clear voices: *"At the call to arms, Russia has risen up to meet the enemy, with iron in her hands and with the cross upon her heart, ready for a feat of valor.... The Lord sees that we have taken up arms not from martial ambition or for the sake of vain earthly glory, but for a just cause—to defend the integrity and safety of our divinely protected Empire...."*[2] [Emphasis added.]

Chapter 8, "Peasants Under Arms," described the bellicose enthusiasm in belligerent nations at the war's outbreak. Initially, war was popular within and across countries, especially among urban crowds. Few peasants in the Austro-Hungarian countryside, however, were sufficiently aroused to offer their lives for their emperor and king. Solzhenitsyn described a similar view among Russian villagers: "People in the village did not discuss the war or even think about it as an event over which anyone had any control or which ought or ought not to be allowed to happen. They accepted the war and the conscription orders issued by the district commandant as the will of God, something like a blizzard or a dust storm, although they could not understand why anyone should volunteer."[3] Resigned to serve in their rulers' wars, peasant men and common folk across the European countryside simply hoped to survive intact. Excluding the desperate poor who sought food, shelter, and clothing in the military, few ordinary men thought they might improve their lives by serving in the war, even if their nation won it.

In 1848, during the revolutionary fervor sweeping Europe, Slovak peasants *did* attempt to improve their lives by fighting and winning. As described in Chapter 2, "The Peasant in Krajné," Slovaks rose up against Magyar rule in initial battles around Myjava. They fought for political autonomy almost a century before the principle became fashionable. Dusan Caplovic wrote, "Despite eventual defeat, the Slovak national uprising of 1848 and 1849 has been recorded with golden letters in the history of Slovakia and the Slovaks."[4]

Slovak histories credit three individuals—Ludovit Štur, Jozef Miloslav Hurban, and Michal Miloslav Hodža—for the intellectual and political leadership of the Slovak revolt.[5] All were Lutherans (Štur had studied theology while Hurban and Hodža were pastors) who were also devoted to developing and promoting the Slovak language within literary, ecclesiastical, and governmental affairs. Seizing the opportunity afforded by the current political turmoil, they signed a political statement, *Žiadosti slovenského národa* (Petition of the Slovak Nation) on May 10, 1848.[6] Their petition presaged Woodrow Wilson's 1918 peace proposal by proposing its *own* fourteen points, including "the recognition and guarantee of national identity; the transformation of Hungary into a state composed of equal nations, each with its own parliament and equal representation in the Hungarian Diet; and the use of Slovak in all Slovak county offices. In addition, it insisted on democratic rights, including universal and equal suffrage, the total abolition of serfdom, the return of the land to the peasants from whom it had been taken away, and the release of Kral and Rotarides [a poet and a teacher involved in a peasant revolt] from prison."[7] The Slovaks addressed their petition to Emperor Ferdinand in Vienna, to the Hungarian Diet, and to other state authorities. At that time, Austria itself was facing revolt from the Hungarians. Its Court had fled to Olmütz (Olomouc, Moravia), and Austria was in no position to reply. The Hungarian Diet responded by issuing warrants for the arrest of leaders Štur, Hodža, and Hurban, who replied by forming a Slovak National Council to coordinate all Slovak political and military activity.[8]

In December, Ferdinand chose his 18-year-old nephew, Franz Josef, to succeed him as Emperor of Austria. The same month, a new batch of Slovak volunteers won some battles against Hungarian troops and in early 1849 took over some land in southwestern Slovakia.[9] In March, the young emperor, still in Olmütz, received leaders of the Slovak National Council, who called for "the creation of an autonomous territory called Slovakia, free of Hungarian control, which would have its own parliament and an administration answering directly to Vienna."[10] Events, however, overtook their efforts. Austria mobilized to crush the Hungarian rebellion, and did so in August 1849, with the aid of Russian troops. Franz Josef then imposed absolute rule in Hungary, which ended Slovak dreams for autonomy—at least in the 19th century.

In 1848, Slovaks dared to dream of autonomy under Habsburg rule, "free of Hungarian control." They did not dare dream of—could not even conceive of—forming a government truly independent of Austria-Hungary. Insofar as they entertained the idea of self-determination, they only envisioned recognition and rights under the monarchy equal to those of the Magyars and other nationality groups. Following World War I, Slovaks gained much more than that.

As reported in Chapter 13, when President Wilson announced his Fourteen Points for peace in January 1918, he did not mention "self-determination." Point No. 10 did address "the peoples of Austria-Hungary," but it only accorded them "the freest opportunity to autonomous development." When Emperor Karl on October 16 desperately tried to retain his empire by proclaiming governmental autonomy for its nationalities in a federal state, Wilson rejected his proposal within the week, saying that mere autonomy was no longer sufficient.[11]

Wilson changed his mind toward the break-up of Austria-Hungary between January 1918 and January 1919 following the campaign orchestrated by Tomáš Masaryk, Edvard Beneš, and Milan Štefánik, who worked to persuade the Allied governments that the Czech and Slovak peoples opposed the war and Habsburg rule. They also sought recognition for their organization, the Czecho-Slovak National Council, and ultimately for the creation of a new country, Czechoslovakia.[12] It would be formed from the Czech-speaking lands (Bohemia and Moravia) in northwest Austria and from the Slovak-speaking land in northwest Hungary.

Their grand words were backed up by the military victories won by tens of thousands of former Czech and Slovak POWs. Kevin McNamara's book *Dreams of a Small Great Nation* explains how Masaryk got permission from the Russian government in July 1917 to organize the POWs into an independent Czecho-Slovak corps to remain militarily under Russian command but politically under the Czecho-Slovak National Council.[13] In December 1917, the National Council got France, Russia's ally, to make them part of the French army, calling them the Czecho-Slovak Legion. (Chapter 12, "Peasants in War," tells of another Czecho-Slovak Legion fighting Austro-Hungarian troops in Italy under Italian command.) After the March 1918 Brest-Litovsk Treaty ended Russia's war with the Central Powers, Russia freed millions of Austro-Hungarian POWs, including about 200,000 Czechs and Slovaks.

Fearing return to Austria-Hungary—either to be shot as deserters, or to be sent to fight for Germany on the Western Front—many Czech and Slovak POWs enrolled in the Legion. They were to travel on trains across Siberia to Vladivostok and shipped to France to fight *against* Germany. *That* they were willing to do. European and American newspapers tracked their adventures across thousands of miles of railway, fighting Russians who turned against them and other Austro-Hungarian POWs who also declined to return home but instead joined their Russian hosts. Alone and ill-supplied in a strange land, the Legionnaires fought valiantly, fiercely, and usually successfully. Aware of the Czecho-Slovak Legion's exploits, crowds in America flocked to Masaryk's personal appearances and responded to his demands for Czech and Slovak independence from Austria-Hungary. McNamara quotes Masaryk as saying, "My plan had been to get the army to France in 1918 and to bring it into action there in 1919. It never reached France, but we had an army and it made itself felt. That was the main thing."[14]

In the United States, Slovak and Czech immigrant organizations paid close attention to Austria-Hungary's role in the war. Chapter 8, "Peasants Under Arms," reported Gregory Ference's content analysis of three Slovak-American newspapers at the war's start. Although the newspaper editors were horrified at the battlefield casualties, they thought that "the war brought about interesting potentials":

> *Slovenský hlásnik* suggested the defeat of the Central Powers would bring about the liberation of the small nationalities from under Austrian-German and Magyar hegemony. It predicted that the end of the fighting would see the fall of empires, the rise of republics, and the end of all wars.
>
> *Jednota* observed that some good could arise from the war.... Although it did not advocate war, the newspaper believed that if peace arrived so early in the conflict it would not be in the interests of the European Slovaks. Instead, it commented that an early peace would cause them greater harm since "only a humbled, exhausted and defeated Austria-Hungary will give freedom to its nations!"[15]

"*Národné noviny*," Ference said, "described in great detail the future changes of the European map," and raised the possibility of an independent Slovakia, or "an intriguing proposal, united with the Czech lands." However, the paper did not consider that a good idea, because "Slovak language and culture would then be assimilated in time by the immensely richer Czech culture. However, it remained quite reserved and skeptical: 'This is not the place to decide.'"[16]

In 1915, the Slovak League and the Czech National Alliance in America had already taken action independently of the Czecho-Slovak National Council in Europe. On October 22, the Slovak and Czech organizations signed the Cleveland Agreement, which provided for "Independence of the Czech lands and Slovakia" and "union of the Czech and Slovak nations in a federative alliance of states with a complete national autonomy of Slovakia."[17] With Cleveland's heavy industries having long provided work for countless Slovak and Czech immigrants, the city was a fitting place for such an agreement.

Heavily industrial Pittsburgh, home to hundreds of thousands of Slavic immigrants, was also a suitable place for a second agreement on May 30, 1918. The Pittsburgh Agreement (also called the Pittsburgh Pact), signed by the same Czech and Slovak organizations (plus the Alliance of Czech Catholics), was similar to but significantly different from the one it superseded in Cleveland. It also differed in being signed by Masaryk himself—representing the Czecho-Slovak National Council in Paris.

Unlike the Cleveland agreement, Pittsburgh's did not advocate independence for Slovakia. Instead, it proposed "to unite the Czechs and Slovaks in an independent state of the Czech lands and Slovakia" in a "Czecho-Slovak state." Within that state, "Slovakia shall have its own administration, its own parliament and its own courts."[18] Slovakia would enjoy governmental autonomy, but it would do so in a federal state, not in an independent nation. As reflected by *Národné noviny's* position reported above, not all Slovaks were pleased by the prospect of joining the Czechs in a federal state instead of seeking a separate, independent state. Most thought, however, that joining with the Czechs offered the best possibility of having the Allied powers grant the Czech and Slovak people governmental autonomy outside of Habsburg rule.

The plan paid off for the Czecho-Slovak National Council. France recognized it as representing the proposed state on June 29, 1918, Britain on August 9, the United States on September 3, and Italy on October 3. On October 28 and October 30 respectively, the Czech National Council in Prague and the Slovak National Council in Martin signed declarations proclaiming Czechoslovakia as a new nation.

Readers today may recall the 1989 collapse of hardened communist governments in eastern Europe. Only Romania ended with a bang; the others fell with scarcely a whimper. When the Habsburg empire collapsed in 1918, the transfer of powers in the Czech and Slovak lands was also anticlimactic. Historian A.J.P. Taylor wrote that the Imperial Governor in Prague invited members of the Czech National Committee to come to the castle. "The Governor handed over his seals and keys. Then he left. The civil servants remained at their desks. Ten minutes of conversation had created Czecho-Slovakia as an independent country."[19] On November 3, 1918, when Austro-Hungary signed an armistice with the Allies in Italy, the independent state of Czecho-Slovakia was already several days old.[20] The transition from empire to republic was remarkably smooth.[21]

Prefacing his book on the Czech and Slovak Legions in Russia, Kevin McNamara held that the Great War produced "much greater consequences in Eastern Europe and Russia than it did in the West," where the combatant nations survived largely intact. He continued: "The war in the east was far more consequential, casting adrift multinational empires, ancient dynasties, and entire societies amidst the collapse of four regimes—Austro-Hungarian, German, Ottoman, and Russian—that governed much of the earth. Governments were deposed, new nations created, old ones destroyed, dictatorships and democracies founded, the map of Europe redrawn, and the twentieth century forever altered."[22]

Czechoslovakia's birth came at the expense of Austria-Hungary's death. Map 14.1 places the new nation within Central Europe. Czechoslovakia's population's ethnic distribution by percentage was estimated to be Czech (51 percent), Slovak (16), German (22), Hungarian (5) and Ruthene (4).[23] With 13.5 million people spread east-west over 140,000 square kilometers, Czechoslovakia became larger than either Hungary or Austria, which were respectively reduced to 93,000 and 84,000 square kilometers. Indeed, Czechoslovakia was created in roughly equal parts out of Austria-Hungary, which was torn asunder by two treaties originating in the 1919 Paris peace conference.

The 1919 Treaty of Saint-Germain eviscerated Austria, taking away 72 percent of its prewar territory and 77 percent of its prewar population. The 1920 Treaty of Trianon dismembered Hungary, stripping away 71 percent of its territory and 64 percent of its population. Czechoslovakia was created from Bohemian, Moravian, and Silesian lands formerly in Austria and from Slovak and Rusyn (Ruthene) lands formerly in Hungary.

Both halves of the former Dual Monarchy became pale shadows of their former selves. On November 12, 1918 (the day after the Allied armistice with Germany) the Austrian half—still with its prewar dimensions—reinvented itself as German Austria (Deutsch-Oesterreich), declaring itself a republic and part of the Republic of Germany.[24] However, the 1919 Treaty of Saint-Germain rescinded both acts and shrank Austria to less than 30 percent of its former size.[25] The treaty renamed the country the Republic of Austria and forbad its union with Germany. Although most Austrians deplored their country's reduced boundaries and its forbidden unification, they were more concerned with its ability to survive as a small state.

Austrians certainly disliked the Treaty of Saint-Germain, but not as much as Hungarians loathed the 1920 Treaty of Trianon. Over the decades, Hungarians have sustained their loathing. In 2015, the American Hungarian Foundation web site called the Treaty of Trianon "The greatest catastrophe to have befallen Hungary since the battle of Mohacs in 1526 [when the Turks defeated a Hungarian king]."[26] Map 14.1 portrays how the treaty partitioned former Hungarian territory. The western half of Czechoslovakia consisted mainly of Bohemia and Moravia, taken from Austria. The eastern half of Czechoslovakia consisted of Slovak and Ruthene lands taken from Hungary. These lands were unmarked because they were not official Hungarian provinces. A huge section of southeast Hungary went to Romania, and a portion of southern Hungary (Croatia) went to Yugoslavia.

The new Hungarian government decried its lost land, but it truly despaired over its lost population, especially its ethnic Magyars. Paul Robert Magocsi estimated that Europe had 8,252,000 Magyars in 1900 and that virtually all of them (8,152,000) had lived in Hungary.[27] In 1900, about half of Hungary's population of 19 million were Magyar. In 1920, despite normal population increases, Hungary's population shrunk to under 8 million as a result of the Treaty of Trianon. Now 90 percent Magyar, Hungary was no longer a multi-national empire.[28] Ironically, millions of Magyars found themselves living outside of Hungary.

In round numbers, over 600,000 Magyars found themselves in Czechoslovakia. Over 1,600,000 were lost to Romania, 300,000 to Serbia, and 200,000 to Ukraine.[29] In one sense, Hungary's new boundaries conformed to the "nationality principle"—country borders should embrace one nationality. That differed from "self-determination"—nationalities have the right to govern themselves. The 600,000 Magyars outside of Hungary and clustered in the southern portions of Slovakia were certainly denied self-determination.

Similarly, the new Austrian government lost three million German-speaking people in Bohemia, Moravia, and Silesia to Czechoslovakia. Masaryk and other founders of the Czech nation acknowledged the heavy German presence in those two provinces, long tied to Czech history, but countered by recalling Austria's long rule over Czech lands. Elisabeth Bakke quoted him as asking rhetorically: "What is most fair—that more than nine million Czechs and Slovaks will be ruled by Germans—or that three million Germans will be ruled by Czechoslovaks?"[30]

Alexander Watson contended that President Wilson "made a fatal mistake in placing the 'self-determination of peoples' at the centre of his post-war vision." He continued,

Map 14.1: PARTITIONING OF HUNGARY BY THE 1920 TREATY OF TRIANON. For good reasons, many Hungarians today detest the 1920 Treaty of Trianon, one of four treaties in addition to the 1919 Versailles Treaty that ended World War I. Forced on Hungary by the Allied Powers, the Treaty of Trianon deprived Hungary of more than a quarter of its territory and its population. The heavy dotted lines in this stylized map delineate Austria-Hungary and the light dotted lines its several provinces. The heavy solid lines bound the new states: (1) The Republic of Austria; (2) the Republic of Hungary; (3) the Republic of Czechoslovakia; (4) Austrian territory annexed by Poland; (5) Hungarian territory annexed by Romania; (6) the Serbo-Croat-Slovene State (Yugoslavia); and (7) Austrian territory annexed by Italy. Credit: "Treaty of Trianon," at https://en.wikipedia.org/wiki/Treaty_of_Trianon. In the public domain.

"The slogan made effective wartime propaganda and contributed to his popularity and moral authority, but it also ensured that his post-war order would be immediately discredited in many eyes. The reason for this was simple: so mixed were the peoples of east-central Europe that not everyone could be permitted to exercise this new right. There would be winners and there would be losers, and *Realpolitik* dictated that the latter would be the two ethnic groups cowed by defeat, the Germans and the Magyars. Both peoples had just reason to feel deeply aggrieved with Wilson."[31] Owing to self-interest and ignorance, "self-determination" was selectively applied for political purposes. As Zara Steiner wrote, "Few in 1919, or at any time after, fully appreciated the racial complexity of eastern Europe."[32] It was impossible to draw boundaries to conform to national lines. For starters, the Treaty of Saint-Germain prohibited Austria—composed of 90 percent German-speakers—from joining Germany, which most Austrians favored. The principle also stopped at Europe's eastern edge. Wilson himself could not imagine applying it to Middle Eastern territories, which were yanked from the Ottoman Empire and divided like cake among the French, British, and Italians. Wilson also failed to view the Irish seeking independence from Britain through the lens of self-determination. And the Paris peace treaties themselves winked at the principle by awarding German-speaking Alsace-Lorraine to victorious France and Austria's ethnically German South Tyrol to victorious Italy.

Margaret MacMillan incisively questioned what Wilson meant by "autonomous development" and later, "self-determination." "Did Wilson merely mean, as sometimes appeared, an extension of democratic self-government? Did he really intend that any people who called themselves a nation should have their own state?"[33] MacMillan said that Wilson's Secretary of State, Robert Lansing (who was present at the peace conference but not a key figure), raised questions of his own: "What, as Lansing asked, made a nation? Was it a shared citizenship, as in the United States, or a shared ethnicity, as in Ireland? If a nation was not self-governing, ought it to be? And in that case, how much self-government was enough? Could a nation, however defined, exist happily within a larger multinational state?"[34] Those questions, she wrote, led to others especially nagging for Central Europe: "What was a 'well-defined' nationalism? Polish? That was an obvious one. But what about Ukrainian? Or Slovak? And what about subdivisions? Ukrainian Catholics, for example, or Protestant Poles? The possibilities for dividing up peoples were unending, especially in central Europe, where history had left a rich mix of religions, languages and cultures. About half the people living there could be counted as members of one national minority or another. How were peoples to be allocated to one country or another when the dividing lines between one nation and another were so unclear?"[35]

In asking whether Slovaks qualified as a "well-defined" nationality, Macmillan raised a serious question in the creation of Czechoslovakia. Thanks to early campaigning by Tomáš Masaryk and Edvard Beneš on behalf of the Czecho-Slovak National Council, the Allied powers recognized Czech nationalism as "well-defined," but Slovak nationalism was not clearly perceived. In 1916, according to MacMillan, Britain's Prime Minister Lloyd George (not known to be up on his geography) asked, "Who are the Slovaks? I can't seem to place them."[36]

In truth, the Slovaks lived in the Czechs' shadows. Lloyd George was among many who could not "place them" or who confused Slovaks with Slovenes, a Slavic group clustered hundreds of miles to the south. Even in Hungary, where Slovaks accounted for over ten percent of the population and lived in a relatively contiguous area, "Slovakia" was not officially recognized as an administrative region. Nor did the government readily acknowledge the nationality of Slovaks, in contrast to the Czechs, Poles, Croats, Romanians, and Serbians. As disclosed in Chapter 3, "The Emperor's Subjects," Slovaks were not credited for having a history. According to Ladislaus Bolchazy, "Magyar nationalists advanced the claim that Slovaks did not constitute a distinct nationality and had no history to speak of."[37] They also denigrated the claim that Slovak was a language of its own, distinct from Czech.

Even educated Czechs denied that Slovak was a different language. Despite having a Slovak father, Masaryk himself regarded Slovak as a "dialect" of Czech.[38] Whether Czech and Slovak were different languages or merely different dialects of the same language was critical to the founding of Czechoslovakia. Language defined ethnicity, and ethnicity was the basis of national self-determination. Could Czechoslovakia exist as a nation if its people spoke different languages?

Elisabeth Bakke said that Czechoslovakia's founders defended its creation with a "state ideology" called *Czechoslovakism*. The concept had at least two meanings: "that Czechs and Slovaks together comprised a Czechoslovak nation with two 'tribes,' Czechs and Slovaks—or also that the Slovaks were actually Czechs, only less developed."[39] Czechs often invoked a "brotherhood" metaphor, implying their responsibility to care for their younger brother. Most Slovak leaders pragmatically accepted such slights in return for escaping from Hungarian rule and gaining a chance at self-government. Eventually, Czechoslovakism failed as a unifying ideology.

Viewed from a historical perspective, World War I resulted in a positive outcome for Slovaks (and Czechs) living in the Austro-Hungarian Empire. Given that most Slovaks were peasants, the positive outcome can be viewed as peasant gains. They gained something for which Slovaks had fought and died when rebelling against Hungarian rule in 1848–49. Seven decades earlier, they merely sought governmental autonomy under Habsburg rule from Vienna. In 1919 they won independence from monarchical rule by uniting with ethnically similar Czechs in neighboring lands within a republican nation. Given that Slovak peasants had been economically oppressed for centuries under Hungarian rule and culturally repressed since 1867 under Magyarization, the peasants collectively gained greatly from the war. Within the new state of Czechoslovakia, Slovaks could speak their own language in their schools, in their workplaces, and in governing themselves.

Individual Slovaks drew satisfaction by asserting their rights and settling scores in local communities across Hungary. They did so in Krajné, Samko's home village. As Ján Lukačka wrote in his 600-year history, Krajné's villagers in November 1918 understood what all Europe knew: the Austro-Hungarian Empire had collapsed, Hungary had collapsed with it, and Slovaks had joined Czechs in a new nation, Czechoslovakia. According to Lukačka, the villagers' "proverbial Slovakian timidity" also collapsed. Soldiers returning home "tore down Hungarian signs" and then rushed to the local tavern to drink. Soon, they focused on the local Magyarone notary, Alojz Nozdrovický, who had held office since 1899, for almost twenty years, and who collected taxes, conducted elections (done openly, not with secret ballots), and generally ran the town.

> Angry people then turned against the notary Nozdrovický and his family. Enraged soldiers came to the council house demanding tobacco. They searched the notary's apartment, leaving after finding tobacco and sugar. The next morning the notary came to the [Lutheran] rectory with his whole family, with a request that the Reverend Bodický save them. After a while, people assembled at the parish and requested the notary to show them the village funds. It was generally thought that the notary wanted to abscond with the funds. Bodický cooled the crowd's passion, and they went to the council house to check the coffers. Shown that there was more money in the treasury than expected, the crowd calmed down. Bodický's charity was manifested again at the police station, where people surrounded the car filled with suitcases and boxes from outgoing representatives of the old regime.[40]

Not satisfied with driving out the notary and his family, the villagers demanded that all Hungarian nobility get out of town. "Among them was the local official Filberger. Bodický here also calmed the crowd and allowed his former detractors to leave. So local officials, the notary, and gendarmes left the village, all representatives of the Hungarian nobility. The existing local council dissolved itself on November 5, 1918." As usually happens in such times of political change, events got out of hand in Krajné before order was restored. "Anarchy occurred for a while…. Thanks to Bodický even this stopped. On his advice, the village set up a 12-member guard, which oversaw order in the village, especially at night…. Later at a gathering before the city hall they voted for new village representatives. The following Sunday, the new representatives swore an oath as Bodický pledged them to be faithful to their Slovak land. After that, as representatives of the new state, police arrived in Krajné and began to establish order."[41]

Samko did not participate in Krajné's rowdy celebrations of Slovak independence from Hungarian rule. According to a letter from the Austrian War Archive to his grandson, John Mozolak, Samko was reported missing on June 19, 1918.[42] He was most certainly lying dead somewhere along Italy's Piave River. What did Samko gain from the Great War? His death and his military service were not even reported in Krajné's village history, for there was no proof of his death. Perhaps he was simply a coward and deserter. Lukačka's book, *Krajné 1392–1992*, listed 75 men from the village who died in World War I by the dates and (for some) the places of their death. It listed another 22 by date but not place of death and named 11 more under the heading, "without more detailed data." Samuel Mozolák was not among them.

According to League of Nations statistics, 19 percent of Hungary's population in 1910 consisted of males between 20 and 49.[43] Applying that percentage to Krajné's population of 2,727 implies that roughly 518 males in Krajné were eligible for conscription. The count of 75 dead means that 14 percent of them were killed in the war. Only four were known to have died during its first five months in 1914, but nineteen deaths were recorded during the war's first full year, 1915. Although the annual toll slowed from 1916 to 1918—seventeen to thirteen to eleven—the total of 75 deaths over 51 months of war amounted to Krajné's losing more than one young man a month, a lot for a small village. *Krajné 1392–1992* reported that most men died in Russia (15), next in Galicia (12), where they were also probably fighting Russians, and some in Italy (8). A few died in Bosnia and Romania (2 each), while single deaths occurred in Serbia, Ukraine, and Dalmatia. One soldier expired of his wounds while at home in Krajné.

Obviously, military records were incomplete at the end of World War I. Perhaps his official status as "missing" prevented Samko from being honored for his service by his home village. In that respect, Samko gained nothing from the war in return for his life. His wife and three children were left to wonder what had become of him and whether he would ever return.

When Samko was reported missing in July 1918, his wife Anna was 40 years old. Their twins Ján and Zuzanna were 12 and a half, and their young brother Samuel had turned 4 in June. Fortunately, his family owned land and was not impoverished. Perhaps Anna could also draw on savings from working in New York from 1907 to 1914. That connection paid social dividends too. At the end of the war, Ján and Zuzanna glorified in their foreign birthplace and in being citizens of the United States of America. It was the country that turned the war to an Allied victory over the Central Powers, the country of Wilson's Fourteen Points and self-determination, the country of freedom and opportunity, the country celebrated in Antonin Dvořák's 1893 *New World Symphony*—indeed the New World itself.

The war also raised the profile of Slovaks in America. As mentioned in Chapter 8, "Peasants Under Arms," many Slovak youths served proudly in the U.S. Army, and their families were equally proud of their service. Chapter 8 mentioned a Slovak-American soldier named Matej Kocak from the village of Gbely, fewer than 40 miles due west of Krajné. Matej shipped out for France on December 8, 1917, the day after the declaration of war against Austria-Hungary. Like Samko, Matej was born in 1882. Like Samko, he died in 1918.

Unlike Samko's military service and death in Italy, however, Matej's military service and death in France did not pass unnoticed. Lt. Colonel Theodore Roosevelt, Jr., commended the Marine Corps sergeant for his bravery near Mont Blanc, where he died attacking a German machine gun nest.[44] Subsequently, Sergeant Kocak was posthumously awarded not one Medal of Honor but two, one from the Navy and one from the Army. Only 119 men received Medals of Honor in World War I, and only 5 received two.[45] See Photo 14.1. Sergeant Kocak also won two Silver Stars and a Purple Heart.

As Slovaks contributed to American life, they acted less like the "birds of passage" described in Chapter 6—returning home after making money in the States—and more like permanent residents in America. Life was good here in the States, they wrote. Although Slovaks in the new Czechoslovakia no longer lived in Hungary under Magyar rule, economic opportunities were better in America than there, where Czechs controlled the government and favored Czech speakers. While Slovak-Americans encouraged Slovaks to come to the United States, Czechs found fewer reasons to leave Czechoslovakia.

Up to 1900, immigrants to the United States were classified by "country of origin," which lumped together Czech and Slovak immigrants as coming from Austria-Hungary.[46] As Konštantín Čulen wrote, that issue led Slovak leaders to meet with President Taft in 1910 to request Congress to add "mother tongue" in the census classification.[47] Their campaign succeeded, requiring the Census Bureau to reprint its 1910 forms and to hastily train census-takers in asking people of foreign stock for their mother tongue—"that is, the language of customary speech in the home prior to immigration."[48] Accordingly, U.S. Census statistics began to separate residents by ethnicity in 1910.[49]

The 1910 Census reported 531,193 Czech speakers versus 281,707 Slovak speakers among America's foreign stock. More Czechs than Slovaks made sense for two reasons: Czechs in Central Europe outnumbered Slovaks by more than three to one, and Czechs started emigrating here about three decades earlier than Slovaks. Oddly, however, the next Census in 1920 found that more residents claimed Slovak than Czech as their mother tongue! Over a span of only ten years, the count of Slovak speakers in the U.S. increased by over 108,000, while that of Czech speakers increased by only 6,000.

Navy Medal of Honor

Army Medal of Honor

Photo 14.1: SERGEANT MATEJ KOCAK, DOUBLE MEDAL OF HONOR WINNER. Slovak Matej Kocak immigrated to the United States in 1907. He enlisted into the Marine Corps the same year and was shipped to France on December 8, 1917. Killed in action, he was posthumously awarded two Medals of Honor for his bravery. Credit: Photo at http://www.homeofheroes.com/photos/6_ww1/kocak.html; used with permission of Home OfHeroes.com.

Such a huge surge in Slovak immigration from 1911 to 1920 was especially suspect given the war's effect on immigration. One source stated that total immigration dropped from 1,200,000 in 1913–1914 to 300,000 in 1915–1916.[50] How could this abrupt shift have happened?

The Census Bureau itself suggested that the 1910 substantially undercounted Slovaks, admitting that census-takers were not properly trained to ask the "mother tongue" question. It seems that they improperly recorded unclassifiable responses, such as "Slavs," "Slavic," "Slavish," and "Slavonians," instead of Slovak.[51] Census-takers were more apt to correctly count Czechs, who were better known in America. So the leap in Slovak speakers in 1920 appears to have come from better field procedures returning a more accurate count.[52]

A different and confusing problem comes when using the 1910 and 1920 Censuses vs. the 1930 Census to estimate immigrants' nationality according to their mother tongues. The 1910 and 1920 censuses asked for the mother tongue of everyone of "foreign white stock, including native white persons of foreign or mixed parentage." The 1930 Census restricted that question to only those who were *foreign-born*—inevitably fewer than those of foreign stock but born here.[53] Consequently, nationality estimates in the first two censuses (for virtually all nationalities) were substantially higher than in 1930.

The 1930 Census also recalculated its 1910 data on mother tongue just for foreign-born and counted only 228,000 Czech and 166,000 Slovak speakers—instead of 531,193 and 218,707 respectively in its original report. Apparently, the huge predominance of Czech over Slovak speakers in 1910 reflected more than a half-century of Czech predominance in immigration prior to that census. Beginning in 1930, the Census Bureau decided to ask the mother tongue only of foreign-born residents. Figure 14.1 reports census data for mother tongue of foreign born from 1910 to 1970.

In any event, the U.S. census data are clear that foreign-born Slovak speakers outnumbered foreign-born Czech speakers by 1920. After 1920, both Czech and Slovak declined as mother tongues due to more restrictive immigration laws, immigrant attrition, and assimilation of immigrant children into American culture. Nevertheless, in every census year from 1920 to 1970, Slovak exceeded Czech as a mother tongue among the foreign-born. These decennial language disparities eventually produced more Slovak-Americans than Czech-Americans. By the 1990 Census, 1.9 million Americans professed Slovak ancestry compared with about 1.3 million claiming Czech roots, while approximately 315,000 considered themselves Czechoslovakian."[54]

Despite the fact that Slovak speakers exceeded Czech speakers in the United States every year since 1920, Slovaks here—as in Europe—lived in the Czechs' shadow. Slovak immigration to the United States seemed to occur without notice. In his obscure 1913 book, *Old Homes of New Americans*, Francis Clark reported on a conversation with "an intelligent American lady, who had traveled widely and was not unacquainted with the history and nationality of Austria-Hungary." He asked her to guess how many Slovaks were in the United States; she guessed twenty thousand. He wrote, "She was only five hundred and eighty thousand out of the way, but I have no doubt her guess was quite as near the truth as would be that of most of her countrywomen, or countrymen either, for that matter."[55]

Data in Figure 14.2 shows how often articles in the *Times*, the leading newspaper in the nation's biggest city, mentioned either "Czechs" or "Slovaks."[56] From 1901 to 1910, the *New York Times* paid little attention to either group. Of only 88 articles during that decade

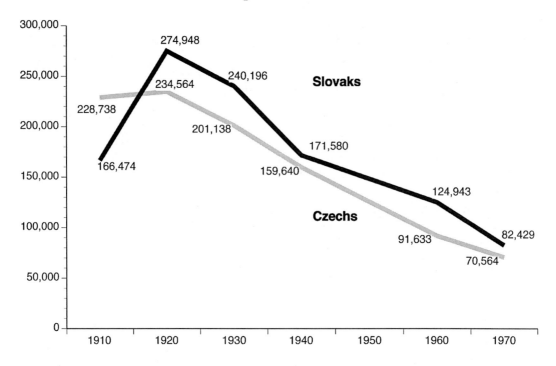

Figure 14.1: Czech and Slovak Speakers, 1910–1970, 1910–1970. In 1910, the U.S. Census began asking respondents what language they spoke as their "mother tongue," but—as explained in the text—field procedures in 1910 undercounted Slovak speakers. The U.S. Census continued reporting counts for mother tongue until 1970 (apparently, the last time the question was asked). The 1910 and 1920 Censuses reported responses by all persons of "foreign stock," but the 1930 Census started to report responses only for those of "foreign birth." However, the 1930 Census recalculated the 1910 and 1920 data to match the 1930 data on foreign birth, thus producing comparable data to 1970. More respondents reported speaking Slovak as their mother tongue in every census except the flawed one in 1910. Data: U.S. Bureau of the Census, "Table 6. Mother Tongue of the Foreign-Born Population: 1910 to 1940, 1960, and 1970," Internet Release date: March 9, 1999.

that mentioned either, 75 percent were about Czechs. In the next decade, encompassing World War I and the creation of Czechoslovakia, the number of stories in the *Times* increased tenfold to 890, and the percentage mentioning Czechs increased to 81. By 1920, when Slovak equaled Czech as a mother tongue in census statistics, the Czech advantage in 689 *Times*' stories climbed to 84 percent. The Czech penumbra extended far over the Slovaks, especially in the metropolitan media.

Two pieces of anecdotal evidence also fit this claim. The first appears in Thomas Čapek's 1920 book, *The Čechs (Bohemians) in America*. In the introduction, Čapek states that "the volume discusses the Čech branch of the Čechoslovak nation only; the Slovaks are not included, for although the two race groups live side by side in several urban centers, each attends its own churches, patronizes its own club-houses, joins its own fraternal and other societies, lives its separate life. The Čech immigration was fully thirty years old when the Slovaks began coming in. Their habitats are not the same."[57] Čapek was not ostensibly anti–Slovak. In fact, American Slovaks in 1905 commissioned him to write *The Slovaks of Hungary, Slavs and Panslavism*.[58] Instead, Čapek was saying, in his way, that Slovaks were different from Czechs and so should not be statistically treated the

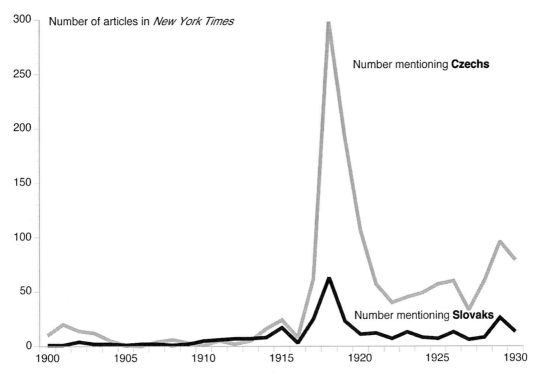

Figure 14.2: "Czechs" and "Slovaks" in the News, 1900–1930. The public knew more about Czechs than Slovaks through newspaper coverage. From 1916 through 1930, the nation's leading newspaper, the *New York Times*, published many more articles mentioning Czechs than Slovaks. Data: Counts of stories came from "CHRONICLE, Visualizing language usage in *New York Times* news coverage throughout its history," at http://nytlabs.com/projects/chronicle.html.

same way. Afterwards, ironically, Czech leaders campaigning to create the new republic of Czechoslovakia held that they would succeed because of the similarity between Czechs and Slovaks.

The second anecdote about Czechs overshadowing Slovaks in American culture, at least in urban cultures, reflects my personal experience. All four of my grandparents immigrated to Chicago before World War I and the birth of Czechoslovakia. They regarded themselves as Bohemians, not Czechs. So did my parents, who stressed that I was Bohemian. They spoke Bohemian (Czech) to my grandparents and English to me. I stubbornly and foolishly refused to learn their language—except for food and other words pertinent to boyhood. With my family, I attended countless Bohemian dinners and dances in Chicago. I do not recall ever meeting a Slovak or hearing my parents discussing the existence of Slovaks.[59]

The patterns of Czech and Slovak immigration help explain why Czechs seemed to be more prevalent than Slovaks in the United States. Czechs, more than Slovaks, tended to settle in urbanized areas, certainly in the major metropolitan areas of Chicago and New York. Čapek reports that in 1910 of the 539,392 foreign-born Bohemians and Moravians in the United States, 124,225 (nearly one-quarter) lived in Illinois, and nearly all of them in Chicago.[60] New York City was second with 40,988 foreign-born Bohemians and Moravians.

M. Mark Stolarik's book, *Immigration and Urbanization: The Slovak Experience,*

1870–1918, reports data for 619,866 Slovaks in the 1920 census. (The 1920 estimate was based on mother tongue of foreign stock.) He found nearly half of them (296,219) in one state: Pennsylvania, where they worked in the mines and in Pittsburgh's steel mills. "Ohio came second with 78,982, then New Jersey with 48,857, New York [state] with 46,209, Illinois with 44,010 and Connecticut with 21,204."[61]

The Czechs in Chicago—like the Irish in Boston and Italians in New York—soon became a force in politics. Anton Cermak (originally Čermák) became an alderman in the city, then president of the county board (1922), head of the country Democratic Party (1928), and mayor of the city (1931). His prominence allowed him to stand next to President-Elect Franklin D. Roosevelt in Miami, where he was killed by a bullet presumably aimed at Roosevelt. Cermak's visible political career in Chicago, along with Tomáš Masaryk's campaign across the U.S. for Czechoslovakia's independence and then his presidency of the new nation, no doubt accounted for many of the articles mentioning Czechs in the *New York Times* in the 1920s. Slovaks lacked comparable political celebrities to garner publicity.

Of course there were plenty of Slovaks in Chicago—25,720 according to the 1920 Census. But they were outnumbered more than 4:1 by 106,428 Czechs, and I do not recall meeting any Slovaks when growing up in Chicago during the late 1930s and early 1940s.[62]

Back in Czechoslovakia after the war, Slovaks knew little and cared less about how they compared with Czechs in the United States. In any event, they were not competing very well with Czechs in their new European nation. Although freed of Magyar rule, Slovaks did not get their own parliament and thus the autonomy they sought. Various socioeconomic conflicts with Czechs and an economic recession in 1921–23 took the luster off their political union.[63] Meanwhile in Krajné, the American twins, Zuzanna and Ján, started to think about capitalizing on their United States citizenship.

Bolder than her brother, Zuzanna at age 17 was the first to emigrate. She applied for a U.S. passport at the U.S. Embassy in Prague on June 18, 1923. That was rather remarkable, for she did not need a passport to enter the United States. Historically, different government agencies had issued passports to validate U.S. citizenship, but prior to World War I, foreigners could enter the country without one.[64] By itself, that helps explain how millions of foreigners immigrated to the United States. Beginning in 1921—after all the war's peace treaties were signed—foreigners could again enter without passports. Ironically, the 1921 Emergency Quota Act limited immigrants from a given country to 3 percent of those already in the U.S. from that country by the 1910 census. The 1924 Immigration Act further restricted immigration to 2 percent of those living here according to the 1890 census, which limited Slovak immigrants to 2,000 per year.[65]

Given that Zuzanna did not need a passport to sail to the United States in 1923, why did she travel 200 miles to Prague to get one? One suspects that she wanted to validate her U.S. citizenship before crossing the ocean. Her mother must have preserved her twins' New York 1906 birth certificate (see Figure 6.1). Presenting that at the embassy would establish Zuzanna's citizenship. Obtaining a passport in her own name allowed her to carry proof that she was a U.S. citizen, and she could return the birth certificate to brother Ján for later use. Applying for citizenship at the embassy in Prague, rather than waiting to do it in the United States, also allowed her to argue her case in Slovak to embassy personnel in Prague who spoke her language, instead of trying to express herself to English-speakers in the United States. Her application was approved on June 20, two days after she applied. It is reproduced in Figure 14.2.

325730

7/18

Form No. 176.—Consular.
(Corrected June, 1922.)

Fee for passport $3.54 $9.00
Fee for administering oath and prepar
... Passport application 3 2 54 ...

DEPARTMENT PASSPORT APPLICATION

NATIVE.

[DEPARTMENT OF STATE PASSPORT — JUL 20 1923 — ISSUED — WASHINGTON]

I, ... Zuzanna Mozolak, ... a NATIVE AND LOYAL CITIZEN

of THE UNITED STATES, hereby apply to the Department of State, at Washington, for a passport for

myself, accompanied by my wife, ..., and minor children as follows:

...., born at ...., on .... (Date.)

...., born at ...., on .... (Date.)

I solemnly swear that I was born at .... New York City ...., in the State of .... New York ....

January 15, 1906 ...., that my father .... Samuel Mozolak (deceased) .... was

born in Vraine, Hungary .... and is now residing died in 191... in U.S. ...., for the

purpose of .... ; that he emigrated to the United States from the port

of .... unknown ...., on or about .... 190... (Date.); that he resided .... 11 .... years

uninterruptedly, in the United States, from .... to 191... New York, N.Y. ...., that

he was naturalized as a citizen of the United States before the .... never naturalized .... Court of

.... , at .... on .... (Date.)

shown by the Certificate of Naturalization presented herewith; that I am the bearer of Passport

No. ...., issued by .... on .... (Date.)

that my legal domicile is in .... Bronx, New York ...., my permanent residence being

1115 Grand Concourse ....; that in the United States I followed the occupation of ....

.... , and last left the United States on .... May, 1906 (Date.)

living at Vraine, Hungary, now Czechoslovakia May, 1906 .... where I am now
(Town, province.) (Country.) (Date.)

residing for the purpose of .... assisting mother ...., on behalf of ....
(Occupation.) (Name, address, and nationality of firm,
corporation, or other organization represented, if any.)

that I have resided outside the United States at the following places for the following periods:

Hungary, now Czechoslovakia .... from .... May, 1906 .... to .... date

.... from .... to ....

.... from .... to ....

that I desire to remain a citizen of the United States and intend to return thereto permanently to

reside and perform the duties of citizenship within ....{months years} or when .... passport obtained

I have not applied elsewhere for a United States passport or for consular registration and been refused.

I desire a passport for use in visiting the countries hereinafter named for the following purpose:

Czechoslovakia, Germany, France .... en route to the United States
(Name of country.) (Object of visit.)

....
(Name of country.) (Object of visit.)

....
(Name of country.) (Object of visit.)

OATH OF ALLEGIANCE.

Further, I do solemnly swear that I will support and defend the Constitution of the United States
against all enemies, foreign and domestic; that I will bear true faith and allegiance to the same; and that
I take this obligation freely, without any mental reservation or purpose of evasion: So help me God.

Zuzanna Mozolak
(Signature of applicant.)

American Consulate .... at .... Prague, Czechoslovakia ....

Sworn to before me this .... 16th .... day of .... June, 1923.
(Date.)

[SEAL AMERICAN CONSULATE] [JUN 18 1923]

.... C.E. Garrity
(Name.)
American Vice Consul.
(Title.)

[Vertical right margin text: CERTIFICATION OF BIRTH CERTIFICATE OR BAPTISM]

Figure 14.2: ZUZANNA MOZOLÁK'S 1923 U.S. PASSPORT APPLICATION. Zuzanna Mozolak's U.S. passport application, obtained in Prague and dated July 20, 1923, two months before sailing from Cherbourg, France, to New York on the SS *Leviathan*.

Note that Zuzanna's passport application had BIRTH CERTIFICATE stamped along its right side. Unfortunately, it did not include her photograph—despite a December 1914 ruling by former Secretary of State Williams Jennings Bryan that required two unmounted 3" by 3" photographs with each application. Passport historian Craig Robertson explained that consuls in foreign countries had "some degree of flexibility" in the matter.[66] Note also that 17-year-old Zuzanna, who spent nearly her entire life in Krajné, took an Oath of Allegiance, swearing "to support and defend the Constitution of the United States."

Zuzanna showed foresight in getting her passport in Prague before sailing to America, and she was audacious in planning her voyage. Although eager to leave Europe, she opted not to depart from the port at Bremen, whence her mother and father had sailed, only 400 miles away. Instead, she traveled more than 800 miles to leave from Cherbourg, France.[67] No one today knows why, but one suspects that she wanted to visit Paris along the way. On September 19, Zuzanna sailed on the SS *Leviathan*, landing at Ellis Island on September 24, 1923. The adventurous nature of the 17-year-old girl fit the flapper era, but the name "Zuzanna" did not. She began to call herself "Sussie," using it on her May 12, 1928, marriage license to first generation Slovak-American John Skaritka in New York. The 1940 census listed her simply as "Susan." Susan and John Skaritka had a son, John, in 1931, and a daughter, Anne, in 1937.

Ján was by nature more conservative than his twin sister. Perhaps that was because he was responsible for the farm. Perhaps he also felt more responsible for his mother, Anna. Things changed, however, after Anna died on April 23, 1926. Three months later, on July 18, 1926, Ján married a 17-year-old servant girl, Zuzana Borik, in Krajné's Lutheran church. Photo 14.2 shows them married in their *kroje*, traditional Slovak folk costumes.

With his mother gone, with a new young wife, with a sister writing encouraging letters from the big city—why not follow his father and go to New York too? Ján was 21 years old when he and

Photo 14.2: JÁN AND ZUZANA MOZOLÁK, 1926 WEDDING. Ján and Zuzana Mozolák on their wedding day, July 18, 1926, in Krajné, Slovakia, within the new nation of Czechoslovakia. Family photo.

Zuzana left for America on November 10, 1927. They embarked from Hamburg on the SS *Cleveland* and arrived in New York on November 21. According to the ship manifest, they traveled as John and Susanna Mozolak, Ján reverting to John as on his birth certificate. Susanna was several months pregnant when she crossed the ocean. John Mozolak, Jr., was born in New York on February 25, 1928. (Back in America, the family dropped using diacritical marks in their names.) Eleven years later, on July 13, 1939, Susan (no longer Susanna) gave birth to a daughter, Anna, named after her grandmother.

Of Samuel and Anna Mozolak's three children, only the youngest, Samuel, remained in Krajné into the 1930s. His father Samko had been killed in the war; his mother had died; and his brother and sister had gone to New York. What kept him in Krajné? For one thing, Samuel, who was born in Krajné in 1914, was only 13 years old when Ján left in 1927. For another, the United States had changed its immigration laws in the 1920s to keep out foreign nationals from Eastern and Southern Europe. But Samuel could claim having American relatives, and at age 23 he sailed from Bremen on June 29 on the SS *Europa*, arriving in New York on July 5, 1937. Fewer than nineteen years after Samko died along the Piave River in his emperor's service, all his children were living in the United States, formerly his emperor's enemy.

His son was not an American citizen, but Samuel fixed that soon after he was drafted into the U.S. Army. He entered service on August 5, 1941, prior to the U.S. entry into World War II, and was naturalized on November 8, 1943, while serving in Italy. Perhaps before the war, perhaps after, Samuel met up with Anna Karlik from the village of Podkylava, two miles northeast of Krajné. Maybe they had arranged to meet in New York, for Anna sailed on the SS *Bremen* on October 1 only three months after Sam. She arrived in New York on October 7 to stay with her aunt in Newark, New Jersey. They married after the war and had a son, Edward Mozolak, on January 4, 1951. Now all the children and grandchildren of the former emperor's conscript were living in the United States as Slovak-American citizens.

Dynastic rulers sought to preserve their realms for their heirs. Inherently conservative, monarchs strived to pass on what they already held. That was their reason for existence. H. Wickham Steed's obituary on Franz Josef in the *London Times* caustically observed, "Beyond his devotion to the dynasty and his desire to transmit its possessions undiminished to his successor, he seems to have had no positive purpose."[68] Monarchs did not necessarily aim to have their heirs live better than they did. Their descendants should just continue to live as well. Often their dynastic heirs were not even their children. Naturally, Emperor Franz Josef had hoped that his son Rudolph would inherit his realm. But unstable Archduke Rudolph committed suicide in 1889. Nevertheless, the old emperor pursued his passion to preserve Habsburg rule over the lands of his Dual Monarchy. Although he did not like his nephew Archduke Franz Ferdinand, at least the archduke continued the Habsburg line. When Franz Ferdinand was assassinated in Sarajevo, a doddering 84-year-old Franz Josef lashed out by declaring war on Serbia.

With war raging, Franz Josef's grandnephew, Archduke Karl, was the next heir in line. Karl was in his late 20s, was not especially close to his granduncle, and was kept completely outside of political affairs. No one knew what would happen if the old emperor died during the war, but everyone feared the consequences. Perhaps Franz Josef feared the end most of all, sensing that he had failed in his mission by igniting the war. Franz Josef died in 1916 at age 86. C.L. Sulzberger wrote that Franz Josef acknowledged on his deathbed: "I took over the throne under the most difficult conditions and I am leaving it under even worse ones."[69] His most intimate biographer, Joseph Redlich, believed that death before the war ended was a gift. The emperor was spared seeing the complete collapse of his empire and his dynasty.

Peasant families, in contrast, did not have "heirs"; they left nothing worthwhile to inherit. They only had children, for whom they wished a better life. By that criterion, Samko was far more successful after death than was Franz Josef. Arguably, his twins— John and Susan—and his namesake, Samuel, lived more comfortable lives in America than they would have led by remaining in Krajné. For starters, they escaped living through World War II and enduring four decades of communist rule. From purely an economic standpoint, they almost certainly enjoyed a higher standard of living in the United States. They kept themselves warmer in the winter and cooler in the summer; they had more and better clothing; and they had more plentiful and nutritious food throughout the year.

Susan and John Skaritka lived at first in New York, where they raised two children— John and Anne. John Skaritka worked mainly in the laundry and cleaning industry, and they owned a motel in Florida for a time. They retired to Sunrise, Florida, living in a modern one-family house in a pleasant community.

John and Susan Mozolak raised their children—similarly named John and Ann— in Manhattan, first in rented apartments on 72th Street and then on 77th Street. Later they bought a brick two-family home in the Bronx, renting out the upper half. John was employed nearly all his life in Manhattan and Brooklyn by Cushman's Bakery and Taystee Bread. He benefitted from a union job and drew a pension on retirement. The Mozolaks later moved to their own modern one-family house in Sunrise, Florida, just two blocks away from the Skaritkas' house and from John's twin sister, Susan. Samuel Mozolak's twins led full lives in the United States. Susan Mozolak lived to age 73, and John to 86. His twin Susan Skaritka died at 82, and her husband John at 95.

Samuel, the twins' younger brother, and his wife, Anna, lived mainly in their own home in New Jersey, where Sam worked for the Ford Motor Company. He died at age 55. His only child, Edward Mozolak, was born April 1, 1951. He enlisted in the U.S. Navy in 1974 and served for four years. Edward became a fireman but died at age 47 on May 10, 1998.

It can be argued that Samuel Mozolák's five grandchildren—Edward Mozolak, John and Anne Skaritka, and John and Ann Mozolak, all born in the United States—also lived better lives than *their* parents. Unlike them, they never toiled in Krajné fields. Unlike their immigrant parents, whose only schooling consisted of a few grades in a Magyar elementary school, the children all had at least a high school education, and three went to college. John Skaritka earned a degree in chemical engineering, worked for major companies, married, and raised three children. Anne Skaritka attended college, married a Lutheran minister, and had four sons.

Ann Mozolak earned a master's degree in Russian language and literature from Indiana University, where she—a second-generation Slovak-American—met Kenneth Janda, a third-generation Czech-American studying for his doctorate in political science. On September 2, 1961, they married in a Slovak-English service at the Holy Trinity Lutheran Church on New York's 20th Street. It was the successor to the city's first Slovak Lutheran church, founded in 1902 on 10th Street. Photo 14.3 shows the Mozolak family with the bride and groom after their wedding.

After Ann Mozolak's marriage, she taught Russian at Chicago's Loyola University

Photo 14.3: ANN MOZOLAK AND KENNETH JANDA, 1961 WEDDING. From left is John Mozolak, Jr., and wife Lily; bride Ann Mozolak Janda and groom Kenneth Janda; and bride's parents Susan and John Mozolak, Sr. Susan and John here are wearing New York evening dress instead of the Slovak costumes they wore in their wedding photo 35 years earlier in Krajné, as shown in Photo 14.2. Family photo.

from 1961 to 1965, and enjoyed a three-decade career in social science data services in the Computing Center and Library at Northwestern University, where Kenneth taught political science. Ann retired in 2006, having raised two daughters, Susan and Kathryn.[70]

John Mozolak, Jr., had a long and noteworthy military career. He enlisted in the Army in January 1947 and retired on January 31, 1967, as sergeant 1st class. Although lacking a college degree, John was uncommonly talented. He became involved in electronic surveillance while serving in the Signal Corps and received an Army Commendation Medal for meritorious service as a radar and electronic countermeasures analyst, authoring a handbook on detecting Soviet vehicles. In the mid–1950s, he worked closely in Japan with Dr. Nick Holonyak, Jr., a Ph.D. in electrical engineering and later inventor of the LED, light-emitting diode.[71] John, a first-generation Slovak-American, got along well with Nick, a first-generation Rusyn-American and prize-winning scholar, and they maintained lifelong contact.

Of all Samko's offspring, John Mozolak, Jr., was the most interested in his Slovak heritage and the most committed to documenting it through numerous visits to Krajné. His extensive genealogical research provided the basis for this book. John's painstaking

Photo 14.4: KRAJNÉ WORLD WAR I MEMORIAL. World War I War Memorial in Krajné, Slovakia, which originally listed in two columns the names of 75 villagers who died in the war, leaving one blank space at the bottom. Providing evidence that Samuel Mozolak also fought in the war, that he won a medal for bravery, and that he died honorably on the battlefield, John Mozolak, Jr. convinced the village authorities to add his name to the memorial and paid to have it chiseled into the 76th space. Family photo.

efforts also provided this chapter's conclusion. Knowing that his grandfather was conscripted into the Austro-Hungarian army and that he died during World War I, John wondered why Samuel Mozolák's name was not included on Krajné's monument honoring the village war dead. Subsequently, John sought and obtained a document from the Austrian State Archives (see Chapter 12, Figure 12.1) that not only verified Sam's service but cited him for bravery during the Romanian campaign.

John then conducted a campaign of his own with Krajné officials to add his grandfather to the list of 75 names engraved in two columns on the village monument to
soldiers who fell in the Great War. Samko's grandson succeeded in having them add
another name to the monument. Given the odd number that died, a blank space existed
at the bottom right of the second column of names. On May 23, 2006, SAMUEL MOZOLÁK
was chiseled into the blank line following JURAJ ZMEKO. As shown in Photo 14.4 of Krajné's World War I Memorial, Samuel Mozolák's death in the old world was remembered
and honored by his grandson, long after all of Samko's progeny followed his example and
immigrated to a new world.

Epilogue: Immigration and Self-Determination

One can draw three conclusions from these two stories about the emperor and the peasant. The story in the odd-numbered chapters confirms that autocratic hereditary rule was ill-suited to 20th-century government and international relations. That in the even-numbered chapters suggests—but does not confirm—that immigrants, even economic migrants, strengthen a nation. Third, both stories together imply that the principle of creating nations according to self-determination of peoples deserves to be pursued, despite problems in implementing the principle. This epilogue illustrates immigrants' contributions to the United States and considers the limitations of self-determination.

Immigration

The Statue of Liberty, a gift from France, was dedicated in 1886. It stands on Liberty Island in Upper New York Bay, less than a mile from Ellis Island, which housed the nation's main immigrant inspection station from 1882 to 1954. The Statue of Liberty bears a sonnet by Emma Lazarus, which ends with these lines:

> *Give me your tired, your poor,*
> *Your huddled masses yearning to breathe free,*
> *The wretched refuse of your teeming shore.*
> *Send these, the homeless, tempest-tost to me,*
> *I lift my lamp beside the golden door!*

The "huddled masses yearning to breathe free" came by the millions, infusing the young nation with willing workers overflowing with energy and ideas. On seeing the Statue of Liberty's welcoming torch, countless immigrants to the United States celebrated the end of their often-perilous ocean voyage.

Unfortunately, American presidents and members of Congress did not always welcome the huddled masses. Edward Prince Hutchinson's *Legislative History of American Immigration Policy, 1798–1965* relates U.S. policy changes over time.[1] From the beginning, statesmen and even politicians acknowledged the need for more inhabitants to work in the vast lands of the new nation. Early immigrants from mostly Protestant countries in northern Europe—e.g., Britain, Germany, Norway, Sweden—were accepted relatively easily. The Irish Catholic immigrants who flocked to the East Coast in the 1840s (averaging 140,000 a year)[2] were less cordially received, but they did not spark wholesale changes in an accommodating immigration policy.

In the latter half of the 19th century, as the flood of immigrants from southern and eastern Europe increased, presidential and congressional concern mounted. Delivering his annual message to Congress in 1903, President Theodore Roosevelt spoke bluntly: "We can not have too much immigration of the right kind, and we should have none at all of the wrong kind. The need is to devise some system by which undesirable immigrants shall be kept out entirely, while desirable immigrants are properly distributed throughout the country."[3] Roosevelt specifically worried about barring anarchists. As he put it in his 1904 message, "Not merely the anarchist, but every man of anarchistic tendencies."[4] Of course, Vice-President Roosevelt became president after an anarchist shot President William McKinley.

President Roosevelt's urging to keep out immigrants "of the wrong kind" was cited in Hutchinson's chapter, "Development of the Regulatory System, 1883–1913." During those years of immigration regulation, Congress was genuinely concerned with migrants' welfare crossing the ocean and after arriving. Stephen Fox's book *The Ocean Railway* cites alarming newspaper stories that complained of conditions for immigrants in steerage, but a congressional investigation in 1873 found the stories overblown.[5] Over the next three decades, according to Fox, "ghastly stories of terrible steerage ordeals" surfaced, and a new investigation in 1908 found much dirtier ship conditions than earlier: "As for the sleeping quarters of a typical steerage, the dirt, air and crowding had again become intolerable: a congestion so intense, so injurious to health and morals that there is nothing on land to equal it. That people live in it only temporarily is no justification of its existence."[6]

What had changed between the 1873 and 1908 congressional investigations? Fox blamed "a fundamental change in the demographics of the emigrants themselves"—or more correctly, the surfacing "of routine, unexamined ethnic and religious prejudices" toward them by those who ran and crewed the steamship lines.[7] In 1880, most immigrants came from Britain, Germany, and Scandinavia—like the ships' officers and crews. Only 8 percent of steerage passengers came from southern and eastern Europe. By 1900, these unfamiliar people accounted for 72 percent. The same seamen regarded their new charges to be "of different stocks, probably inferior, and surely not worthy of respect."[8] Fox quoted Edward Steiner, a 1906 Slovak emigrant to America, about traveling as a steerage passenger: "His position is part of his lot in life; the ship is just like Russia, Austria, Poland or Italy. The cabin passengers are the lords and ladies, the sailors and officers are the police and the army, while the captain is the king or czar."[9]

Hutchinson wrote that changes in the immigrants' complexion shifted how Congress viewed immigration: "A darker side of the discussion of this and other immigration measures during the period in question was what now would be considered strongly racist and ethnocentric sentiments. It was a time when beliefs about race and ethnicity superiority or inferiority were common, and these beliefs come out strongly in the discussion of immigration questions."[10] Hutchison's next chapter, titled "From Regulation to Restriction, 1913–1929," chronicled changes in immigration policy.

To most members of Congress, Chinese immigrants were clearly the wrong kind. Representative Everis A. Hayes (Republican from California) agreed, but he had a far broader conception of the wrong kind of immigrants. Hayes proposed a bill titled: "To regulate the coming into and the residence within the United States of Chinese, Japanese, Koreans, Tartars, Malays, Afghans, East Indians, Lascars, Hindoos, and persons of Chinese, Japanese, Korean, Tartar, Malayan, Afghan, East Indian, Lascar, Hindoo, or other

Mongolian extraction."[11] Although Hayes's bill was buried in the Committee on Foreign Affairs, it reflected the public's growing concern over immigrants' racial composition. Congress responded by passing the Emergency Quota Act of 1921, which Roger Daniels said "marked the first time a numerical cap had been placed on immigration and represents a pivotal point in the history of American immigration policy."[12]

Immigration quotas in the 1921 Act were based on 3 percent of the U.S. population from individual foreign countries according to the 1910 Census. Hutchinson stated: "Estimates set the quota as so determined at about 337,000 for northwestern Europe and 255,000 for other countries. On this point it was stated that the need was not to exclude all immigrants, but to check immigration from southern and eastern Europe, from which the greater part of current immigration was coming."[13] Congress then decided that the 1921 quotas permitted too many immigrants from southern and eastern Europe and revised the quota formula in the 1924 Immigration Act. It limited the annual number of immigrants from any country to 2 percent of foreign residents according to the *1890* Census. Daniels explained why Congress relied on older information and not on the available 1920 Census: "The reasons for this were frankly stated; from the restrictionists' point of view, the existing law was allowing in too many of the wrong kinds of people—non–Protestant eastern and southern Europeans. Updating to the 1920 census would have allowed in even more."[14] Daniels reported that a leader of extreme restrictionist forces in the House "calculated that instead of the 42,000 Italian and 31,000 Polish annual quota spaces created by using a 2 percent quota based on the 1920 census, a similar quota based on the 1890 census would cut the numbers to 4,000 Italians and 6,000 Poles."[15]

After World War II and the emergence of the Cold War, Congress was obsessed with communism and national security. That obsession underlay the Immigration and Nationality Act of 1952, which "expanded the power of the federal government to exclude, deport, and detain aliens deemed subversive or seen as holding subversive views."[16] The controversial act, passed over President Truman's veto, also continued national quotas but relied on the 1920 Census and using a different formula. However, it ended the near-blanket exclusion of Asians.

The United States did not abandon national immigration quotas until the 1965 Immigration and Naturalization Act. This Act was, in Hutchinson's view, "a turning point in American immigration policy—a turning point, that is, in the system of selection of immigrants for admission. It brought to an end the selection of immigrants on the basis of their national origin, a basis of selection introduced by the 1924 Act.... And along with national origins it did away with any selection, more often called discrimination, on the basis of race or ancestry.... The new criteria were, first and principally, relationship to a citizen or lawfully resident alien; second and less heavily weighted, personal qualifications of ability and training; and finally chronological order of application for admission."[17]

The 1965 Act was modified and expanded by the 1990 Immigration Act, which "significantly increased the total level of immigration to 700,000, increasing available visas 40 percent. The act retained family reunification as the major entry path, while more than doubling employment-related immigration."[18] It also created a lottery system to provide for the admission of immigrants from "underrepresented" countries. Subsequent immigration legislation tended to focus on issues of border control and amnesty for illegal aliens. Essentially, immigrants today enter under the outlines of the 1990 Immigration Act.

According to data from the Department of Homeland Security, 79,483,571 persons obtained lawful resident status in the United States between 1820 and 2013.[19] The 2010 Census reported that since 1970 the foreign-born population has continued to increase in size and percent of the total population. In 2015, the National Academies of Sciences stated that the 41 million immigrants constituted 13.1 percent of the U.S. population.[20] Foreigners can achieve citizenship through the process of "naturalization," which requires noncitizens to meet certain statutory requirements, such as length of residence; ability to speak, read, and write basic English; understand fundamental aspects of U.S. history and government; show good moral character; and demonstrate support of the principles and ideals of the U.S. Constitution.

The United States naturalizes about 680,000 people annually.[21] Almost half, 44 percent, of the foreign-born become naturalized U.S. citizens. U.S.-born children of immigrants represent another 37.1 million citizens, or 12 percent of the population. About 1 in 4 children under 18 in families had at least one foreign-born parent. The Academies' report concluded: "Thus, together the first and second generations account for one out of four members of the U.S. population. Whether they are successfully integrating is therefore a pressing and important question."[22]

In recent decades, most immigrants have come from Latin America and Asia. According to the 2010 Census, specific countries accounting for the most foreign-born (in millions) were Mexico (12); China, India, and Philippines (2 each); Vietnam, El Salvador, Cuba, and Korea (1 each). These recent immigrants contrast sharply with those who arrived at the end of the 19th century and the beginning of the 20th. Then they came from eastern and southern Europe—Poland, Russia, Italy, Czechoslovakia, Greece. Earlier they came from central and northern Europe—Germany, Ireland, Sweden, the Netherlands, Norway.

More recently, immigration has increased from the Middle East and North Africa (MENA). To document their presence in the United States, citizens from these areas lobbied to include MENA as a race and ethnicity in the 2020 Census.[23] In so doing, they behaved much like the Slovaks did when they lobbied President Taft and Congress to add "mother tongue" to the 1910 Census to document their numbers in America. (See the discussion in Chapter 14.) Some people forget that American citizens of German, Irish, Swedish, Dutch, or Norwegian stock were also immigrants, but perhaps three or four generations earlier than those from Latin America, Asia, the Middle East, or North Africa.

Garrison Keillor, who for decades hosted the popular radio program *The Prairie Home Companion* on National Public Radio, often poked fun at the old-fashioned lifestyle of the Norwegian bachelor farmer in Minnesota, where Keillor's program originated. Norwegian immigration to the United States began in large numbers in the mid–1850s. By 1910, the nation had a million Norwegian immigrants.[24] Today, Norwegian-Americans account for about 16 percent of the State of Minnesota's population. No wonder its football team is the Minnesota Vikings.

Unlike Samko, who crossed the ocean in a steamship in 1902, most of the Norwegian immigrants crossed in sailing ships fifty years earlier. Unlike Samko, who settled safely in a bustling city with a subway and electric lights, many Norwegian immigrants suffered hardships of primitive living in sod houses. After weeks crossing the ocean, they traveled by train to the Midwest, perhaps to Chicago, and then by wagon to the Minnesota prairies. Some pushed on further west. Ole Edvart Rølvaag's 1927 novel *Giants in the Earth* recounted the hardships immigrants suffered as they settled in the remote Dakota territory, days away by horse from stores that sold basic provisions.[25]

Most immigrants today enjoy indoor plumbing, heating and refrigeration, electric lights, automobiles, and television. Nevertheless, they encounter their own hardships adjusting to a new life in the 21st century. In his cover story in the July 4, 1988, issue of *Newsweek*, Garrison Keillor called today's immigrants his "Heroes":

> Heroes, all of them, at least they're my heroes, especially the new immigrants, especially the refugees. Everyone makes fun of the New York cab drivers who can't speak English: they're heroes.
>
> To give up your country is the hardest thing a person can do: to leave the old familiar places and ship out over the edge of the world to America and learn everything over again different than you learned as a child, learn the new language that you will never be so smart or funny in as in your true language. It takes years to start to feel semi-normal.
>
> And yet people still come from Russia, Vietnam and Cambodia and Laos, Ethiopia, Iran, Haiti, Korea, Cuba, Chile, and they come on behalf of their children, and they come for freedom. Not for our land (Russia is as beautiful), not for our culture (they have their own, thank you), not for our system of government (they don't even know about it, maybe not even agree with it), but for freedom.
>
> They are heroes who make an adventure on our behalf, showing by their struggle how precious beyond words freedom is, and if we knew their stories, we could not keep back the tears.[26]

In the summer of 2015, Felix Okema, who emigrated from the Ivory Coast 20 years earlier as a student, took his citizenship oath in Brooklyn from federal magistrate judge Steven I. Locke, whose great-great-grandfather had emigrated from Lithuania. Mr. Okema, who earned separate M.A. degrees in finance and accounting, told a reporter: "You can come from a deep forest in Africa, you don't have the support you can find here—this country is uniquely equipped to give you the educational tools, the financial tools, to accomplish things. You have a system that opens its doors to opportunity, to others. You hear people talking about it. It's real. The vibe, the intelligence, the special blast of the people here—it's going to make the country better."[27]

Of course, immigrants' characteristics today are very different from immigrants in the early 20th century. The National Academies' 2015 report noted, "European immigrants in 1910 came with very little education and had, on average, half the education of native-born Americans of that time, with high rates of illiteracy in many groups."[28] Today, both the immigrants' countries of origin and their educational attainments are quite diverse, "with Asia and Africa sending relatively more immigrants with high educational attainment, while Latin America and the Caribbean send relatively more immigrants with low attainment."[29] Those with the highest education come from Asia, followed closely by Africa, Canada, and Europe.

Even first-generation immigrant groups with low education gain substantially by the second generation. The report found: "Among Mexican American men, for instance, average education rises from 9.4 years to 12.6 years in the second generation. Among women the average education rises from 9.5 to 12.8 years."[30] Even immigrants who came with little education seemed to acquire more after their arrival. For example, Felix Okema (above) earned M.A. degrees in finance and accounting after arriving from the Ivory Coast before becoming a naturalized citizen in 2015. According to the U.S. Census in 2010, the percentage of the foreign-born over 25 years of age with at least a bachelor's degree was almost identical to that of the total population, 27 versus 28 percent.[31]

Immigrant employment today is also far different from the early 20th century, when hordes of poorly educated European immigrants found ready and steady work in industrial states as laborers or, in far fewer cases, as skilled craftsmen. Relatively few immigrants from central and southern European nations (e.g., Slovaks) sought to be farmers. The National Academies' 2010 statistics on employment, however, showed that foreign-born workers age 25–64 were more likely than U.S. born workers to be engaged in agricultural occupations.

The entries in Figure E.1 are "index" values based on the ratio of foreign-born to U.S.-born workers in broad occupational categories of the U.S. Census. Although only about one percent of the U.S. working population was engaged in "Farming, forestry, and fishing" in 2010, the foreign-born were 85 percent more likely to be employed in that category (mainly as agricultural workers) than the U.S.–born. They were also 30 percent more likely to work in service occupations in private households, food preparation, buildings, and health facilities.

While the foreign-born were 14 percent less likely to be employed in managerial and professional occupations, they were more likely than the U.S.-born to be in specific professions as natural scientists; physicians and other health specialists; engineers, architects, and surveyors; writers; and mathematical and computer scientists—as shown in Figure E.2.

The report found that "the overrepresentation of immigrants in areas of exceptional contribution to American society has shifted over time from cultural and artistic fields (Writers, Artists, Entertainers, and Athletes) in the period 1950–1980 to engineering, computing, and scientific professions since 1980."[32] A companion report in 2016, *The Economic and Fiscal Consequence of Immigration*, said:

> Importantly, immigration is integral to the nation's economic growth. Immigration supplies workers who have helped the United States avoid the problems facing stagnant economies created by unfavorable demographics—in particular, an aging (and, in the case of Japan, a shrinking) workforce. Moreover, the infusion by high-skill immigration of human capital has boosted the nation's capacity for innovation, entrepreneurship, and technological change. The literature on immigrants and innovation suggests that immigrants raise patenting per capita, which ultimately contributes to productivity growth. The prospects for long-run economic growth in the United States would be considerably dimmed without the contributions of high-skilled immigrants.[33]

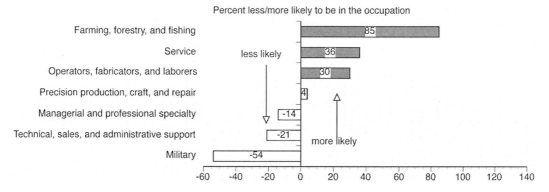

Figure E.1: RELATIVE OCCUPATIONAL CONCENTRATION OF IMMIGRANTS, 2010. **Studies of immigrants' occupations in 2010 show that they were most likely took jobs in the broad census category, "Farming, forestry, and fishing," which means that they worked on farms, mostly harvesting crops. Immigrants were also more likely to work in services and in nonfarm jobs as operators, fabricators, and laborers. Data: National Academies of Sciences, Engineering, and Medicine,** *The Integration of Immigrants into American Society* **(Washington, D.C.: The National Academies Press, 2015), Table 6–6.**

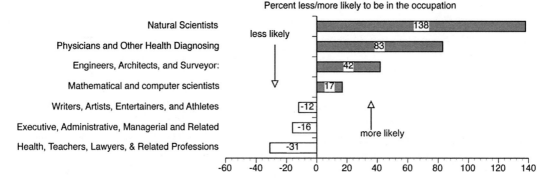

Figure E.2: Concentration of Immigrants in Professions, 2010. Although—as shown in Figure E.1—immigrants were less likely than nonimmigrants to be employed in professions, those who did work in professional occupations were more likely to be scientists, physicians, engineers, and mathematicians than nonimmigrants. Data: National Academies of Sciences, Engineering, and Medicine, *The Integration of Immigrants into American Society* (Washington, D.C.: The National Academies Press, 2015), Table 6–6.

Contrary to widespread belief, increased immigration is associated with lower, not higher, crime rates. The National Academies found: "Foreign-born males age 18–39 are incarcerated at one-fourth the rate for the native-born. Cities and neighborhoods with greater concentrations of immigrants have much lower rates of crime and violence than comparable nonimmigrant neighborhoods."[34] Like their European predecessors, today's immigrants are contributing to America, not detracting from it.

Self-Determination

Self-determination of peoples was not among President Woodrow Wilson's original Fourteen Points for ending the war, but he embraced the concept in making the peace.[35] Defined as the "the right of peoples or nations to choose how they live their collective lives and structure their communities based on their own norms, laws, and cultures,"[36] that principle was invoked after the war to create Czechoslovakia and Yugoslavia from the former Austro-Hungarian Empire. Yet neither nation exists today. The lesson from these stories is that the noble principle of self-determination—like peace among nations—is difficult to implement yet is essential to pursue.

Although Czechoslovakia and Yugoslavia were formed under the guise of self-determination of people, "the people" did not create these nations; international leaders did. Leaders created Czechoslovakia first. Backed by the Allied powers, separate leadership groups in separate cities on separate dates declared the existence of Czechoslovakia. The Czech National Council issued its proclamation in Prague on October 28, 1918, and the Slovak National Council issued its proclamation on October 30 in Martin. Neither group asked the Czech and Slovak people to consent to their actions.

Neither did international leaders ask the Serbians, Croats, Slovenes, and several other mostly Slavic peoples whether they wished to be bundled together in a "south Slav" nation informally called Yugoslavia ("yugo" meaning south). On December 1, 1918, a Serbian dynasty had already proclaimed a Kingdom of Serbs, Croats, and Slovenes absorbing parts of Austria-Hungary. Because its ethnic composition conflicted with guidelines in the Paris peace conference, the nation was reshaped on November 12, 1920, by the Treaty of Rapallo between the Kingdom of Italy and the Kingdom of Serbs, Croats, and Slovenes. It was officially renamed Yugoslavia on October 3, 1929. Serbs had such a large plurality of Yugoslavia's population that the U.S. State Department said: "As Serbia was the dominant partner in this state, the U.S. Government has considered the Kingdom of Serbs, Croats, and Slovenes and then later, Yugoslavia, as the successor government to the original Government of Serbia."[37]

By creating Yugoslavia as a nation for the southern Slavs, the Allied leaders at the Paris peace conference thought that they were fulfilling the principle of self-determination: a Slav is a Slav is a Slav, no? Instead of unifying common people in a nation, the leaders joined together ethnic groups that had fought one another for decades if not centuries. Yugoslavia endured a turbulent history from 1920 through World War II until the death of Communist leader Josip Broz Tito in 1980. After much political tension and maneuvering, Slovenia, Croatia, and Macedonia declared their independence in 1991. Vicious civil wars broke out as Serbs sought to retain control. Bosnia and Herzegovina declared independence in 1992.

By 2003, Yugoslavia was reduced to the Union of Serbia and Montenegro, and Montenegro split away in 2006. Today, seven nations—Serbia, Slovenia, Croatia, Bosnia and Herzegovina, Macedonia, Montenegro, and Kosovo—stand in place of the former Yugoslavia. After World War II, Yugoslavia officially honored Archduke Franz Ferdinand's assassin, Gavrilo Princip, "for having struck a blow that led to the breakup of the empire and Bosnia's reincarnation as part of Yugoslavia.[38] In 2014, on the 100th anniversary of the assassination, visitors to Sarajevo, Bosnia, found mixed messages about the assassin whose act launched World War I. They were "left to decide whether he was a liberator, an anarchist killer or a terrorist motivated by sectarian and ethnic hatreds."[39] Ethnic Serbs in East Sarajevo expressed their own opinion by unveiling a monument to Gavrilo Princip, their national hero.[40]

The Allies in Paris also mistakenly acted under the cloak of self-determination when creating Czechoslovakia as a nation for Czechs and Slovaks. As Caroline Barker said, "Beneš had managed to persuade the Allies that his London-based government-in-exile represented both the Czech and Slovak nations."[41] Beneš did have both Czech and Slovak leaders in his Czecho-Slovak National Council. Virtually all Czech leaders valued the nation's creation as an end in itself, and so did some Slovak leaders. Masaryk, who was born in Slovakia, was himself caught up in "Czechoslovakism"—an ideological commitment to blend the Czechs and Slovaks into a common culture, albeit with a Czech flavor. Other Slovak leaders regarded the creation of Czechoslovakia only as a means to an end—a means to escape Magyar domination and gain some degree of autonomy.[42]

Created as a unitary state, Czechoslovakia in 1918 had a population of 13 million, roughly composed of 6 million Czechs versus 2 million Slovaks—placing them third after 3 million Germans. The rest of Czechoslovakia consisted of 750,000 Hungarians and almost 500,000 Ruthenians, among others.[43] Together, the Czechs and Slovaks had a clear majority, but Slovaks were a minority within the majority. Article 1 of the new Language Law stated: "The Czecho-Slovak language is the state (official) language of the Republic."[44] Of course, there was and is no Czecho-Slovak language. The Czech and Slovak languages are similar but different. For instance, they use different vocabularies and spellings. Because Czechs dominated the new government, the law meant that Czech would be the official language.

Kirschbaum quoted a Czech delegate at the Paris conference as claiming "an international mandate to create a Czechoslovak political nation with the entry of the Slovaks in the Czech political nation."[45] Note that the delegate allowed Slovaks entry into the *Czech* nation, in line with the Czechs' view of Slovaks as their "little brothers." Kirschbaum cited a typical Slovak response to the "little brother" depiction: "A Slovak does not want to be a Czechoslovak, he does not want to be shoved behind a foreign facade, he wants to be himself, independent and equal."[46] Elisabeth Bakke explained why the ruling Czechs could not recognize Slovaks' desire to have governmental autonomy: "Bearing in mind that the government did acknowledge the principle of national self-determination (according to which Czechoslovakia was founded), recognizing the Slovaks as a separate nation would mean recognizing their right to autonomy—or in the final instance even to secession. Conversely, allowing autonomy would mean recognizing the Slovaks as a nation, which in turn would undermine the status of Czechoslovakia as a nation-state."[47] Consistent with Czechoslovakism, the national 1921 Census did not count Czechs and Slovaks separately but together as Czechoslovaks.

According to A.J.P. Taylor, leaders at the Paris peace conference hoped that self-determination would be self-fulfilling: "The Czechs and Slovaks would become one people, as the Piedmontese and Neapolitans had become Italian; Serbs, Croats, and Slovenes would merge into Yugoslavia, as Prussians, Saxons, and Bavarians had merged into Germany. The analogy was near; not near enough to prove true."[48] Although grudgingly admitting that the Czechs and Slovaks were not one people, the Allies, according to Taylor, expected that they "would come together as the English and Scotch had done."[49] But by the mid–1940s, he observed that decades of living together had made Czechs and Slovaks "more distinct, not less."[50] For many Slovaks, the problem was a lack of respect. Slovaks resented that "foreigners usually referred to the inhabitants of Czechoslovakia as 'the Czechs,' as foreigners often refer to the inhabitants of Great Britain as 'the English'; though the Slovaks were no more Czechs than the Scots are English."[51]

Certainly before 1918, there was no solid evidence of widespread nationalism among the Slovak people.[52] The "Slovak masses," according to Caroline Barker, "identified primarily with their local region or town" and had limited interest in outside events.[53] Anthropologist Janet Pollak wrote, "Until the 20th century, it was difficult to mobilize Slovaks as an ethnic group since any elites they may have generated were constantly co-opted and assimilated by Hungarians or Germans."[54] She also might have mentioned that the Czechs co-opted Tomáš Masaryk and Milan Štefánik. Both were born in Slovakia but came to embrace Czechoslovakism, not "Slovakism."

Joseph Grisak, who immigrated to Baltimore in 1901, recalled in his autobiography, "There was not much incentive to inculcate culture into the daily lives of the peasants. Each family lived their own crude style of existence. National or patriotic songs did not receive much attention and were not popular."[55] Moreover, their prominent indigenous leaders did not appeal to Slovak national sentiment. By the late 1920s, a Slovak intelligentsia had grown large enough to run Slovak affairs and—reacting to the 1929 economic crisis—began to campaign for "Slovaks first" in employment.[56] For good reasons and poor ones, Slovaks saw themselves as economically disadvantaged, and pressed for governmental autonomy.

Slovakia got its legal autonomy in 1939 when Nazi Germany recognized the Slovak Republic. In return, Slovakia became Germany's client state, while Bohemia and Moravia were absorbed as German protectorates. Legacies from World War II stained Czech and

Slovak relations when Czechoslovakia became reconstituted as the "third republic" in 1945. After the communists took over in 1948, Czech and Slovak relations suffered under the byzantine politics of communist rule until the Velvet Revolution in 1989. The creation of a democratic Czechoslovakia with a federal form of government presented the opportunity for a new start.

Recreated as a federal state, the ethnic composition of Czechoslovakia in 1990 was quite different from that of 1918. Roughly speaking, its 15.5 million people were mostly Czech (63 percent) but Slovaks (31 percent) were now the second largest group.[57] Fewer than 50 thousand Germans remained, nearly all being forced out after the war. The only other sizable group was a half million Magyars (4 percent). Still, Czechs outnumbered Slovaks two to one. In the new federal state, 99 percent of the Czechs lived in the Czech Republic and 93 percent of the Slovaks lived in the Slovak Republic. Most Czechoslovaks lived separately as Czechs and Slovaks.

Seventy years after the creation of Czechoslovakia in 1918, the Czechs and the Slovaks failed to become one people. Meanwhile, Slovak leaders became more assertive of Slovak aspirations. In 1968, during the communist era, Czechoslovakia was changed to a federal system. Slovaks got their own republic and parliament, but the whole country was under rule of the Communist Party. After the fall of communism in 1989, Slovak leaders wanted their own identity and a greater share of the national resources. In the June 1990 parliamentary elections for the federal and republic assemblies, some leaders on both sides threatened separation. Unlike those of 1918, leaders in the 1990s had to reckon with public opinion, but public opinion was unclear.

Opinion polls on Czechoslovakia's political unity or separation showed similar results.[58] In two surveys during September and October 1990, Prague's Public Opinion Research Institute reported that only 11 percent of Czechs and 12 percent of Slovaks favored separation in each survey.[59] Figures E.3 to E.5 graphs the results for three other public opinion surveys in 1990, 1991, and 1992.[60]

Figures E.3 to E.5 showed surprisingly consistent results. In each of the three polls, about 40 percent of Czechs versus about 15 percent of Slovaks favored a unitary state. Such a state would increase the concentration of power at the center and dilute the power of both republics, but further weaken the less populous one, Slovakia. Another 20 to 30 percent of Czechs and about 30 to 40 percent of Slovaks favored the existing federal system. Only about 10 to 20 percent of Czechs versus almost 40 percent of Slovaks favored either a confederation (separate republics with veto power) or outright independence.

Neither a majority of Czechs or of Slovaks favored any single option, but substantial proportions of Czechs favored either keeping the existing federal system or making the central government stronger. Lesser proportions of Slovaks favored making it weaker or splitting into independent countries. Thus, public opinion was split over the options within the two ethnic groups. Czechs leaned toward preserving the status quo; Slovaks were more ambivalent.

Even in democracies, governmental leaders sometimes fail to heed majority sentiment even when it is clear. Leaders exercise considerably more latitude when public opinion is unclear. In June 1992 Václav Klaus's party won parliamentary elections in the Czech Republic, making him its prime minister. Vladimír Mečiar's party won simultaneous elections in the Slovak Republic, and he became its prime minister. Despite polls showing relatively few Czechs favoring a split, Klaus chose separation, which he thought encouraged foreign investment.[61] Mečiar's personal position on the fate of Czechoslovakia was

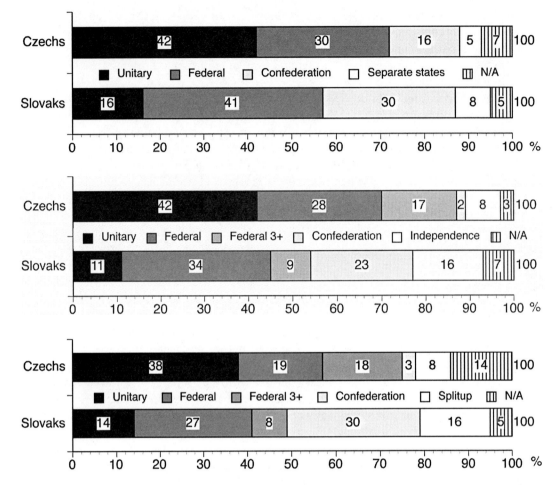

Top: **Figure E.3:** June 1990 Poll on Separating Czechoslovakia. **Data:** June 1990 Poll: *Radio Free Europe*, October 5, 1990. *Middle:* **Figure E.4:** August 1991 Poll on Separating Czechoslovakia. **Data:** 1991 Poll: "Hojda sa stat, hojda…," *Smena*, 28 August 1991. *Bottom:* **Figure E.5:** Summer 1992 Poll on Separating Czechoslovakia. **Data:** October 30, 1992 poll, *Radio Free Europe*.

Like many other polls taken in the early 1990s on the possible dissolution of Czechoslovakia, the results were generally consistent: Czech respondents were far more likely to favor continuing the union than Slovaks, who tended to favor a confederation or complete split. (The "Federal 3+" option allowed for Moravia and perhaps Silesia to be governmental units.)

less clear—as was Slovak public opinion.[62] Observers argue over why Mečiar came around to independence, but in a meeting in Brno on August 26, 1992, both sides agreed to dissolving Czechoslovakia on January 1, 1993.[63]

According to the existing constitution, secession from the federation had to be approved in referenda, which neither Klaus nor Mečiar wanted to hold.[64] Instead, both sides prevailed on their supporters in the Federal Assembly to pass a law on November 25 that dissolved the federation, despite a constitutional requirement for a referendum.[65] In 1918, Czech and Slovak leaders had also created Czechoslovakia without assessing the state of public opinion, but at least Czech and Slovak intelligentsia supported the action. As Caroline Barker wrote, the case in 1992 was different, especially for the Slovaks. This time, the intelligentsia "were never a part of the push for independence from the Czechs; indeed many, if not most, opposed it." She added, "This, like the creation of the wartime state, was a matter decided between a few politicians. Granted, there was no vassal status to the new Slovakia that was created; but, equally, there was no plebiscite, no referendum, no voice for the people in the formation of this new state. It was handled by a political elite and engineered by the two prime ministers, Vaclav Klaus and Vladimir Mečiar."[66]

Following what was dubbed "the velvet divorce"—the separation occurred without violence—observers expected the Czech economy to prosper while the Slovak struggled.[67] That occurred for the first few years, but a decade later, financial writers were touting Slovakia's economic successes. For 2011–2015, the World Bank estimated similar figures for gross domestic product per capita: $19,502 for the Czech Republic and $18,500 for Slovakia.[68] Reporting in 2014 for *The New Statesman*, Andrew Roxburgh wrote, "Czechs and Slovaks appear to get on better now than they did when they shared a country, constantly bickering as they did (just like the Scots and English) over whether one "subsidised" the other or "dictated policy."[69]

Roxburgh, the *New Statesman* reporter, invoked the Scot/English and Slovak/Czech analogy in 2014, just as A.J.P. Taylor did decades earlier in the mid–1940s. But Taylor's reference was metaphorical; Roxburgh's was not. On September 18, 2014, Scotland held a referendum on independence from Britain. In heavy voting, the Scots rejected independence by a vote of 55 to 45 percent. In contrast to Czechoslovakia's split in 1993, leaders in the United Kingdom allowed people to determine for themselves how they wished to be governed. Scots in 2014 chose the status quo—for the time being.

In other countries, ethnic regions are cueing up to hold referenda on self-determination. In January 2011, over 98 percent of voters in southern Sudan chose independence, creating the new nation, South Sudan. In Crimea on March 16, 2014—under warlike conditions—over 90 percent of Crimeans voted to join Russia rather than stay in Ukraine. Spain has been grappling with two disgruntled regions: Catalonia on the east and the Basque Country in the north. Smaller nationalist movements in Belgium (Flanders), Italy (South Tyrol, Veneto and Sardinia), and France (Brittany) are also angling for referenda.[70] In the 21st century, self-determination seems to be settled by citizens voting rather than by leaders agreeing.

Creating states through popular vote seems preferable to creating them through civil war or by leaders' agreements, but the evidence is not clear. The breakup of Czechoslovakia, done by leaders' agreement, worked out well so far for both the Czech Republic and Slovakia. The creation of South Sudan, done by referendum, spawned a civil war killing more than a million people. The jury is still out on Crimea, and on Ukraine for that matter. And Scotland may have another go at independence by referendum.

Where will self-determination end? A *Washington Post* cartoonist outlined an expanse of land with its interior borders drawn according to race, religion, ethnicity, sect, language, and custom. The result was that everyone ended up in his own country.[71] We can draw our conclusion about self-determination from A.J.P. Taylor's assessment of President Wilson's effort to end the Great War with a "just and lasting" peace. His plan was based in part on the self-determination of peoples: "Self determination, on national lines, did not work out as simply as President Wilson had once expected. Nationalities were mixed up; often the real national allegiance could not be discovered even by a plebiscite. Ingenious lines of national division cut across railway lines and areas economically tied together.… The frontiers were not perfect even from the national point of view. Still, fewer people were under an alien national sovereignty than ever before in European history."[72] Like just and lasting peace among nations, practical self-determination of nations is an elusive but worthwhile goal. Living under the government of people who share your culture and values is far better than living under rulers who do not.

A.J.P. Taylor also provides a fitting end to our stories: "Before the war there had been only one republic in Europe, France; or counting Portugal, after 1908, two. [Three, counting non-belligerent Switzerland.[73]] After the war there were more republics than monarchies in Europe. Before the war there had been four empires in Europe; after it, there was none. The Habsburg Monarchy broke up into national states; the core of the Ottoman Empire emerged as national Turkey; Russia and Germany survived somewhat diminished, but not Empires at any rate in name."[74] European government improved without emperors, American society and government improved with the influx of millions of European immigrants, and government across the world is more promising if based on self-determination than on denying self-determination.

Chapter 13, "Imperial Losses," referred to John Deak's judgment, "The real tragedy of the First World War, and of the twentieth century itself, may actually be a Habsburg story: the Great War ended the possibilities of multinationalism in Europe."[75] Other scholars were not so sanguine about Austria-Hungary's success with multinational government. What is clear is that the Great War enhanced the promise of multinationalism in the United States. Already a nation of Anglo-Saxon, Nordic, and German immigrants, the United States welcomed millions of new immigrants fleeing economic deprivations and social chaos. A 2015 study by the Pew Research Center found "the U.S. has—by far—the world's largest immigrant population, holding about one-in-five of the world's immigrants."[76]

Exercising a global form of "self-determination," the immigrants found a better life by emigrating out of their old country to a new land. By the twenty-first century, the United States had blossomed into a *Nation of Nations*, to cite the title of Tom Gjelten's 2015 book, which he subtitled *A Great American Immigration Story*.[77] Multinationalism failed in the Austria-Hungary monarchy, but it reemerged in a different form in the United States republic. The story of Samuel Mozolák's immigration to the United States along with millions of other Slovaks is just one chapter in the Great American Immigration Story.

Chapter Notes

Prologue

1. "Franz Joseph I of Austria: biography," http://www.fampeople.com/cat-franz-joseph-i-of-austria_5.

2. John Deak, *Forging a Multinational State: State Making in Imperial Austria from the Enlightenment to the First World War* (Stanford: Stanford University Press, 2015), 4.

3. Economic and Financial Section, League of Nations, *International Statistical Yearbook, 1926* (Geneva: League of Nations, 1927), Table 1, 14.

4. League of Nations, Economic and Financial Section, *International Statistical Year-Book, 1926* (Geneva: Publications of the League of Nations, 1927), 14.

5. "Austria-Hungary: Linguistic Distribution." *Wikipedia*, at http://en.wikipedia.org/wiki/Austro–Hungarian_Empire#Linguistic_distribution.

6. Especially "dusty and unread" were books published during or soon after the war. One wartime example is Roger Maria Hermann Bernhard Rességuier, *Francis Joseph and His Court: From the Memoirs of Count Roger de Rességuier* (New York: John Lane, 1917). A postwar example is Albert Margutti, *The Emperor Francis Joseph and His Times* (New York: George H. Dooran, 1921). A more recent book specifically on the Habsburgs is A.J.P. Taylor, *The Habsburg Monarchy, 1809–1918: A History of the Austrian Empire and Austria-Hungary* (London: Hamish Hamilton, 1948).

7. Alan Sked, *The Decline and Fall of the Habsburg Empire 1815–1918*, 2nd ed. (Harlow, Essex: Longman, 2001), 2.

8. Sked, 3.

9. The usual spelling is "Habsburg," but some write "Hapsburg." See Arthur J. May, *The Passing of the Hapsburg Monarchy, 1914–1918*, vols. 1 and 2 (Philadelphia: University of Pennsylvania Press, 1966). Winston Churchill also used Hapsburg in *The World Crisis*, his monumental five-volume set chronicling the war. Nevertheless, the official funeral website for the eldest son of the last emperor used Habsburg in both the German and English versions.

10. Taylor, *The Habsburg Monarchy*, 8.

11. "Rudolf I of Germany" at http://en.wikipedia.org/wiki/Rudolf_I_of_Germany#King_of_Germany and "House of Habsburg" at https://en.wikipedia.org/wiki-Hugh Thomas, /House_of_Habsburg.

12. Thomas Hugh, *World Without End: Spain, Philip II, and the First Global Empire* (New York: Random House, 2015).

13. Ferdinand Schevill, *A History of Europe from the Reformation to the Present Day* (New York: Harcourt, Brace, 1954), 115.

14. Robert Pick, *Empress Maria Theresa: The Earlier Years, 1717–1757* (New York: Harper & Row, 1966).

15. Karen Wilkin, "An Empire's True Wealth," *Wall Street Journal* (August 6, 2015), D5.

16. Oscar Jászi, *The Dissolution of the Habsburg Monarchy* (Chicago: University of Chicago Press, 1961; originally published in 1929), 34.

17. Gordon Brook-Shepherd, *The Austrians: A Thousand-Year Odyssey* (New York: Carroll & Graf, 1998), xiv–xv.

18. See Ferdinand Schevill, *A History of Europe from the Reformation to the Present Day* (New York: Harcourt, Brace, 1954), 74.

19. Historians differ on the territories gained and lost, and also on the dates. For example, most scholars agree that the Habsburg empire was founded on the Archduchy of Austria in 1282, but the Archduchy's composition is disputed. Most agree that it included what is today called Lower Austria and Styria, but Upper Austria had a hazy relationship to the Archduchy. Brook-Shepherd's map included it in the Archduchy; others did not. This map somewhat arbitrarily adds Upper Austria to Habsburg lands in 1506, under Emperor Maximilian I. See "Habsburger" in http://www.land-oberoesterreich.gv.at/24411.htm.

20. Geoffrey Wawro, "The Masque of Command: Bad Generals and Their Impact," *Historically Speaking* 6 (November/December 2004): 5–6.

21. Jászi, 106.

22. Margaret MacMillan, *The War that Ended Peace: The Road to 1914* (New York: Random House, 2013), 220.

23. Christopher Clark, *The Sleepwalkers: How Europe Went to War in 1914* (New York: Harper, 2013), 65.

24. Chang and Eng Bunker, at https://en.wikipedia.org/wiki/Chang_and_Eng_Bunker.

25. Pieter M. Judson, *The Habsburg Empire: A New History* (Cambridge, MA: Belknap Press, 2016), 44.

26. Judson, 24 and 43.

27. May, 822–823.

28. May, 820.

29. "Ruthene" was the term used most frequently at the time. Today, "Rusyn" or "Carpatho-Rusyn" is preferred.

30. Barbara Tuchman, *The Guns of August* (New York: Ballantine Books, 1994), index entries on pages 578 and 585: Austria-Hungary: mobilization, 85; bombards Belgrade, 85; ultimatum to Serbia, 85, 100; declares war on Serbia, 85, 164; fleet at Pola a "paper tiger," 166; defeat at Lemberg, 365. Franz Ferdinand, Archduke of Austria (1863–1914), 3; assassination of, 85. Franz Josef, Emperor (1830–1916), 3; opinion of Leopold II, 29.

31. Tuchman, xxiii–xxiv.

32. James J. Sheehan, "The Bloody Detail: Who Was to Blame for World War I?" *Commonweal* (May 2, 2014), 20–22.

33. Sked, 274.

34. Sheehan reviewed Clark, *The Sleepwalkers*; Max Hastings, *Catastrophe 1914: Europe Goes To War* (New York: Alfred A. Knopf, 2013); MacMillan, *The War that Ended Peace*; and Sean McMeekin, *July 1914: Countdown to War* (New York: Basic Books, 2013). Austria-Hungary is also discussed extensively in two other books: T.G. Otte, *July Crisis: The World Descent into War, Summer 1914* (Cambridge, UK: Cambridge University Press, 1914); and Geoffrey Wawro, *A Mad Catastrophe: The Outbreak of World War I and the Collapse of the Habsburg Empire* (New York: Basic Books, 2014).

35. Dominic Lieven, *The End of Tsarist Russia: The March to World War I and Revolution* (New York: Viking, 2015), 2.

36. Lieven, 2.

37. Winston Churchill, *The Unknown War: The Eastern Front* (New York: Scribner's, 1931), 76.

38. Erich Maria Remarque, *Im Western nichts Neues* (published in English as *All Quiet on the Western Front*) (New York: Little, Brown, 1929).

39. Maureen Healy, *Vienna and the Fall of the Habsburg Empire: Total War and Everyday Life in World War I.* (Cambridge, UK: Cambridge University Press, 2004), 98.

40. Healy, 101.

41. Healy, 99.

42. One hundred thirty-nine films appear on the "List of World War I Films," *Wikipedia*, at https://en.wikipedia.org/wiki/List_of_World_War_I_films. Statistics reported here were computed from that listing.

43. See David Mermelstein, "Unquiet on the Western Front," *Wall Street Journal* (July 31, 1914), D5, for films primarily about the familiar Western Front.

44. J.M. Winter, *The Experience of World War I* (New York: Oxford University Press, 1989), 240–245.

45. Calculated from "WWI Casualty and Death Tables," at http://www.pbs.org/greatwar/resources/casdeath_pop.htm.

46. Churchill's history of World War I came out over a number of years by different publishers under the collective title *The World Crisis*. Volumes 1–4 were subtitled by years. Volume 5 appeared as *The Unknown War* or *The Eastern Front* or a concatenation of both. Citations herein are to *The Unknown War: The Eastern Front* (New York: Scribner's, 1931). Volume 4 was issued in two parts, so the set consisted of six physical books. In addition, a single-volume abridged edition was published as *The World Crisis: 1911–1918*.

47. Alan Palmer, *The Gardeners of Salonika* (New York: Simon & Schuster, 1965), inside front cover, identified these five fronts in addition to the Western and Eastern Fronts.

Chapter 1

1. This follows the practice in Winston Churchill, *The Unknown War: The Eastern Front* (New York: Scribner's, 1931), xi. In the same place Churchill announced, "For convenient brevity the word 'Austrian' is nearly always used to cover the Austro-Hungarian Empire." That practice was indeed common to many writers, especially when discussing the war, but it will not be followed here. Austria-Hungary will be used when referring to the empire.

2. See "Emperor," *Wikipedia*, at http://en.wikipedia.org/wiki/Emperor#Distinction_from_other_monarchs.

3. Shmuel N. Eisenstadt, "Empires," in David L. Sills, ed., *International Encyclopedia of Social Sciences*, vol. 5 (New York: Macmillan and The Free Press, 1968), 41.

4. Miranda Carter, *George, Nicholas, and William: Three Royal Cousins and the Road to World War I* (New York: Alfred A. Knopf, 2010), 43.

5. Joseph Redlich, *Emperor Francis Joseph of Austria:*

A Biography (Hamden, CT: Archon Books, 1965); reprint of 1929 Macmillan edition, 23. Redlich's career and political influence before and after World War I are profiled in Fredrik Lindström, *Empire and Identity: Biographies of the Austrian State Problem in the Late Habsburg Empire* (West Lafayette, IN: Purdue University Press, 2008), Part Three.

6. Carter, *George, Nicholas, and William*, xxiii.

7. Carter, *George, Nicholas, and William*, 48.

8. Walter Bagehot, *The English Constitution* (Boston: Little, Brown, 1873), 173.

9. There were two Habsburgs called Ferdinand I. Ferdinand I of Austria (1793–1875) came roughly three hundred years after Ferdinand I of the Holy Roman Empire (1503–1564).

10. These remarks appear in various writings. See "Ferdinand I of Austria," *Wikipedia*, at http://en.wikipedia.org/wiki/Ferdinand_I_of_Austria.

11. Pieter M. Judson, *The Habsburg Empire: A New History* (Cambridge, MA: Belknap Press, 2016), 189.

12. Redlich, *Emperor Francis Joseph of Austria*, 31.

13. Alan Palmer, *Twilight of the Habsburgs: The Life and Times of Emperor Francis Joseph* (New York: Grove Press, 1994), 3.

14. Redlich's quotations on page 31 differ from those in Alan Palmer, 47.

15. Palmer, 52–53.

16. John Deak, *Forging a Multinational State: State Making in Imperial Austria from the Enlightenment to the First World War* (Stanford: Stanford University Press, 2015), 37.

17. Victor S. Mamatey, *The United States and East Central Europe, 1914–1918: A Study in Wilsonian Diplomacy and Propaganda* (Princeton, NJ: Princeton University Press, 1957), 10.

18. Éva Somogyi, "The Age of Neoabsolutism, 1849–1867," in Peter F. Sugar, Péter Hanák, and Tibor Frank, eds., *A History of Hungary* (Bloomington: Indiana University Press, 1990), 235.

19. For a more charitable interpretation of the Bach era, which emphasizes its administrative efficiency, see Deak, *Forging a Multinational State*, 99–138.

20. "Constitution of the Empire of Austria," at http://www.hoelseth.com/royalty/austria/austrianconst18490304.html#Constitution.

21. R.W. Seton-Watson, *Racial Problems in Hungary* (New York: Howard Fertig, 1972 edition, originally published in 1908). Later during the war, Seton-Watson served Britain's "Enemy Propaganda Department," according to Ian F.W. Beckett, *The Great War 1914–1918* (Harlow, UK: Longman, 2001), 287.

22. In 1911, the U.S. Immigration Commission used "race" to mean "nationality," recommending that "the limitation of each [race] arriving each year be limited to a certain percentage of that race arriving during a given period of years." Quoted in Roger Daniels, *Not Like Us: Immigrants and Minorities in America, 1890–1924* (Chicago: Ivan R. Dee, 1997), 132. As late as 1931, Winston Churchill commented on the "Mixture of different races" and that "officers of German race" predominated in the Austro-Hungarian army. See *The Unknown War*, 230.

23. Deak, 167–169.

24. John Lukacs, *Budapest 1900: A Historical Portrait of a City and Its Culture* (New York: Weidenfeld & Nicolson, 1988), 177.

25. Lindström, *Empire and Identity*, 133–134.

26. A twelve-minute version of the film is at https://www.youtube.com/watch?v=zPkWH3L9s7Y. A two-minute version at https://www.youtube.com/watch?v=lQjNSdy44Cs. I thank Dr. László Vass for telling me about this film.

27. Stefan Zweig, *The World of Yesterday* (New York:

Viking Press, 1945). Soon after finishing this work in 1941, Zweig committed suicide, after killing his wife.

28. Zweig, 71.

29. In his history of the monarchy, A.J.P. Taylor grappled with what to call the two parts of the empire, "Austria" in particular. Interestingly, he does not mention Transleithania and Cisleithania, which also do not appear in his index. See *The Habsburg Monarchy, 1809–1918: A History of the Austrian Empire and Austria-Hungary* (London: Hamish Hamilton, 1948), 8.

30. Gordon Brook-Shepherd, *The Austrians: A Thousand-Year Odyssey* (New York: Carroll & Grad, 1998), 93. Thomas Čapek wrote, "Austria received Bohemia, Moravia, Silesia, Bukovina, Dalmatia, Galicia, Carinthia, Carniola, Trieste and vicinity, Goritz and Gradiska, Istria, Lower Austria, Upper Austria, Salzburg, Styria, Tyrol, Voralberg. Hungary secured as her part of the bargain Hungary Proper, Transylvania, Fiume, Croatia, Slavonia, and the Military Frontier": *Bohemia under Hapsburg Misrule; A Study of the Ideals and Aspirations of the Bohemian and Slovak Peoples, As They Relate To and are Affected By the Great European War* (New York: Fleming H. Revell, 1915), 68.

31. Ladislaus J. Bolchazy, ed., *Illustrated Slovak History: A Struggle for Sovereignty in Central Europe* (Wauconda, IL: Bolchazy-Carducci, 2006), 327.

32. Hilde Spiel, *Vienna's Golden Autumn, 1866–1938* (New York: Weidenfeld & Nicolson, 1987), 18.

33. Robert Musil, *The Man without Qualities* (New York: Coward-McCann, 1953), 94.

34. Joseph Roth, *The Radetzky March* (New York: Alfred A. Knopf, 1996).

35. Joseph Roth, *The Collected Stories of Joseph Roth* (New York: W.W. Norton, 2003; translated by Michael Hofmann).

36. Jeff Shaara, *To the Last Man: A Novel of the First World War* (New York: Ballantine Books, 2004), 115.

37. Brook-Shepherd, *The Austrians*, 68.

38. Deak, *Forging a Multinational State*, 245.

39. Brook-Shepherd, *The Austrians*, 135.

40. Konštantín Čulen, *History of Slovaks in America* (translated from the 1942 Slovak edition by Daniel C. Nečas) (St. Paul, MN: Czechoslovak Genealogical Society International, 2007), 265.

41. MacMillan, *The War that Ended Peace*, 234.

42. Brook-Shepherd, *The Austrians*, 71.

43. Tertius Chandler, *Four Thousand Years of Urban Growth* (Lewiston, NY: St. David's University Press, 1987), 492.

44. Spiel, *Vienna's Golden Autumn*, 120.

45. Zweig, 12.

46. "Hofburg Imperial Palace," at http://www.cityscouter.com/travelguides/vienna/Hofburg-Imperial-Palace.html.

47. Zweig, 21.

48. MacMillan, *The War that Ended Peace*, 223.

49. Chandler, 492.

50. "Timeline of railway history," at http://en.wikipedia.org/wiki/Timeline_of_railway_history.

51. Edwin A. Pratt, *The Rise of Rail-Power in War and Conquest, 1833–1914* (Philadelphia: J.B. Lippincott, 1916).

52. "Austria-Hungary," *Wikipedia*, at http://en.wikipedia.org/wiki/Austro-Hungarian_Empire#Telegraph.

53. "Telegraphy," *Wikipedia* at http://en.wikipedia.org/wiki/Telegraph.

54. See Simon Winchester, *Krakatoa: The Day the World Exploded: August 27, 1883* (New York: HarperCollins, 2003), 182.

55. "Austria-Hungary: Telegraph," *Wikipedia* at http://en.wikipedia.org/wiki/Austro-Hungarian_Empire#Telegraph.

56. "Incandescent light bulb," *Wikipedia* at http://en.wikipedia.org/wiki/Incandescent_light_bulb#Early_pre-commercial_research.

57. MacMillan, *The War that Ended Peace*, 4–5.

58. Geoffrey Drage, *Austria-Hungary* (London: John Murray, 1909), p. 53.

59. Steven Erlanger and Stephen Castle, "Elizabeth Becomes Britain's Longest-Serving Monarch," *New York Times* (September 10, 2015), A10.

60. Zweig, 205.

Chapter 2

1. Ján Lukačka's *Krajné: 1392–1992* (Bratislava: Bratislava Press, 1992) has 117 pages in double-column format with black-and-white and color illustrations. Printed in Slovak, it is also available in English on the village's website at http://www.krajne.sk/ using the translation capabilities of an Internet browser.

2. "Elizabeth Báthory in Popular Culture," *Wikipedia*, at http://en.wikipedia.org/wiki/Elizabeth_Báthory_in_popular_culture#Film.

3. Lukačka, 26.

4. *Ibid.*, 34.

5. Lukačka, 51 and 102.

6. *Ibid.*, 51.

7. *Cram's Unrivaled Atlas of the World* (Chicago: Geo F. Cram, 1911), 549.

8. "Mesto Myjava," at http://www.myjava.sk/http://www.myjava.sk/historia/.

9. Issues leading to the Slovak uprising in 1848 are set forth by Daniel Rapant, "Slovak Politics in 1848–1849," *Slavonic and East European Review* (1948), 67–90, especially p. 85.

10. Gregory C. Ference, *Sixteen Months of Indecision: Slovak American Viewpoints toward Compatriots and the Homeland from 1914 to 1915 as Viewed by the Slovak Language Press in Pennsylvania* (Selinsgrove, PA: Susquehanna University Press, 1995), 26.

11. Anton Spiesz, "The Revolution of 1848–1849," in Ladislaus J. Bolchazy, ed., *Illustrated Slovak History: A Struggle for Sovereignty in Central Europe* (Wauconda, IL: Bolchazy-Carducci, 2006), 115–117.

12. Lukačka, 35.

13. John Lukacs, *Budapest 1900: A Historical Portrait of a City and Its Culture* (New York: Weidenfeld & Nicolson, 1988), 60.

14. Lukacs, 73.

15. Lukacs, 63.

16. Lukacs, 43.

17. Lukacs, 14.

18. Lukacs, 31.

19. This building belonged to Samuel Borik, Ann Mozolak's uncle on her mother's side. It was probably used as a stable. It was certainly used only for animals in 1971, during our visit to Krajné.

20. Zuzana Bielikova and Ján Kubíček, *Krajné v spomienkach* (Krajné Memories) (Krajné, Slovakia: City of Krajné, 2010), 10–17, discussed house construction.

21. Joe M. Samson, "Keeping Warm in Orava and the Slovak Carpathians," *Slovakia* 18 (Summer 2004), 3.

22. Information about the Mozolák family in the 19th century comes from government documents and church records in Slovak, German, and Hungarian studied by John Mozolak, Jr., Samko Mozolák's grandson.

23. From the 1869 Census Mozoláci Kopanice, translated by grandson John Mozolak.

24. Andrew C. Janos, *The Politics of Backwardness in Hungary, 1825–1945* (Princeton, NJ: Princeton University Press, 1982), 121.

25. Bielikova and Kubíček, *Krajné v spomienkach*, 54.

26. Keely Stauter-Halsted, *The Nation in the Village: The Genesis of Peasant National Identity in Austrian Poland, 1848–1914* (Cornell University Press, 2001), 9.

27. Eva Somogyi, "The Age of Neoabsolutism, 1849–1867," in Sugar, Hanâk, and Frank, eds., *A History of Hungary*, 235–251, at p. 237; Somogyi, 238.

28. Stauter-Halsted, 10.

29. Werner Roesener, *The Peasantry of Europe* (Oxford, UK: Blackwell, 1994), 18.

30. Roesener, 19.

31. Bernard Wasserstein, *Barbarism and Civilization: A History of Europe in Our Time* (UK: Oxford University Press, 2007), 17.

32. Wasserstein, 18.

33. Wasserstein, 18.

34. Janos, *The politics of Backwardness in Hungary*, 85.

35. Ference, 32.

36. Anton Spiesz, "The Era of a Dual Monarchy (1867–1918)," in Ladislaus J. Bolchazy, ed., *Illustrated Slovak History*, 171.

37. Jânós Bak, "The Late Medieval Period, 1382–1526," in Sugar, Hanâk, and Frank, eds., *A History of Hungary*, 78.

38. Andrew C. Janos, *The Politics of Backwardness in Hungary, 1825–1945* (Princeton, NJ: Princeton University Press, 1982), 23.

39. Spiesz, "The Era of a Dual Monarchy (1867–1918)," 144.

40. The figure was 3 percent according to Miklos Molnar, *A Concise History of Hungary*, translated by Anna Magyar (Cambridge, UK; New York: Cambridge University Press, c2001), 218. In 1839, it was 5 percent, according to Andrew C. Janos, *The Politics of Backwardness in Hungary*, 18. Tibor Frank put the number under 1 percent in 1910 in "Hungary and the Dual Monarchy, 1867–1890," in Sugar, Hanâk, and Frank, *A History of Hungary*, 275.

41. The figure is 23 percent according to Géza Jeszenszky, "Hungary Through World War I and the End of the Dual Monarchy," in Sugar, Hanâk, and Frank, 273. It is 27 percent according to Miklos Molnar, *A Concise History of Hungary*, 218.

42. Zsigmond Móricz, *The Torch (A Fâkly)* (New York: Alfred A. Knopf, 1931; originally published in 1917), 46.

43. Móriciz, 98.

44. Suzanna Maria Mikula, "Milan Hodža and the Slovak National Movement, 1898–1918" (Ph.D. diss., Syracuse University, 1974), 24–25.

45. Ference, 32.

46. *Ibid.*

47. Thomas Čapek, *The Slovaks of Hungary, Slavs and Panslavism* (New York: The Knickerbocker Press, 1906), 165–166.

48. Lukačka, 46.

49. "Magyarization," *Wikipedia*, at https://en.wikipedia.org/wiki/Magyarization#Education.

50. "Kingdom of Hungary (Austria-Hungary)," *Wikipedia*, at http://en.wikipedia.org/wiki/Kingdom_of_Hungary_(Austria-Hungary).

51. Jeszenszky, Géza, "Hungary Through World War I and the End of the Dual Monarchy," in Sugar, Hanâk, and Frank, *A History of Hungary*, 270.

52. Čulen, *History of Slovaks in America*, 39.

53. Čulen, 37.

54. Michael J. Grisak, *The Grisak Family* (Merrillville, IN: unpublished 98-page autobiography of Joseph Grisak, 1978), available at http://www.carpathorusynsociety.org/Genealogy/Grisak.pdf.

55. Čulen, 265.

56. "Pozsony County," *Wikipedia*, at http://en.wikipedia.org/wiki/Pozsony_County#1900.

57. John Keegan, *The First World War* (New York: Alfred A. Knopf, 1999), 156.

Chapter 3

1. Pieter M. Judson, *The Habsburg Empire: A New History* (Cambridge, MA: Belknap Press, 2016), 51.

2. Judson, 34.

3. Judson, 35.

4. Judson, 19.

5. Judson, 38.

6. Judson, 123.

7. Judson, 122.

8. Judson, 211.

9. Judson, 247.

10. Judson, 43.

11. MacMillan, *The War that Ended Peace*, 217.

12. Jászi, *The Dissolution of the Habsburg Monarchy*, 237.

13. Shmuel N. Eisenstadt, "Empires," in Sills, ed., *International Encyclopedia of Social Sciences*, vol. 5, 41.

14. "Austria-Hungary," *Wikipedia*, at http://en.wikipedia.org/wiki/Austro-Hungarian_Empire#Name_in_official_languages_of_Austria-Hungary.

15. A Google search in June 2014 for "Austro-Hungarian Empire" returned 559,000 hits versus 56,5000 for "Austro-Hungarian Monarchy."

16. The 1937 *Oxford Universal English Dictionary* listed eleven different meanings for "country," including "an expanse of land" and "the territory or land of a nation."

17. Dankwart A. Rustow, "Nation," in Sills, ed., *International Encyclopedia of the Social Sciences*, vol. 11, 7–14.

18. Arthur J. May, *The Passing of the Hapsburg Monarchy, 1914–1918*, vol. 1 (Philadelphia: University of Pennsylvania Press, 1966), p. 5.

19. "Austria-Hungary," *Wikipedia* at http://en.wikipedia.org/wiki/Austro-Hungarian_Empire#Linguistic_distribution. Z.A.B. Zeman said that the Austrian Censuses from 1880 to 1910 did not ask one's "mother tongue" but "*Umgangssprache*" (the language of common intercourse), which generated more German speakers in the German economy. See his "The Four Austrian Census and Their Political Consequences," in Mark Cornwall, ed., *The Last Years of Austria-Hungary 1908–1918* (Exeter: University of Exeter Press, 1990), 31–39 at p. 32.

20. Some historians doubt that 55 percent of the population was ethnically Magyar. Judson (p. 309) said that the Statistical Office described "mother tongue" as the language that "the respondent considers his own and which he speaks the most fluently and freely." It was not necessarily one's first language.

21. Zeman (*ibid.*) said that Hungarian censuses did use mother tongue.

22. The terms Ruthenians, Ruthenes, Rusyns, and Ukrainians are often used interchangeably. According to the "Internet Encyclopedia of Ukraine" at http://www.encyclopediaofukraine.com, they refer to the same ethnic group, except that Ruthenians, Ruthenes, and Rusyns were Ukrainians who lived in Habsburg lands, in the Carpathian Mountains. In contrast, a pamphlet, *Carpatho-Rusyns* (Carpatho-Rusyn Research Center, 2012), contends that Carpatho-Rusyns are a distinct nationality.

23. "Austria-Hungary," *Wikipedia* at https://en.wikipedia.org/wiki/Austria-Hungary.

24. Stanislav J. Kirschbaum, *A History of Slovakia: The Struggle for Survival* (New York: St. Martins' Griffin, 1995), 34.

25. Gordon Brook-Shepherd, *The Austrians: A Thousand-Year Odyssey* (New York: Carroll & Grad, 1998), 116.

26. *Ibid.*, 117.

27. Janos, *The Politics of Backwardness in Hungary*, 125.

28. Appendix III, "The Law of Nationalities," in Seton-Watson, *Racial Problems in Hungary*, 432.

29. Judson, 39.

30. http://en.wikipedia.org/wiki/Magyarization. Pieter Judson's "new history" of the Habsburg empire employs "Hungarianization" instead of "Magyarization," which he refers to as "ethnically inflected." See Judson, ix, and 303.

31. See Seton-Watson, *Racial Problems in Hungary*, Chapter 5; and Kirschbaum, *A History of Slovakia*, 109 and elsewhere.

32. John Palka, *My Slovakia, My Family* (Minneapolis: Kirk House, 2012), 174.

33. Janos, 126.

34. Spiesz, Caplovic, and Bolchazy, ed., *Illustrated Slovak History*, 155. See Appendix XXVI, "The Magyarization of Family Names and Official Pressure," in Seton-Watson, *Racial Problems in Hungary*. The examples of name changes come from Konštantín Čulen, *Dejiny Slovákov v Amerike* (Bratislava: Slovak League Publishing House, 1942), translated by Daniel C. Nečas and published as *History of Slovaks in America* (St. Paul: Czechoslovak Genealogical Society International, 2007). All citations will be to Nečas's English translation. These examples appear on p. 231.

35. How Slovaks strived to develop their own written language is documented in Kirschbaum, *A History of Slovakia*.

36. *Ibid.*, 101.

37. Appendix VII, 437, in Seton-Watson, *Racial Problems in Hungary*. Seton-Watson's Appendices contain some arithmetical errors. For example, the two right-hand columns of Appendix IV, "Hungarian population by race," do not sum to the stated total, 19,122,340. In fact, each sum to different totals, 19,948,562 and 18,922,340.

38. Seton-Watson, 438.

39. Janos, 47. However, Sked, *The Decline and Fall of the Habsburg Empire*, 211, claims Janos "deliberately underplays the significance of the nationality question in his writings in favour of the socio-political consequences of economic backwardness."

40. Deak, *Forging a Multinational State*, 2.

41. MacMillan, *The War that Ended Peace*, 217.

42. Géza Jeszenszky, "Hungary Through World War I and the End of the Dual Monarchy," in Sugar, Hanâk, and Frank, *A History of Hungary*, 289.

43. Judson, 28.

44. "Magyarization," at http://en.wikipedia.org/wiki/Magyarization#Education.

45. Brook-Shepherd, 116.

46. "Kingdom of Hungary," *Wikipedia* at http://en.wikipedia.org/wiki/Kingdom_of_Hungary_(Austria-Hungary).

47. Béla Zombory-Moldován, *The Burning of the World: A Memoir of 1914* (New York: New York Review Books, 2014), x.

48. Geoffrey Drage, *Austria-Hungary* (London: John Murray, 1909), 565.

49. "The most wretched of Hungary's subject peoples, however, were the Slovaks and the Ruthenes (or Ukrainians) in the northern and northeastern counties of the Kingdom." Victor S. Mamatey, *The United States and East Central Europe, 1914–1918: A Study in Wilsonian Diplomacy and Propaganda* (Princeton, NJ: Princeton University Press, 1957), 15.

50. Drage, 290.

51. See Julianna Puskás, "Hungarian Migration Patterns, 1880–1930: From Macroanalysis to Microanalysis," in Ira A. Glazier and Luigi De Rosa, eds., *Migration across Time and Nations: Population Mobility in Historical Contexts* (New York: Holmes & Meier, 1986), 231–254, at p. 232.

52. Northwestern University Library posted 260 League of Nations statistical and disarmament documents online at http://digital.library.northwestern.edu/league/.

53. Seton-Watson, *Racial Problems in Hungary*, viii.

54. Puskás's long endnote 3 on page 252 details sources in German, Magyar, and Slovak reporting sources and problems. This chapter reports more accessible early sources available more readily in English.

55. Seton-Watson wrote, "I approached the subject with the conventional views of a British admirer of Louis Kossuth [former Governor-President of Hungary], and have gradually and reluctantly revised my opinion on almost every problem of Austrian or Hungarian politics." *Racial Problems in Hungary*, vii.

56. Z.A.B. Zeman, *The Break-up of the Habsburg Empire, 1914–1918* (London, New York: Oxford University Press, 1961), 185.

57. Zeman, 43.

58. Your Correspondent for Austria-Hungary. "Hungarian Social Legislation," *London Times*, 25 Sept. 1907: 6. The Times Digital Archive. Web. 4 Aug. 2015.

59. Čulen, *History of Slovaks in America*.

60. Most of the data reported here come from Appendix XIII, 470, in Seton-Watson, *Racial Problems in Hungary*. Seton-Watson criticized Hungarian governmental policies toward non-Magyars but cited official Hungarian statistical sources. One might question the reliability of Hungary's emigration statistics or Seton-Watson's selections. However, the data he reported for 1896 to 1906 matched almost exactly data reported by the Slovak author and Magyar opponent, Čulen, in *History of Slovaks in America*, 34. Inconsequential differences occurred only for the years 1897, 1899, 1901, and 1903.

61. Čulen, *History of Slovaks in America*, 36.

62. Čulen, *History of Slovaks in America*, 40.

63. Čulen, *History of Slovaks in America*, 42.

64. Appendix XIII, 470, in Seton-Watson, *Racial Problems in Hungary*.

65. Puskás, 233. Puskás relied heavily on Walter F. Wilcox. "International Emigration According to National Statistics: Europe," *International Migrations, Volume I: Statistics* (Washington, D.C.: National Bureau of Economic Research, 1929), 85–136; especially his data on page 92, showing 38 percent of Hungarians repatriating from 1908 to 1913.

66. Čulen, *History of Slovaks in America*, 39.

67. Walter F. Wilcox. "Statistics of Migrations, National Tables, United States," *International Migrations*, vol. 1: *Statistics* (Washington, D.C.: National Bureau of Economic Research, 1929), 372–498 at p. 389.

68. Wawro, *A Mad Catastrophe*, 42.

69. "Says Pan-Serb Move Is All In Austria," *New York Times*, July 30, 1914, 3.

70. Dorothy Giles, *The Road through Czechoslovakia* (Philadelphia: Penn Publishing Co., 1930), 298.

71. Jeszenszky, "Hungary Through World War I and the End of the Dual Monarchy," at p. 283.

72. May, 412.

73. May, 414–415.

74. Jászi, *The Dissolution of the Habsburg Monarchy*, 7.

75. Henry Wickham Steed, *The Hapsburg Monarchy*, 3rd ed. (London: Constable, 1914), 30.

76. May, 230.

77. Ference, *Sixteen Months of Indecision*, 32.

78. Studies of 19th-century immigration suggest that good economic conditions in the country targeted for immigration pulled immigrants more than they were pushed out by poor economic conditions. See Adolph Jensen, "Migration Statistics of Denmark, Norway and Sweden," in Walter F. Willcox, ed., *International Migrations*, vol. 2: *Interpretations* (Washington, D.C.: National Bureau of Economic Research, 1931), 283–312 at p. 296.

79. Stephanie Saxon-Ford, *The Czech Americans* (New York: Chelsea House, 1989), 47.

80. United States, Department of Homeland Security. *Yearbook of Immigration Statistics: 2008* (Washington, D.C.: U.S. Department of Homeland Security, Office of Immigration Statistics, 2009), Table 2. Data were not reported consistently for Austria and Hungary in all years.
81. MacMillan, xxvii.

Chapter 4

1. Jozef Cíger-Hronský, *Jozef Mak* (originally published in Slovak in 1933; translated by Andrew Cincura; Columbus, OH: Slavica, 1985), Cincura's endnote 30 attached to page 220.
2. Timrava, "That Alluring Land," in Norma L. Rudinsky (editor and translator), *That Alluring Land: Slovak Stories by Timrava* (Pittsburgh: University of Pittsburgh Press, 1992), 97–98. Timrava was the pen name of Božena Slančiková, who wrote this story in 1907.)
3. Timrava, "That Alluring Land," 105.
4. Timrava, "That Alluring Land," 117.
5. Thomas Čapek, *The Čzechs in America* (New York: Arno Press and The New York Times, 1969; originally published by Houghton Mifflin, 1920), 33.
6. Carl Wittke, "The Business of Encouraging Immigration," in Jeff Hay, *Immigration* (San Diego: Greenhaven Press, 2001), 49–55 at 53.
7. M. Mark Stolarik, *Where Is My Home? Slovak Immigration to North America (1870–2010)* (Bern: Peter Lang, 2012), 11.
8. Felix Klezl wrote that the 1867 Constitution limited freedom of emigration "by the liability to do military service." See "Austria," in Willcox, *International Migrations*, vol. 2, 392.
9. The manifest for SS *Rhein*, which sailed from Bremen on January 18, 1902, and arrived in New York on February 3, listed a passenger, Samuel Mozolák, from Hungary. The passenger's year of birth is shown as 1885, not 1882, but such errors were common. Unfortunately, the passenger's home town and contact person are illegible.
10. Čulen, *History of Slovaks in America*, 43.
11. Grisak, *The Grisak Family*, available at http://www.carpathorusynsociety.org/Genealogy/Grisak.pdf. at p. 74.
12. Philip Taylor, *The Distant Magnet: European Emigration to the U.S.A.* (New York: Harper & Row, 1971), 151.
13. "Norway-Heritage," http://www.norwayheritage.com/p_ship.asp?sh=rheil.
14. SS *Rhein* (2) at http://www.norwayheritage.com/p_ship.asp?sh=rheil. See also "Our Litwack Family History, The Trip Over," http://litwackfamily.com/ships.htm.
15. Taylor, 151.
16. Description attributed to August Bolino and reported by Albert Misenko, "Immigrant Journeys," in *Slovakia* 12 (Spring 1998): 4.
17. United States. Department of Homeland Security. *Yearbook of Immigration Statistics: 2008* (Washington, D.C.: U.S. Department of Homeland Security, Office of Immigration Statistics, 2009), Table 2.
18. Čulen, *History of Slovaks in America*, 44.
19. Craig Robertson, *The Passport in America: The History of a Document* (Oxford: Oxford University Press, 2010), 187.
20. Robertson, 204.
21. Edward Prince Hutchinson, *Legislative History of American Immigration Policy, 1798–1965* (Philadelphia: University of Pennsylvania Press, 1981), 536–537.
22. Robertson, 169.
23. "10 Things to Know: Passenger Lists," http://c.mfcreative.com/offer/immigration/2011/imm2011_10things2know.pdf.
24. *Ibid.*
25. Robertson, 169.
26. Manifests had only 22 columns from 1893 to 1906. See "Answers," at http://wiki.answers.com/Q/What_were_the_13_main_topics_about_on_29_questions_immigrants_passing_through_Ellis_Island_answered_on_the_ships_manifest. PIP #1 Manifest Extract Forms, http://web.archive.org/web/20050207195925/http://www.rootsweb.com/~ilpiplgs/manifest_extract_forms.htm
27. Bureau of the Census, *Fourteenth Census of the United States Taken in the Year 1920*, vol. 2: *Population, General Report and Analytical Tables* (Washington, DC: Department of Commerce, 1922), Table 11, "Mother Tongue of the Foreign White Stock," 1008. The 1910 and 1920 censuses said, "The foreign white stock comprises the aggregate white population which is foreign either by birth or by parentage. It embraces three classes, namely, foreign born whites, native whites both of whose parents were foreign born, and native whites having one foreign and one native parent" (p. 967). It includes "only immigrants and the native children of immigrants," so does not count those who came earlier. Foreign white stock embraces "foreign born" and so is greater.
28. "Among the 528,000 Hungarians, who reached the United States between 1876 and 1877 and 1901–02, there were only 655, or one-tenth of one per cent who exercised a calling demanding a high degree of intelligence (teacher, minister, artist, musician, architect, engineer, lawyer, or physician). This is a smaller percentage than in the other countries of Europe except Scandinavia and Russia." From Gustav Thirring, "Hungarian Migration of Modern Times," in Willcox, *International Migrations*, vol. 2, 427.
29. Ference, *Sixteen Months of Indecision*, 32.
30. Ference, 39.
31. Ference, 40.
32. Ference, 41.
33. Ference, 40.
34. Ference, 36.
35. "Slavs of New York," http://nycslav.blogspot.com/2006/01/slovaks-in-new-york-city.html. The Holy Trinity Church moved to 332 East 20th Street in 1911. See "Holy Trinity Slovak Lutheran Church," http://www.nycago.org/organs/nyc/html/holytrinityslovakluth.html.
36. Ference, 37. Sometimes C.S.P.S. is translated as the Bohemian-Slavic Assistance Society; sometimes as the Czech and Slovak Protective Society.
37. Ference, 37.
38. Sokol New York website at http://sokolnewyork.org/about/history.
39. Ed Chlanda, librarian at New York Sokol, outlined the early Sokols in New York in his email of March 16, 2026.
40. Quoted in Elsie Gergor-Umleaf, "Jeronym No. 120," *ČSA Journal* (June 1994).
41. Christopher Gray, "On East 73rd Street, a Lingering Vestige of a Czech Heritage," *New York Times* (March 15, 1987), 14R.
42. Clark, *The Sleepwalkers*, 3–13.
43. Clark, 14–15.
44. Clark, 48.
45. "Top Ten Cities of the Year 1900," http://geography.about.com/library/weekly/aa011201f.htm.
46. "Of the 377,527 Slovaks who entered the United States between 1889 and 1910, 26,351 gave Illinois as their final destination; 35,729 gave Jersey; 48,310 gave New York; 30,785 gave Ohio. The largest number 195,632 were headed for Pennsylvania.... The great majority of entering Slovaks worked in the steel mills and coal mines. M. Mark Stolarik, "The Role of American Slovaks in the Creation of Czecho-Slovakia, 1914–1918," *Slovak Studies* 8, Historica 5 (1968): 7–82 at p. 14.
47. *Fourteenth Census of the United States Taken in the Year 1920*, vol. 2: *Population, General Report and Analytical*

Tables, Table 7, "Mother Tongue of the Foreign White Stock," 984.

48. Čulen, 67.
49. Čulen, 68.
50. Marian Mark Stolarik, *Immigration and Urbanization: The Slovak Experience, 1870–1918* (New York: AMS Press, 1989), 111–112.
51. Robert J. Gordon, *The Rise and Fall of American Growth: The U.S. Standard of Living Since the Civil War* (Princeton, NJ: Princeton University Press, 2016), 75.
52. Thomas Bell, *Out of This Furnace* (Boston: Little, Brown, 1941), 3.
53. Bell, 21.
54. Bell, 44.
55. Bell, 123.
56. Bell, 123.
57. Peter Roberts, *The New Immigration: A Study of the Industrial and Social Life of Southeastern Europeans in America* (New York: Macmillan, 1912), 70.
58. Roberts, 366.
59. See "The Inflation Calculator," at http://www.west egg.com/inflation/infl.cgi or http://www.usinflationcalcu lator.com.
60. "How much do Americans earn in 2015? A comprehensive look at household income and individual earnings. GDP disconnects from household income," at http://www.mybudget360.com/how-much-do-americans-earn-in-2015-household-income-wages-real-income-gdp/.
61. Estimates for per person median income at that time are hard to come by. The U.S. Embassy in Germany reported that the average income for occupations across all industries was $438 in 1900 and $574 in 1910. That would calculate to roughly $500 in 1906. See http://usa.usembassy.de/etexts/his/e_prices1.htm.
62. Roberts, 166.
63. "Austro-Hungarian krone," *Wikipedia* at http://en.wikipedia.org/wiki/Austro-Hungarian_krone#Historic_exchange_rates_and_prices.
64. Jászi, *The Dissolution of the Habsburg Monarchy*, 231.
65. Timrava, "That Alluring Land," 129.
66. Ference, 34.
67. Stolarik, *Immigration and Urbanization*, 43.

Chapter 5

1. Richard F. Hamilton and Holger H. Herwig, *Decisions for War, 1914–1917* (Cambridge: Cambridge University Press, 2004), 239.
2. Hamilton and Herwig, 15.
3. Carter, *George, Nicholas, and William*; Giles MacDonogh, *The Last Kaiser: The Life of Wilhelm II* (New York: St. Martin's Press, 2001); Alan Palmer, *Twilight of the Habsburgs: The Life and Times of Emperor Francis Joseph* (New York: Grove Press, 1994); Edvard Radzinsky, *The Life and Death of Nicholas II* (New York: Doubleday, 1992, translated from the Russian by Marian Schwartz); Joseph Redlich, *Emperor Francis Joseph of Austria: A Biography* (Hamden, CT: Archon Books, 1965; reprint of 1929 Macmillan edition); John Röhl, *Wilhelm II: Into the Abyss of War and Exile, 1900–1941* (Cambridge, UK: Cambridge University Press, 2014); Virginia Rounding, *Alix and Nicky: The Passion of the Last Tsar and Tsarina* (New York: St. Martin's Press, 2011).
4. Clark, *The Sleepwalkers*; Niall Ferguson, *The Pity of War: Explaining World War I* (New York: Basic Books, 1999); Janos, *The Politics of Backwardness in Hungary*; Keegan, *The First World War*; MacMillan, *The War that Ended Peace*; Hilde Spiel, *Vienna's Golden Autumn, 1866–1938* (New York: Weidenfeld & Nicolson, 1987); and Barbara Tuchman, *The Guns of August* (New York: Dell Books, 1962).

5. Deak, *Forging a Multinational State*, 79.
6. Spiel, 18.
7. Hamilton and Herwig, 239.
8. Redlich, 245.
9. Palmer, 16.
10. Palmer, 309.
11. MacMillan, 76.
12. Carter, 83.
13. Carter, 189.
14. Hamilton and Herwig, 237.
15. Janos, 88.
16. Palmer, 62.
17. Redlich, 412.
18. Palmer, 89.
19. MacMillan, 76.
20. Hamilton and Herwig, 239.
21. Carter, 93.
22. MacMillan, 182.
23. Carter, 326.
24. The title "Tsesarevich" was created in 1797 for the tsar's heir apparent. The similar and more common term, "tsarevich," applied to any tsar's son. See https://en.wikipedia.org/wiki/Tsesarevich.
25. Redlich, 18.
26. Rounding, 94.
27. Rounding, 94.
28. Redlich, 319.
29. Otte, *July Crisis*, 513.
30. Palmer, 169.
31. Redlich, 23 and 42.
32. Palmer, 19.
33. Palmer, 21.
34. Redlich, 246–247.
35. Palmer, 224.
36. Jászi, *The Dissolution of the Habsburg Monarchy*, 154.
37. MacDonogh, 39.
38. John C.G. Röhl, *Young Wilhelm: The Kaiser's Early Life, 1859–1888* (Cambridge, UK: Cambridge University Press, 1998), 292.
39. Tuchman, *The Guns of August*, 7.
40. MacDonogh, 58.
41. Carter, 76.
42. MacMillan, 345.
43. Carter, 56.
44. Carter, 59.
45. Carter, 103.
46. Carter, 182.
47. Carter, 254.
48. Rounding, 77.
49. Radzinsky, 55.
50. Carter, 44–45.
51. Carter, 328–329.
52. Carter, 325.
53. Robert K. Massie, *Peter the Great: His Life and World* (New York: Wings Books, 1991), 67–68.
54. Carter, 61.
55. MacMillan, 275.
56. Gallup Poll, "American Continue to Express Highest Confidence in Military," at http://www.gallup.com/poll/192917/americans-continue-express-highest-confidence-military.aspx?g_source=confidence%20military&g_medium=search&g_campaign=tiles.
57. MacMillan, 221.
58. MacDonogh, 214 and 126.
59. MacMillan, 433.
60. Tuchman, 55.
61. Tuchman, 48.
62. Redlich, 226.
63. MacMillan, *The War that Ended Peace*, 433.
64. Hamilton and Herwig, 54.

65. Hamilton and Herwig, 47.
66. "Who Said, "War Is Too Important to Be Left to Generals?" at http://askville.amazon.com/'war-important-left-generals'/AnswerViewer.do?requestId=3893805.
67. Redlich, 319.
68. Hamilton and Herwig, 239.
69. Hamilton and Herwig, 246.
70. Otte, 511.
71. "Bush: 'I'm the decider' on Rumsfeld," at http://www.cnn.com/2006/POLITICS/04/18/rumsfeld/.
72. Clark, *The Sleepwalkers*, 222.

Chapter 6

1. Robert Coit Chapin, *The Standard of Living among Workingmen's Families in New York City* (New York: Charities Publication Committee, 1909).
2. Chapin, 39.
3. Chapin, 59.
4. Chapin's Table 10 on sources of income indicates that the male (father) contributed 90 percent of the family's income, 63.
5. Chapin, 44.
6. Chapin, 235.
7. Chapin, 231.
8. Chapin, 231–232.
9. Čulen, *History of Slovaks in America*, 162.
10. Čulen, 163.
11. Walter Littlefield, "Inside Story of the Morocco Imbroglio," *New York Times* (June 25, 1905), SM2.
12. Čulen, 63.
13. Maurice R. Davie, *World Immigration: With Special Reference to the United States* (New York: Macmillan, 1936), 126.
14. Davie, 367.
15. On her 1923 passport application, U.S. citizen Zuzanna Mozolák said that she was returning to the United States, having left in May 1906. The infant born earlier that year would have sailed with her parents and twin brother, John.
16. Peter Roberts, *The New Immigration: A Study of the Industrial and Social Life of Southeastern Europeans in America* (New York: Macmillan, 1912), 13.
17. Čulen, 42.
18. Sean Dennis Cashman, "Settlement and Work for the New Immigrants," in Jeff Hay, *Immigration*, 92–99, at p. 96.
19. Wilcox. "International Emigration According to National Statistics: Europe," *International Migrations*, vol. 1, 85–136, at p. 92.
20. Searching the passenger lists at the Northeast Region of National Archives, John Mozolak, Jr., reported that he found this information on reel 876, 44., lines 1–2: "SS Gera (North German Lloyd), Lv Bremen April 12, 1907; Arr NYC April 25, 1907. Samuel 25, laborer and wife Anna, 27. Previously in U.S. 1901–1906. To stay with friend Paul Bucala at 101 ?Galtore or _?_orton Ave."
21. "Triple Enente," at http://gluedideas.com/content-collection/encyclopedia-americana-27/Triple-Entente_P1.html.
22. Gordon Brook-Shepherd, *The Austrians: A Thousand-Year Odyssey* (New York: Carroll & Grad, 1998), 196.
23. Wawro, *A Mad Catastrophe*, 25.
24. Redlich, *Emperor Francis Joseph of Austria*, 394.
25. Gordon Brook-Shepherd, *Royal Sunset: The European Dynasties and the Great War* (Garden City, NY: Doubleday, 1987), 149.
26. Brook-Shepherd, *Royal Sunset*, 150.
27. "The Bulgarian Declaration of Independence, 1908," at https://www.mtholyoke.edu/acad/intrel/boshtml/bos129.htm.

28. Brook-Shepherd, *The Austrians*, 140.
29. "The Annexation of Bosnia-Herzegovina, 1908," at https://www.mtholyoke.edu/acad/intrel/boshtml/bos127.htm.
30. "Balkan Wars," *Encyclopaedia Britannica*, at http://www.britannica.com/EBchecked/topic/50300/Balkan-Wars.
31. MacMillan, *The War that Ended Peace*, xxxi.
32. MacMillan, 418.
33. Mark Wansa, *The Linden and the Oak* (Toronto: World Academy of Rusyn Culture, 2009), 50.
34. Norman Angell, *The Great Illusion* (New York: Putnam, 1910).

Chapter 7

1. Carter, *George, Nicholas, and William*, 101.
2. Carter, 102.
3. Clark, *The Sleepwalkers*, xxv.
4. Clark, xxvii.
5. Carter, xxiv.
6. MacMillan, *The War that Ended Peace*, 73.
7. MacMillan, 73–74.
8. MacMillan, 76.
9. Martin Kitchen, *The Cambridge Illustrated History of Germany* (London: Cambridge University Press, 1996), 216–217.
10. Röhl, *Wilhelm II*, 416.
11. Kitchen, 223–224.
12. Röhl, *Wilhelm II*, xvii.
13. Keegan, *The First World War*, 28.
14. Brook-Shepherd, *The Austrians*, 155.
15. Reported by CNN on April 18, 2006, at http://www.cnn.com/2006/POLITICS/04/18/rumsfeld/.
16. Mark D. Steinberg and Vladimir M. Khrustalëv, *The Fall of the Romanovs: Political Dreams and Personal Struggles* (New Haven: Yale University Press, 1995), 18.
17. Carter, 51.
18. Steinberg and Khrustalëv, 19.
19. Clark, 219.
20. Clark, 267.
21. Carter, 103.
22. Clark, 177–178.
23. Clark, 176.
24. MacMillan, 366.
25. Clark, 178.
26. MacMillan, 603.
27. Deak, *Forging a Multinational State*, 140.
28. Brook-Shepherd, *The Austrians*, 79.
29. Redlich, *Emperor Francis Joseph of Austria*, 428.
30. Wawro, *A Mad Catastrophe*, 6.
31. Ferguson, *The Pity of War*, 117.
32. Wawro, *A Mad Catastrophe*, xix.
33. Alan Palmer, *Twilight of the Habsburgs: The Life and Times of Emperor Francis Joseph* (New York: Grove Press, 1994), p 57.
34. Palmer, 314.
35. Avner Offer makes a similar distinction in "Going to War in 1914: A Matter of Honor?" *Politics & Society*, 23 (1995), 213–241.
36. Frank Maloy Anderson and Amos Shartle Hershey, *Handbook of Diplomatic History of Europe, Asia, and Africa 1870–1914* (Washington, D.C.: Government Printing Office, 1918), 473.
37. Yale Law School Avalon Project at http://avalon.law.yale.edu/imt/partviii.asp.
38. James Davenport Whelpley, *American Public Opinion* (New York: E.P. Dutton, 1914), 264.
39. Sidney Bradshaw Fay, *The Origins of the World War*, vol. 1: *Before Sarajevo: Underlying Causes of the War* (New York: Macmillan, 1928). Digitized by the Internet Archive

in 2014 and available at https://archive.org/details/origin-sofworldwa01sidn.

40. Sidney Bradshaw Fay, *The Origins of the World War*, vol. 2: *After Sarajevo: Immediate Causes of the War* (New York: Macmillan, 1928).

41. Fay, vol. 1, 49.

42. Fay, vol. 2, 558.

43. Fay, vol. 2, 550.

44. Gallup Poll, Apr, 1944. Retrieved Oct-1-2014 from the iPOLL Databank, The Roper Center for Public Opinion Research, University of Connecticut. http://www.ropercenter.uconn.edu/data_access/ipoll/ipoll.html. Later polls asked similar questions and produced similar results.

45. Fritz Fischer, *Griff nach der Weltmacht* (Düsseldorf: Droste, 1961), published in English as *Germany's Aims in the First World War* (London: Chatto & Windus, 1967).

46. Hamilton and Herwig, *Decisions for War*, 67.

47. Richard F. Hamilton and Holger H. Herwig, eds., *The Origins of World War I* (Cambridge: Cambridge University Press, 2003).

48. Hamilton and Herwig, *Decisions for War*.

49. Sheehan, "The Bloody Details," 20.

50. MacMillan, xxv.

51. Clark, *The Sleepwalkers*, xxvii.

52. Clark, xxviii.

53. Geert Mak, *In Europe: Travels Through the Twentieth Century* (New York: Pantheon Books, 2007), 80.

54. Mak, 81–82.

55. Clark devotes a chapter to the assassination: "Murder in Sarajevo," 367–403.

56. MacMillan, 107.

57. Hilde Spiel, *Vienna's Golden Autumn, 1866–1938* (New York: Weidenfeld & Nicolson, 1987), 195.

58. MacMillan, xxxi.

59. MacMillan, 418.

60. MacMillan, 107.

61. Otte, 336.

62. "Liveblogging World War I: July 28, 1914: The Austrian Declaration of War and Manifesto," http://delong.typepad.com/sdj/2014/07/liveblogging-world-war-i-july-28-1914-the-austrian-declaration-of-war-and-manifesto.html.

63. Avner Offer, "Going to War in 1914: A Matter of Honor?" 215.

64. Bertha von Suttner, *Lay Down Your Arms: The Autobiography of Martha von Tillings*, 2nd ed. (New York: Longmans, Green, 1908). The book was originally published in German in 1889. Baroness von Suttner was the first woman to receive the Nobel Peace Prize.

65. Louis Harris & Associates, Harris Survey, Dec. 1980 [survey question]. USHARRIS.010881.R4. Louis Harris & Associates [producer]; Storrs, CT: Roper Center for Public Opinion Research, iPOLL [distributor], accessed Feb-27-2015.

66. Gallup Organization. Gallup Poll, May 2012 [survey question]. USGALLUP.12MAY003.R09. Gallup Organization [producer]; Storrs, CT: Roper Center for Public Opinion Research, iPOLL [distributor], accessed Feb-27-2015.

67. István Deák, *Beyond Nationalism: A Social and Political History of the Habsburg Officer Corps, 1848–1918* (New York: Oxford University Press, 1990), 127.

68. Gunther E. Rothenberg, *The Army of Francis Joseph* (West Lafayette, IN: Purdue University Press, 1976), 182.

69. Brook-Shepherd, *The Austrians*, 152. Of course, Franz Josef spoke in German. Others have translated his statement differently. "If the Monarchy is doomed to perish, at least perish decorously," is how Offer reports it, 227. However, Deák's translation on p. 45, "If we must perish, we should do so with honor," is very close to Brook-Shepherd's.

70. Readily available on the Internet, this political cartoon is variously attributed to a Canadian publication and more specifically to the *Brooklyn Eagle* sometime in July 1914. My search of all issues of the *Brooklyn Eagle* from the last two weeks in June and the first two in August 1914 failed to find it. My email exchange with Samantha Samel, current managing editor of the newspaper, produced this response on December 1, 2014: "You have our permission to use the drawing and the attribution, though we cannot account for the authenticity of the Internet source."

71. Dates, times and text are from "Historia.ro" at http://www.historia.ro/exclusiv_web/general/articol/willy-nicky-telegrams. The exchange is also in Michael S. Neiberg, ed., *The World War I Reader* (New York: New York University Press, 2007), 46–49.

72. Röhl, *Wilhelm II*, 1065.

73. Winston Churchill's *The Unknown War: The Eastern Front* stands as an exception. He devoted three pages to the exchange, beginning on page 107.

74. Lieven, *The End of Tsarist Russia*, 336.

75. Isabel V. Hull, *The Entourage of Kaiser Wilhelm II, 1888–1918* (Cambridge: Cambridge University Press, 1982), 259.

76. Offer, 225.

77. Quoted in Offer, 226.

78. Keegan, *The First World War*, 65.

79. "The July 1914 Crisis: Chronology of Events," at http://www2.uncp.edu/home/rwb/July_Crisis_1914_Chronology.htm.

80. Norman Stone, *The Eastern Front: 1814–1917* (New York: Scribner's, 1975), 75.

81. David Fromkin, *Europe's Last Summer: Who Started the Great War in 1914?* (New York: Knopf, 2004), 299.

82. Churchill, 87.

83. All dates come from Marshall Cavendish Corporation, *History of World War I*. vol. 1: *War and Response, 1914–1916* (New York: Marshall Cavendish, c2002), 84–85.

84. The war's spread across the world is chronicled in Ian F.W. Beckett, *The Great War 1914–1918* (Harlow, UK: Longman, 2001), 67–68.

85. Zweig, *The World of Yesterday*, 430.

86. Otte, 513.

87. Churchill, 101–102.

Chapter 8

1. Jaroslav Hašek, *The Good Soldier Švejk and His Fortunes in the World War* (London: Penguin Books, 1973).

2. Sean McMeekin, *July 1914: Countdown to War* (New York: Basic Books, 2013), 28–29.

3. Clark, *The Sleepwalkers*, 379 and 381.

4. Palka, *My Slovakia, My Family*, 245.

5. Palka, 247.

6. Anton Spiesz, "The Era of a Dual Monarchy (1867–1918)," in Bolchazy, *Illustrated Slovak History*, 166.

7. A.J.P. Taylor, *War by Time-Table: How the First World War Began* (London: Macdonald, 1969), 119.

8. Documentation cited in Gregory C. Ference, "The American Slovaks and the Start of the Great War," paper presented at 27th World Congress of the Czechoslovak Society of Arts & Science (SVU) (Plzeň, Czech Republic, June 29–July 4, 2014), 1.

9. Čulen, *History of Slovaks in America*, 365.

10. Ference, "The American Slovaks and the Start of the Great War." Much of what Ference reported in his paper appeared in his earlier book, *Sixteen Months of Indecision*.

11. Mayynne Sternstein, *Images of Czechs in America* (Charleston, SC: Arcadia, 2008), 71.

12. Wawro, *A Mad Catastrophe*, 114.

13. Hamilton and Herwig, *Decisions for War*, 55.

14. Hamilton and Herwig, 67.

15. Anja Johansen, *Soldiers as Police: The French and Prussian Armies and the Policing of Popular Protest, 1889–1914* (Burlington, VT: Ashgate, 2005), 1.

16. István Deák, "The Habsburg Army in the First and Last Days of World War I: A Comparative Analysis" in Béla K. Király and Nándor F. Dreisziger, eds., *East Central European Society in World War I* (Boulder: Social Science Monographs Vol. 19; Highland Lakes: Atlantic Research and Publications; New York Distributed by Columbia University Press, 1985), 301–312, at p. 304.

17. Judson, *The Habsburg Empire*, 365.

18. According to the account on page 128 in Michal Dugáček and Ján Gálik, eds., *Myjava* (Myjava: Obzor Publisher, 1985), residents of the nearby town of Myjava were rousted by drummer on July 26 to hear that Austria-Hungary was mobilizing its forces.

19. Timrava, "Great War Heroes," in Norma L. Rudinsky (editor and translator), *That Alluring Land: Slovak Stories by Timrava* (Pittsburgh: University of Pittsburgh Press, 1992), 214–216.

20. Timrava, 229.

21. Timrava, 230.

22. Christon I. Archer, John R. Ferris, Holger H. Herwig, and Timothy H.E. Travers, *World History of Warfare* (Lincoln, NE: University of Nebraska Press, 2002), 485.

23. David Laskin, *The Long Way Home* (New York: HarperCollins, 2010).

24. Laskin, xi.

25. Laskin, 138.

26. Laskin, 139.

27. Ferguson, *The Pity of War*, 204–207.

28. Zweig, *The World of Yesterday*, 223.

29. Hastings, *Catastrophe 1914*, 118.

30. Ferguson, *The Pity of War*, 189.

31. Dániel I. Szabó, "The Social Basis of Opposition to the War in Hungary," in Király and Dreisziger, *East Central European Society in World War I*, 135–144, at p. 136.

32. Wawro, *A Mad Catastrophe*, 122.

33. Timrava, 234–235.

34. Rudinski, 270.

35. Deák, "The Habsburg Army in the First and Last Days of World War I," 305.

36. Letter to John Mozolak from Österreichisches Staatsarchiv Kriegsarchiv of November 11, 2004.

37. J.S. Lucas, *Austro-Hungarian Infantry, 1914–1918* (New Malden, UK: Almark Publications, 1973), 107–108.

38. Lucas, 54.

39. Rothenberg, *The Army of Francis Joseph*, 165.

40. Lucas, 7–8.

41. Zweig, 225.

42. Stone, *The Eastern Front*, 126.

43. Deák, *Beyond Nationalism*, 105–106.

44. Lucas, *Austro-Hungarian Infantry*, 19.

45. Lucas, 7–8.

46. Richard Georg Plaschka, "Doberdo: The Army and Internal Conflict in the Austro-Hungarian Empire, 1918," in Király and Dreisziger, *East Central European Society in World War I*, 338–351 at p. 339.

47. Alexander Watson, *Ring of Steel* (New York: Basic Books, 2014), 249.

48. Deák, *Beyond Nationalism*, 101.

49. Keegan, *The First World War*, 156. These percentages are identical to those in Lucas, 4. Winston Churchill's *The Unknown War: The Eastern Front* gave similar but somewhat different figures: "The personnel of the army was 25 per cent German, 23 per cent Magyar, 17 per cent Czecho-Slovak, 11 per cent Serb, Croat and Slovenes, 8 percent Polish, 8 per cent Ukranian [*sic*], 7 per cent Roumanian and 1 per cent Italian." Presumably, the later figures are more accurate.

50. Rothenberg, *The Army of Francis Joseph*, 151.

51. Lucas, *Austro-Hungarian Infantry*, 4.

52. Lucas, 17.

53. Lucas, 6.

54. Stone, *The Eastern Front*, 125.

55. Erich Maria Remarque, *All Quiet on the Western Front* (New York: Random, 1958), 19–20.

56. Remarque, 21.

57. Andrew Krivak, *The Sojourn* (New York: Bellevue Literary Press, 2011), 132–133.

58. May, *The Passing of the Hapsburg Monarchy*, vol. 1, 410–411.

59. Alexander Solzhenitsyn, *August 1914* (New York: Farrar Straus, and Giroux, 1972), 143.

60. Remarque, 203.

61. Remarque, 205.

62. Clark, *The Sleepwalkers*, 229.

63. Clark, 232.

64. Carter, *George, Nicholas, and William*, 202.

65. Carter, 203.

66. Clark, 227.

67. Stephen Fischer Galati, "East Central Europe in World War I," in Király and Dreisziger, *East Central European Society in World War I*, 593–597, at p. 595.

68. Galati, 595.

Chapter 9

1. J.S. Lucas, *Austro-Hungarian Infantry, 1914–1918* (New Malden, UK: Almark Publications, 1973), 4.

2. Brook-Shepherd, *The Austrians*, 134.

3. Redlich, *Emperor Francis Joseph of Austria*, 483.

4. Rothenberg, *The Army of Francis Joseph*, 200.

5. Keegan, *The First World War*, 156.

6. Peter Jung, *The Austro-Hungarian Forces in World War I: 1914–1916 (1)* (Oxford: Osprey, 2003), 3.

7. J.S. Lucas, *Austro-Hungarian Infantry*, 12.

8. Jung, *(1)*, p. 4.

9. Holger H. Herwig, *The First World War: Germany and Austria-Hungary, 1914–1918* (London: Arnold, 1997), 13.

10. Lucas, 6.

11. Rothenberg, *The Army of Francis Joseph*, 128. Rothenberg said there were two Slovak regiments, but Lucas named only one.

12. Wawro, *A Mad Catastrophe*, 34–35.

13. Rothenberg, 130.

14. Stone, *The Eastern Front*, 126.

15. Deák, *Beyond Nationalism*, 179.

16. Jozef Cíger-Hronský, *Jozef Mak* (Columbus, OH: Slavica, 1985; originally published in Slovak in 1933; translated by Andrew Cincura), 108.

17. Deák, 183.

18. Peter H. Wilson, "Defining Military Culture," *The Journal of Military History* 72 (January 2008): 11–41, at p. 24.

19. Tibor Hajdu, "Army and Society in Hungary in the Era of World War I," in Király and Dreisziger, *East Central European Society in World War I*, 112–123, at pp. 113–117.

20. Éva Somogyi, "The Hungarian *Honvéd* Army and the Unity of the Habsburg Empire: The *Honvéd* Reform of 1904," in Király and Dreisziger, *East Central European Society in World War I*, 273–279, at p. 276.

21. Somogyi, 276.

22. Somogyi, 274.

23. Judson, *The Habsburg Empire*, 363.

24. Deak, 303–304.

25. Hamilton and Herwig wrote: "The ethnic conflicts in Austria-Hungary blocked provision of requisite funds for modernization of the armed forces." Hamilton and Holger H. Herwig, *Decisions for War*, 16.

26. Palmer, 282.

27. Arthur J. May used this term, but not specifically in this context, in *The Passing of the Hapsburg Monarch*, vol. 1, 6.

28. Wawro, *A Mad Catastrophe*, 35.

29. Clark, *The Sleepwalkers*, 217.

30. Gunther Rothenberg, "The Hungarian Army in the First World War: 1914–1918," in Király and Dreisziger, *East Central European Society in World War I*, 289–300, at p. 290.

31. Discussing the 1912 recruitment law, Rothenberg gave these figures: 136,000 troops in the common army, 20,715 in the Austrian *Landwehr*, and 17,500 in the Hungarian *Honvédseg* (p. 165). Those numbers would total to about 175,000, which is considerably less than the 335,000 given by Wawro for 1913 (pp. 35–36). They are also less than and the 415,000 cited by Jung (p. 4).

32. János Decsy, "The Hungarian Army on the Threshold of Total War," in Király and Dreisziger, *East Central European Society in World War I*, 280–288, at p. 284.

33. J.S. Lucas, *Austro-Hungarian Infantry*, 8.

34. The data appear in the Spartacus Educational website created by John Simpkin. See "Armies, 1914," at http://spartacus-educational.com/FWWarmies1914.htm.

35. Zombory-Moldován, *The Burning of the World*, 40.

36. Hastings, *Catastrophe 1914*, 503.

37. János Decsy, "The Hungarian Army on the Threshold of Total War," in Király and Dreisziger, *East Central European Society in World War I*, 280–288, at p. 284.

38. Zombory-Moldován, 47.

39. Decsy, 284.

40. Decsy, 284.

41. J.S. Lucas, *Austro-Hungarian Infantry*, 96–99.

42. Jung *(1)*, 6.

43. Descsy, 296.

44. Albert A. Nofi, "Comparative Divisional Strengths During World War I: European Belligerents and Theaters," in Király and Dreisziger, *East Central European Society in World War I*, 263–270.

45. Nofi also reported the number of Turkish divisions in the Eastern theaters. These Turkish divisions are not included with the Central Powers in the graph for Turkish troops were engaged on six different fronts: Gallipoli, Syria-Egypt, Arabia, Mesopotamia, Persia, and the Caucasus. Figures for Russia also include divisions engaged in areas, primarily against the Ottoman Empire.

46. Hastings, *Catastrophe 1914*, 56.

47. Edwin A. Pratt, *The Rise of Rail-Power in War and Conquest, 1833–1914* (Philadelphia: J.B. Lippincott, 1916).

48. Pratt, 2.

49. Pratt, 9.

50. Pratt, 10.

51. Pratt, 104.

52. Pratt, 105–106.

53. Pratt, 110.

54. Pratt, 138.

55. Clark, *The Sleepwalkers*, 336.

56. Pratt, 100.

57. Colette Hooper, *Railways of the Great War* (London: Bantam Press, 2014), 20.

58. Hooper, 30–31.

59. Hooper, 29.

60. Hooper, 32.

61. Clark, 331.

62. See "Russian Railways" at http://eng.rzd.ru/statice/public/en/rzdeng?STRUCTURE_ID=30#1.

63. Economic and Financial Section, *International Statistical Year-Book 1926* (Geneva: League of Nations, 1927), Table 79, page 122.

64. Economic and Financial Section, Table 1, page 14.

65. David Stevenson, *Cataclysm: The First World War as Political Tragedy* (New York: Basic Books, 2004), 24.

66. In an email of October 31, 2016, noted historical geographer Paul Robert Magocsi kindly shared his maze of existing European railroad lines in 1914, which is too detailed to reproduce here.

67. Rothenberg, *The Army of Francis Joseph*, 160.

68. MacMillan, *The War that Ended Peace*, 355.

69. Wawro, *A Mad Catastrophe*, 91.

70. David Stevenson, "War by Timetable? The Railway Race Before 1914," *Past and Present*, 162 (1991), 163–194, at pp. 161–162.

71. Peter Englund, *The Beauty and the Sorrow: An Intimate History of the First World War* (New York: Alfred A. Knopf, 2011), 343.

72. Herwig, 74.

73. Tuchman, *The Guns of August*, 101–102.

74. Stevenson, 162.

75. Keegan, *The First World War*, 24–25.

Chapter 10

1. Dániel I. Szabó, "The Social Basis of Opposition to the War in Hungary," in Király and Dreisziger, *East Central European Society in World War I*, 140.

2. Szabó, 141.

3. Szabó, 135–144.

4. Lukačka, *Krajné: 1392–1992*, 42–44, original in Slovak.

5. See Ina Zweiniger-Bargielowska, Rachel Duffett, and Alain Drouard, eds., *Food and War in Twentieth Century Europe* (Burlington, VT: Ashgate, 2011).

6. Szabó, 139.

7. May, *The Passing of the Hapsburg Monarchy*, vol. 1, 398–399.

8. Martin Franc, "Bread from Wood: Natural Food Substitutes in the Czech Lands during the First World War," in Ina Zweiniger-Bargielowska, Rachel Duffett, and Alain Drouard, eds., *Food and War in Twentieth Century Europe* (Burlington, VT: Ashgate, 2011), 73–97, at p. 74.

9. Gary W. Shanafelt, *The Secret Enemy: Austria-Hungary and the German Alliance, 1914–1918* (Boulder, CO: East European Monographs, 1985), 135.

10. Alexander Watson, *Ring of Steel* (New York: Basic Books, 2014), 345.

11. May, *The Passing of the Hapsburg Monarchy*, vol. 1, 6.

12. Healy, *Vienna and the Fall of the Habsburg Empire*, 50.

13. Healy, 47.

14. Healy, 49.

15. Healy, 50.

16. Hastings, *Catastrophe 1914*, 505.

17. Englund, *The Beauty and the Sorrow*, 216–217.

18. Herwig, *The First World War*, 108.

19. Herwig, 434.

20. Peter Lummel, "Food Provisioning in the German Army of the First World War," in Zweiniger-Bargielowska, Duffett, and Drouard, *Food and War in Twentieth Century Europe*, 19.

21. Mark Wansa, *The Linden and the Oak* (Toronto: World Academy of Rusyn Culture, 2009), 182.

22. Krivak, 92–93.

23. Hašek, 724.

24. Horst Haselsteiner, "The Habsburg Empire in World War I: Mobilization of Food Supplies," in Király and Dreisziger, *East Central European Society in World War I*, 87–102, at pp. 88–89.

25. Marshall Cavendish Corporation, *History of World War I*, vol. 3: *Home Fronts/Technologies of War* (New York: Marshall Cavendish, c2002), 874.

26. J.S. Lucas, *Austro-Hungarian Infantry, 1914–1918*. (New Malden, UK: Almark Publications, 1973), 18.
27. Lucas, 18–19.
28. Lucas, 18.
29. Keegan, *The First World War*, 33.
30. Zombory-Moldován, *The Burning of the World*, 27.
31. Herwig, *The First World War*, 56.
32. Deák, *Beyond Nationalism*, 193–194.
33. Winston S. Churchill, *The World Crisis, 1911–1918*, abridged and revised edition (London: Macmillan, 1941), 157.
34. Remarque, *All Quiet on the Western Front*, 59.
35. Beckett, *The Great War 1914–1918*, 44.
36. MacMillan, *The War that Ended Peace*, 330.
37. Tuchman, *The Guns of August*, 48.
38. Stephen Van Evera, "The Cult of the Offensive and the Origins of the First World War," *International Security* 9 (Summer 1984): 58–107, at pp. 58 and 60.
39. Herwig, *The First World War*, 53.
40. MacMillan, *The War that Ended Peace*, 330.
41. Jung, *The Austro-Hungarian Forces in World War I: 1914–1916 (1)*; Peter Jung, *The Austro-Hungarian Forces in World War I: 1916–1918 (2)* (Oxford, UK: Osprey, 2003).
42. Englund, *The Beauty and the Sorrow*, 14.
43. Rothenberg, *The Army of Francis Joseph*, 150.
44. Englund, *The Beauty and the Sorrow*, 343.
45. Carter, *George, Nicholas, and William*, 387.
46. Hastings, *Catastrophe 1914*, 392.
47. Churchill, *The Unknown War*, 287.
48. Remarque, 138.
49. Stephen Currie, *World War I: Life in the Trenches* (San Diego, CA: Lucent Books, 2002), 82.
50. E. Norman Gladden, *Across the Piave: A Personal Account of the British Forces in Italy, 1917–1919* (London: Her Majesty's Stationery Office, 1971), 30.
51. Gladden, 90.
52. Jaroslav Hašek, *The Good Soldier Švejk and His Fortunes in the World War* (London: Penguin Books, 1973), 598 to 661.
53. *Oxford Universal Dictionary*, 1937.
54. Remarque, 7–8.
55. Remarque, 62.
56. Hašek, 598.
57. Kirchberger, 881.
58. Zweig, *The World of Yesterday*, 223.
59. Hew Strachan, "Economic Mobilization: Money, Munitions, and Machines," in Hew Strachan, ed., *World War I: A History*. Oxford (New York: Oxford University Press, 1998), 134–148, at p. 137.
60. Strachan, 137.
61. Currie, 20.
62. Churchill, *The World Crisis*, 300.
63. Original reads: "OFFICIAL PHOTOGRAPH TAKEN ON THE BRITISH WESTERN FRONT IN FRANCE. Some shell cases on the roadside in the front area, the contents of which have been despatched over into the German lines." National Library of Scotland, taken circa 1918. No known copyright restrictions.
64. Leonard V. Smith, "Narrative and Identity at the Front: Theory and the Poor Bloody Infantry," in Jay Winter, Geoffrey Parker, and Mary R. Habeck, eds., *The Great War and the Twentieth Century* (New Haven: Yale University Press, 2000), 132–165 at p. 138.
65. Wawro, *A Mad Catastrophe*, 8.
66. Stone, *The Eastern Front*, 13.
67. Marshall Cavendish Corporation, *History of World War I*. vol. 2: *Victory and Defeat, 1917–1918* (New York: Marshall Cavendish, c2002), 479.
68. Beckett, *The Great War 1914–1918*, 258.
69. Strachan, 145; J.S. Lucas in *Austro-Hungarian Infantry 1914–1918* reports increases in its machine-gun sections, but the numbers are difficult to compare.
70. Healy, 107.
71. Timrava, "Great War Heroes," in Norma L. Rudinsky (editor and translator), *That Alluring Land: Slovak Stories by Timrava* (Pittsburgh: University of Pittsburgh Press, 1992), 296.
72. Timrava, 302–303.
73. Hastings, *Catastrophe 1914*, 402.
74. Dorothy Giles, *The Road through Czechoslovakia* (Philadelphia: Penn Publishing Co., 1930), 43.

Chapter 11

1. Robert K. Massie, *Peter the Great: His Life and World* (New York: Alfred A. Knopf, 1980), 306.
2. Massie, 307.
3. "Battle of Solferino," at http://en.wikipedia.org/wiki/Battle_of_Solferino.
4. MacMillan, *The War that Ended Peace*, 320.
5. MacMillan, 321.
6. Taylor, *War by Time-Table*.
7. Brook-Shepherd, *Royal Sunset*, 313.
8. Clark, *The Sleepwalkers*, 178.
9. Röhl, *Wilhelm II*, 1009.
10. Carter, *George, Nicholas, and William*, 384.
11. Röhl, 1011.
12. MacDonogh, *The Last Kaiser*, 3.
13. Röhl, 1011.
14. Churchill, *The Unknown War*, 324.
15. Churchill, *The World Crisis*, 749–750.
16. Carter, *George, Nicholas, and William*, 407.
17. Shanafelt, *The Secret Enemy*, 108.
18. Herwig, *The First World War*, 381.
19. Carter, *George, Nicholas, and William*, xxi.
20. C.L. Sulzberger, *The Fall of Eagles* (New York: Crown, 1977), 376.
21. Carter, *George, Nicholas, and William*, 386.
22. Alexander Solzhenitsyn, *August 1914* (New York: Farrar Straus, and Giroux, 1972), 587.
23. Solzhenitsyn, 586.
24. Carter, 386–387.
25. Carter, 388.
26. Churchill, *The Unknown War*, 378.
27. Carter, 398.
28. Churchill, *The Unknown War*, 375.
29. John W. Boyer, "The End of an Old Regime: Visions of Political Reform in Late Imperial Austria," *Journal of Modern History* 8 (March 1986): 171.
30. Clark, *The Sleepwalkers*, 183.
31. Lieven, *The End of Tsarist Russia*, 92.
32. Palmer, *Twilight of the Habsburgs*, 312.
33. Samuel R. Williamson, Jr., "Influence, Power, and the Policy Process: The Case of Franz Ferdinand, 1906–1914," *The Historical Journal* 17 (June 1974): 417–434, at p. 419.
34. Spiel, *Vienna's Golden Autumn*, 196.
35. Ferguson, *The Pity of War*, 148.
36. Hastings, *Catastrophe 1914*, xxix.
37. Wawro, *A Mad Catastrophe*, 95.
38. Williamson, Jr., "Influence, Power, and the Policy Process," 417–434, at p. 434.
39. McMeekin, *July 1914*, 391.
40. Redlich, *Emperor Francis Joseph of Austria*, 530.
41. May, *The Passing of the Hapsburg Monarchy*, vol. 1, 61–62.
42. Shanafelt, *The Secret Enemy*, 37.
43. Redlich, *Emperor Francis Joseph of Austria*, 533.
44. Redlich, 533–534.
45. Film footage of Franz Josephs funeral at https://www.youtube.com/watch?v=KE3e6Y7MkKc.

46. May, *The Passing of the Hapsburg Monarchy*, vol. 1, 422–432.

47. May, 424–425.

48. Deák, *Beyond Nationalism*, 60.

49. Herwig, *The First World War*, 8.

50. Herwig, 273.

51. Judson, *The Habsburg Empire*, 341.

52. John Deak, "The Great War and the Forgotten Realm: The Habsburg Monarchy and the First World War," *The Journal of Modern History* 86, No. 2 (June 2014): 336–380.

53. Judson, 343.

54. Deak's essay mentions the "Dual Monarchy" 10 times, and "Austria-Hungary" 31 times, making it seem that he was addressing both halves of the Habsburg realm. Inspection of the text, however, shows that he was really writing about Austria. Apart from its mention 31 times in the country name, "Hungary" appears in only two sentences—and only incidentally—in the entire essay of 40+ pages.

55. Wawro, 15.

56. Palmer, *Twilight of the Habsburgs*, 285.

57. Karl has an alternative spelling as Charles. Authors in the period, such as Joseph Redlich, referred to him as Karl, and some contemporary German historians, such as Holger Herwig, still do so. Authors today sometimes call Austria-Hungary's last emperor Charles to distinguish him from Archduke Karl von Habsburg, the grandson of Charles I, born in 1961.

58. Shanafelt, *The Secret Enemy*, 103.

59. Herwig, 229.

60. Shanafelt, 193.

61. Herwig, 436.

62. Sulzberger, *The Fall of Eagles*, 350.

63. Sulzberger, 350.

64. Zweig, *The World of Yesterday*, 283.

65. *The Fall of Eagles*, a BBC TV series of 13 episodes at http://www.imdb.com/title/tt0207885/.

66. Beckett, *The Great War 1914–1918*, 51.

67. Michael S. Neiberg, *Fighting the Great War: A Global History* (Cambridge: Harvard University Press, 2005), 40–41.

68. Alexander Watson, *Ring of Steel* (New York: Basic Books, 2014), 160–161.

69. Wawro, *A Mad Catastrophe*, 51.

70. William C. Fuller, Jr., "The Eastern Front," in Jay Winter, Geoffrey Parker, and Mary R. Habeck, eds., *The Great War and the Twentieth Century* (New Haven: Yale University Press, 2000), 30–68 at p. 34.

71. Churchill, *The World Crisis*, 114.

72. Churchill, *The World Crisis*, 83.

73. David Stevenson, *Cataclysm: The First World War as Political Tragedy* (New York: Basic Books, 2004), 24.

74. Terrence Zuber, "The Schlieffen Plan Reconsidered," *War in History* 6 (July 1999), 262–305, especially p. 305: "There never was a 'Schlieffen plan.'"

75. David Fromkin, *Europe's Last Summer: Who Started the Great War in 1914?* (New York: Knopf, 2004), 34; Christon I, Archer, John R. Ferris, Holger H. Herwig, and Timothy H.E. Travers, *World History of Warfare* (Lincoln, NE: University of Nebraska Press, 2002), 485.

76. See Zuber, 304.

77. Watson, 107.

78. Herwig, *The First World War*, 9.

79. Rothenberg, *The Army of Francis Joseph*, 139.

80. Stone, *The Eastern Front*, 306.

81. Röhl, *Wilhelm II*, 1019.

82. Stone, *The Eastern Front*, 76.

83. János Decsy, "The Hungarian Army on the Threshold of Total War," in Király, and Dreisziger, *East Central European Society in World War I*, 280–288, at p. 283.

84. D.E. Showalter, "Manœuvre Warfare: The Eastern and Western Fronts, 1914–1915," in Hew Strachan, ed., *World War I*, 39–53 at p. 47.

85. Churchill, *The Unknown War*, 132.

86. Keegan, *The First World War*, 28.

87. Palmer, *Twilight of the Habsburg*, 305.

88. Beckett, *The Great War 1914–1918*, 50.

89. Shanafelt, *The Secret Enemy*, 32.

90. Shanafelt, 32.

91. Jeff Shaara, *To the Last Man: A Novel of the First World War* (New York: Ballantine Books, 2004), 117.

Chapter 12

1. "Verzeichnis über beantragte (verliehene) Auszeichnungen [Registry of requested (awarded) commendations]," December 13, 1917.

2. Lucas, *Austro-Hungarian Infantry*, 54.

3. Churchill, *The World Crisis*, 155.

4. The story was datelined Northern France, December 30. It was rerun under "Topics of the Times," *New York Times* (February 10, 1915), 10.

5. Stanley Weintraub, *Silent Night: The Story of World War I Christmas Truce* (New York: The Free Press, 2001), see "Sources" at the end.

6. Weintraub, xvii.

7. "Topics of the Times," *New York Times* (February 10, 1915), 10.

8. Weintraub, 170–172.

9. Hastings, *Catastrophe 1914*, 556.

10. Hastings, 557.

11. *Ibid.*

12. Kevin J. McNamara, *Dreams of a Great Small Nation: The Mutinous Army that Threatened a Revolution, Destroyed an Empire, Founded a Republic, and Remade the Map of Europe* (New York: Public Affairs, 2016), 57.

13. May, *The Passing of the Hapsburg Monarchy*, vol. 1, 121–122.

14. Herwig, *The First World War*, 244.

15. Herwig, 105.

16. Neiberg, *Fighting the Great War*, 59; "Serbian Campaign of World War I" at http://en.wikipedia.org/wiki/Serbian_Campaign_of_World_War_I#Austro-Hungarian.

17. Fromkin, *Europe's Last Summer*, 301.

18. Churchill, *The World Crisis*, 512.

19. In *The Unknown War*, Winston Churchill wrote on page 356: "In their rejoicings over the campaign against Serbia there had mingled a strong strain of irritation. This longed-for event had in the end been a German achievement."

20. Christine Hatt, *World War I 1914–1918* (Danbury, CT: Franklin Watts, 2001), 23.

21. Alan Palmer, *The Gardeners of Salonika* (New York: Simon & Schuster, 1965), p 71.

22. Jan Slomka, *From Serfdom to Self-Government: Memoirs of a Polish Village Mayor, 1842–1927* (London: Minerva, 1941), 207.

23. Slomka, 213.

24. Beckett, *The Great War 1914–1918*, 58.

25. Rothenberg, "The Hungarian Army in the First World War," in Király and Dreisziger, *East Central European Society in World War I*, 289–300 at p. 293.

26. Shanafelt, *The Secret Enemy*, 46.

27. Christon I. Archer, John R. Ferris, Holger H. Herwig, and Timothy H.E. Travers, *World History of Warfare* (Lincoln, NE: University of Nebraska Press, 2002), 483.

28. Jan Slomka, *From Serfdom to Self-Government*, 232.

29. Slomka, 221.

30. Watson, *Ring of Steel*, illustration 5 between pages 392 and 393.

31. Watson, 153–154.

32. Watson, 154.

33. Watson, 170–181.

34. Watson, 181–182.

35. R.A. Reiss, *Report Upon the Atrocities Committed by the Austro-Hungarian Army During the First Invasion of Serbia,* trans. F.S. Copeland (London: Simpkin, Marshall, Hamilton, Kent, 1916).

36. Stéphane Audoin-Rouzeau and Annette Becker, eds., *14–18: Understanding the Great War* (New York: Hill and Wang, 2002), 47.

37. May, *The Passing of the Hapsburg Monarchy,* 131–132.

38. The book is Miroslav Honzik and Hana Honzikóvá, *1914/1918: Léta zkázy a naděje [Thee years of destruction and hope]* (Nejnovější vydání, 1984).

39. John Reed quoted in Neiberg, 57.

40. Remarque, *All Quiet on the Western Front,* 113.

41. Wansa, *The Linden and the Oak,* 153.

42. Timrava, "Great War Heroes," 284.

43. William Philpott, *The War of Attrition: Fighting the First World War* (New York: Overlook Press, 2014), 47.

44. Timothy Snyder, *The Red Prince: The Secret Lives of a Habsburg Archduke* (New York: Basic Books, 2008), 82.

45. Watson, 283.

46. Joe H. Kirchberger, *The First World War: An Eyewitness History* (New York: Facts on File, 1992), 877–878.

47. Herwig, 296.

48. Herwig, 296.

49. Leo van Bergen, *Before My Helpless Sight: Suffering, Dying and Military Medicine on the Western Front, 1914–1918* (Burlington, VT: Ashgate, 2009), 16. Translated from Dutch edition 1999.

50. Van Bergan, 16–17.

51. Van Bergen, 166–167. A similar figure of 76 percent German casualties in 1917 from artillery fire was cited by Ian Kershaw, *To Hell and Back: Europe, 1914–1949* (New York: Viking, 2014), 64.

52. Van Bergen, 446. Kershaw claimed only 0.1 percent of German soldiers in 1917 died due to hand-to-hand fighting, 64.

53. Herwig, 296.

54. Van Bergen, 33.

55. Edward A. Gutiérrez, *Doughboys on the Great War: How American Soldiers Viewed Their Military Service* (Lawrence: University of Kansas, 2014), 121.

56. Van Bergen, 167.

57. Van Bergen, 451.

58. Van Bergen, 4501–451.

59. Van Bergen, 408.

60. Gabriel Chevallier, *Fear: A Novel of World War I* (New York: New York Review Books, 2014; originally published in 1930, translated from the French by Malcolm Imrie), 211.

61. Philpott, 232.

62. Philpott, 213.

63. Reference to the 10th *Honved* is not clear. One source states that the 10th Infantry Division was sent to Italy before this battle. (See http://thoughtsonmilitaryhistory10.weebly.com/64---631-south.html.) Some 10th brigades and regiments participated in the battle, but no divisions had that number. Perhaps 10th is a miss type of 70th.

64. "The Brusilov Offensive, June 4, 1916," at http://thoughtsonmilitaryhistory10.weebly.com/64---631-north.html.

65. Watson, 305.

66. Philpott, 240.

67. Zweig, *The World of Yesterday,* 249–250.

68. Today, Ružomberok has a large, modern hospital and also operates a military hospital.

69. Samko's grandson, John Mozolak, Jr., reported on conversations with his father, the young Ján who visited his father in the hospital.

70. Neiberg, *Fighting the Great War,* 204.

71. Watson, 16.

72. Liviu Rebreneau, "We'll See What You Do There..." in Peter Ayrton, ed., *No Man's Land: Fiction from a World at War: 1914–1918* (New York: Pegasus Books, 2014), 278–284 at pp. 281–282.

73. Peter Pastor, "The Home Front in Hungary, 1914–18," in Király and Dreisziger, *East Central European Society in World War I,* 124–134 at p. 130.

74. Herwig, 218.

75. "The Battle of Oituz in Romania 8–28 August 1917," at http://1914–1918.invisionzone.com/forums/index.php?/topic/117786-the-battle-of-oituz-in-romania-8-28-august-1917/.

76. Glenn E Torrey, *The Romanian Battlefront in World War I* (Lawrence: University of Kansas Press, 2011), 257.

77. Torrey, 265.

78. Peter Hart, *The Great War: A Combat History of the First World War* (Oxford, UK: Oxford University Press, 2013), 378.

79. "Austro-Hungarian Armies, Southwest Front/Italian Theater, 15 June 1918," at http://www.cgsc.edu/CARL/nafziger/918AFAA.pdf.

80. Neiberg, *Fighting the Great War,* 252.

81. *Encyclopædia Britannica* at http://www.britannica.com/EBchecked/topic/296437/Battles-of-the-Isonzo.

82. Ernest Hemingway, *A Farewell to Arms* (New York: Scribner, 1957), 186.

83. Bernard Wasserstein, *Barbarism and Civilization: A History of Europe in Our Time* (UK: Oxford University Press, 2007), 62.

84. Englund, *The Beauty and the Sorrow,* 401.

85. Wasserstein, 62.

86. Herwig, 344.

87. Deák, *Beyond Nationalism,* 192.

88. Shanafelt, *The Secret Enemy,* 149.

89. Watson, 512.

90. Deák, "The Habsburg Army in the First and Last Days of World War I," in Király and Dreisziger, *East Central European Society in World War I,* at p. 309.

91. Mike Bennighof, "Austria-Hungary's Last Offensive: Summer 1918," *Strategy and Tactics* (July–August 2000): 4–14, at p. 6.

92. Bennighof, 11.

93. Austin West, "Foe's Dead Block Defiles: Mountain Slopes Black With Bodies of Austrian Storming Troops," *New York Times* (June 19, 1918) pg. 1.

94. David Raab, *Battle of the Piave: Death of the Austro-Hungarian Army, 1918* (Pittsburgh: Dorrance, 2003), 75.

95. Douglas Wilson Johnson, *Battlefields of the World War* (New York: Oxford University Press, 1921), 534.

96. Bennighof, 10.

97. Johnson, 535.

98. Bennighof, 11.

99. Raab, 76.

100. Andrew Krivak, *The Sojourn* (New York: Bellevue Literary Press, 2011), 126.

101. Bennighof, 11.

102. Raab, 77.

103. "The Italian Victory," *The Advertiser* (June 27, 1918): 5; at http://trove.nla.gov.au/ndp/del/article/5567657.

104. Shanafelt, 197.

105. Zeman, *The Break-up of the Habsburg Empire,* 56.

106. Campbell Stuart, *Secrets of Crewe House: The Story of a Famous Campaign* (London: Hodder and Stoughton, 1921), 8–17.

107. Stuart, 39.

108. Stuart, original inserted between pages 176 and 177; translation on page 250.

109. Victor S. Mamatey, *The United States and East Central Europe, 1914–1918: A Study in Wilsonian Diplomacy and Propaganda* (Princeton, NJ: Princeton University Press, 1957), 247.

110. Stuart, 20.

111. Mark Cornwall, *The Undermining of Austria-Hungary: The Battle for Hearts and Minds* (New York: St. Martin's Press, 2000), 433.

112. Cornwall, 362–364.

113. Rothenberg, *The Army of Francis Joseph*, 214.

114. Cornwall, 408.

Chapter 13

1. Herwig, *The First World War*, 112.

2. Herwig, 120.

3. Victor S. Mamatey summarized the German rescues of Austro-Hungarian troops on p. 21 of *The United States and East Central Europe*: "The German High Command directed the successful campaign that resulted in driving the Russians out of Poland (May–September 1915). The Germans also directed the punitive campaign against Serbia (October 1915 to January 1916). "They also saved the situation when the Russians broke through the Austrian lines at Lutsk and lunged forward into Galicia again (the Brusilov offensive, June–July 1916). They also hastened to the rescue of the Austrians when little Rumania entered the war and invaded Transylvania (August–September 1916)."

4. Herwig, 105.

5. That quotation appears in many places. See "World War I: Opening Campaigns," at http://militaryhistory.about.com/od/worldwari/a/wwi1914_2.htm.

6. Watson, *Ring of Steel*, 558.

7. Shanafelt, *The Secret Enemy*.

8. Shanafelt, 53.

9. Shanafelt, 56.

10. Shanafelt, 65.

11. May, *The Passing of the Hapsburg Monarchy*, 428.

12. Brook-Shepherd, *The Austrians*, 184.

13. Brook-Shepherd, 191.

14. Watson, 374.

15. Watson, 278.

16. Herwig, 313.

17. Watson, 463.

18. Herwig, 384.

19. Neiberg, *Fighting the Great War*, 208.

20. Herwig, 392.

21. Watson, 524.

22. John Richard Schindler, "A Hopeless Struggle: The Austro-Hungarian Army and Total War, 1919–1918" (Ph.D. diss., McMaster University, 1995), 228.

23. Schindler, 237, 265.

24. Watson, 526–527.

25. Shanafelt, 202.

26. Herwig, 425.

27. As edited from the summary, at "Woodrow Wilson," *History Learning Site*, at http://www.historylearningsite.co.uk/woodrow_wilson1.htm. Points 10 and 11 dropped the phrase "self-determination," which was not in Wilson's Fourteen Points. The complete set is given at "President Wilson's Fourteen Points," at http://avalon.law.yale.edu/20th_century/wilson14.asp.

28. U.S. State Department at https://history.state.gov/milestones/1914–1920/fourteen-points.

29. Zara Steiner, "The Peace Settlement," in Hew Strachan, ed., *World War I: A History* (New York: Oxford University Press, 1998), 291–304.

30. May, *The Passing of the Hapsburg Monarchy*, 561.

31. David Lloyd George, "British War Aims," Statement of January 5, 1918, to the British Trades Union League, Authorized Version as published by the British Government (New York: George H. Doran, 1918), at http://wwi.lib.byu.edu/index.php/Prime_Minister_Lloyd_George_on_the_British_War_Aims.

32. Wansa, *The Linden and the Oak*, 318.

33. Rothenberg, *The Army of Francis Joseph*, 210.

34. See "The Great War Timeline," at http://www.greatwar.co.uk/timeline/ww1-events-1918.htm.

35. Judson's *The Habsburg Empire* makes a similar claim. Judson said that the imperial state was "increasingly justifying its existence in terms of its ability to promote the development of its constituent nations" (p. 270), and said of the Habsburg empire: "Its distinctiveness may lie in the positive ways that empire sought to negotiate the cultural differences that became a key factor in political life and ultimately in the ways it sought to make political and social institutions organized around such differences function effectively" (p. 452).

36. Deak, "The Great War and the Forgotten Realm," 336–380. See also his *Forging a Multinational State*.

37. Deak, *Forging a Multinational State*, 226.

38. Although John Deak's essay "The Great War and the Forgotten Realm" was on "the Habsburg Monarchy," Deak really only discussed the Austrian half of the Dual Monarchy. Apart from its mention 31 times in the country name, "Hungary" appears in only two sentences—and only incidentally—in the entire essay. Similarly, his comprehensive book *Forging a Multinational State* focuses only on "imperial Austria," rarely discusses discrimination of non-German minorities in Austria, and never mentions discrimination against non-Magyars in Hungary.

39. Herwig, 425.

40. Stone, *World War I*, 177–179.

41. May, *The Passing of the Hapsburg Monarchy*, 250–286.

42. "Czechoslovak National Council," at http://en.wikipedia.org/wiki/Czechoslovak_National_Council.

43. Stolarik, "The Role of American Slovaks in the Creation of Czecho-Slovakia," 7–82.

44. Alan Palmer, *Victory 1918* (New York: Atlantic Monthly Press, 1998), 268.

45. Zeman, *The Break-up of the Habsburg Empire*, 185.

46. Cornwall, *The Undermining of Austria-Hungary*, 11.

47. Cornwall, 40–41.

48. Seton-Watson, *Racial Problems in Hungary*; Henry Wickham Steed, *The Hapsburg Monarchy*, 3rd ed. (London: Constable and Company, 1914).

49. László Péter, "R.W. Seton-Watson's Changing Views on the National Question of the Habsburg Monarchy and the European Balance of Power," *Slavonic and East European Review* 82 (July 2004): 655–679 at p. 665.

50. Zeman, 185.

51. James Ramon Felak, "Review of Jan Rychlík, Thomas D. Marzik, and Miroslav Bielik, eds., *R.W. Seton-Watson and His Relations with the Czechs and Slovaks: Documents 1906–1951/ R.W. Seton-Watson a jeho vztahy k Cechum a Slovakum: dokumenty 1906–1951*." HABSBURG, H-Net Reviews. March 1998, at http://www.h-net.org/reviews/showrev.php?id=1819.

52. Indeed, historian John Deak wrote, "One hundred years later, depictions of the Habsburg monarchy in studies of the Great War still owe much more to wartime propaganda than to actual historical research." See Deak, "The Great War and the Forgotten Realm," 336–380.

53. Zeman, 215.

54. C.L. Sulzberger, *The Fall of Eagles* (New York: Crown, 1977), 348–349.

55. Timothy Snyder, *The Red Prince: The Secret Lives*

of a Habsburg Archduke (New York: Basic Books, 2008), 117.

56. Palka, *My Slovakia, My Family*, 251–252.
57. Herwig, 436.
58. Herwig, 437.
59. Palka, 252.
60. Judson, 433.
61. Mamatey, *The United States and East Central Europe*, 344.
62. Taylor, *The Habsburg Monarchy*, 251.
63. Neiberg, 356.
64. The terms of the armistice are given at http://www.firstworldwar.com/source/armisticeterms.htm.
65. Nieberg, 361.
66. Laurence Rees, *Hitler's Charisma: Leading Millions into the Abyss* (New York: Pantheon Books, 2012), 14.
67. Beckett, *The Great War 1914–1918*, 396.
68. Gunther Rothenberg, "The Hungarian Army in the First World War: 1914–1918," in Király and Dreisziger, *East Central European Society in World War I*, 289–300, at p. 297.
69. Mike Bennighof, "Austria-Hungary's Last Offensive: Summer 1918," *Strategy and Tactics* (July–August 2000): 4–14 at p. 14.
70. Rees, 14.
71. Many Internet sources mention this quotation by the German chancellor. One is "Popular Myths and the Conspiracy Theory: 'the stab in the back' 1918," at http://general-history.com/popular-myths-and-the-conspiracy-theory-the-stab-in-the-back-1918/.
72. Margaret MacMillan, *Paris 1919: Six Months That Changed the World* (New York: Random House, 2002).
73. MacMillan, illustration 4, seating chart.
74. MacMillan, 53.
75. BYU Library, World War I Document Archive, http://wwi.lib.byu.edu/index.php/Conventions_and_Treaties.
76. MacMillan, 192.
77. Quoted in MacMillan, 467.
78. John Maynard Keynes, *The Economic Consequences of Peace* (London: Macmillan, 1919).
79. MacMillan, 493.
80. Quoted in MacMillan, 469.
81. Although this map is titled *Peace Map of Europe: July 4, 1918*, the date must be merely symbolic, for the map depicts the "final battle line, Nov. 11, 1918." Still, the map, which bears 1919 as the year of publication, appears to have been drawn before the 1920 Treaty of Trianon finalized the boundaries of Hungary and other countries.
82. "First World War Casualties," at http://www.historylearningsite.co.uk/?s=casualties1.
83. Stolarik, *Where Is My Home?*, 15.
84. League of Nations, Economic and Financial Section, *International Statistical Year-Book, 1927* (Geneva: Publications of the League of Nations, 1928), Table 1, page 14. These data are available online from Northwestern University Library's digital collection, "League of Nations Statistical and Disarmament Documents," which contains the full text of 260 League of Nations documents. See http://digital.library.northwestern.edu/league/le0262ad.pdf.
85. Primary Documents, Emperor Karl I's Abdication Proclamation, 11 November 1918, at http://www.firstworldwar.com/source/abdication_karl.htm.
86. "Habsburg Law" at http://en.wikipedia.org/wiki/Habsburg_Law.
87. "Zita of Bourbon-Parma; Obituary," *Times* [London] (March 15, 1989). *Academic OneFile* on the Internet.
88. "Charles I of Austria" at http://en.wikipedia.org/wiki/Charles_I_of_Austria#Proclamation_of_11_November.

89. Historian Arthur May discussed the archduke's plan to rule a Polish state, but neglected to mention his training of his sons, saying only "two of whose daughters had married Polish aristocrats, and who had himself effectively cultivated the good will of the Poles." See May, *The Passing of the Hapsburg Monarchy*, 155 and 167.
90. Timothy Snyder, *The Red Prince: The Secret Lives of a Habsburg Archduke* (New York: Basic Books, 2008).
91. Snyder, 89.
92. Snyder, 101.
93. Snyder, 119.
94. Snyder, *Ibid.*
95. "Zita of Bourbon-Parma; Obituary."
96. "Otto von Habsburg; Scion of the Austro-Hungarian imperial dynasty who served as a dedicated MEP and championed the ideal of European spiritual unity." *London Times* (July 5, 2011), 50; *Academic OneFile* on the Internet, July 14, 2015.

Chapter 14

1. Rothenberg, *The Army of Francis Joseph*, 218.
2. Solzhenitsyn, *August 1914*, 10. Italics added.
3. Solzhenitsyn, 13.
4. Dusan Caplovic, "An Afterword," in Bolchazy, *Illustrated Slovak History*, 283.
5. Kirschbaum, *A History of Slovakia*, 99–101.
6. Palka, *My Slovakia, My Family*, 173. Palka translated the Slovak text as "Petition of the Slovak Nation" and cited Štúr, Hodža, and Hurban as principal authors. Kirschbaum translated the Slovak as "The Demands of the Slovak Nation" and credited Štúr as the principal author.
7. Kirschbaum, 117.
8. Kirschbaum, 119.
9. Kirschbaum, 120.
10. Kirschbaum, 120.
11. Rothenberg, *The Army of Francis Joseph*, 215–216.
12. "Czechoslovak National Council," at http://en.wikipedia.org/wiki/Czechoslovak_National_Council.
13. McNamara, *Dreams of a Great Small Nation*, 133.
14. McNamara, 322.
15. Ference, "The American Slovaks and the Start of the Great War," 8.
16. Ference, 8 and 9.
17. Elisabeth Bakke, *Doomed to Failure? The Czechoslovak Nation Project and the Slovak Autonomist Reaction 1919–1938* (Oslo: Series of dissertations submitted to the Department of Political Science, Faculty of Social Sciences, University of Oslo, No. 11/99, 1999), 182.
18. Bakke, 187.
19. Taylor, *The First World War*, 244.
20. Spiesz, Caplovic, and Bolchazy, *Illustrated Slovak History*, 171.
21. Judson wrote, "Yet, as imperial symbols fell, imperial administrators, police officers, and even many military officers often remained in their posts," 434.
22. Kevin J. McNamara, xiii.
23. "Czechoslovakia" at http://en.wikipedia.org/wiki/Czechoslovakia.
24. Walter R. Roberts, "Years of Self-inflicted Disasters—Austria before Annexation in 1938," *American Diplomacy* (May 2012), at http://www.unc.edu/depts/diplomat/item/2012/0106/ca/roberts_austria2.html.
25. "Republic of German-Austria," at http://en.wikipedia.org/wiki/Republic_of_German-Austria.
26. "The Treaty of Trianon: A Hungarian Tragedy–June 4, 1920," which quotes a passage in a book by Bryan Cartledge, *The Will to Survive: A History of Hungary* (New York: Columbia University Press, 2011); see http://www.americanhungarianfederation.org/news_trianon.htm.
27. Paul Robert Magocsi, *Historical Atlas of East Cen-*

tral Europe (Seattle: University of Washington Press, 1993), 97.

28. "Demographics of Hungary," at http://en.wikipedia.org/wiki/Demographics_of_Hungary#Post-Trianon_Hungary.

29. See http://www.americanhungarianfederation.org/news_trianon.htm.

30. Bakke, 184.

31. Watson, *Ring of Steel*, 561.

32. Zara Steiner, "The Peace Settlement" in Strachan, *World War I: A History*, 291–304 at 301.

33. MacMillan, *Paris 1919*, 11.

34. MacMillan, 11–12.

35. MacMillan, 12.

36. MacMillan, 42.

37. Bolchazy, *Illustrated Slovak History*, ix.

38. Bakke, 183.

39. Bakke, 179.

40. Lukačka, *Krajné: 1392–1992*, 46.

41. Lukačka, 44–45.

42. Österreichisches Staatsarchiv Kriegsarchiv letter GZ 20966/001-KA/2004 dated November 11, 2004.

43. League of Nations, Economic and Financial Section, *International Statistical Year-Book, 1927* (Geneva: Publications of the League of Nations, 1928), Table 6, 33.

44. David Laskin, *The Long Way Home* (New York: HarperCollins, 2010), 279.

45. "List of Medal of Honor recipients for World War I," at http://en.wikipedia.org/wiki/List_of_Medal_of_Honor_recipients_for_World_War_I. TDouble awards were ended in February 1919.

46. Marian Mark Stolarik, *Immigration and Urbanization: The Slovak Experience, 1870–1918* (New York: AMS Press, 1989), 59, said that a group of Slovaks worked to have the census forms changed to include "mother tongue."

47. Čulen, *Dejiny Slovákov v Amerike*, 329–333.

48. *Fifteenth Census of the United States—1930—Population*, vol. 2: *General Report, Statistics by Subject* (Washington, D.C.: U.S. Bureau of the Census, 1933), 341.

49. Campbell J. Gibson and Emily Lennon, "Historical Census Statistics on the Foreign-born Population of the United States: 1850–1990," *Population Division Working Paper No. 29* (Washington, D.C.: U.S. Bureau of the Census, February 1999), Table 6.

50. Daniels, *Not Like Us*, 79–80.

51. Stolarik, 59. *The Fourteenth Census of the United States*—vol. 2, *General Report and Analytical Tables 1920 Census*, supports this interpretation on p. 968: "At the preceding census it also included the small number of Wendish shown by the returns, but was then composed mainly of persons who were reported, contrary to the instructions given the enumerators, as 'Slavs' 'Slavic,' 'Slavish,' or 'Slavonian.' Some of those persons should doubtless have been reported as Slovak or Slovenian. (These two languages are also sometimes confused with each other and must be considered as having a larger margin of error than perhaps than other languages in the regular classification.) The figures for "Slavic, not specified" for 1910 are not, therefore, comparable with those for 1920.

Also, note the difference between "Mother Tongue of Foreign-Born Population and Table 11, "Mother Tongue of the Foreign White Stock," p. 1008. The 1910 and 1920 censuses said, "The foreign white stock comprises the aggregate white population which is foreign either by birth or by parentage. It embraces three classes, namely, foreign born whites, native whites both of whose parents were foreign born, and native whites having one foreign and one native parent" (p. 967). It includes "only immigrants and the native children of immigrants," so does not count those who came earlier. Foreign white stock is necessarily greater than "foreign born," which it embraces.

52. Czech emigration from Bohemia and Moravia may also have been curtailed with the creation of Czechoslovakia in 1918, but that would account for only two years of the decade.

53. The Census Bureau noted other qualifications in the 1930 data: (1) "No tabulation of mother tongue was made for cities of less than 25,000 nor for counties." (2) Mother tongue was "tabulated only for white persons, since most persons … of the other races speak one characteristic language—Spanish for the Mexicans, Chinese for the Chinese, Japanese for the Japanese, etc."

54. Bureau of the Census, *Census '90: Detailed Ancestry Groups for States* (Washington, D.C.: 1990 CP-S-1-2), Table 3. Persons Who Reported at Least One Specific Ancestry Group: 1990.

55. Francis E. Clark, *Old Homes of New Americans: The Country and the People of the Austro-Hungarian Monarchy and Their Contribution to the New World* (Boston: Houghton Mifflin, 1913), 212–213.

56. "CHRONICLE, Visualizing language usage in New York Times news coverage throughout its history," at http://chronicle.nytlabs.com/.

57. Thomas Čapek, *The Čechs (Bohemians) in America* (Boston: Houghton Mifflin, 1920; reprinted by New York: Arno Press and the New York Times, 1969), ix.

58. Thomas Čapek, *The Slovaks of Hungary, Slavs and Panslavism* (New York: The Knickerbocker Press, 1906). Stolarik, *Immigration and Urbanization*, 214, attributed the commissioning to the National Slovak Society in 1905.

59. The first time I recall ever meeting a bona fide Slovak-American was in graduate school in 1960, when I met Ann Mozolak, whom I married in 1961 in a Slovak Lutheran Church on 20th Street in New York.

60. Čapek, 60 and 62.

61. Stolarik, *Immigration and Urbanization*, 36.

62. Kenneth Janda, "More Slovaks in the U.S. Than Czechs? Who Says? When and Where?" Paper prepared for delivery at the 28th World Congress of the Czechoslovak Society of Arts & Sciences; Bratislava, Slovakia, September 1–4, 2016.

63. Bakke, 377–437.

64. "Passport Applications," National Archives, https://www.archives.gov/research/passport/#intro.

65. Bolchazy, *Illustrated Slovak History*, 340.

66. Robertson, *The Passport in America*, 89.

67. The German ports of Bremen and Hamburg handled most of Hungary's 239,000 people who emigrated overseas in 1911–13. Bremen accounted for 43 percent and Hamburg for 31 percent. Less than 1 percent sailed from Cherbourg, Zuzanna Mozolák's embarkation choice. See Gustav Thirring, "Hungarian Migration of Modern Times," in Willcox, *International Migrations*, vol. 2, 418. Comparable data were not available for 1923, but World War I did not destroy the port. In fact it gained new facilities, which suggests that Bremerhaven was still the most used. See "World Port Source, Port of Bremerhaven," at http://www.worldportsource.com/ports/review/DEU_Port_of_Bremerhaven_2764.php.

68. Quoted in May, *The Passing of the Hapsburg Monarchy*, 432.

69. Sulzberger, *The Fall of Eagles*, 281.

70. Susan earned her M.A. in viola from Northwestern and plays with the Minnesota Opera. Kathryn received her Ph.D. in energy resources from Berkeley and is senior researcher in the Environmental Change Institute at England's University of Oxford.

71. "Nick Holonyak, Jr., Biography," http://ethw.org/Nick_Holonyak,_Jr.

Epilogue

1. Edward Prince Hutchinson, *Legislative History of American Immigration Policy, 1798–1965* (Philadelphia: University of Pennsylvania Press, 1981).
2. Stephen Fox, *The Ocean Railway* (London: Harper Perennial, 2003), 171.
3. Hutchinson, 134.
4. Hutchinson, 136.
5. Fox, *The Ocean Railway*, 327.
6. Fox, 333.
7. Fox, 330.
8. *Ibid.*
9. Fox, 334.
10. Hutchinson, 157.
11. Hutchinson, 149.
12. Daniels, *Not Like Us*, 134.
13. Hutchinson, 175.
14. Daniels, 135.
15. *Ibid.*
16. "Immigration Act of 1952," http://encyclopedia.densho.org/Immigration_Act_of_1952/.
17. Hutchinson, 377.
18. "Historical Overview of Immigration Policy," http://cis.org/ImmigrationHistoryOverview.
19. Department of Homeland Security, "Yearbook of Immigration Statistics: 2013," at http://www.dhs.gov/yearbook-immigration-statistics-2013-lawful-permanent-residents, Table 1.
20. National Academies of Sciences, Engineering, and Medicine, *The Integration of Immigrants into American Society* (Washington, D.C.: The National Academies Press, 2015); Summary, 1.
21. Jim Dwyer, "From All Corners of the World, Becoming Fellow Americans," *New York Times* (July 1, 2015), A21.
22. *Ibid.*
23. Tara Bahrampour, "Census Could Get Specific on Ethnicity," *Minneapolis Star-Tribune* (October 22, 2016), A3.
24. "Norwegian American," at http://en.wikipedia.org/wiki/Norwegian_American#Historical_population_by_year.
25. Ole Edvart Rølvaag, *Giants in the Earth* (New York: Harper, 1927).
26. Garrison Keillor, "Heroes," in "Laying on Our Backs Looking Up at the Stars," *Newsweek* (July 4, 1988), 30ff. Used with permission of Prairie Home Productions.
27. Dwyer, 21.
28. National Academies of Sciences, Engineering, and Medicine, *The Integration of Immigrants into American Society*, 6–2.
29. *Ibid.*, 6–3.
30. *Ibid.*, 6–4.
31. United States Census, "The Foreign-Born Population in the United States," at https://www.census.gov/prod/2012pubs/acs-19.pdf.
32. *Ibid.*, 6–16.
33. Francine D. Blau and Christopher Mackie, eds., *The Economic and Fiscal Consequences of Immigration* (Washington, D.C.: National Academies Press, 2016), 18, online at http://www.nap.edu/23550.
34. *Ibid.*, Summary, 6.
35. As explained in Chapter 13, the term "self-determination" was used by British Prime Minister David Lloyd George.
36. Jennifer E. Dalton, "Self Determination," in George Thomas Kurian, ed., *The Encyclopedia of Political Science*, vol. 5 (Washington, D.C.: CQ Press, 2011), 1530.
37. Office of the U.S. State Department Historian, at https://history.state.gov/countries/kingdom-of-yugoslavia.

38. John F. Burns, "Revelry in Sarajevo, Where Shots Started a World War," *New York Times* (June 20, 2014), A4.
39. Burns, *ibid.*
40. "Sarajevo Serbs Unveil Monument to Gavrilo Princip, The Assassin Who Triggered WWI," at http://www.breitbart.com/national-security/2014/06/28/29-jun-14-world-view-sarajevo-serbs-unveil-monument-to-gavrilo-princip-who-triggered-world-war-i/.
41. Caroline Barker, "Slovak Nationalism: Model or Mirage?" *New England Journal of Public Policy* 14 (Fall/Winter 1998): 45–71 at 52.
42. M. Mark Stolarik, "The Role of American Slovaks in the Creation of Czecho-Slovakia, 1914–1918," *Slovak Studies*, VIII, Historica 5 (Cleveland-Rome: Slovak Institute, 1968), 7–82.
43. "Ethnic Minorities in Czechoslovakia," at https://en.wikipedia.org/wiki/Ethnic_minorities_in_Czechoslovakia.
44. Kirschbaum, *A History of Slovakia*, 169.
45. Kirschbaum, 170–171.
46. Kirschbaum, 259–260.
47. Bakke, *Doomed to failure?* 517.
48. Taylor, *The Habsburg Monarchy*, 253.
49. Taylor, *The Habsburg Monarchy*, 254–255.
50. A.J.P. Taylor, "National Independence and the 'Austrian Idea,'" *Political Quarterly* 16 (July 1945): 234–24 at p. 219.
51. *Ibid.*
52. Jan Slomka, mayor of Dzikow, the Polish village in Galicia, said that its inhabitants also thought little about nationalism. Writing after the Great War, he said, "They lived their own life, forming a wholly separate group, and caring nothing for the nation. I myself did not know that I was a Pole till I began to read books and papers, and I fancy, that other villagers came to be aware of their national attachment much in the same way." Jan Slomka, *From Serfdom to Self-Government: Memoirs of a Polish Village Mayor, 1842–1927* (London: Minerva, 1941), 171.
53. Barker, 55.
54. Janet Pollak, "Slovak Nationalism and Ethnicity: Testing the Boundaries of Political Identity," paper presented at the 16th Annual European Studies Conference, University of Nebraska at Omaha (October 10–12, 1991), 6.
55. Grisak, "History of the Grisak family," 70.
56. Bakke, 518.
57. "Demographics of Czechoslovakia," *Wikipedia* ar https://en.wikipedia.org/wiki/Demographics_of_Czechoslovakia.
58. These are accessible at Archiv—Centrum pro výzkum veřejného mínění (Archive—Center for Public Opinion Research) at cvvm.archiv@soc.cas.cz and http://cvvm.soc.cas.cz. See also the results in Abby Innes, *Czechoslovakia and the Short Goodbye* (New Haven: Yale University Press, 2001), 287n.
Innes said "Slovak public opinion divided fairly evenly over models for a common state" in 1992 (p. 56) and independence was "discordant with public opinion" in the Czech Republic (p. 59).
59. I. Tomek and V. Forst, "Czechoslovak Citizens Attitudes Towards Federation," *PORI Information* (November 12, 1990).
60. Poll data for 1990 and 1992 were reported in Jon Elster, "Transition, constitution-making and separation in Czechoslovakia," *European Journal of Sociology/Archives Europennes de Sociologie* 36 (1995): 105–134; poll data for 1991 came from Kirschbaum, 266. To enhance comparability across polls, some of the reported options were rephrased or simplified. For example, the "unitary" option in the 1990 poll replaced "common state with large powers vested in central government," and the "federal" option

replaced "common state with large powers vested in Czech and Slovak governments." The "Federal +3" option in 1991 replaced "a union of associated republics," which allowed for Moravia (or other regions) to become republics. The "Federal +3" option replaced the "Federation of more than two republics" in 1992. Also, the 1990 and 1992 polls did not report "no answers." Values were entered to make the totals sum to 100 percent and thus match the 1991 data.

61. Elster, "Transition, constitution-making and separation in Czechoslovakia," 105–134 at 120.

62. M. Mark Stolarik said that Mečiar favored a confederation. See his book, *Where Is My Home?*, 291.

63. Abby Innes, *Czechoslovakia and the Short Goodbye* (New Haven: Yale University Press, 2001), 192.

64. Elster, "Transition, constitution-making and separation in Czechoslovakia," 119.

65. Elster, 120.

66. Barker, 65.

67. See "The Break-Up of Czechoslovakia," at http://www.slovakia.org/history-breakup.htm for a subdued Slovak perspective.

68. "GDP per capita (current U.S.$)" at http://data.worldbank.org/indicator/NY.GDP.PCAP.CD.

69. Angus Roxburgh, "Slovakia: Life after the Velvet Divorce," *New Statesman* (March 2014) at http://www.newstatesman.com/politics/2014/03/slovakia-life-after-velvet-divorce.

70. Adam Taylor, "2014: The Year Referendums Reshaped the World," *Washington Post* (September 10, 2014) at http://www.washingtonpost.com/blogs/worldviews/wp/2014/09/10/2014-the-year-referendums-reshaped-the-world/.

71. Tom Toles, July 18, 2014, *Washington Post*.

72. Taylor, *The First World War*, 208.

73. Ian Kershaw, *To Hell and Back: Europe, 1914–1949* (New York: Viking, 2014), 13.

74. Taylor, 218.

75. Deak, "The Great War and the Forgotten Realm," 336–380.

76. Mark Hugo Lopez, Jeffrey Passel, and Molly Rohal, *Modern Immigration Wave Brings 59 Million to U.S., Driving Population Growth and Change Through 2065* (Washington, D.C.: September 2015), 7.

77. Tom Gjelten, *A Nation of Nations: A Great American Immigration Story* (New York: Simon & Schuster, 2015).

Bibliography

Biographies

Alzo, Lisa A. *Three Slovak Women*, 2nd ed. Lisa Alzo, 2013.

Grisak, Michael J. *The Grisak Family*. Merrillville, IN: unpublished, 1978.

Laskin, David. *The Long Way Home*. New York: HarperCollins, 2010.

Lindström, Fredrik. *Empire and Identity: Biographies of the Austrian State Problem in the Late Habsburg Empire*. West Lafayette, IN: Purdue University Press, 2008.

MacDonogh, Giles. *The Last Kaiser: The Life of Wilhelm II*. New York: St. Martin's Press, 2001.

Margutti, Albert. *The Emperor Francis Joseph and His Times*. New York: George H. Dooran, 1921.

Massie, Robert K. *Peter the Great: His Life and World*. New York: Wings Books, 1991.

May, Arthur J. *The Passing of the Hapsburg Monarchy, 1914–1918*, 2 vols. Philadelphia: University of Pennsylvania Press, 1966.

Mikula, Suzanna Maria. "Milan Hodža and the Slovak National Movement, 1898–1918." Ph.D. diss., Syracuse University, 1974.

Palka, John. *My Slovakia, My Family*. Minneapolis, MN: Kirk House, 2012.

Palmer, Alan. *Twilight of the Habsburgs: The Life and Times of Emperor Francis Joseph*. New York: Grove Press, 1994.

Pick, Robert. *Empress Maria Theresa: The Earlier Years, 1717–1757*. New York: Harper & Row, 1966.

Radzinsky, Edvard. *The Life and death of Nicholas II*. Translated by Marian Schwartz. New York: Doubleday, 1992.

Redlich, Joseph. *Emperor Francis Joseph of Austria: A Biography*. Hamden, CT: Archon Books, 1965; reprint of 1929 Macmillan edition.

Rees, Laurence. *Hitler's Charisma: Leading Millions into the Abyss*. New York: Pantheon Books, 2012.

Röhl, John. *Wilhelm II: Into the Abyss of War and Exile, 1900–1941*. Cambridge, UK: Cambridge University Press, 2014.

Rounding, Virginia. *Alix and Nicky: The Passion of the Last Tsar and Tsarina*. New York: St. Martin's Press, 2011.

Steinberg, Mark D., and Vladimir M. Khrustalëv. *The Fall of the Romanovs: Political Dreams and Personal Struggles*. New Haven: Yale University Press, 1995.

General History

Bagehot, Walter. *The English Constitution*, rev. ed. Boston: Little, Brown, 1873.

Bolchazy, Ladislaus J., ed. *Illustrated Slovak History: A Struggle for Sovereignty in Central Europe*. Wauconda, IL: Bolchazy-Carducci, 2006.

Brook-Shepherd, Gordon. *The Austrians: A Thousand-Year Odyssey*. New York: Carroll & Grad, 1998.

_____. *Royal Sunset: The European Dynasties and the Great War*. Garden City, NY: Doubleday, 1987.

Čapek, Thomas, ed. *Bohemia under Hapsburg Misrule*. New York: Fleming H. Revell, 1915.

_____. *The Čechs (Bohemians) in America*. Boston: Houghton Mifflin, 1920; reprinted by New York: Arno Press and the *New York Times*, 1969.

_____. *The Slovaks of Hungary, Slavs and Panslavism*. New York: The Knickerbocker Press, 1906.

Carter, Miranda. *George, Nicholas, and William: Three Royal Cousins and the Road to World War I*. New York: Alfred A. Knopf, 2010.

Chapin, Robert Coit. *The Standard of Living among Workingmen's Families in New York City*. New York: Charities Publication Committee, 1909.

Clark, Francis E. *Old Homes of New Americans: The Country and the People of the Austro-Hungarian Monarchy and Their Contribution to the New World*. Boston: Houghton Mifflin, 1913.

Cornwall, Mark, ed. *The Last Years of Austria-Hungary 1908–1918*. Exeter, 1990.

_____. *The Undermining of Austria-Hungary: The Battle for Hearts and Minds*. New York: St. Martin's Press, 2000.

Čulen, Konštantín. *History of Slovaks in America*. Translated by Daniel C. Nečas. St. Paul, MN: Czechoslovak Genealogical Society International, 2007.

Deak, John. *Forging a Multinational State: State Making in Imperial Austria from the Enlightenment to the First World War*. Stanford: Stanford University Press, 2015.

Drage, Geoffrey. *Austria-Hungary*. London: John Murray, 1909.

Dugáček, Michal, and Ján Gálik, eds. *Myjava* (Myjava: Town Council, 1985.

Fay, Sidney Bradshaw. *The Origins of the World War*, vol. 1: *Before Sarajevo: Underlying Causes of the War*. New York: Macmillan, 1928.

_____. *The Origins of the World War*, vol. 2: *After Sarajevo: Immediate Causes of the War*. New York: Macmillan, 1928.

Ference, Gregory C. *Sixteen Months of Indecision: Slovak American Viewpoints toward Compatriots and the Homeland from 1914 to 1915 as Viewed by the Slovak Language Press in Pennsylvania*. Selinsgrove, PA: Susquehanna University Press, 1995.

Glenny, Misha. *The Balkans: Nationalism, War, and the Great Powers, 1804–1999*. New York: Viking, 2000.

Gordon, Robert J. *The Rise and Fall of American Growth: The U.S. Standard of Living Since the Civil War*. Princeton, NJ: Princeton University Press, 2016.

Gutiérrez, Edward A. *Doughboys on the Great War: How American Soldiers Viewed Their Military Service*. Lawrence: University of Kansas Press, 2014.

Hamilton, Richard F., and Holger H. Herwig. *Decisions for War, 1914–1917*. Cambridge, UK: Cambridge University Press, 2004.

Healy, Maureen. *Vienna and the Fall of the Habsburg Empire: Total War and Everyday Life in World War I*. Cambridge, UK: Cambridge University Press, 2004.

Home, John, ed. *State, Society and Mobilization in Europe during the First World War*. Cambridge, UK: Cambridge University Press, 1997.

Honzik, Miroslav, and Hana Honziková. *1914/1918: Léta zkázy a naděje* [The years of doom and hope]. Nejnovější vydání, 1984.

Innes, Abby. *Czechoslovakia and the Short Goodbye*. New Haven: Yale University Press, 2001.

Jászi, Oscar. *The Dissolution of the Habsburg Monarchy*. Chicago: University of Chicago Press, 1961; originally published in 1929.

Janos, Andrew C. *The Politics of Backwardness in Hungary, 1825–1945*. Princeton, NJ: Princeton University Press, 1982.

Johansen, Anja. *Soldiers as Police: The French and Prussian Armies and the Policing of Popular Protest, 1889–1914*. Burlington, VT: Ashgate, 2005.

Judson, Pieter M. *The Habsburg Empire: A New History*. Cambridge, MA: Belknap Press, 2016.

Kennedy, Paul M. *The Rise and Fall of the Great Powers: Economic Change and Military Conflict from 1500 to 2000*. New York, NY: Random House, 1987.

Keynes, John Maynard. *The Economic Consequences of Peace*. London: Macmillan, 1919.

Kirschbaum, Stanislav J. *A History of Slovakia: The Struggle for Survival*, 2nd ed. New York: Palgrave Macmillan, 2005.

Lieven, Dominic. *The End of Tsarist Russia*. New York: Viking, 2015.

Lukačka, Ján. *Krajné: 1392–1992*. Bratislava: Bratislava Press, 1992.

Lukacs, John. *Budapest 1900: A Historical Portrait of a City and Its Culture*. New York: Weidenfeld & Nicolson, 1988.

Mamatey, Victor S. *The United States and East Central Europe, 1914–1918: A Study in Wilsonian Diplomacy and Propaganda*. Princeton, NJ: Princeton University Press, 1957.

Molnar, Miklos. *A Concise History of Hungary*. New York: Cambridge University Press, c. 2001; translated by Anna Magyar.

Palmer, Alan. *Victory 1918*. New York: Atlantic Monthly Press, 1998.

Roesener, Werner. *The Peasantry of Europe*. Oxford, UK: Blackwell, 1994.

Rothenberg, Gunther E. *The Army of Francis Joseph*. West Lafayette, IN: Purdue University Press, 1976.

Saxon-Ford, Stephanie. *The Czech Americans*. New York: Chelsea House, 1989.

Schevill, Ferdinand. *A History of Europe from the Reformation to the Present Day*. New York: Harcourt Brace, 1954.

Seton-Watson, R.W. *Racial Problems in Hungary*. New York: Howard Fertig, 1972 edition; originally published 1908.

Shanafelt, Gary W. *The Secret Enemy: Austria-Hungary and the German Alliance, 1914–1918*. Boulder, CO: East European Monographs, 1985.

Snyder, Timothy. *The Red Prince: The Secret Lives of a Habsburg Archduke*. New York: Basic Books, 2008.

Spiel, Hilde. *Vienna's Golden Autumn, 1866–1938*. New York: Weidenfeld & Nicolson, 1987.

Stauter-Halsted, Keely. *The Nation in the Village: The Genesis of Peasant National Identity in Austrian Poland, 1848–1914*. Cornell University Press, 2001.

Steed, Henry Wickham. *The Hapsburg Monarchy*, 3rd ed. London: Constable and Company, 1914.

Stevenson, David. *Cataclysm: The First World War as Political Tragedy*. New York: Basic Books, 2004.

Stuart, Campbell. *Secrets of Crewe House: The Story of a Famous Campaign*. New York: Hodder and Stoughton, 1921.

Sugar, Peter F., Péter Hanâk, and Tibor Frank, eds. *A History of Hungary*. Bloomington, IN: Indiana University Press, 1990.

Sulzberger, C.L. *The Fall of Eagles*. New York: Crown, 1977.

Taylor, A.J.P. *The Habsburg Monarchy, 1809–1918: A History of the Austrian Empire and Austria-Hungary*. London: Hamish Hamilton, 1948.

Wasserstein, Bernard. *Barbarism and Civilization: A History of Europe in Our Time*. Oxford, UK: Oxford University Press, 2007.

Watson, Alexander. *Ring of Steel: German and Austria-Hungary in World I*. New York: Basic Books, 2014.

Whelpley, James Davenport. *American Public Opinion*. New York: E.P. Dutton, 1914.

Winchester, Simon. *Krakatoa: The Day the World Exploded: August 27, 1883*. New York: HarperCollins, 2003.

Winter, Jay, Geoffrey Parker, and Mary R. Habeck, eds. *The Great War and the Twentieth Century*. New Haven: Yale University Press, 2000.

Zeman, Z.A.B. *The Break-up of the Habsburg Empire, 1914–1918*. London, New York: Oxford University Press, 1961.

_____. *The Twilight of the Habsburgs: The Collapse of the Austro-Hungarian Empire*. New York: American Heritage Press, 1971.

Zweiniger-Bargielowska, Ina, Rachel Duffett, and Alain Drouard, eds. *Food and War in Twentieth Century Europe*. Burlington, VT: Ashgate, 2011.

World War I

Angell, Norman *The Great Illusion*. New York: Putnam, 1910.

Archer, Christon I., John R. Ferris, Holger H. Herwig, and Timothy H.E. Travers. *World History of Warfare*. Lincoln, NE: University of Nebraska Press, 2002.

Audoin-Rouzeau, Stéphane, and Annette Becker, eds. *14–18: Understanding the Great War*. New York: Hill and Wang, 2002.

Banks, Arthur S. *A Military Atlas of the First World War*. Heinemann, 1975.

Barrett, Michael B. *Prelude to Blitzkrieg: The 1916 Austro-German Campaign in Romania*. Bloomington: Indiana University Press, 2013.

Beckett, Ian F.W. *The Great War 1914–1918*. Harlow, UK: Longman, 2001.

Boot, Max. *War Made New: Technology, Warfare, and the Course of History, 1500 to Today*. New York: Gotham Books, [2007], c. 2006.

The Britannica Book of the War. New York: Encyclopædia Britannica, 1914.

Buchan, John. *A History of the Great War*, vols. 1–4. Boston: Houghton Mifflin, 1923.

Burg, David F. and L. Edward Purcell. *Almanac of World War I*. Lexington, KY: University of Kentucky Press, 1998.

Churchill, Winston S. *The Unknown War: The Eastern Front*. New York: Scribner's, 1931.

_____. *The World Crisis, 1911–1918*, abridged and revised edition. London: Macmillan, 1941.

Clark, Christopher. *The Sleepwalkers: How Europe Went to War in 1914*. New York: Harper, 2013.

Currie, Stephen. *World War I: Life in the Trenches*. San Diego, CA: Lucent Books, 2002.

Deák, István. *Beyond Nationalism: A Social and Political History of the Habsburg Officer Corps, 1848–1918*. New York: Oxford University Press, 1990.

Ferguson, Niall. *The Pity of War: Explaining World War I*. New York: Basic Books, 1999.

Fischer, Fritz. *Griff nach der Weltmacht*. Düsseldorf: Droste, 1961, published in English as *Germany's Aims in the First World War*. London: Chatto & Windus, 1967.

Fromkin, David. *Europe's Last Summer: Who Started the Great War in 1914?* New York: Knopf, 2004.

Grant, R.G., *World War I: The Definitive Visual History, from Sarajevo to Versailles*. New York: DK, 2014.

Halsey, Francis Whiting, ed. *The Literary Digest History of the World War*, vol. 9. New York: Funk & Wagnalls, 1919.

Hart, Peter, *The Great War: A Combat History of the First World War* (Oxford, UK: Oxford University Press, 2013).

Hastings, Max. *Catastrophe 1914: Europe Goes to War*. New York: Alfred A. Knopf, 2013.

Hatt, Christine. *World War I: 1914–1918*. Danbury, CT: Franklin Watts, 2001.

Herwig, Holger. *The First World War: Germany and Austria-Hungary, 1914–1918*. London: Arnold, 1997.

History of World War I. vol. 1: *War and Response, 1914–1916*. New York: Marshall Cavendish, c2002.

History of World War I. vol. 2: *Victory and Defeat, 1917–1918*. New York: Marshall Cavendish, c2002.

History of World War I. vol. 3: *Home Fronts/Technologies of War*. New York: Marshall Cavendish, c2002.

Hooper, Colette. *Railways of the Great War*. London: Bantam Press, 2014.

Johnson, Douglas Wilson. *Battlefields of the World War*. New York: Oxford University Press, 1921.

Jukes, Geoffrey. *The First World War: The Eastern Front, 1914–1918*. Botley, UK: Osprey, 2002.

Jung, Peter. *The Austro-Hungarian Forces in World War I: 1914–1916* (1). Oxford, UK: Osprey, 2003.

Keegan, John. *The First World War*. New York: Alfred A. Knopf, 1999.

_____. *A History of Warfare*. New York: Knopf, 1993.

_____. *An Illustrated History of the First World War*. New York: Alfred A. Knopf, 2001.

Kershaw, Ian. *To Hell and Back: Europe, 1914–1949*. New York: Viking, 2014.

King, Charles A., and A.E. Potts, eds. *Harper's Pictorial Library of the World War*, vol. 3: *Battles, Sieges and Campaigns*. New York: Harper & Brothers, 1920.

Lucas, J.S., *Austro-Hungarian Infantry, 1914–1918*. New Malden, UK: Almark, 1973.

_____. *Fighting Troops of the Austro-Hungarian Army 1868–1914*. New York: Hippocrene Books, 1987.

MacMillan, Margaret. *The War That Ended Peace: The Road to 1914*. New York: Random House, 2013.

McNamara, Kevin J., *Dreams of a Great Small Nation: The Mutinous Army that Threatened a Revolution, Destroyed an Empire, Founded a Republic, and Remade the Map of Europe*. New York: Public Affairs, 2016.

Miller, Steven E., Sean M. Lynn-Jones, and Stephen Van Evera. *Military Strategy and the Origins of the First World War*. Princeton, NJ: Princeton University Press, 1991.

Morrow, John H. Jr. *The Great War: An Imperial History*. London: Routledge, 2004.

Neiberg, Michael S. *Fighting the Great War: A Global History*. Cambridge: Harvard University Press, 2005.

Palmer, Alan. *The Gardeners of Salonika*. New York: Simon & Schuster, 1965.

Philpott, William. *The War of Attrition: Fighting the First World War*. New York: Overlook Press, 2014.

Pratt, Edwin A. *The Rise of Rail-Power in War and Conquest, 1833–1914*. Philadelphia: J.B. Lippincott, 1916.

Raab, David. *Battle of the Piave: Death of the Austro-Hungarian Army, 1918*. Pittsburgh: Dorrance, 2003.

Schindler, John Richard. "A Hopeless Struggle: The Austro-Hungarian Army and Total War, 1919–1918." Ph.D. diss., McMaster University, 1995.

Simkins, Peter. *Chronicles of the Great War: The Western Front 1914–1918*. Surrey, UK: Colour Library, 1997.

Stone, Norman. *The Eastern Front: 1914–1917*. New York: Scribner's, 1975.

Taylor, A.J.P. *The First World War: An Illustrated History*. London: Hamish Hamilton, 1963.

_____. *War by Time-Table: How the First World War Began*. London: Macdonald, 1969.

Torrey, Glenn E. *The Romanian Battlefront in World War I*. Lawrence: University of Kansas Press, 2011.

Tuchman, Barbara, *The Guns of August*. New York: Dell Books, 1962.

van Bergen, Leo. *Before My Helpless Sight: Suffering, Dying and Military Medicine on the Western Front, 1914–1918*. Surrey, UK: Ashgate, 2009; translated from a Dutch edition, 1999.

The War of the Nations: A Pictorial Portfolio of World War I. New York: New York Times Company, 1919; reissued by the Arno Press, 1977, with the 1919 copyright.

Wawro, Geoffrey. *A Mad Catastrophe: The Outbreak of World War I and the Collapse of the Habsburg Empire*. New York: Basic Books, 2014.

Winter, J.M. *The Experience of World War I*. New York: Oxford University Press, 1989.

Memoirs

Bednár, Štefan, et al. *Myjava, Našej jari [Myjava, Our Spring].* Bratislava: Obzor, 1968.

Bielikova, Zuzana, and Ján Kubíček, eds. *Krajné v spomienkach [Krajné Memories].* Krajné, Slovakia: City of Krajné, 2010.

Englund, Peter. *The Beauty and the Sorrow: An Intimate History of the First World War.* New York: Alfred A. Knopf, 2011.

Fussell, Paul. *The Great War and Modern Memory.* New York: Oxford University Press, c2000.

Giles, Dorothy. *The Road through Czechoslovakia.* Philadelphia: Penn, 1930.

Gladden, E. Norman. *Across the Piave: A Personal Account of the British Forces in Italy, 1917–1919.* London: Her Majesty's Stationery Office, 1971.

Jünger, Ernst. *The Storm of Steel.* New York: Howard Fertig, 1966; originally published in 1929.

Kirchberger, Joe H. *The First World War: An Eyewitness History.* New York: Facts on File, 1992.

Palmer, Svetlana, and Sarah Wallis, eds. *Intimate Voices from the First World War.* New York: W. Morrow, c2003.

Rességuier, Roger Maria Hermann Bernhard. *Francis Joseph and His Court: From the Memoirs of Count Roger de Rességuier.* New York: John Lane, 1917.

Slomka, Jan. *From Serfdom to Self-Government: Memoirs of a Polish Village Mayor, 1842–1927.* London: Minerva, 1941.

Zweig, Stefan. *The World of Yesterday.* New York: Viking Press, 1945.

Geography and Maps

Cram's Unrivaled Atlas of the World: New Census Edition. New York: Geo F. Cram, 1911.

Gilbert, Martin. *The Routledge Atlas of the First World War.* London: Routledge, 2002.

Magocsi, Paul Robert. *Historical Atlas of East Central Europe.* Seattle: University of Washington Press, 1993.

Obrien, Patrick, ed. *Atlas of World History,* 2nd ed. Oxford University Press, 2010.

Westwood, John N. *The Historical Atlas of World Railroads.* Buffalo, NY: Firefly Books, 2009, c2008.

Book Chapters

Bak, János. "The Late Medieval Period, 1382–1526," in Peter F. Sugar, Péter Hanák, and Tibor Frank, eds., *A History of Hungary.* Bloomington: Indiana University Press, 1990, 54–82.

Caplovic, Dusan, "An Afterword," in Ladislaus J. Bolchazy, ed., *Illustrated Slovak History: A Struggle for Sovereignty in Central Europe.* Wauconda, IL: Bolchazy-Carducci, 2006, 262–299.

Cashman, Sean Dennis. "Settlement and Work for the New Immigrants," in Jeff Hay, *Immigration.* San Diego: Greenhaven Press, 2001, 92–99.

Crampton, R.J. "The Balkans, 1914–1918," in Hew Strachan, ed., *World War I: A History.* New York: Oxford University Press, 1998, 66–79.

Dalton, Jennifer E. "Self Determination," in George Thomas Kurian, ed., *The Encyclopedia of Political Science,* vol. 5. Washington, D.C.: CQ Press, 2011, 1530.

Deák, István, "The Habsburg Army in the First and Last Days of World War I: A Comparative Analysis," in Béla K. Király and Nándor F. Dreisziger, eds., *East Central European Society in World War I.* Boulder: Social Science Monographs, Vol. 19. Highland Lakes: Atlantic Research and Publications; Distributed by Columbia University Press, 1985, 301–312.

_____. "The Revolution and the War of Independence, 1848–1849," in Peter F. Sugar, Péter Hanák, and Tibor Frank, eds., *A History of Hungary.* Bloomington: Indiana University Press, 1990, 209–234.

Decsy, János. "The Hungarian Army on the Threshold of Total War," in Béla K. Király and Nándor F. Dreisziger, eds., *East Central European Society in World War I.* Boulder: Social Science Monographs, Vol. 19. Highland Lakes: Atlantic Research and Publications; Distributed by Columbia University Press, 1985, 280–288.

Deist, Wilhelm. "The Military Collapse of the German Empire," in Michael S. Neiberg, ed., *The World War I Reader.* New York: New York University Press, 2007, 297–311.

Dreisziger, Nándor F., "The Dimensions of Total War in East Central Europe, 1914–18," in Béla K. Király and Nándor F. Dreisziger, eds., *East Central European Society in World War I.* Boulder: Social Science Monographs, Vol. 19. Highland Lakes: Atlantic Research and Publications; Distributed by Columbia University Press, 1985, 3–23.

Eksteins, Modris. "Memory and the Great War," in Hew Strachan, ed., *World War I: A History.* New York: Oxford University Press, 1998, 305–317.

Englander, David. "Mutinies and Military Morale," in Hew Strachan, ed., *World War I: A History.* New York: Oxford University Press, 1998, 191–203.

Farkas, Márton. "Doberdo: The Habsburg Army on the Italian Front, 1915–16," in Béla K. Király and Nándor F. Dreisziger, eds., *East Central European Society in World War I.* Boulder: Social Science Monographs, Vol. 19. Highland Lakes: Atlantic Research and Publications; Distributed by Columbia University Press, 1985, 313–337.

Franc, Martin. "Bread from Wood: Natural Food Substitutes in the Czech Lands during the First World War," in Ina Zweiniger-Bargielowska, Rachel Duffett, and Alain Drouard, eds., *Food and War in Twentieth Century Europe.* Burlington, VT: Ashgate, 2011, 73–97.

Frank, Tibor, "Hungary and the Dual Monarchy, 1867–1890," in Peter F. Sugar, Péter Hanák, and Tibor Frank, eds., *A History of Hungary.* Bloomington: Indiana University Press, 1990, 252–266.

Fuller, William C., Jr. "The Eastern Front," in Jay Winter, Geoffrey Parker, and Mary R. Habeck, eds., *The Great War and the Twentieth Century,* New Haven: Yale University Press, 2000, 30–68.

Galati, Stephen Fischer "East Central Europe in World War I," in Béla K. Király and Nándor F. Dreisziger, eds., *East Central European Society in World War I.* Boulder: Social Science Monographs, Vol. 19. Highland Lakes: Atlantic Research and Publications; Distributed by Columbia University Press, 1985, 593–597.

Habeck, Mary R. "Technology in the First World War: The View from Below," in Jay Winter, Geoffrey Parker, and Mary R. Habeck, eds., *The Great War and the Twentieth Century.* New Haven: Yale University Press, 2000, 99–131.

Hajdu, Tibor. "Army and Society in Hungary in the Era of World War I," in Béla K. Király and Nándor F. Dreisziger, eds., *East Central European Society in World War I*. Boulder: Social Science Monographs, Vol. 19. Highland Lakes: Atlantic Research and Publications; Distributed by Columbia University Press, 1985, 112–123.

Haselsteiner, Horst. "The Habsburg Empire in World War I: Mobilization of Food Supplies," in Béla K. Király and Nándor F. Dreisziger, eds., *East Central European Society in World War I*. Boulder: Social Science Monographs, Vol. 19. Highland Lakes: Atlantic Research and Publications; Distributed by Columbia University Press, 1985, 87–102.

Herwig, Holger H. "Of Men and Myths: The Use and Abuse of History and the Great War," in Jay Winter, Geoffrey Parker, and Mary R. Habeck, eds., *The Great War and the Twentieth Century*. New Haven: Yale University Press, 2000, 299–330.

Howard, Michael. "The First World War Reconsidered," in Jay Winter, Geoffrey Parker, and Mary R. Habeck, eds., *The Great War and the Twentieth Century*. New Haven: Yale University Press, 2000, 13–29.

Jeszenszky, Géza. "Hungary Through World War I and the End of the Dual Monarchy," in Peter F. Sugar, Péter Hanák, and Tibor Frank, eds., *A History of Hungary*. Bloomington: Indiana University Press, 1990, 267–294.

Kalvoda, Josef. "The Origins of the Czechoslovak Army, 1914–18," in Béla K. Király and Nándor F. Dreisziger, eds., *East Central European Society in World War I*. Boulder: Social Science Monographs, Vol. 19. Highland Lakes: Atlantic Research and Publications; Distributed by Columbia University Press, 1985, 419–435.

Katalin, Péter. "The Later Ottoman Period and Royal Hungary, 1606–1711," in Peter F. Sugar, Péter Hanák, and Tibor Frank, eds., *A History of Hungary*. Bloomington: Indiana University Press, 1990, 100–120.

Lummel, Peter. "Food Provisioning in the Germany Army of the First World War," in Ina Zweiniger-Bargielowska, Rachel Duffett, and Alain Drouard, eds., *Food and War in Twentieth Century Europe*. Burlington, VT: Ashgate, 2011, 3–25.

Makkai, László. "The Hungarians' Prehistory, Their Conquest of Hungary and Their Raids to the West to 955," in Peter F. Sugar, Péter Hanák, and Tibor Frank, eds., *A History of Hungary*. Bloomington: Indiana University Press, 1990, 8–22.

Mamatey, Victor S. "The Czech Wartime Dilemma: The Habsburgs or the Entente?" in Béla K. Király and Nándor F. Dreisziger, eds., *East Central European Society in World War I*. Boulder: Social Science Monographs, Vol. 19. Highland Lakes: Atlantic Research and Publications; Distributed by Columbia University Press, 1985, 103–111.

McKercher, B.J.C. "Economic Warfare," in Hew Strachan, ed., *World War I: A History*. New York: Oxford University Press, 1998, 119–133.

Neiberg, Michael S., ed. "The 'Willy-Nicky' Telegrams," in *The World War I Reader*. New York: New York University Press, 2007, 46–49.

Nofi, Albert A. "Comparative Divisional Strengths During World War I: European Belligerents and Theaters," in Béla K. Király and Nándor F. Dreisziger, eds., *East Central European Society in World War I*. Boulder: Social Science Monographs, Vol. 19. Highland Lakes: Atlantic Research and Publications; Distributed by Columbia University Press, 1985, 263–270.

Pastor, Peter. "The Home Front in Hungary, 1914–18," in Béla K. Király and Nándor F. Dreisziger, eds., *East Central European Society in World War I*. Boulder: Social Science Monographs, Vol. 19. Highland Lakes: Atlantic Research and Publications; Distributed by Columbia University Press, 1985, 124–134.

Plaschka, Richard Georg. "Doberdo: The Army and Internal Conflict in the Austro-Hungarian Empire, 1918," in Béla K. Király and Nándor F. Dreisziger, eds., *East Central European Society in World War I*. Boulder: Social Science Monographs, Vol. 19. Highland Lakes: Atlantic Research and Publications; Distributed by Columbia University Press, 1985, 338–351.

Prior, Robin, and Trevor Wilson. "Eastern Front and Western Front, 1916–1917," in Hew Strachan, ed., *World War I: A History*. New York: Oxford University Press, 1998, 179–190.

Rebreneau, Liviu. "To the Romanian Front," in Peter Ayrton, ed., *No Man's Land: Fiction from a World at War: 1914–1918*. New York: Pegasus Books, 2014, 270–277.

_____. "We'll See What You Do There..." in Peter Ayrton, ed., *No Man's Land: Fiction from a World at War: 1914–1918*. New York: Pegasus Books, 2014, 278–284.

Rothenberg, Gunther. "The Hungarian Army in the First World War: 1914–1918," in Béla K. Király and Nándor F. Dreisziger, eds., *East Central European Society in World War I*. Boulder: Social Science Monographs, Vol. 19. Highland Lakes: Atlantic Research and Publications; Distributed by Columbia University Press, 1985, 289–300.

Showalter, D.E. "Manœuvre Warfare: The Eastern and Western Fronts, 1914–1915," in Hew Strachan, ed., *World War I: A History*. New York: Oxford University Press, 1998, 39–53.

Smith, Leonard V. "Narrative and Identity at the Front: Theory and the Poor Bloody Infantry," in Jay Winter, Geoffrey Parker, and Mary R. Habeck, eds., *The Great War and the Twentieth Century*. New Haven: Yale University Press, 2000, 132–165.

Somogyi, Éva. "The Age of Neoabsolutism, 1849–1867," in Peter F. Sugar, Péter Hanák, and Tibor Frank, eds., *A History of Hungary*. Bloomington: Indiana University Press, 1990, 235–251.

_____. "The Hungarian Honvéd Army and the Unity of the Habsburg Empire: The Honvéd Reform of 1904," in Béla K. Király and Nándor F. Dreisziger, eds., *East Central European Society in World War I*. Boulder: Social Science Monographs, Vol. 19. Highland Lakes: Atlantic Research and Publications; Distributed by Columbia University Press, 1985, 273–279.

Spiesz, Anton. "The Era of a Dual Monarchy (1867–1918)," in Ladislaus J. Bolchazy, ed., *Illustrated Slovak History: A Struggle for Sovereignty in Central Europe*. Wauconda, IL: Bolchazy-Carducci, 2006, 142–188.

_____. "The Revolution of 1848–1849," in Ladislaus J. Bolchazy, ed., *Illustrated Slovak History: A Struggle for Sovereignty in Central Europe*. Wauconda, IL: Bolchazy-Carducci, 2006, 102–123.

Steiner, Zara. "The Peace Settlement," in Hew Strachan, ed., *World War I: A History*. New York: Oxford University Press, 1998, 291–304.

Strachan, Hew, "Economic Mobilization: Money, Munitions, and Machines," in Hew Strachan, ed., *World War I: A History*. New York: Oxford University Press, 1998, 134–148.

Szabó, Dániel I. "The Social Basis of Opposition to the War in Hungary," in Béla K. Király and Nándor F. Dreisziger, eds., *East Central European Society in World War I*. Boulder: Social Science Monographs, Vol. 19. Highland Lakes: Atlantic Research and Publications; Distributed by Columbia University Press, 1985, 135–144.

Szakály, Ferenc. "The Early Ottoman Period, Including Royal Hungary, 1526–1606," in Peter F. Sugar, Péter Hanák, and Tibor Frank, eds., *A History of Hungary*. Bloomington: Indiana University Press, 1990, 83–99.

Turner, J.A. "The Challenge to Liberalism: The Politics of the Home Front," in Hew Strachan, ed., *World War I: A History*. New York: Oxford University Press, 1998, 163–178.

Verhey, Jeffrey. "'War Enthusiasm': Volunteers, Departing Soldiers, and Victory Celebrations," in Michael S. Neiberg, ed., *The World War I Reader*. New York: New York University Press, 2007, 148–157.

Wilson, Woodrow. "The Fourteen Points," in Michael S. Neiberg, ed., *The World War I Reader*. New York: New York University Press, 2007, 291–293.

Winter, J.M. "Propaganda and the Mobilization of Consent," in Hew Strachan, ed., *World War I: A History*. New York: Oxford University Press, 1998, 216–226.

Sources on Immigration

Blau, Francine D., and Christopher Mackie, eds. *The Economic and Fiscal Consequences of Immigration*. Washington, D.C.: National Academies Press, 2016.

Daniels, Roger. *Not Like Us: Immigrants and Minorities in America, 1890–1924*. Chicago: Ivan R. Dee, 1997.

Davie, Maurice R. *World Immigration: With Special Reference to the United States*. New York: Macmillan, 1936.

Fox, Stephen. *The Ocean Railway*. London: Harper Perennial, 2003.

Gjelten, Tom. *A Nation of Nations: A Great American Immigration Story*. New York: Simon & Schuster, 2015.

Hutchinson, Edward Prince. *Legislative History of American Immigration Policy, 1798–1965*. Philadelphia: University of Pennsylvania Press, 1981.

Janda, Kenneth. "More Slovaks in the U.S. Than Czechs? Who Says? When and Where?" Paper prepared for delivery at the 28th World Congress of the Czechoslovak Society of Arts & Sciences; Bratislava, Slovakia, September 1–4, 2016.

Jensen, Adolph. "Migration Statistics of Denmark, Norway and Sweden," in Walter F. Willcox, ed., *International Migrations*, vol. 2: *Interpretations*. Washington, D.C.: National Bureau of Economic Research, 1931, 283–312.

Klezl, Felix. "Austria," in Walter F. Willcox, ed., *International Migrations*, vol. 2, 390–410.

Lopez, Mark Hugo, Jeffrey Passel, and Molly Rohal. "Modern Immigration Wave Brings 59 Million to U.S., Driving Population Growth and Change Through 2065." Washington, D.C.: Pew Research Center, September 2015.

Misenko, Albert. "Immigrant Journeys." *Slovakia* 12 (Spring 1998): 4.

Perec, Georges, with Robert Bober. "Ellis Island: The First Stop for Most immigrants," in Jeff Hay, *Immigration*. San Diego: Greenhaven Press, 2001, 86–91.

Puskás, Julianna. "Hungarian Migration Patterns, 1880–1930: From Macroanalysis to Microanalysis," in Ira A. Glazier and Luigi De Rosa, eds., *Migration across Time and Nations: Population Mobility in Historical Contexts*. New York: Holmes & Meier, 1986, 231–254.

Roberts, Peter. *The New Immigration: A Study of the Industrial and Social Life of Southeastern Europeans in America*. New York: Macmillan, 1912.

Robertson, Craig. *The Passport in America: The History of a Document*. Oxford: Oxford University Press, 2010.

Sternstein, Malynne. *Images of Czechs in America*. Charleston, SC: Arcadia, 2008.

Stolarik, Marian Mark. *Immigration and Urbanization: The Slovak Experience, 1870–1918*. New York: AMS Press, 1989.

_____. "The Role of American Slovaks in the Creation of Czecho-Slovakia, 1914–1918." *Slovak Studies 8, Historica 5* (1968): 7–82.

_____. *Where Is My Home? Slovak Immigration to North America (1870–2010)*. Bern: Peter Lang, 2012.

Taylor, Philip. *The Distant Magnet: European Emigration to the U.S.A.* New York: Harper & Row, 1971.

Thirring, Gustav. "Hungarian Migration of Modern Times," in Walter F. Willcox, ed., *International Migrations*, vol. 2, 411–439.

United States Bureau of the Census. *Fifteenth Census of the United States—1930—Population*, vol. 2: *General Report, Statistics by Subject*. Washington: U.S. Bureau of the Census, 1933.

United States Department of Homeland Security. *Yearbook of Immigration Statistics: 2008*. Washington, D.C.: U.S. Department of Homeland Security, Office of Immigration Statistics, 2009.

Willcox, Walter F., ed. *International Migrations*, vol. 1: *Statistics*. Washington, D.C.: National Bureau of Economic Research, 1929.

_____, ed. *International Migrations*, vol. 2: *Interpretations*. Washington, D.C.: National Bureau of Economic Research, 1931.

_____. "International Emigration According to National Statistics: Europe," in Walter F. Willcox, ed., *International Migrations*, vol. 1, 85–136.

Wittke, Carl. "The Business of Encouraging Immigration." in Jeff Hay, *Immigration*. San Diego: Greenhaven Press, 2001, 49–55.

Articles and Papers

Bairoch, Paul. "Europe's Gross National Product: 1800–1975." *Journal of European Economic History* 5 (Fall 1976): 273–340.

Bennighof, Mike, "Austria-Hungary's Last Offensive: Summer 1918." *Strategy and Tactics* (July–August 2000): 4–14.

Boyer, John W. "The End of an Old Regime: Visions of Political Reform in Late Imperial Austria." *The Journal of Modern History* 58 (March 1986): 159–193.

Deak, John. "The Great War and the Forgotten Realm: The Habsburg Monarchy and the First World War." *The Journal of Modern History* 86, No. 2 (June 2014): 336–380.

Eisenstadt, Shmuel N. "Empires," in David L. Sills, ed., *International Encyclopedia of Social Sciences*, vol. 5. New York: Macmillan and The Free Press, 1968, 41–48.

Farrell, Theo. "Culture and military power." *Review of International Studies* 24 (July 1998): 407–416.

Felak, James Ramon. "Review of Jan Rychlík, Thomas D. Marzik, and Miroslav Bielik (eds.), *R.W. Seton-Watson and His Relations with the Czechs and Slovaks: Documents 1906–1951*" [*R.W. Seton-Watson a jeho vztahy k Cechum a Slovakum: dokumenty 1906–1951*], *HABSBURG, H-Net Reviews.* March 1998. URL: http://www.h-net.org/reviews/showrev.php?id=1819.

Ference, Gregory C. "The American Slovaks and the Start of the Great War." Paper presented at 27th World Congress of the Czechoslovak Society of Arts & Science (SVU) (Plzeň, Czech Republic, June 29–July 4, 2014.

Keillor, Garrison. "Heroes," in "Laying on Our Backs Looking Up at the Stars." *Newsweek* (July 4, 1988), 30ff.

Offer, Avner. "Going to War in 1914: A Matter of Honor?" *Politics & Society* 23 (1995): 213–241.

Pollak, Janet. "Slovak, "Nationalism and Ethnicity: Testing the Boundaries of Political Identity." Paper Presented at the 16th Annual European Studies Conference, University of Nebraska at Omaha, October 10–12, 1991.

Rapant, Daniel. "Slovak Politics in 1848–1849." *Slavonic and East European Review* (1948): 67–90.

Rustow, Dankwart A. "Nation," in David L. Sills, ed., *International Encyclopedia of the Social Sciences*, vol. 11. New York: The Free Press and Macmillan, 1968, 7–14.

Seton-Watson, R.W. "Review of Joseph Redlich, Emperor Francis Joseph of Austria: A Biography." *The Slavonic and East European Review* 7 (March 1929): 748–752.

Sheehan, James J. "The Bloody Detail: Who Was to Blame for World War I?" *Commonweal* (May 2, 2014): 20–22.

Stevenson, David. "War by Timetable? The Railway Race Before 1914." *Past and Present* 162 (1991): 163–194.

Stone, Norman. "Army and Society in the Habsburg Monarchy, 1900–1914." *Past and Present* 33 (April 1966): 95–111.

_____. "Hungary and the Crisis of July 1914," *Journal of Contemporary History* 1 (1966): 153–170.

Taylor, A.J.P. "National Independence and the 'Austrian Idea,'" *Political Quarterly* 16 (July 1945): 234–246.

Tomek, I., and V. Forst. "Czechoslovak Citizens' Attitudes Towards Federation." *PORI Information* (November 12, 1990).

Wawro, Geoffrey. "The Masque of Command: Bad Generals and Their Impact." *Historically Speaking* 6 (November/December 2004): 5–6.

Williamson, Samuel R. "Influence, Power, and the Policy Process: The Case of Franz Ferdinand, 1906–1914." *The Historical Journal* 17 (June 1974): 417–43.

Wilson, Peter H. "Defining Military Culture." *The Journal of Military History* 72 (January 2008): 11–41.

Zeman, Z.A.B. "The Four Austrian Census and Their Political Consequences," in Mark Cornwall, ed., *The Last Years of Austria-Hungary 1908–1918.* Exeter: University of Exeter Press, 1990, 31–39.

Zuber, Terrence. "The Schlieffen Plan Reconsidered." *War in History* 6 (July 1999): 262–305.

Government Documents

Anderson, Frank Maloy, and Amos Shartle Hershey. *Handbook of Diplomatic History of Europe, Asia, and Africa 1870–1914.* Washington, D.C.: Government Printing Office, 1918.

Blau, Francine D., and Christopher Mackie, eds. *The Economic and Fiscal Consequences of Immigration.* Washington, D.C.: National Academies Press, 2016.

Gibson, Campbell J., and Emily Lennon: "Historical Census Statistics on the Foreign-born Population of the United States: 1850–1990." Washington, D.C.: Population Division, U.S. Bureau of the Census, February 1999.

League of Nations, Economic and Financial Section. *International Statistical Year-Book, 1926* Geneva: Publications of the League of Nations, 1927.

League of Nations, Economic and Financial Section. *International Statistical Year-Book, 1927* Geneva: Publications of the League of Nations, 1928.

National Academies of Sciences, Engineering, and Medicine. *The Integration of Immigrants into American Society.* Washington, D.C.: The National Academies Press, 2015.

Novels

Ayrton, Peter, ed. *No Man's Land: Fiction from a World at War: 1914–1918.* New York: Pegasus Books, 2014.

Barker, Pat. *Regeneration.* New York: Viking Press, 1991.

Bell, Thomas. *Out of This Furnace.* Boston: Little, Brown, 1941.

Chevallier, Gabriel. *Fear: A Novel of World War I.* New York: New York Review Books, 2014; originally published in 1930, translated from the French by Malcolm Imrie.

Cíger-Hronský, Jozef, *Jozef Mak.* Columbus, OH: Slavica, 1985; originally published in Slovak in 1933; translated by Andrew Cincura.

Hašek, Jaroslav. *The Good Soldier Švejk and His Fortunes in the World War* [*Osudy dobrého vojáka Švejka za světové války*]. London: Penguin Books, 1973; originally published in sections from 1921 to 1923.

Hemingway, Ernest. *A Farewell to Arms.* New York: Scribner, 1957.

Krivak, Andrew. *The Sojourn.* New York: Bellevue Literary Press, 2011.

Móricz, Zsigmond. *The Torch* [*A Fáklya*]. New York: Alfred A. Knopf, 1931; originally published in 1917.

Musil, Robert. *The Man without Qualities.* New York: Coward-McCann, 1953.

Remarque, Erich Maria. *All Quiet on the Western Front.* New York: Random, 1958.

Rølvaag, Ole Edvart. *Giants in the Earth.* New York: Harper, 1927.

Roth, Joseph. *The Collected Stories of Joseph Roth.* New York: W.W. Norton, 2003; translated by Michael Hofmann.

_____. *The Radetzky March.* New York: Alfred A. Knopf, 1996.

Shaara, Jeff. *To the Last Man: A Novel of the First World War.* New York: Ballantine Books, 2004.

Solznenitsyn, Aleksandr. *August 1914.* New York: Farrar, Straus and Giroux, 1972.

Timrava. "Great War Heroes," in Norma L. Rudinsky, ed. and trans., *That Alluring Land: Slovak Stories*. Pittsburgh: University of Pittsburgh Press, 1992, 214–320. Timrava was the pen name of Bozena Slanciková (1867–1951).
_____. "That Alluring Land [Tá zem vábna]," in Rudinsky, *That Alluring Land*, 95–129.
von Suttner, Bertha. *Lay Down Your Arms: The Autobiography of Martha Von Tillings*, 2nd ed. New York: Longmans, Green, 1908.
Wansa, Mark. *The Linden and the Oak*. Toronto: World Academy of Rusyn Culture, 2009.

Newspaper Headlines

June 12, 1903: "King and Queen of Servia Slain," *New York Times*, 1.
Apr. 30, 1905: "Russian Ruler Grants Freedom of Religion," *New York Times*, 2.
May 30, 1905: "Czar's Seapower Is Annihilated," *New York Times*, 1.
June 25, 1905: "Inside Story of the Morocco Imbroglio," *New York Times*, Sm2.
Jan. 15, 1906: "Russians Expect a Bad Year," *New York Times*, 5.
Apr. 1, 1906: "Morocco Conference Ends with Agreement," *New York Times*, 4.
May 9, 1906: "William's Visit to Vienna," *New York Times*, 5.
Oct. 6, 1908: "Powers Hope to Avoid War," *New York Times*, 1.
Oct. 7, 1908: "Austria Takes Two Provinces," *New York Times*, 1.
Oct. 8, 1908: "Russia And England Clash," *New York Times*, 1.
Oct. 10, 1908: "Servians Still Eager to Fight," *New York Times*, 1.
Oct. 10, 1908: "Austria Fears A Servian War," *New York Times*, 1.
June 29, 1914: "Heir to Austria's Throne Is Slain with His Wife by a Bosnian Youth to Avenge Seizure of His Country," *New York Times*, 1.
July 30, 1914: "Says Pan-Serb Move Is All in Austria," *New York Times*, 3.
June 19, 1918: "Foe's Dead Block Defiles: Mountain Slopes Black with Bodies of Austrian Storming Troops," *New York Times*, 1.

Newspaper Articles

Bahrampour, Tara. "Census Could Get Specific on Ethnicity." *Minneapolis Star-Tribune* (October 22, 2016), A3.
Burns, John F. "Revelry in Sarajevo, Where Shots Started a World War." *New York Times* (June 20, 2014), A4.
Dwyer, Jim. "From All Corners of the World, Becoming Fellow Americans." *New York Times* (July 1, 2015), A21.
Gray, Christopher. "On East 73rd Street, a Lingering Vestige of a Czech Heritage." *New York Times* (March 15, 1987), 14R.
"The Italian Victory." *The Advertiser* (June 27, 1918), 5.
Littlefield, Walter. "Inside Story of the Morocco Imbroglio." *New York Times* (June 25, 1905), SM2.
Mermelstein, David. "Unquiet on the Western Front." *Wall Street Journal* (July 31, 1914), D5.

"Otto von Habsburg; Scion of the Austro-Hungarian imperial dynasty who served as a dedicated MEP and championed the ideal of European spiritual unity," *Times* (London), (July 5, 2011): 50. *Academic OneFile*. Web. July 14, 2015.
"Says Pan-Serb Move Is All In Austria." *New York Times* (July 30, 1914), 3.
"Topics of The Times." *New York Times* (February 10, 1915), 10.
Wilkin, Karen. "An Empire's True Wealth." *Wall Street Journal* (August 6, 2015), D5.
Your Correspondent for Austria-Hungary. "Hungarian Social Legislation." *Times* (London, England), 25 Sept. 1907: 6. The Times Digital Archive. Web. 4 Aug. 2015.
"Zita of Bourbon-Parma; Obituary." *Times* (London, England) (March 15, 1989). *Academic OneFile*. Web. (July 13, 2015).

Movies, Opera, Operettas and Television

Movie	1916	*Mágnás Miska* (*Magnate Mike*; Hungarian)
Movie	1918	*Hotel Imperial* (Hungarian silent)
Movie	1925	*Battleship Potemkin* (Russian)
Movie	1927	*Hotel Imperial* (Hollywood silent remake of Hungarian film)
Movie	1930	*All Quiet on the Western Front* (German)
Movie	1932	*A Farewell to Arms*
Movie	1933	*Duck Soup*
Movie	1937	*The Grand Illusion* (French)
Movie	1939	*Hotel Imperial* (Hollywood remake as a sound film)
Movie	1951	*The African Queen*
Movie	1957	*A Farewell to Arms* (remake)
Movie	1962	*Lawrence of Arabia*
Movie	1964	*Dr. Strangelove or: How I Learned to Stop Worrying and Love the Bomb*
Movie	1965	*The Sound of Music*
Movie	1969	*Oh! What a Lovely War* (British)
Movie	1981	*Gallipoli* (Australian)
Movie	1999	*The Death Triangle* (Romanian)
Movie	2006	*Ode to Joy* (Japanese)
Movie	2008	*120* (Turkish)
Movie	2011	*War Horse*
Movie	2014	*The Grand Budapest Hotel*
Opera	2012	*Silent Night*
Operetta	1905	*The Merry Widow*
Operetta	1908	*The Chocolate Soldier*
Operetta	1911	*Der Rosenkavalier*
Operetta	1924	*The Student Prince*
TV Series	1974	*The Fall of Eagles*

Internet Sources

"The Annexation of Bosnia-Herzegovina, 1908," at https://www.mtholyoke.edu/acad/intrel/boshtml/bos127.htm.
"Answers," at http://wiki.answers.com/Q/What_were_the_13_main_topics_about_on_29_questions_immigrants_passing_through_Ellis_Island_answered_on_the_ships_manifest.
Archiv—Centrum pro výzkum veřejného mínění

(Archive—Center for Public Opinion Research) at cvvm.archiv@soc.cas.cz and http://cvvm.soc.cas.cz.

"Armies, 1914," at http://spartacus-educational.com/FWWarmies1914.htm.

"Austria-Hungary," Wikipedia at http://en.wikipedia.org/wiki/Austro-Hungarian_Empire#Linguistic_distribution.

"Austria-Hungary," Wikipedia at https://en.wikipedia.org/wiki/Austria-Hungary.

"Austria-Hungary," Wikipedia, at http://en.wikipedia.org/wiki/Austro-Hungarian_Empire#Name_in_official_languages_of_Austria-Hungary.

"Austria-Hungary: Linguistic Distribution," Wikipedia at http://en.wikipedia.org/wiki/Austro-Hungarian_Empire#Linguistic_distribution.

"Austro-Hungarian krone," Wikipedia at http://en.wikipedia.org/wiki/Austro-Hungarian_krone#Historic_exchange_rates_and_prices.

"Balkan Wars," Encyclopaedia Britannica, at http://www.britannica.com/EBchecked/topic/50300/Balkan-Wars.

"Battle of Solferino," at http://en.wikipedia.org/wiki/Battle_of_Solferino.

"British War Aims," Statement of January 5, 1918, at http://wwi.lib.byu.edu/index.php/Prime_Minister_Lloyd_George_on_the_British_War_Aims.

Brooklyn Daily Eagle at http://bklyn.newspapers.com/image/54213771

"The Bulgarian Declaration of Independence, 1908," at https://www.mtholyoke.edu/acad/intrel/boshtml/bos129.htm.

"Charles I of Austria" at http://en.wikipedia.org/wiki/Charles_I_of_Austria#Proclamation_of_11_November.

"CHRONICLE, Visualizing language usage in New York Times news coverage throughout its history," at http://chronicle.nytlabs.com/.

CNN on April 18, 2006, at http://www.cnn.com/2006/POLITICS/04/18/rumsfeld/.

"Constitution of the Empire of Austria," at http://www.hoelseth.com/royalty/austria/austrianconst184903 04.html#Constitution.

"Content of the Austro-Hungarian Ultimatum to Serbia," at http://en.wikipedia.org/wiki/July_Crisis#Content_of_the_Austro-Hungarian_ultimatum_to_Serbia.

"Czechoslovak National Council," at http://en.wikipedia.org/wiki/Czechoslovak_National_Council.

"Czechoslovakia" at http://en.wikipedia.org/wiki/Czechoslovakia.

"Demographics of Hungary," at http://en.wikipedia.org/wiki/Demographics_of_Hungary#Post-Trianon_Hungary.

Department of Homeland Security, "Yearbook of Immigration Statistics: 2013," at http://www.dhs.gov/yearbook-immigration-statistics-2013-lawful-permanent-residents, Table 1.

"Elizabeth Báthory in Populat Culture," Wikipedia, at http://en.wikipedia.org/wiki/Elizabeth_Báthory_in_popular_culture#Film.

"Emperor," Wikipedia, at http://en.wikipedia.org/wiki/Emperor#Distinction_from_other_monarchs.

Emperor Karl I's Abdication Proclamation, 11 November 1918, at http://www.firstworldwar.com/source/abdication_karl.htm.

"Ethnic Minorities in Czechoslovakia," at https://en.wikipedia.org/wiki/Ethnic_minorities_in_Czechoslovakia.

"Facts and Figures, Income and Prices 1900–1999," at http://usa.usembassy.de/etexts/his/e_prices1.htm

The Fall of Eagles, BBC-TV series of 13 episodes at http://www.imdb.com/title/tt0207885/.

"Ferdinand I of Austria," Wikipedia, at http://en.wikipedia.org/wiki/Ferdinand_I_of_Austria.

Film footage of Franz Joseph's funeral at https://www.youtube.com/watch?v=KE3e6Y7MkKc.

"First World War Casualties," at http://www.historylearningsite.co.uk/?s=casualties1.

"Four Steps to War, June-Aug 1914," at http://www.johndclare.net/causes_WWI4.htm

"Franz Joseph I of Austria: biography," at http://www.fampeople.com/cat-franz-joseph-i-of-austria_5.

"The Great War Timeline," at http://www.greatwar.co.uk/timeline/ww1-events-1918.htm.

The Grisak Family, available at http://www.carpathorusynsociety.org/Genealogy/Grisak.pdf.

HABSBURG, H-Net Reviews. March 1998. URL: http://www.h-net.org/reviews/showrev.php?id=1819.

"Habsburg Law" at http://en.wikipedia.org/wiki/Habsburg_Law.

"Historia.ro" at http://www.historia.ro/exclusiv_web/general/articol/willy-nicky-telegrams.

"Historical Overview of Immigration Policy," http://cis.org/ImmigrationHistoryOverview.

"A History of the First World War in 100 Moments: Austro-Hungarian army executes civilians in Serbia," at http://www.independent.co.uk/news/world/world-history/history-of-the-first-world-war-in-100-moments/a-history-of-the-first-world-war-in-100-moments-the-execution-of-civilians-in-serbia-9244674.html.

"Holy Trinity Slovak Lutheran Church," at http://www.nycago.org/organs/nyc/html/holytrinityslovakluth.html.

"House of Habsburg" at https://en.wikipedia.org/wiki-iHugh Thomas, /House_of_Habsburg.

"House of Habsburg" at http://en.wikipedia.org/wiki/House_of_Habsburg.

"How much do Americans earn in 2015? A comprehensive look at household income and individual earnings. GDP disconnects from household income," at http://www.mybudget360.com/how-much-do-americans-earn-in-2015-household-income-wages-real-income-gdp/.

"Immigration Act of 1952," http://encyclopedia.densho.org/Immigration_Act_of_1952/.

"Immigration in America," at http://immigrationinamerica.org/455-czech-and-slovakian-immigrants.html.

"Immigration Records," at http://www.archives.gov/research/immigration/passenger-arrival.html

"Imperial War Museums," at http://www.iwm.org.uk/collections/search

"Internet Encyclopedia of Ukraine," at http://www.encyclopediaofukraine.com.

iPOLL Databank, at http://www.ropercenter.uconn.edu/data_access/ipoll/ipoll.html.

"The July 1914 Crisis: Chronology of Events," at http://www2.uncp.edu/home/rwb/July_Crisis_1914_Chronology.htm.

"Kingdom of Hungary (1526–1867)," at http://en.wikipedia.org/wiki/Kingdom_of_Hungary_(Habsburg).

"Kingdom of Hungary (Austria-Hungary)," Wikipedia, at http://en.wikipedia.org/wiki/Kingdom_of_Hungary_(Austria-Hungary).

League of Nations documents at http://digital.library. northwestern.edu/league/le0262ad.pdf.

"List of Medal of Honor recipients for World War I," at http://en.wikipedia.org/wiki/List_of_Medal_of_ Honor_recipients_for_World_War_I.

"List of World War I Films," Wikipedia, at https:// en.wikipedia.org/wiki/List_of_World_War_I_films.

"Magyarization," Wikipedia, at https://en.wikipedia. org/wiki/Magyarization#Education.

"Magyarization," at http://en.wikipedia.org/wiki/Mag yarization#Education

"Mesto Myjava," at http://www.myjava.sk/http://www. myjava.sk/historia/.

"Military Records in Upper Hungary (Slovakia)," at http://www.iabsi.com/gen/public/military_records_ in_upper_hungar.htm

"Mother Tongue of the Foreign-Born Population: 1910 to 1940, 1960, and 1970," athttp://www.census.gov/ population/www/documentation/twps0029/tab06. html

"Nick Holonyak, Jr., Biography," at http://ethw.org/ Nick_Holonyak,_Jr.

"Norway-Heritage," at http://www.norwayheritage. com/p_ship.asp?sh=rheil.

"Norwegian American," at http://en.wikipedia.org/ wiki/Norwegian_American#Historical_popula tion_by_year.

Office of the U.S. State Department Historian, at https: //history.state.gov/countries/kingdom-of-yugosla via.

"Our Litwack Family History, The Trip Over," http:// litwackfamily.com/ships.htm.

"Photos of the Great War," at http://www.gwpda.org/ photos/

"Pozsony County," Wikipedia at http://en.wikipedia. org/wiki/Pozsony_County#1900.

"President Wilson's Fourteen Points," at http://avalon. law.yale.edu/20th_century/wilson14.asp.

"Primary Documents, 1914," at http://www.firstworld war.com/source/1914.htm

"Researching WWI A Handbook," at http://www.acad emia.edu/4562141/Researching_WWI_A_Hand book

"Rudolf I of Germany" at http://en.wikipedia.org/wiki/ Rudolf_I_of_Germany#King_of_Germany.

"Sarajevo Serbs Unveil Monument to Gavrilo Princip, The Assassin Who Triggered WWI," at http://www. breitbart.com/national-security/2014/06/28/29-jun-14-world-view-sarajevo-serbs-unveil-monument-to-gavrilo-princip-who-triggered-world-war-i/.

"See the Inflation Calculator," at http://www.westegg. com/inflation/infl.cgi or http://www.usinflationcal culator.com.

"Serbian Campaign of World War I," at http://en. wikipedia.org/wiki/Serbian_Campaign_of_World_ War_I#Austro-Hungarian.

"Slavs of New York," at http://nycslav.blogspot.com/ 2006/01/slovaks-in-new-york-city.html.

"States and Nationalities in Europe, 1848–1900, Aus-tria," at https://www.mtholyoke.edu/courses/rsch wart/hist151/StatesNationalities1848&later/album/ Austria/slides/Languages%20of%20Austro-Hun gary.html

"Succession to the Aaudi Arabain throne," at https:// en.wikipedia.org/wiki/Succession_to_the_Saudi_Ar abian_throne#Abdulaziz_.22Ibn_Saud.22.

The terms of the armistice: http://www.firstworldwar. com/source/armisticeterms.htm.

"Top Ten Cities of the Year 1900," http://geography. about.com/library/weekly/aa011201f.htm.

"The Treaty of Trianon," at http://www.americanhun garianfederation.org/news_trianon.htm.

"Triple Entente," at http://gluedideas.com/content-collection/encyclopedia-americana-27/Triple-Entente_P1.html.

United States Census, "The Foreign-Born Population in the United States," at https://www.census.gov/ newsroom/pdf/cspan_fb_slides.pdf.

"Who Declared War on Who in WWI," at http:// schoolworkhelper.net/who-declared-war-on-who-in-wwi/

"Who Said, 'War Is Too Important to Be Left to Gen-erals?'" at http://askville.amazon.com/'war-import ant-left-generals'/AnswerViewer.do?requestId=389 3805.

"Woodrow Wilson," History Learning Site, at http:// www.historylearningsite.co.uk/woodrow_wilson1. htm.

"The World of the Habsburgs," http://www.habsburger. net/en/portrait.

"World War I: Opening Campaigns," at http://military history.about.com/od/worldwari/a/wwi1914_2.htm.

"WWI Casualty and Death Tables," at http://www.pbs. org/greatwar/resources/casdeath_pop.htm.

Yale Law School Avalon Project at http://avalon.law. yale.edu/imt/partviii.asp.

Index

Numbers in **bold italics** indicate pages with illustrations

97, 99, 108, 158; travel 75; war
powers 79–80
Nikolaevich, Nikolai 99, 155
Nitra, Slovak Republic 29, 38, 53–
54
Nofi, Albert 131–133
North German Lloyd Line 60
Northwestern University 225
Nozdrovický, Alojz 37, 139, 214

Oberlin College 55
Ode to Joy 13
Offer, Avner 104
Oh! What a Lovely War 191
Oituz, Romania, battle of 178, 180–
184, 191, 206
Okema, Felix 232
Olympic 59
120 (One Hundred Twenty) 13
operettas 21, 78
Oppenheim, Louis 190
Orolando, Vittorio 197
Otte, T.G. 75, 80, 109
Otto 160, 205
Ottoman Empire 42, 100, 159, 161,
197–198, 213, 240
Out of the Furnace 65–66

Palka, John **30**
Palmer, Alan 72–73, 75, 100, 155, 159
Pavlovic, Darko 144
Peasant building **32**
Péter, Lászo 194
Peter the Great 75, 77–78, 151
Philpott, William 176
Piave River, battle of 180–181, **182**,
183–**184**, 185, 191, 206, 215
Pick, Robert 6
Pilsudski, Jozef 205
Podkylava, Slovak Republic 223
Poland 205
Pollak, Janet 236
population changes, in European
countries **203**
Potiorek, Oskar 172–173
Pozony
(Bratislava/Prešporok/Pressburg),
Slovak Republic 39, 117
Prairie Home Companion 231
Pratt, Edwin 134
Princip, Gavrilo 103, 235
propaganda: Italian message
intended for Czech troops **185**
Putnik, Radomit 105

Raab, David 183
Radetzky, Joseph 18
Radetzky March 22
Radzinsky, Edvard 77
railways, principal **136**
Rebreneau, Liviu 177
Redlich, Joseph 15, 72, 75–76, 80,
123, 156–157, 159–160
Reed, John 172
Rees, Laurence 196
Reiss, R.A. 172
Remarque, Erich Maria 120–121,
145–147, 192
Renoir, Jean 11
S.S. *Rhein* 59–**60**, 61–**62**; passenger
manifest **62**

Ripper, Jack D. 80
Roberts, Peter 66
Robertson, Craig 61, 222
Rodzianko, Mikhail 154
Roesener, Werner 34
Rogers, Daniel 230
Röhl, John 98, 105, 152–153, 163
Rølvaag, Ole 231
Romania: declaration of war 178,
189
Romanian Front in 1916–1917 **178**
Romanovs 160; Alexander III 76–
78; Alexandra 155; Alexie 75;
Catherine the Great 75, 99;
Nicholas I 18, 154; Nicholas II *see*
Nicholas II; Peter the Great 75,
77–78, 151
Romberg, Sigmund 21
Roosevelt, Franklin D. (president-
elect) 220
Roosevelt, Theodore 72, 194, 229
Roosevelt, Theodore, Jr. 216
Der Rosenkavalier 19
Roth, Joseph 22
Rothenberg, Gunther 119, 123, 125,
127, 136, 170, 185
Roxburgh, Andrew 239
Royal Castle 31
royal courts 96; inbreeding 16
royal palaces and castles: Buda
Castle 25; Gödöllő Palace 24;
Habsburg Castle 6; Hofburg
Palace 23–**24**, 32; Laxenburg Cas-
tle 24; Royal Castle 31; Schön-
brunn Palace 23, **25**, 158–160;
Tsarskoe Selo 77
royal titles: archduke 110–111; duke
v. earl 110, 129; emperor, kaiser,
and tsar 15
Ružomberok, Slovak Republic 177
Rudolph 26, 76, 159, 223
Rudolph II 45
Rumsfeld, Donald 80
Russia: army divisions 131–133;
demographics 4; railroads 135–
137; March 1917 revolution 154;
Serbia's protector 105, 113, 117,
121, 163, 168; Stavka, Russian mil-
itary headquarters 154
Russian Empire 240
Russian generals: Alekseyev,
Mikhail 154; Brusilov, Aleksei
176; Nikolaevich, Nikolai 99, 155;
Tatishev, Ilya 107; Yanushkevich
154
Russian political leaders: Izvolski,
Alexander 90–91; Lenin 154, 194
Ruthene/Rusyn/Carpatho-Rusyn
241*n*29, 244*n*22

Salonika 168
Sarikamis, battle of 13
Saxon-Ford, Stephanie 55
Schlieffen, Alfred von 135, 161
Schlieffen Plan **162**
Schönbrunn Palace 23, **25**, 158–160
Schwarzenberg, Prince Felix of 17
Second Balkan War, 1913 92–93, 95
self-determination 192, 211, 213,
228, 234–236, 240; Crimea 239;
Czechoslovakia 239; nationality

principle 211; referenda 239; Scot-
land 239; Sudan 239
separation of Czechoslovakia, pub-
lic opinion polls on **238**
Serbia 10, 64, 102–104, 168
Seton-Watson, R.W. 18–19, 49, 51–
52, 54–55, 184, 194
Shaara, Jeff 22, 165
Shanafelt, Gary 140, 153, 156, 159–
160, 164, 170, 180, 188
Sheehan, James 10, 102
Shepherd, William R. 45
Showalter, D.E. 163
Sigismund, King 29
Silent Night 167
Sixtus Affair 160, 181, 188–189, 204
Skaritka, Anne 222, 224
Skaritka, John, and Susan 222–224
Sked, Alan 6, 10
Slančiková, Božena 57
Slomka, Jan 168, 170–171
Slovak immigrants: census 62, 65,
86, 216–218; culture 63; employ-
ment 65–67; military service 117;
Ohio 65; Pennsylvania 65–66;
settlement in America 14, 65,
219–220
Slovak League in America 209
Slovak National Council in Martin,
1918 195, 208, 210, 234; in
Vienna, 1848 30
Slovak newspapers 82; *Jednota* 112;
Národné noviny 112; *Slovenský
hlásnik* 112; *Slovenský týždenník*
112
Slovak political leaders: Hodža,
Michal Miloslav 207–208; Hodža,
Milan 111; Mečiar, Vladiir 237–
239; notaries 36–37, 114; public
offices 36; Stefánik, Milan 193,
208, 236; Štur, Ludovit 207–208
Slovak Republic 236
Slovak towns and counties: Myjava
30–31, 39, 54, 207; Nitra 29, 38,
53–54; Pozony (Bratislava/ Preš-
porok /Pressburg) 39, 117;
Ružomberok 177; Spiš 38;
Trenčín 117
Slovak villages: Gbely 114, 215; Hra-
chovište 67–68, 87; Podkylava
223
Slovakia: economy 239; emigration
51, 53, 57–58; nationalism 213,
236; peasants **32**, 34, 36, 149;
revolt of 1848 207, 214
Slovenský hlásnik 112
Slovenský týždenník 112
Smith, Leonard 148
Smuts, Jan 198
Snyder, Timothy 173, 204–205
The Sojourn 120, 183
Sokol athletic organizations 63, 67
Solferino, battle of 1859 100, 134,
151
Solzhenitsyn, Alexander 121, 154,
207
Somogyi, Éva 126
Sophia, Archduchess 18–19
Sophie, Duchess of Hohenberg 27,
102
Sound of Music 12